THE LIMITS OF GLOBALIZATION

In the media and in political debate we are continually reminded of the emergence of global competition or even of a global culture. At the same time we hear cries of alarm that such forces combined with increasingly unrestrained and unregulated markets are destroying communities, undermining local values and weakening the ability of nation states to regulate their affairs and maintain a sense of common national identity. These two views frequently convey contradictory messages. The first demands our submission to the inexorable logic of emerging global forces; the second calls for a renewal of political projects which can defend 'society' and 'community' against such forces. These debates have found an echo in the increasingly influential theory of globalization.

The limits of globalization assesses the claims made by globalization theorists from a variety of perspectives and disciplines, and through a mixture of case studies and theoretical reflections. It asks to what extent assumptions from the wider public debate have been absorbed into the social sciences and whether we are not perpetuating what some refer to as the 'rhetoric' and others the 'myth' of globalization. Using a broad selection of examples, ranging from the struggle over the future of Berlin's Potsdamer Platz to the regulation of international air transport, the contributors examine the complexity of so-called processes of globalization. They identify not merely its 'limits' but also the countervailing forces which contest or channel social and political change.

The contributions are gathered under four headings: contesting global forces; homogenized culture or enduring diversity?; the national, the international and the global; and theoretical reflections. Case studies cover cultural analysis, international relations, industrial relations, and economic and urban policy. Theoretical contributions offer an analysis of the emergence of the concept of the globe and the global, an examination of ethnic homogenization and fragmentation, and an analysis of the impact of disembedded markets upon society.

Alan Scott is Senior Lecturer in Sociology at the University of East Anglia.

INTERNATIONAL LIBRARY OF SOCIOLOGY
Founded by Karl Mannheim
Editor: John Urry
Lancaster University

THE LIMITS OF GLOBALIZATION

Cases and arguments

Edited by Alan Scott

London and New York

First published 1997
by Routledge
11 New Fetter Lane, London EC4P 4EE

Simultaneously published in the USA and Canada
by Routledge
29 West 35th Street, New York, NY 10001

© 1997 selection and editorial matter, Alan Scott;
individual chapters, the contributors.

Typeset in Baskerville by Florencetype Ltd, Stoodleigh, Devon
Printed and bound in Great Britain by
Biddles Ltd, Guildford and King's Lynn

British Library Cataloguing in Publication Data
A catalogue record for this book is available from the British Library

Library of Congress Cataloging in Publication Data
A catalogue record for this book has been requested

ISBN 0–415–10565–X (hbk)
ISBN 0–415–10566–8 (pbk)

CONTENTS

CONTENTS

Part III The national, the international and the global

Part IV Theoretical reflections: social theory, cultural subjectivism and disembedded markets

FIGURES

TABLES

NOTES ON CONTRIBUTORS

Elmar Altvater is Professor of Political Science, Free University Berlin. He has published extensively on capitalist development, state theory, development politics, debt crises, and ecology. Recent Publications include *Die Armut der Nationen*, (1987), *Die Zukunft des Marktes* (second edition, 1992) translated as *The Future of the Market* (Verso, 1991), *Der Preis des Wohlstands* (1992) and, as co-author with Birgit Mahnkopf, *Die Grenzen der Globalisierung* (1996).

Mike Bowker is Lecturer in Politics and International Relations, University of East Anglia. He is author of *Russian Foreign Policy and the End of the Cold War* (Dartmouth, 1997), co-author of *Superpower Détente: a Reappraisal* (Sage, 1988) and co-editor of *From Cold War to Collapse* (CUP, 1993).

Howard Caygill is Professor of Cultural History, Goldsmiths College, University of London. He writes on philosophy and social theory, on art and architecture, and the sociology of law. He is author of *Art of Judgement* (Blackwell, 1989) and *A Kant Dictionary* (Blackwell, 1995), and co-editor of *The Fate of the New Nietzsche* (Avebury, 1993). His latest book, *Walter Benjamin: the colour of experience*, will be published by Routledge in 1998.

Philip Garrahan is Professor and Head of the School of Social, Political and Economic Studies at the University of Northumbria at Newcastle. He was formerly Senior Lecturer in Politics at Sunderland University and Principle Lecturer at Teesside University. He is co-author of The *Nissan Enigma* (Mansell, 1992).

Ahmed Gurnah was formally Lecturer in Sociology, Sheffield Halam University and is currently an Educational Officer in Sheffield Education Department. He has written widely on sociological theory as well as on social and educational policy. He is co-author of *The Uncertain Science* (Routledge, 1992) and is currently editing a book entitled *Culture for Social Renewal*. He has been a guest editor of *Adults Learning* and *Language Issues*.

Alan Harding is Professor of Urban Policy and Politics, European Institute of Urban Affairs, Liverpool John Moores University. He is co-author of

Urbanization and the Functions of Cities in the European Community (Commission of the European Union) and co-editor of *European Cities in the 1990s: Profiles, Policies and Prospects* (Manchester University Press, 1994).

Wai-Nang Ho is Lecturer in the Department of Public and Social Administration, City University of Hong Kong. He teaches China studies and social policy and administration. Recent publications include 'Individual Economy in the Pearl River Delta Region: The Case of Dongguan, Zhongshan, Nanhai and Guangzhou' in S. MacPherson and J. Chang (eds) *Development in the Pearl River Delta Region* (Edward Arnold, 1996).

Rajika Jalan studied English and American Literature at the University of East Anglia before taking an MA in 'Culture and Communications'. After leaving university, she began working in publishing at the Harvill Press, and is currently a publicist at Fourth Estate.

Richard Kilminster is Lecturer in Sociology, University of Leeds. He is author of *Praxis and Method* (Routledge, 1979), *The Sociological Spiral* (Routledge, forthcoming) and numerous articles on sociological theory, the sociology of knowledge and Norbert Elias; co-editor with Ian Varcoe of *Culture, Modernity and Revolution: Essays in Honour of Zygmunt Bauman* (Routledge, 1996). Member of the Editorial Board of *Sociology* (1985–88); co-convenor of the Sociological Theory Group of the British Sociological Association (1993–9). Associate Editor, *Theory, Culture and Society*; Corresponding Editor for the UK of 'Figurations', twice-yearly Newsletter of the Norbert Elias Foundation, Amsterdam.

Hussein Kassim is Lecturer in Politics in the Department of Politics and Sociology, Birkbeck College, University of London. He has written on aspects of European integration, EU decision-making and air transport policy, and is co-editor of *The European Union and National Industrial Policy* (Routledge, 1996).

Patrick Le Galès is CNRS Senior Research Fellow at CEVIPOF (FNSP, Paris) and Associate Professor of Sociology and Politics, Institut d'Etudes Politiques de Paris. He works on comparitive urban politics and urban and regional sociology in Britain, France and Italy. Author of *Politique Urbaine et Développement Local, une Comparison Franco-Britannique* (L'Harmattan, 1993) and co-editor (with Mark Thatcher) of *Les réseaux de politique publique* (L'Harmattan, 1995). His latest book (with Christian Lequesne) *Regions in Europe* will be published by Routledge in 1998.

Birgit Mahnkopf is Professor for European Social Policy [Europäische Gesellschaftspolitik] at the Fachhochschule für Wirtschaft, Berlin. Her publications include *Die Legende vom Ende des Proletariats* (1985), as co-author with Elmar Altvater, *Die Grenzen der Globalisierung* (1996), as editor, *Der gewandelte Kapitalismus. Kritische Beiträge zur Theorie der Regulation* (1988) and as co-editor, *Gewerkschaften vor der europäischen Herausforderung* (1993).

Cesare Poppi is an anthropologist and Deputy Director of the Sainsbury Research Unit for the Arts of Africa, Oceania, Asia and the Americas at the University of East Anglia. He has conducted research on ethnicity in the Dolomites and on the cult of masks in North West Ghana. Recent publications include 'Building Difference: the Political Economy of Tradition in the Latin Carnival of the Val di Fassa' in J. Boissevain (ed.) *Revitalising European Rituals*' (Routledge, 1992) and 'The contention of tradition: legitimacy, culture and ethnicity in Southern Tyrol', in *Biblioteca Comunale di Trento* (a cura di) *Por Padro Frumenzio ghettu, O.f.M. eh ... In Onore del Settantesimo Compleanno* (1991).

Sasha Roseneil is University Research Fellow in Sociology at the University of Leeds. She is author of *Disarming Patriarchy: Feminism and Political Action at Greenham* (Open University Press, 1995) and co-editor of *Stirring it: Challenges for Feminism* (Taylor and Francis, 1994). Her latest book, *Common Women, Uncommon Lives*, will be published by Cassell in 1997.

Alan Scott is Senior Lecturer in Sociology, University of East Anglia. He writes on political sociology and social theory. Publications include *Ideology and the New Social Movements* (Routledge, 1990) and, as co-author, *The Uncertain Science* (Routledge, 1992).

Paul Stewart was formally Senior Lecturer in Sociology at Sunderland University and, until 1995, Lecturer in Japanese Management at the Cardiff Business School. He is now a Research Fellow in Organizational Sociology, Cardiff Business School, University of Wales. He is co-author of *The Nissan Enigma* (Mansell, 1992) and author of *Working Harder and Smarter in the Automobile Industry* (Mansell, 1997).

John Street is Senior Lecturer in Politics, University of East Anglia. Author of *Rebel Rock* (Blackwell, 1986), *The Politics of Technology* (Macmillan, 1992), *The Politics of Popular Culture* (Polity Press, 1997) and co-author of *Deciding Factors in British Politics* (Routledge). He also writes regularly for *The Times* on popular music.

Julia Tao is Associate Professor and Dean of the Faculty of Humanities and Social Sciences, City University of Hong Kong. She is also Director of the University's Contemporary China Research Centre. Her Publications include 'The moral foundations of welfare in Chinese society: between virtues and rights' in G. Becker (ed.) *Ethics in Business and Society* (Springer, 1996) and 'The contestation of values in welfare reform in China' in T. Wing Lo and J. Cheng (eds) *Social Welfare Development in China: Constraints and Opportunities* (Imprint, 1996).

ACKNOWLEDGEMENTS

For their detailed comments on the Introduction, I would like to thank John Street and Richard Kilminster and, for some very valuable suggestions on the translation of Chapter 14, Brigitte Scott and Andrew Chitty. Mari Shullaw at Routledge has been an encouraging and patient editor. A sabbatical leave granted by UEA enabled me to work on this and other projects.

1

INTRODUCTION

Globalization: social process or political rhetoric?

Alan Scott

The danger of the rhetoric of globalization is that it reduces the scope of democratic political life to marginal adjustments in the management of market institutions. It thereby closes the political process to questions about the contribution made by market institutions to the satisfaction of human needs ... [An effective opposition] must question this model and expose the desolation wrought on communities by policies that have no justification apart from the spurious claim that they are forced on us by an inexorable historical process. In doing so it will assume a responsibility relinquished by contemporary Conservatism – that of ensuring through political action that the workings of market institutions are compatible with the satisfaction of the human need for a life in common.

(Guardian, 4 January 1994: 18)

The new hegemony of the capital markets – and with it new-right pro-market ideas – means the current imperatives are to cut budget deficits, reduce social costs and scale back welfare provision. Worse, all forms of public action are prohibited by the injunction that the private is not only more efficient but also the state has reached the limits of what it can afford to do ...

The left and liberal conservatives everywhere have a responsibility to keep a different vision of society and economy alive. Taxation, welfare systems and regulation serve the larger cause of social cohesion; and while ideas of public ownership and planning need to be recast, they, too, serve the same cause. Such heresies need to be said aloud and a political tradition preserved. History demands no less.

(Guardian, 4 January 1994: 13)

These two extracts from articles appearing in the same newspaper on the same day are strikingly similar. They express concern that market forces are

1

destroying community and social solidarity. The authors criticize the idea that globalization is an unstoppable historical force in the face of which politics is helpless, and they call for a renewal of political projects that can defend society against markets. Both are, in brief, demanding a politics that can resist the subordination of the political and social to the economic. But this consensus is arrived at via quite different political assumptions.

The first quotation is from an article written by the political theorist John Gray who has greatly contributed to the dissemination of new right ideas, particularly in Britain. It expresses what might be called 'second thoughts' on the impact of the new right's project. The argument he makes here and has elaborated elsewhere (see Gray 1993) recognizes the market's social destructiveness and appeals to traditional conservatism to protect community. The second quotation is by Will Hutton, then the *Guardian*'s Economics Editor and a leading left-of-centre economic commentator. Hutton derives the idea that markets destroy social cohesion not from conservatism but from Karl Polanyi, one of the earliest and most trenchant critics of the free market economics of von Mises and Hayek. Polanyi's analysis was written as a response to the rise of European fascism, and Hutton speculates that contemporary manifestations of ultra-right nationalism can similarly be interpreted as a last ditch defence against market logic. Like Polanyi, he calls for social democratic planning as a means of holding the destructive force of the market in check before it is met by some much more desperate political reaction (see also Hutton 1995). So there is a further neat, if ironic, parallel between Gray and Hutton. Both are appealing to pre-existing political positions, namely conservatism and social democracy; the very political ideologies and policies against which the new right ranged its intellectual armoury in the first place.

What Gray here calls the 'rhetoric of globalization' is as common in contemporary debate in political science and sociology as it is in politics or journalism. The question thus arises, do Hutton's and Gray's criticisms of globalization in political debate apply equally to the social sciences? First, is social science as prone as political punditry to interpreting globalization as historically inevitable and unstoppable? Second, have the social sciences in their diagnosis of late- or post- modernity, of which the theory of globalization is a key element, been sufficiently aware of the extent to which globalization is a *political project*? If the answer to the first question is 'yes' and to the second 'no', then a further question arises. Gray and Hutton are at the very least implying that it is precisely the *belief* of key political and economic actors, even those who oppose its effects, that globalization is inevitable which contributes to its political puissance. The question for social scientists then becomes to what extent are we contributing to a self-fulfilling prophecy by assuming the same inevitablist logic which Gray and Hutton argue has incapacitated political opposition? Expressed differently, are we assisting the process of globalization by providing people with persuasive arguments to the effect that little can be done in the face of these enormous economic, political and social developments?

In this introduction I wish to elaborate somewhat on the ramifications of these questions. I shall suggest that globalization can be interpreted either diagnostically or politically and that this difference may be more fundamental than that, say, between Marxist and non-Marxist perspectives. Later chapters will examine globalization in political analysis, in international relations, in cultural theory, in urban sociology and in political economy. Here I will focus on globalization as a theme in recent social theory (see also Chapter 12). The arguments found in social theory are frequently 'diagnostic' in the sense that they attempt to develop a general theory of contemporary social, political and economic developments; a '*Zeitdiagnose*' – a 'diagnosis of our times'. I hope to provide both a brief overview of the current state of the debate and to highlight the issues which this collection seeks to address.

DIAGNOSTIC APPROACHES: GLOBALIZATION, MODERNITY AND POSTMODERNITY

> We know that we are caught within these more complex global networks, because we palpably suffer the prolongations of corporate space everywhere in our daily lives. Yet we have no way of thinking about them, of modelling them, however abstractly, in our mind's eye.
>
> Fredrick Jameson

> One of the most widespread diseases is diagnosis.
>
> Karl Kraus

Recent discussion within sociology and political science has been careful to distinguish globalization theory from the theory of modernization on the one hand and from accounts of colonialism on the other. The concept of globalization should not act simply as a synonym for a new phase of modernization or for Westernization. At the same time, globalization theorists have sought to avoid explanations they consider reductionist or determinist, i.e. which appear to reduce divergent aspects of a complex process to some set of fundamental causes or to some single societal sub-system (e.g., the economy). Thus in the literature one frequently encounters a critique of world-systems theory on the grounds that it subordinates cultural and political developments to the logic of capitalism (e.g. Robertson 1992b, ch.4; Boyne 1990), and we find no less frequently a discussion of 'aspects' of globalization in which these aspects are treated if not as autonomous then at least as non-reducible. Similarly, Marxist analysts have tended to argue that while one might explain globalization as an outcome of the logic of

3

capitalism, that logic is itself always mediated through political and social forms. In some respects, then, globalization theory has emerged cautiously by defining its own projects negatively: as the avoidance of the limitations of theories of colonialism, earlier Marxist accounts and modernization theory.

This caution is balanced by very bold claims focusing on the assertion that the nation state is losing its historical role as society's chief organizing principle and that it is being replaced by human, technological, communicative, political, economic and financial networks which have liberated themselves from the territorial limitations of the nation state. Globalization theorists have identified the task for social science as likewise to liberate itself from its own territorial assumptions; to avoid 'state-centred' approaches (Sklair 1991: 144), to 'go beyond the category of "the state"' (Holloway 1994: 25), and to desist from its implicit but more-or-less automatic equation of 'society' with 'nation' (e.g. Robertson 1992b: 112; also Picciotto 1991). For some, the full appreciation of the impact of globalizing tendencies demands no less than a revolution in the way in which social science conceptualizes its object and a complete rethinking of its most basic categories: society, *Gemeinschaft* (community), nation, state, etc. Thus, for example, Zygmunt Bauman questions the 'modern' and 'orthodox' concept of 'society' with its unavoidable assumption of unification of the means of violence, administration and even cultural homogeneity within a given territory:

> It seems that most sociologists of the era of modern orthodoxy believed that – all being said – the nation state is close enough to its own postulate of sovereignty to validate the use of its theoretical expression – the 'society' concept – as an adequate framework for sociological analysis.
>
> (1992: 57)

This assumption, so the argument goes, is no longer appropriate for an era in which the state has largely abandoned its mission to create a unified culture within its territory (Ernest Gellner's 'cultivated culture') and left culture to the market with its drive to create new niches through fragmentation. Clearly, this would have quite radical implications for basic social scientific concepts. It may no longer, for example, be possible to define, as Weber famously did, the state as that institution which claims a monopoly over the legitimate use of violence (and exercises unified administration) *within a given territory* (cf. Hoffman 1995). But for Bauman, more radically still, the notion through and with which sociology has defined itself and its boundaries (society) must likewise be abandoned.

The substantive analysis which lies behind and is thought to warrant such dramatic proposals rests upon a general diagnosis of late/postmodernity which focuses not on increasing cultural homogeneity and universalism – as the theory of modernity typically did – but upon diversity and fragmentation.

It is this emphasis which has drawn globalization theory into the general domain of the social theory of postmodernity.[1]

Globalization and (late/post) modernity

The question of the relationship between alleged processes of globalization and more familiar accounts of modernity and modernization has been highly problematic. Anthony Giddens, for example, asserts simply that 'modernity is inherently globalising' (1990: 63 and 177). Roland Robertson is more cautious. While claiming that 'the problem of modernity has been expanded to – in a sense subsumed by – the problem of globality' (1992b: 66), Robertson also warns that the 'present concern with globality and globalization cannot be comprehensively considered simply as an aspect or outcome of the Western "project" of modernity or, except in very broad terms, enlightenment' (1992b: 27). These proclaimed differences become apparent when we examine the terms with which globalization might be thought to be associated but which its theorists say it is not, namely Americanization or cultural imperialism.

It has been a central contention of recent debate that it is no longer a specific societal model which is being exported or globalized (e.g. the 'American way'). Even those whose analysis has emerged out of development theory, and who are therefore sensitized to the exportation of Western models, stress that the relationship of globalization to Americanization is by no means a straightforward one. In this spirit Leslie Sklair notes: 'capitalist consumerism is mystified by reference to Americanization, while Americanization, the method of the most successfully productive society in human history, gives its imprimatur to capitalist consumerism' (1991: 134). Globalization is not, in other words, a polite way of saying Americanization.

It is thought to be characteristic of late modernity that highly diverse cultural practices and material (from world music to world religion) might provide the source of exportable commercialized culture. Indeed commercialized culture can be sold all the more effectively where it can be tailored to the local context or, alternatively, where it has an 'exotic feel'. What is being sold in all cases is the idea of selling – of consumerism – itself; the idea that the world is a market of cultural artefacts and resources from whose vast range the consumer must choose. Sklair's notion of the 'culture-ideology of consumerism' is intended to draw attention to this aspect:

> The specific task of the global capitalist system in the Third World is to promote consumerism among people with no regard for their own ability to produce for themselves, and with only an indirect regard for their ability to pay for what they are consuming.
>
> (1991: 131)

Similarly, Lash and Urry argue that a globalized culture of consumption cannot be subsumed under any one dominant substantive ideology:

'contemporary developments do not produce a straightforwardly dominant ideology, that is sets of *ideas* which in some way involve legitimation, dissimulation, unification, fragmentation and reification' (1994: 306).

Thus, not only is globalization thought not to be tied to any substantive notion of the 'Good Society', it may, according to its critics, even preclude any discussion of what such a society might look like. As objects of consumption and transmission all social forms are equal. It is the individual as sovereign consumer who must decide on the basis of his/her own preferences what is good 'for them':

> Junk culture is the spoilt brat of affluence, but in its ceaseless acts of proliferation and unprincipled celebrations of novelty, it also denies the possibility of any debate on the Good Society predicates as that must be on enduring, if contested, principles and on rational discourse for their contestation.

> (Archer 1990: 102)

Margaret Archer's observation here suggests that modernization and globalization are really quite distinct indeed. The ethnocentric assumptions of the modernizers have been replaced by the relativism of a market in which consumer preferences rather than any form of public discourse establish the criteria by which the Good Society is to be judged. In Lash and Urry's terms, a postmodern 'network of communication and information' replaces an at least partially rational discourse of ideology. While the claims of modernizers could at least be challenged by holding up some alternative societal model, consumerism and technology claim neutrality and impartiality. They profess to be merely the most efficient mechanisms for placing bets on which societal forms are preferable, the outcome being determined by the aggregate of individual choices.

Of course, this difference may be more apparent than real because (as Sklair's comments on 'imprimatur' imply) it is the market itself, and the idea of the market as the appropriate medium for social interaction, which comes to embody (Archer might say 'usurp') a substantive conception of the Good Society. Globalization and modernization may not be so different after all. The notion of the consumer as an isolated individual with sets of preferences upon which basis choices are made can be held to embody quite specific values and assumptions. Later I shall suggest that sociological accounts of globalization have sometimes tended to take the claims of markets and of technology to neutrality *vis-à-vis* specific societal models at face value.

Globalization and/or fragmentation?

A second theme which has permeated recent discussions is the claim that processes of globalization and fragmentation are complementary. This, too, is thought to distinguish globalization from modernization. No longer is it claimed that the world is converging upon a consensus (cf. Kerr *et al.* 1960). Nor is it argued, in the style of modernization theory, that we are moving from particularism to universalism. Rather, globalization is held to be a complex interaction of globalizing and localizing tendencies (so-called 'glocalization'); a synthesis of particularistic and universalistic values. As Robertson notes, 'we are, in the late twentieth century, witnesses to – and participants in – a massive, twofold process involving *the interpenetration of the universalization of particularism and the particularization of universalism*' (1992b. 100). Likewise, Ulf Hannerz argues that globalization is characterized by the 'organization of diversity rather than by a replication of uniformity' (1990: 237) while Jonathan Friedman claims that 'ethnic and cultural frag-mentation and modernist homogenization are not two arguments, two opposing views of what is happening in the world today, but two constitutive trends of global reality' (1990: 311).

The point Hannerz and Friedman make about the heterogeneity of global culture has also been made about the global economy. Thus Anthony McGrew argues that 'globalization is highly uneven in its scope and highly differentiated in its consequences' (1992: 23), while Bob Jessop is even more explicit:

> whereas Fordism could plausibly be interpreted in terms of the diffusion of the American model to other national economies, there is currently no single hegemonic growth model (Japanese, American, and West German models are in competition) and even more extensive financial and industrial internationalization makes it even more important for most national economies to find distinctive niches in the world-wide division of labour.
>
> (1988: 160)

The suggestion here is that globalization is occurring in the absence of either a cultural or an economic 'hegemon' and that processes of standardization and diversification, and unification and fragmentation, are occurring simul-taneously.

In the sphere of cultural analysis perhaps the most influential version of this argument is the one advanced by Arjun Appadurai (1990) through his now well-known distinctions between 'ethnoscapes', 'mediascapes', 'technoscapes', 'financescapes' and 'ideoscapes'. Appadurai's argument is that globalization is characterized precisely by the divergence of these aspects; by the fact that these 'scapes' 'follow increasingly non-isomorphic paths' (1990: 301). With these distinctions Appadurai theorizes the compat-ibility and simultaneity of convergence and fragmentation which is thought to distinguish both the recent debate from the earlier notions of simple convergence which characterized theories of modernization and the most recent from earlier phases of societal development.

But is this broadly postmodern sensitivity to the differences between modernization and globalization and to the complexity of the interaction of globalizing and localizing tendencies sufficient to avoid what John H. Goldthorpe once called the 'recrudescence of historicism' within the theory of industrial society (Goldthorpe 1971)? On the one hand, are diagnostic approaches by dint of their own logic and the manner in which they assert truth claims inclined to overestimate the power and underestimate the limitations of the processes they identify? On the other hand, are they prone to neglect the extent to which globalization is a quite specific project? – that is to say, a project that is much more specific than can be captured by the notions of modernity, late or high modernity or postmodernity, which have displaced the now somewhat unfashionable notion of industrial society, but which may have carried over some of its epistemological assumptions.

I have already suggested that there may at least be a difference of emphasis or interpretation between the kinds of diagnostic analysis discussed above and a more political reading of the type offered by Gray and Hutton. I want next to identify what these differences of interpretation or emphasis might be. Since I think Hutton is right to see Karl Polanyi as a key figure for understanding the contemporary changes which are captured under the label 'globalization', I shall develop the point by re-examining the arguments he developed in the 1930s and 1940s.

GLOBALIZATION, DEREGULATION AND THE LOGIC OF MARKETS

Laissez-faire was planned.

Karl Polanyi

In the following discussion I hope to show that there are at least three reasons why in the context of current social-scientific debate it is worth revisiting Polanyi. First, he provides an analysis of the globalizing tendencies of market societies with a concrete analysis of their political and regulative institutions. Second, he does not equate globalization with the logic of either capitalism or modernity *per se*, but sees it rather as one possibility for a modern capitalist society, the realization of which requires conditions that are both contingent and political. Third, at a time when many social scientists seem to believe that the possibility of a critical engagement with liberalism has disappeared, with the near collapse of Marxism as a paradigm and of communism as a viable alternative to capitalism, Polanyi's arguments suggest that we may not, after all, have to abandon ourselves to a Bacchanalian celebration of consumerism, cultural fragmentation and unrestrained individualism.

Polanyi's analysis, though developed through detailed historical and anthropological argument, is based upon a model which is both simple and elegant.

Indeed, it might be reduced to a series of straightforward claims or hypotheses. The first is that markets destroy social relations or, more precisely, the organization of economic life, which historically has typically taken the form of complex, localized relations of reciprocal obligation, is usurped by markets in which transactions are mediated through monetary exchange and in which social relations are regulated by contract. This argument, which has earlier echoes in Marx's analysis of the labour contract, is intended to point to the fact that economic life does not naturally, always, or even normally consist in the transactions of rational egotists. The second core argument is that markets come into being through the activity of political organizations and, in the modern period, specifically through the actions of states. This reinforces the anti-naturalistic analysis of the market. Markets do not arise spontaneously from our nature as animals inclined to 'truck and trade', but in a conscious planned fashion: as the outcome of political action and decision. In Polanyi's terms, the free market is a utopian conception, all markets are regulated in the sense that their parameters are established by state institutions. Finally, Polanyi's historical analysis is also intended to show that the socially disruptive nature of markets is so strong that it will result either in social collapse or authoritarianism as actors desperately try to resist its effects upon community, or – more hopefully – in the re-introduction of political mechanisms for regulating the market and protective restrictions on its scope of operation. In other words, society will delimit, either irrationally or rationally, the area in which markets operate 'freely' in order to protect 'itself'.

Although these arguments were developed to explain the rise and nature of the first 'free market utopia' (Britain as it was conceived by Manchester economics), and although what gave urgency to Polanyi's work was the rise of European fascism, the three essentially straightforward general points he makes remain relevant to what might be called the 'second free market utopia' (i.e. a single global market as it is conceived by contemporary neoliberalism). The implications of these propositions for analysing globalization are as follows: first, ideas are important, and perhaps as important as societal processes and economic trends; second, globalization necessarily remains a contested and ultimately unrealizable project.

Ideas, not (just) societal processes and economic trends

Polanyi's analysis suggests that no matter how careful one is in avoiding teleology and determinism, it remains insufficient to analyse globalization exclusively as though it were the outcome of social and economic *processes*, however complex. Globalization must be seen in part at least as the outcome of an idea, and specifically the idea of a free market; 'free' in the sense of freed from all political, social or '*gemeinschaftlich*' constraint. In contemporary terms, globalization on such a view is the realization or side-effect of economic deregulation and the lowering of social costs within national communities. Part of the aim of Polanyi's analysis was to suggest a reversal of the direction of causality: not from economic development to political response but from political philosophy to economic relations. Polanyi here seems to be taking the injunction that 'social life is the expression of ideas' (cf. Winch 1958) as methodological counsel. Deregulation on such an interpretation is not a *response* to competition but a means of extending it into areas which were previously protected, or partially protected, from commodification. It is deregulation that undermines the ability of nation states to protect themselves and the community they represent from the social destructiveness of markets, but it is also the nation state that is the key actor in bringing deregulation about both internally (e.g. through privatization and lowering social costs within its borders) and externally (e.g. by participating in and agreeing to proposals emerging from international fora – GATT negotiations etc.). On such a view, contemporary neo-liberalism has been successful because it has persuaded many politicians, and perhaps voters also, that the direction of causality runs from economic development to political response and thus presents itself merely as an objective or at least neutral diagnosis rather than as a contributor to the emergence of the very conditions it purports to analyse. If this criticism is valid, one might, echoing Karl Kraus's observations on psychoanalysis, characterize deregulation as that disease which purports to be its own cure. My worry about diagnostic approaches in political science and sociology is that they may have unwittingly accepted this 'spurious claim' (Gray 1994).

The alternative interpretation emerging from Polanyi's analysis ascribes considerable significance to neo-liberal political philosophy. It would almost define globalization, as Hutton and Gray have, as the new right's project. In other words, causal significance is ascribed to political belief. This goes against the grain of diagnostic approaches whether of a Marxist or non-Marxist type. With respect to Marxism it suggests that globalization is not the result of capitalism *per se*, nor the outcome of a logic of capitalism however 'mediated through historically specific institutional forms' (Jessop 1988: 151). Rather, Polanyi's analysis assumes both interdependence of and permanent contest between markets and states. What neo-liberalism has done, he would have argued, is to tip the balance in favour of markets by convincing political actors, who may not yet be fully aware of the political and social consequence, that they should deregulate markets, if for no better reason than that they are persuaded that there is no alternative. What Sklair has called 'transnational practices' are facilitated by neo-liberalism's political project. While, to retain Sklair's terminology, the 'transnational capitalist class' (to the extent that such a thing exists) may have benefited, it is not by itself able to bring these conditions about. In so far as nation states are in decline – and some of the subsequent chapters question the extent to which they are – this is not so much because they die of natural causes (i.e. as a consequence of market expansion), but rather they consent to voluntary euthanasia by releasing market forces from political constraint,

Particularly, Marxist and neo-Marxist analysts have been wary of such explanations not simply because they are thought to ascribe too much significance to ideas and to the political, but also because they do not address what appears to be the key question. As John Holloway notes, 'to explain the changes in terms of the influence of neo-liberal thought simply raises the question of why neoliberals should have gained such influence in different countries at this particular time' (1994: 25). But the answer to at least the first part of this question is quite straightforward: it is neo-liberalism which is an intrinsically globalizing project; it will have influence either almost nowhere or almost everywhere. Although new right ideas are popularly associated with Hayek and Friedman, its inherently globalizing logic – the opposition to each and every territorial and political constraint on markets – is already evident in the earliest expressions of modern neo-liberalism, namely in the work of Ludwig von Mises:

> If, for instance, all important restrictions were lifted today, the greatest difficulty would be evident for a short time, but there would soon be an unprecedented rise in the productivity of human labor. These inevitable frictions cannot be mitigated through an orderly lengthening of the time taken for such a reduction of the protection, nor are they always aggravated by such lengthening. However, in the case of government interference with prices, a slow and gradual reduction, when compared with their immediate abolition, only prolongs the time during which the undesirable consequences of the intervention continue to be felt.
>
> (1977 [1929]: 62–3)

It is thus no coincidence that Polanyi's analysis may be useful now. If the political context of his work was the emergence of European fascism, its intellectual context was the 'Austrian economics' of von Mises and Hayek, whose arguments re-emerged in the 1970s and 1980s as the core economic ideas of the new right.

That neo-liberalism and deregulation are entwined is evident, but its significance may have been lost in diagnostic accounts of globalization. In pointing to the significance of political belief in the emergence of globalization we are suggesting that the claim that 'capital, by its nature, knows no special bounds' (Holloway 1994: 30) while in one sense true (capital flows across borders) is not helpful because the real question is how tightly the political organizations which territorially constrain the globalizing tendency of capitalism will continue to hold in the reins. This question must be addressed not only conjecturally but also through an understanding of the beliefs which guide decision-making. There is a simple logical point here. Precisely, if the globalizing tendencies of capitalism (or indeed of modernity) are as ubiquitous as Holloway and others maintain, then the solution to the riddle of

11

globalization must make reference to something other than inherent economic tendencies. In other words, Holloway's criticism of explanations in terms of political ideas can be turned against socio-economic diagnosis: 'if capitalism is inherently globalizing then why are its globalizing tendencies not always equally and evenly apparent?' Precisely the same question can be addressed to the claim that modernity is intrinsically globalizing (as nation states are modern inventions then presumably modernity is, and was always, also intrinsically fragmenting). If we are to avoid falling into the same inevitablism as the proponents of neo-liberalism then we need something stronger than the notion of historical and institutional mediation of the logic of capitalism (or of modernity). We need to go beyond such formulations as 'even at high levels of abstraction, the basic forms of the capitalist relations do not determine the course of accumulation. For the latter also depend on a variety of social practices' (Jessop on the ambiguities of French regulation theory, 1990: 177) to the full realization of what this 'dependency on social [and political] practices [and beliefs]' means.

The necessarily incomplete project of globalization

The second broad implication of a political reading of globalization is that it lays greater emphasis upon the contestation of globalizing processes and upon the limits placed upon them. This follows from what I identified above as the first and third Polanyian thesis: markets destroy social relations, and there will inevitably be societal or political reactions which attempt to redress this balance. Polanyi is arguing that there is an incompatibility between the logic of market relations (based upon free exchange between rational egotists) and social relations (based upon a degree of trust and reciprocity between social actors). While a market logic can dominate social logic, as happens where forms of neo-liberalism are hegemonic, it can only do so at considerable cost and to a limited degree. As Hutton (1995) argues, ultimately markets themselves, and the transactions which underlie them, rely upon the very trust they undermine. This is essentially Durkheim's (and before him Rousseau's) argument: one cannot build into any contract a binding clause to the effect that contracts should be respected (Durkheim 1933 [1893]). The pre-contractual 'contract' for Durkheim is a *'conscience collective'* which is itself non-rational. In the context of this debate we might take Durkheim to be saying that even the transactions of rational egotists must be underpinned by trust and underwritten by a 'community' embodied in social institutions, not least states.[2] The problem Polanyi identifies is the tension between this pre-contractual (social) element and the asocial nature of the contractual relations themselves.

In order to understand the implications of this it is necessary to have a much more nuanced view of what states are and what they do than is to be found either in a realist view of them as power-hungry actors, as instruments of capitalism or merely as mechanisms for the regulation of capital. Regulatory bodies such as nation states have a double, and essentially contradictory, role. On the broadly Polanyian/Durkheimian view I am proposing here, on the one hand states have been instrumental in establishing markets and market parameters (and thus have assisted the destruction of communities), on the other they have also acted as protection against the effects of markets. What applies to states also applies to larger scale political bodies as is vividly illustrated in EU policy, which simultaneously deregulates and regulates, and appears to view – much to the consternation or even incomprehension of recent British governments – this dual track policy not as an inconsistency but as part of an integrated and coherent whole. There is no need to be particularly sentimental about the forms of social protection offered by nation states. Mary Douglas' warning applies all the more to national and super-national communities: 'let us be careful not to idealize community. It does not always deal kindly with its members' (1992: 104). Nor, one might add, does it always deal kindly with non-members. But it is also necessary to recognize that however narrowly nation states have defined the (it has now become customary to say 'imagined') communities they protect, their weakening would entail the increased exposure of classes of actors (including workers) to market forces. The point is especially clear with regard to 'decommodification'. Both Walter Korpi (1983) and Gösta Esping-Andersen (1990) have argued that the workers' strategy in pursuing narrowly economic interests (e.g. for wage increases) merge into more political demands for a social wage (e.g. welfare and unemployment benefits) in order to protect them from market forces (to decommodify their labour). It is the nation state towards which such demands are directed. Thus a weakening of nation states also entails a weakening of the position of labour and increases the likelihood of its recommodification. What can be said of labour might also be said of all other societal relations which can be commodified. This reinforces the general and widely recognized point that there is an internal relation between deregulation and the exposure of social groups and classes to globalizing forces of competition.

But there is a further and perhaps more important implication which, on Polanyi's analysis, would follow from this: globalization is not merely a political project it is also necessarily an unrealizable one. Just as Bauman (1992) has argued that the modernist project of imposing order upon chaos is ultimately unachievable, Polanyi is suggesting that the opposite strategy – what Peter Marcuse has dubbed the 'attempt to impose chaos on order' (1995: 241) – is not a realizable option either. The claim that were market logic allowed to become totally dominant over the non-rational logic of social relations it would corrode the very social and political conditions of its own possibility has specific implications for our understanding of the future direction in which globalization processes are likely to head. Rather than continuing to develop in its current direction and at its current speed in destroying social networks, economic globalization is always meeting resistance and approaching its limits. This resistance is not necessarily only or primarily the heroic resistance of popular mobilization. Indeed, in Polanyi's analysis such mobilizations may take on a very undesirable form (the essentially reactionary defence of rigid communal boundaries, possibly on the basis of nationality or race). Rather, one might expect new regulatory bodies to emerge at local and/or the interstate level as the power of nation states to control markets declines.

The argument here is essentially this: the deregulation and the marketization of society produces a series of catastrophes and potentially catastrophic developments which can be addressed in the short to medium term without constraining the market but in the longer run will entail the imposition of limits upon it. Some of these catastrophes are social: growing inequality, the impoverishment of sections of the population within and between national communities, urban decline, environmental degradation, etc. While these potential social catastrophes can be 'dealt with' to a degree and while markets enable states to reduce the areas for which they are held responsible (and hence distance themselves from the effects of their own policies), the potential for heading off possible crises in this manner is not inexhaustible. But perhaps more important is the fact that not all these potential catastrophes are social. Some are economic. The collapse of the Bank of Credit and Commerce International and the even more dramatic collapse of Barings Bank provide evidence enough that deregulated (or weakly regulated) markets are not so much crisis prone as catastrophe prone. But the complimentary argument is that these catastrophes are part of a (somewhat painful) societal learning process. Polanyi characterized the emergence of modern systems of social protection (including welfare states) as a learned response to the catastrophes of industrialization. Not least because planning has been partially effective (and because it brings with it problems of its own), these lessons may have been forgotten. But if deregulated markets and societies are disaster prone the lessons will have to be relearnt. There is an implicit catastrophe-learning-regulation model in Polanyi (and we may have to add a forgetting-deregulation-relearning-reregulation cycle to it).[3] Such a model is now re-emerging in the arguments of those who are worried by the effects of deregulation but by no means necessarily from a traditional leftist or Marxist position – John Gray for example, or the communitarians.

If Polanyi's learning model is valid this has significant implications for any would-be 'diagnosis of our times'; implications which contradict the globalization scenario. The most likely development on this view could not be continued unrestrained economic globalization but, as Hirst and Thompson (1992 and 1996) have argued, the increasing influence of geo-political organizations larger than the nation state but smaller than the globe (the EU, Pacific Basin Region, the American Trade Area, etc.). While these may initially appear as trade agreements (as 'common markets') their continued evolution entails a mix of de- and re-regulation (including social transfers) as well as attempts to build political bodies, civil societies and cultural identities at a level higher than that of the nation state – not, as for Bauman, the end of the cultivation of a coherent (if not necessarily homogenous) identity, but the re-integration of existing identities within larger communities. On such a view, new restrictions and limitations on markets will come to replace those in decline. Thus while financial flows and the information super highway may be global in *range*, their *scope* of influence will become the object of regulation and restriction. If we are to retain notions of a logic of capital at all, then we must also speak of a competing and opposing 'logic of politics'. The globalizing logic of capital is always and already engaged in a struggle to escape political regulation, while politics is constantly fighting to keep economic activity under its control.

Polanyi's analysis is in a strict sense social and democratic. We can accept that the total victory of the political over the economic leads to the kinds of inefficiencies manifested by no longer actually existing socialism while arguing that the kind of once-and-for-all victory envisaged by neo-liberalism for the economy over the social and political could only be achieved at a high social cost (cf. Bottomore 1996). This would support the essentially moderate conclusions drawn by Habermas (1990) from the collapse of communism. Habermas argued that communism's demise, even were it to demonstrate the greater efficiency of the market as a means of organizing economic life, does not of itself uphold neo-liberalism's claim that the logic of market relations should supplant all other principles of social organization beyond and outside the economic sphere. There can be no once-and-for-all victory for either the economic or the political. Here again globalization theory may have underestimated the contradictory character of social change. While globalization theorists have emphasized the complementary nature of globalization and fragmentation and of universalizing and partic-ularizing tendencies, they may have fallen into an historicist trap by viewing this, to adapt another Polanyian metaphor, 'double movement' (or simulta-neous de- and re-regulation) as something new or as itself evidence of globalization rather than simply a phase of the struggle between the opposing (but mutually interdependent) logics of the economic and the socio-political at a time when the balance of forces lay with the former.

ISSUES ADDRESSED IN THE COLLECTION

Polanyi's work is a striking illustration of the way in which the social sciences, or at least most of sociology and much of political science, emerged as a critical response to liberalism. In what I have called diagnostic approaches to globalization, analysis and critique have become detached and in the process some of the assumptions of neo-liberalism – including the inevitab-lism criticized by Gray – have been absorbed. The much heralded collapse of 'grand narratives' (often a code for the putative collapse of the Marxist paradigm and of an alternative to capitalism) lies behind this disengagement. But such an analysis ignores the fact that the sociological critique of liberalism has not necessarily or always been conducted from a position outside it. Thus, for example, Durkheim (especially 1969 [1898]) defends liberalism but not in its most utilitarian (for him 'egotistic') form, while Weber offers a defence of liberal institutions which is not grounded in liberal individualism (e.g. Weber 1994 [1918]). This makes Polanyi an instructive figure even now. His critique of *laissez-faire* capitalism combines Weber's recognition that commercial activity and individualist beliefs are compatible with bureaucratic domination (see Scott 1996) and Durkheim's concern about the impact of an unrestricted (or 'forced') division of labour upon social solidarity. Given the conflation of a critique of utilitarian liberalism with the critique of capitalism *per se*, for which we must hold Marxism partly responsible, it is perhaps less surprising that an impasse of the totalizing critique of capitalism should issue in such a strong reaction in the opposite direction: resignation in the face of, unquestioning attitude towards, or even celebration of consumerism, materialism and subjectivism (for a critique of which, see Poppi, Chapter 13). In contrast to the broad-brush diagnostic approach of much recent social theory, where the analysis of globalization has focused on its concrete manifestations, as for example in Saskia Sassen's analysis of global markets in financial services (1991), the connection of globalization to the kinds of beliefs and political projects briefly discussed above again becomes apparent, as does the contestation and manipulation of globalizing processes as well as their possible limitation. In other words, it is through more specific or concrete exploration that a general analysis which is both analytic and critical may again emerge.

To shift debate away from general diagnosis by relocating the social sciences in the context of the critical response to liberalism suggests that we might take Hirst and Thompson's well-supported argument that the notion of globalization has taken on something of the character of a 'myth' (Hirst and Thompson 1996) one stage further by suggesting that in its diagnostic form globalization theory may have become 'ideological', not in the highly problematic sense of 'false consciousness' but in Karl Mannheim's sense: an idea whose purpose is to assist or resist social change. Ideology in this sense, or some equivalent but less 'contaminated' term, would seem indispensable for characterizing those ideas which produce, or seek to produce, the effects they purport merely to reflect. The suggestion here, and it largely repeats Gray's assertion with which I opened the discussion, is that globalization *theory* may itself be part of the globalization *process*. Where an idea becomes established as an unquestioned orthodoxy it too might might be said (as Altvater and Mahnkopf say about the logic of markets and money in Chapter 14) to have taken on a life of its own and come to exercise an objective compulsion over actors. But the validity of the assertion that globalization theory may have taken on something of the character of a political rhetoric or ideology cannot be established purely through an appeal to the authority of a major social theorist of a previous generation, however distinguished. We need to assess the coherence and validity of the central claims it makes. It is to this project that the present work hopes to contribute.

The aim of this collection is to examine from a variety of perspectives (i) the limits or boundaries placed upon globalizing processes and (ii) the degree of flexibility or permeability of those boundaries. This, we believe, can be done most effectively through a mixture of theoretical reflection and more empirically focused case studies. Furthermore, because of the all-embracing nature of alleged globalizing processes which are said to encompass the social, political and cultural as well as the economic, assessing the claims requires an interdisciplinary or cross-disciplinary approach, a variety of perspectives and the adoption of diverse argumentative and presentational approaches. The case studies are not intended as mere 'illustrations' of theoretical argument. In part this is because they may be informed by distinct theoretical agendas of their own. Explicit theoretical discussion is not the only, nor indeed inevitably the most effective, way of conveying a theoretical argument. However, and more importantly, first, it is in the articulation of general globalizing tendencies with specific instances that the utility of globalization theory as a research programme can be examined; second, it is in the case studies that it becomes most apparent just how far globalization, in so far as we can speak of it at all, is uneven, problematic and contested. Recognizing this is particularly important where, as here, a research programme is so largely dependent upon general diagnostic or prognostic assertions, and so heavily reliant upon theoretical argument. We hope to redress the balance somewhat by presenting theoretical debate and empirical material in a way in which each can feed productively off the other; in which the often rigid boundaries between the two can be loosened.[4] If the more explicitly theoretical chapters were to be read merely to 'cull' core arguments, or if the case studies were taken either as illustrative or as something for specialists alone, then the collection would have failed in one of its key aims: to focus debate down onto a plane in which 'great transformations' and 'big processes' meet with the actions and intentions of institutional, collective or individual actors.

If the desire to focus debate is one rationale for the present collection, then the other can be expressed through the various senses in which the authors have taken the term *limit*. Above I have used Polanyi's arguments to explore a most general sense of the limits of globalization, but the term has a number of more specific implications. I shall finally set out briefly the distinct senses of 'limits' to globalization as they appear in this collection.

Limits due to contestation and resistance

That globalizing processes are contested is generally acknowledged, but the full significance of such contestation becomes most apparent when we examine specific cases, as do Howard Caygill (Chapter 2) and Sasha Roseneil (Chapter 3) in Part I ('Contesting global forces'). The two chapters provide contrasting examples. In the case of Berlin's Potsdamer Platz the combined economic power of major corporations and the cultural power of leading architects and firms proved too strong for local social movement opposition. In Caygill's account, it is the local authorities that embody the conflict, sometimes representing the interests of sections of the affected populations, at other times those of developers. But even here, the existence of opposition at least forces elaborate programmes of 'selling' the corporate project to the local population in the process of which the plans, though ultimately never abandoned, are to a degree transformed. Caygill leaves us with the provocative suggestion that the apparent victory of the combined global force of international architecture and capital may presage its local failure on a site which has many times seen grand and triumphalist schemes.

In Roseneil's account of the Greenham Common peace movement the outcome is likewise open-ended. The failure of its immediate political ends did not, she argues, nullify its broader cultural and political achievements. One point to emerge from both discussions is that local movements may be, in Charles Tilly's sense (Tilly 1978), 'reactive', but they are not thereby simply rolled over by globalizing forces, or even in so far as they are, they do not leave those forces unchanged. As Roseneil observes, these movements 'were at the same time both the product of globalization and productive of globalization' (p. 70). Roseneil is concerned with the ways in which 'globalization' can be moulded to the projects of collective actors, i.e. the senses in which it does not go on 'behind their backs' – as is sometimes assumed – but can be incorporated into the language and strategy of social movements. In other words, the rhetoric of globalization is not the exclusive property of the powerful. This links directly to a second sense in which globalizing processes may be said to be limited.

The complexity of culture and agency as a limit

Part II ('Homogenized culture or enduring diversity?') examines the possibility that continued cultural diversity is not a mere remnant, but is and will remain a feature of social life however advanced globalization may become in other spheres.

John Street (Chapter 4), taking the example of the music industry where one might expect cultural globalization to be most advanced, argues that the notion of a global popular culture is largely mythical and that nation states retain a higher degree of policy and economic control over their cultural industries than is generally recognized. In this way they may continue to act to protect what they understand to be 'their' national culture. The issues of the powers remaining to nation states is taken up further in Part III (see below).

If Caygill and Roseneil are concerned with collective and more-or-less systematic responses, Ahmed Gurnah's account (Chapter 6) of the ways in which young Zanzibaris in the 1950s and 1960s reinterpreted American culture (e.g. films and music) focuses upon the less intentionally organized but none the less effective ways in which actors adapt and deploy exported cultural material to their own ends. Rejecting simplistic 'cultural imperialism' models, Gurnah draws out the nature of culture not merely as another object to be exported, but as a means of communication; something not merely 'received' but transformed and re-transmitted. No matter how determined the attempt to transmit homogenous and uniform cultural material, actors are too knowing and culture too complex for any process of cultural exchange – no matter how unequal – to be exclusively one-way. One implication here may be that it is the complexity of culture itself rather than the greater flexibility of globalization as compared to so-called 'Americanization' that explains the eclecticism of cultural exchange; such eclecticism being the normal condition of cultural interaction irrespective of the ways in which inequalities of power mould those interactions.

In a different theoretical guise the issue of the complexity of cultural material appears again in Rajika Jalan's discussion (Chapter 5). Taking very specific cultural images which might be thought to typify the influence of 'Western' culture, she demonstrates the complexity and ambiguity of cultural icons when they become re-formed in the process of being taken up by Asian magazines and their readers. The point is made all the more vivid by the fact that she selects what appears to be a highly 'Westernised' magazine and readership. The complexity of texts in their inter-texuality (e.g. multiplicity of references to other media) makes not merely their *use* but also their *reading* a complex process. Jalan does not stop at making this point theoretically, but demonstrates it by using techniques of reading informed by post-structuralist literary analysis. In doing so she opens out the multiple significance of what at first glance appears familiar material. Again, the idea of simple exportation without transformation of the material is called into question.

What is true of texts is – perhaps more surprisingly – true of economic behaviour in Julia Tao's and Wai-Nang Ho's account of Chinese entrepreneurship (Chapter 7). While China's new economic zone and growth in the East Asian economies generally may in some respects appear to be a paradigmatic response (and stimulus) to economic globalization, the kinds of cultural resources upon which its success depends are shown to be intensely local. 'Enterpreneurialism' too is complex and the question is not, as it was for an earlier generation of modernization theorists, merely one of its presence or absence, but of its form. The case is particulary significant because it suggests (as Weber did) that even economic behaviour is culturally grounded. Their argument, which echoes that of Stewart and Garrahan (Chapter 10), may support Polanyi's claim that economic disembedding is restrained by the degree of economy's own dependence upon the very social resources from which it seeks to break free.

The resilience of the nation state as a limit

In Part III ('The national, the international and the global') the issue already raised by John Street is examined in a variety of spheres. Nation states, as Hirst and Thompson (1992 and 1996) have forcefully argued, are not the mere victims of globalization, but active participants in shaping and deter- mining its scope and reach. The nation state may well continue to be an active agent in steering these processes and able, with varying degrees of success, to position itself within a changing world order. This view is gener- ally supported in the discussion of urban policy by Alan Harding and Patrick Le Galès (Chapter 8), of air transport by Hussein Kassim (Chapter 9) and of industrial relations and policy by Paul Stewart and Philip Garrahan (Chapter 10). As Harding and Le Galès remark 'the constitutional, legisla- tive and financial power of national governments continues to give them a decisive role in central–local government relations and in determining the structures and modes of operation of subordinate tiers and agencies of the state' (p. 198). Kassim uses the ideal type developed by Hirst and Thompson (1996) to show that air transport liberalization and deregulation have not entailed the full globalization of the industry in the sense of giving it autonomy from political regulation. And even in the case of auto manufacture in which the power of the Japanese industry and the influence of its style of industrial relations appears almost as a paradigm case of globalization, Stewart and Garrahan argue that 'there is no evidence to suggest that international restructuring follows the certainties of the glob- alization theorists in their assumption of convergence' (p. 235–6).

Continuing the theme of the relationship of globalization to the nation state, in his discussion of the fate of the former Soviet Union Mike Bowker (Chapter 11) challenges both the most pessimistic and the most optimistic interpretations of the ethnic fragmentation which is held to characterize a post-nation state world. He too questions the sometimes glib assumption that the nation state model with its culturally homogenizing project is no longer valid when he concludes 'the nation state represents the only chance for peace and stability in this troubled region' (p. 253). Like Poppi (Chapter 13), Bowker questions assumptions that are increasingly taken for granted within contemporary social scientific debate.

Locating globalization

Part IV consists of theoretical reflections from a variety of perspectives on globalization which link the current debate to general social theory on the one hand, and longer-term social change on the other. Each piece is thus an attempt to locate globalization and globalization theory critically in a wider context. Richard Kilminster (Chapter 12) offers a very useful guide to the pre-history of the concept and of its antecedents in philosophy before going on to interpret more recent developments through a perspective informed by Norbert Elias's theory of social evolution.

Globalization theorists have drawn attention to the growing fragmentation of identity and have argued that such fragmentation is compatible with (or even a manifestation of) globalizing tendencies. There are clear overlaps here with post-Marxist arguments that better theorized social divisions – particularly class – are losing some of the significance previously ascribed to them (see, for example, Laclau and Mouff 1985; Laclau 1992). But how are we to understand and assess such claims? Cesare Poppi (Chapter 13) offers a critique of what he calls the 'New Subjectivism' of much recent social analysis, namely the reification of culture and its treatment as free-floating. By discussing ethnic identity Poppi takes that area of analysis, with its emphasis on dissolution of identity, where the influence of postmodernist social theory is perhaps strongest and challenges those narratives of discontinuity which insist on the uniqueness and novelty of contemporary cultural fragmentation.

Finally, Elmar Altvater and Birgit Mahnkopf (Chapter 14) develop aspects of Marx's analysis of money and Polanyi's analysis of markets to trace the current phase of capitalist society through its longer-term historical development. They show how the logic of money and markets has taken on a life of its own and how it can come to dominate the social relations from which it has broken loose (become 'disembedded'). They do this in a way which recognizes both the specific (e.g. political and ideological as well as economic) conditions under which this 'disembedding process' can take place, and the limits set by the ultimate infeasibility of full market autonomy. They thus offer a synthesis of Marx's analysis of the tendency of economic relations to become independent and dominant with Polanyi's recognition that the logic of money and market can never achieve the kind of total domination to which it aspires.

NOTES

1 Indeed, Bauman's discussion of the redundancy of the 'society concept' takes place in the context of an account of postmodernity rather than globalization.
2 For a fuller discussion of the implications of arguments from the Durkheimian school for the assessment of modern social relations, including commercial ones, see Scott 1997.

3 A very similar but much more developed model of the process by which societies learn the necessity for the provision of public goods (including those of regulation and social transfers) and learn how to overcome the free-rider problems which act as barriers to such provisions can be found in Abram de Swaan's work on welfare (1988).

4 This proximity of theoretical reflection and presentation of case study material is also demonstrated by the fact that several chapters explicitly shift between the two levels.

Part I

CONTESTING GLOBAL FORCES

2

THE FUTURES OF BERLIN'S POTSDAMER PLATZ

Howard Caygill

INTRODUCTION

The locus of power is an empty place, it cannot be occupied – it is such that no individual and no group can be consubstantial with it – and it cannot be represented.
(Claude Lefort, *The Question of Democracy*)

Architecture may be defined as the taking-place of the political, the process by which public space is constituted and configured. It is by no means a purely aesthetic phenomenon, since buildings do not simply 'reflect' given social and political structures but form part of their constitution. This constitutive aspect of architecture contributes to the peculiar temporality of architectural judgement. Buildings do not simply happen once and for all but embody their imagined pasts, presents and futures. Architecture is a temporal art which defines the present occupation and configuration of a site in terms of its imagined pasts and futures. It is also a political art in so far as it orients itself within a present riven by competing and perhaps irreconcilable hopes and memories.

Where architecture stands with respect to politics and time is itself an object of dispute, and one which involves the very nature of the profession. Should architecture be open-ended, its buildings occupying a provisional present – rising, changing, collapsing – or should it be monumental, drawing together past and future into an unchanging present which exhausts the history past and future of a site? This is a question not only of architecture, but also of politics, since the two views of architecture – the provisional and the monumental – are aligned with two understandings of architectural politics. In the first, civil society is taken to constitute and empower itself in the process of building its environment, while in the second, buildings are handed down from above, disempowering the community. In the first case architecture in process is an integral part of the local community, while in the second it is spectacular, working at the level of the abstract design forms of global architecture. There are clear grounds for conflict between the saturated time of the local community, occupying a site laden with memories and aspirations, and the abstract speed of world architecture, whose avant-garde dynamic tends to fold past and future into a monumental present suited to spectacular imposition.

In terms of architectural judgement and decision-making, an inverse rule prevails in which architecture as process claims an infinitely extended, and monumental architecture an infinitesimally reduced, time for judgement and decision. The first requires time to make provisional judgements and decisions about the configuration of a site, while the second makes an almost instantaneous decision meant to hold for all time. The question then arises as to whether the monumental mode of architecture will always prevail by virtue of the advantages of speed and spectacle, its ability to condense the time of judgement into a moment of decision. And if it does so prevail, may that be taken as a judgement upon the democratic credentials and possibilities of architecture, if not even the architectural credentials and possibilities of democracy?

The case of Berlin's Potsdamer Platz exemplifies many of these problematic affinities between architectural judgement, time and the political. It provides a rare opportunity for an analysis of the political and aesthetic issues enmeshed in the process of architectural judgement and decision-making. It is exemplary for other reasons as well, since its local history is that of a contested site for monumental and provisional architecture, between official and popular definitions of urban space, between local and world politics (whether in their fascist, socialist, or capitalist variants) and specifically, since 1989, between corporate/world architecture and the local community. It may indeed be argued with respect to the development of Potsdamer Platz in the months immediately following the 1989 Revolution that if local control failed here, in Berlin, with its entrenched and unprecedented organization of the local 'alternative' community in the west of the city, and with the Green 'Alternative List' (AL) participating in city government, even controlling the department of Urban Development and Environmental Protection, it is hard to see it having much chance of succeeding anywhere else.

THE PHANTASMAL SITE

> I can't find Potsdamer Platz ... It was a lively place! Trams, horse-drawn buses and two cars, mine and the one from Hamann's chocolate shop. The Wertheim department store was here too. And then suddenly there were flags, there ... The whole place was covered with ... And the people weren't friendly any more, nor were the police. But I won't give up searching until I have found Potsdamer Platz!
>
> (Wim Wenders and Peter Handke, screenplay from *Der Himmel über Berlin*)

Figure 2.1 Views of Potsdamer Platz, 1901–1953
Source: Postcard by Kunst und Bild, Berlin

Shortly after the Revolution in 1989 I received two excited postcards from friends in Berlin telling me about the November events. One featured a view of the Brandenburg Gate, the other a collage of historical photographs with the caption: 'Berlin – Potsdamer Platz – in Changing Times'. The image of the Brandenburg Gate seemed to collect the past, present and future of Germany into a single time and place – a monumental *Jetztzeit* – while that of Potsdamer Platz seemed to fragment and disperse the present into a number of pasts and, more subtly, possible futures. Framed in black, the Potsdamer Platz postcard contrasted two colour images of Potsdamer Platz, one at the height of its modernity in 1929, the other after the erection of the Wall. In between the two colour images was a series of four dated, black and white photographs, 1901, 1930, 1945 ('Zero Hour'), and 1953 (the East German Uprising). It was hard to imagine that these two viewcards pictured sites only ten minutes walk from each other, one hard to miss, the other hard to find.

Berlin's Potsdamer Platz has always occupied a special place in the German political and architectural imagination. While the Brandenburger Tor is given over to celebrations of achievement and success, Potsdamer Platz evokes risk and failure. It has always been a non-place – literally a utopia – a site upon which to project fantasies of desire and fear, power and powerlessness. Its existence was never planned; it emerged as the name given to the undefined area outside the city's Potsdam Gate, and became the unofficial inverse of the formal, baroque Octagon or 'Leipziger Platz' on the inside of the gate. Its extent remained indefinite, eventually spreading to include both the Potsdam gate and the official square behind it. Its ambiguous spatial character was matched by its phantasmal presence in time: Potsdamer Platz always seemed be on a point of transition from the past to the future.

The phantasmal character of Potsdamer Platz may be traced to the peculiar fusion of politics and architecture which has characterized its history. Since the late eighteenth century the area around the Potsdam Gate has been the site for an uncanny encounter between architectural and political fantasy. Beginning with Friedrich Gilly's visionary plans for a monument to Frederick the Great in 1797 and Karl Friedrich Schinkel's proposal in 1814 for a vast cathedral commemorating the German War of National Liberation, Potsdamer Platz has been repeatedly called to embody architecturally the political ambitions of its masters. As a result its *genii loci* have undergone as many bewildering changes of identity as the German polity, hosting the local, national and world political conflicts of the past two centuries.

In the course of decades Potsdamer Platz changed from a semi-rural idyll on the outskirts of the city to the residential quarter of the Imperial bureaucracy and financial bourgeoisie. It became a centre of metropolitan consumption, the 'busiest road junction in Europe' and symbol of the Weimar Republic's technocratic modernity. Following the destruction of the Weimar Republic it became the monumental *Machtzentrum* of the National Socialists and after its destruction in the bombings and street battles of the Second World War was called to embody the 'Landscape of Rubble' (*Trümmerlandschaft*) of the so-called 'Zero Hour' of German history in 1945. Soon after it became the main corridor between the 'East' and the 'West' zones of the city and a symbol for the espionage and black marketeering of the immediate post-war years.

It was on Potsdamer Platz in 1953 that the troops of the Western Allies watched as Soviet tanks crushed the East Berlin Workers' Uprising, and in 1961 it was transformed into the deserted 'moonscape' of the 'death strip' between the Berlin Walls. In this inverted monument, the time of Potsdamer Platz was frozen into a moment of desolation intended to last until the resumption of the world proletarian revolution. Thereafter, even though it no longer physically existed, Potsdamer Platz became one of West Berlin's main tourist attractions, viewed from a vast wooden gantry on the western side of the wall. And it was not before the wall was finally breached at Potsdamer Platz in 1989 that the changes in the GDR were perceived as both profound and irreversible, and the unification of the German states became the order of the day.

28

While the Brandenburger Tor has become the place to re-celebrate the ecstasies of unification, Potsdamer Platz has lived up to its mournful history by becoming the site of intense political and architectural controversy. The re-invention of the place after 1989, described by Walter Momper, the then reigning Mayor of West Berlin, as the 'architectural decision of the century', has generated fundamental debate about not only architecture but also the future of Germany and German democracy. The intensity of these debates was heightened to near fever pitch by the decision of the Bundestag on 20 June 1991, by an 18 vote majority, to transfer the Federal capital from Bonn to Berlin.

With this decision the already highly charged debates around the future of Potsdamer Platz took on even greater significance. They were marked by several overlapping conflicts between different social, political, economic, ecological and aesthetic visions of the future, and how to reach it. The decision about the future of Potsdamer Platz assumed not only local, but also national and international significance. It would be a statement about not only the future of the two parts of the divided city, but also the two parts of the divided nation, and the future role of Germany as a mediator on a world stage between the capitalist states of the 'West' and the ex-socialist states of the 'East'. Once again, Potsdamer Platz has become the focus of the aspirations of world politics, this time those of capitalism and liberal democracy. Once again Potsdamer Platz was called to embody the challenges and the risks facing the German polity: it became the site of an encounter between different visions of the German future. It is also a stretch of derelict land in the middle of a capital city about which a decision must be made, whether to build or not to build, and if to build, then how? This is a 'decision' haunted not only by a history of past failures, but also by fundamentally different imaginations of the future. Potsdamer Platz is again a site of ambivalence, haunted by ghosts of the past and perplexed by desires for the future.

THE HAUNTING OF POTSDAMER PLATZ

> Noisy, matter-of-fact Berlin, the city of work and the metropolis of business, nevertheless has more, rather than less, than some others, of those places and moments when it bears witness to the dead, shows itself full of the dead.
>
> (Walter Benjamin, *A Berlin Chronicle*)

The origins of Potsdamer Platz lie in the late seventeenth-century expansion of Berlin under the 'Great Elector' Frederick William. In the Edict of Potsdam (1685), Frederick William placed the marshland to the south west of the city at the disposal of the Huguenot refugees from religious persecution in France. In 1688 the rectangular grid street plan characteristic of

European military-colonial city foundations was laid between the roughly north–south/east–west axis of Friedrich Straße and Leipzigerstraße, forming the 'new town' of Friedrichstadt. This along with the other seventeenth-century foundation Dorotheenstadt was incorporated into Berlin in 1709.

The development of Friedrichstadt was accelerated under the reign of the 'soldier king' Frederick William I, and especially during the 1730s. In 1732 Philipp Gerlach articulated the urban expansion to the south west with the centre of Berlin by means of an avenue joining three geometrically planned public squares known on early plans as *das Rondel* (the circle), *das Achteck* (the octagon), and *das Viereck* (the square). Each square was situated behind the main southerly gates in the proposed city wall, the so-called 'customs wall' built after 1735 in order to control the collection of customs duties (the '*akzise*' tax) and to prevent desertion from the city's vast garrison. The three baroque squares and their gates became the main symbolic axis of Berlin absolutist architecture: the Rondel, later 'Belle Alliance' later 'Mehring Platz' adjoined the Halle Gate, the Octagon, later Leipziger Platz, was behind the Potsdam Gate, while the Square, later Pariser Platz adjoined the Brandenburg Gate.

By 1740 the area before the Potsdam Gate became known as 'the place in front of the Potsdam Gate' (*Platz vor dem Potsdamer Tore*) but it did not appear on maps as Potsdamer Platz before the nineteenth century. It is conspicuously absent from Selter's map of 1804, but present on a map of 1834 and the revised version of Selter in 1841. It had disappeared again according to Reimer's map of 1850, but by this time the entire area including the gate and two areas before and behind it was known as 'the place around the Potsdam Gate'; in other words, the popular genius of the place had overcome its official.

In 1797 Friedrich Gilly described the site for his proposed Monument to Frederick the Great simply as 'the octagon on the Potsdam Gate'. His uncanny and still disturbing proposal unites both sides of the Gate into an architectural and political unity which combines, under the aegis of a mausoleum, both the popular space without and the official space within the Gate (see Watkin and Mellinghof 1987: 66). While Gilly's explication of his drawing alludes to the benign presence of the dead monarch in the midst of the current prosperity of his subjects – they who will thankfully perpetuate his memory as they walk and drive through the Potsdam Gate in their wagons – the drawing itself seems to transform Potsdamer Platz into the vestibule of a necropolis.[1] Its claustrophobic quality arises from the absence of any human figures that might give scale to the architecture; the only available reference point is the memory of classical proportion and architectural typology. The place has become a theatre of political and architectural memory.[2]

Gilly's proposal was never realized, nor was Karl Friedrich Schinkel's project for a cathedral on the site to commemorate the Prussian victory over

Figure 2.2 Friedrich Gilly, perspective of the monument to Fredrick the Great, 1797
Source: Kunstbibliothek Preussischer Kulturbesitz.

Napoleonic France in the Wars of Liberation in 1814. In two memoranda to the Monarch in 1814 and 1815, Schinkel described the cathedral as a 'living' monument, through which 'something is to be established by the people, which by the very nature of its installation, will live on and bear fruit'. Schinkel intended the building of the cathedral to provide a focus not only for the regeneration of art and industry, but also for the union of architectural and political order.

This project gave rise to a tension, characteristic of Schinkel's entire oeuvre between the politically formative activity of building (as for example in his 1836 painting 'View of Greece in its Prime', National Gallery, Berlin), and the politically repressive character of monumental buildings. In the case of Potsdamer Platz this is figured in the contrast between the open character and human scale of his sketches of the cathedral as a project under construction, and the oppressive painting of its completed state glimpsed through a vast triumphal arch under which the masses are dwarfed by the figures of mounted monarchs.[3] Although Schinkel's project was never realized, the *Spannungsfeld* between Potsdamer Platz as an incomplete architectural and political project with an open future and as a completed, monumental work occupying an eternal present characterized much of its subsequent history, and indeed continues to do so.

Gilly and Schinkel's extravagant visions of the futures of Potsdamer Platz gave way to a more subtle colonization of the place by politics and architecture. The area between the Brandenburg and Potsdam Gates became the residential quarter of the ministers, bureaucrats and bankers of the Prussian, later Imperial state. Potsdamer Platz and Leipziger Straße in the period of frantic building and speculation, known as the *Gründerzeit*, following Imperial Unification in 1871 became a service and retail centre first for the locality, and then for the city as a whole. The area became one of the main traffic knots of Berlin, an intersection of road and rail networks, and was the preferred site for large retail developments such as the Wertheim Department Store, built according to Messel's plans between 1896 and 1904.

Already before the First World War Potsdamer Platz was represented by the expressionist painter Ernst Ludwig Kirchner as a nightmare of metropolitan modernity. But during the 1920s under the Weimar Republic its modernity was celebrated; it was Potsdamer Platz above all that justified Berlin's claim to be the New York of Europe. Its traffic control tower, the first in Europe – shown hovering high above the earth like a satellite in Otto Arpkes photomontage of 1929 – and the hi-tech lines of Erich Mendelssohn's Columbus Haus (1932) (soon to serve as an SS inner-city detention camp) all contributed to making Potsdamer Platz the representative site for the Weimar Republic's technocratic modernity.

The futuristic traffic control tower embodied the Republic's modernist ideology of solving social and political problems through rational and

Figure 2.3 Karl Friedrich Schinkel's Triumphal Arch, 1817
Source: Berlin-Schloss Charlottenburg.

sachlich 'social engineering'. The Weimar Republic's architectural plans for Potsdamer Platz, above all those of the Berlin planner Martin Wagner subscribed to the prevailing engineer's aesthetic of *Die Schönheit der Technik*, the beauty of technology. Wagner in 1929 saw the beauty of the place to consist of its functional impermanence; because of the 'limited lifespan of a metropolitan square . . . the buildings around [Potsdamer Platz] will possess no permanent economic or architectural value. No town planner or traffic engineer would be able to predict the growth of traffic over the next 25 years' (Wagner cited in Knieper et al. 1991: 16).

Elements of this modernist ideology persisted in certain factions of the National Socialist Party after its seizure of power and establishment of a dictatorship in 1933. Even though the regime was confident that it could predict not only the next 25 but even the next 1,000 years, it was still possible in 1935 for Otto Kohtz to imagine Potsdamer Platz 'beautified' with an impressively articulated ensemble of skyscrapers. However, the area quickly became adapted to the monumental purposes of the new regime, being surrounded by ministerial buildings and Albert Speer's Monumental Reichs Chancellery on Voßstraße. The pace of the decision to build the Chancellery and its execution was intended to oppress: Hitler ordered its construction in 1938 and saw it completed within a year.

In Speer's megalomaniac plans for the Capital of the 1,000-year Reich – Berlin was to be renamed 'Germania' – Potsdamer Platz was destined to play an important role in the architectural complex of the triumphant regime.[4] It was to lead into a 156-metre-wide street running from north to south which culminated in a gigantic domed 'Soldiers Hall' dedicated to the glorious dead of the wars that were to come. Preparatory demolition work commenced in 1940 but ceased in 1942 when it was succeeded by the saturation bombing of the Allied Air Forces.

The proximity of the National Socialist centres of power meant that Potsdamer Platz became one of the most intensively bombed areas of Berlin. The bombing and the battle for Hitler's Bunker left the area a burnt-out shell in 1945, a memorial landscape far more effective than those planned by Gilly and Schinkel.[5] In the following years 'Potsdamer Platz', under the allied agreements for the division of Berlin, was known as the 'three-way corner', bordering the Russian, British and American Zones of the city. There children would beg in three languages, and goods, information and people shuttled illicitly between the zones. With the currency reforms in the western sectors of the city in 1948, Potsdamer Platz become the main site of black market dealing in currency, cigarettes, cameras, watches, and other 'goods and services'.

Apart from demolition, the main architectural innovation of the post-war period before the building of the Berlin Wall in 1961 consisted in raising hoardings for the propaganda war between East and West. In 1953 Potsdamer Platz was one of the main theatres of the Workers' Uprising, and

Figure 2.4 Potsdamer Platz and the remains of Schinkel's gates, March 1946
Source: Berlin-Landesbildstelle. From A. Balfour (1990) *Berlin: The Politics of Order*,
New York: Rizzoli International

became the place where, for the first time, workers fought against the forces of a worker's state and the tanks of its fraternal ally. And once again the place played host to an ambiguous victory in defeat, defeat in victory. The uprising was defeated, but at the price of the legitimacy of the SED regime, which was shown having to rely upon Soviet force to support its regime against its own citizens.

The collapse of the SED's legitimacy and the departure of many of its young skilled workers across the open border in Berlin culminated in the decision to erect an 'anti-fascist protection wall' in August 1961. The Wall was in fact two walls enclosing a 'death strip' which was mined and policed by armed border guards with orders to shoot to kill anyone attempting to cross it. Potsdamer Platz now straddled the death strip, and what was once the main place to be seen in Berlin became the place where to be seen meant death. The surviving buildings in the death strip were demolished, and by the 1980s all that remained of Potsdamer Platz were a pair of forlorn tram lines heading nowhere and the ghostly traces of the former street plan now colonized by rabbits. Once again Potsdamer Platz took up its role as a memorial landscape combining architectural and political symbolism, but this time featuring as the front line of the global Cold War.

Figure 2.5 Potsdamer Platz from the air, Fall 1935
Source: Berlin-Landesbildstelle. From A. Balfour (1990) *Berlin: The Politics of Order*,
New York: Rizzoli International

In spite of the desolation and the physical extinction of Potsdamer Platz, it continued to exist as a tourist attraction in the West. Coachloads of Wessies would draw up, climb the gantry, stare for a while, buy a souvenir and an ice-cream, and then return to the Ku'Damm. A genre of superior Berlin humour developed which featured the inane comments made by the visitors on the gantry, who were often unsure about what they were meant to be looking at. The area of the Wall at Potsdamer Platz was also the preferred site for unofficial political protest, such as the action against the Census in 1987 when protesters stuck their census forms to the Wall. Even though architecturally the place was now only a wasteland between two stretches of wall, it nevertheless continued to exist in memory and political imagination.[6] In the 1980s it disappeared from East Berlin maps and the authorities attempted to defuse the area's significance by dedicating it to housing. A proposal for housing developments on the Western side, proposed as part of the Internationale Bauausstellung (IBA), was rejected by the Senate in 1982.

The building programme in the East of the area was one of the first casualties of the 1989 Revolution. Building workers, many of them conscripted from the provinces to work in the capital, downed tools on the prefabricated housing and went home. One of the first signs of the renewed architectural significance of the area came in December 1989 with an official decision by the East German city authorities to suspend the existing building project. In the meantime Potsdamer Platz had rejoined the Brandenburger Tor as a focus for German political aspirations. On 9 November the political collapse of the Wall was celebrated at the Brandenburger Tor, while on 12 November at Potsdamer Platz the architectural seal was given by the dismantling of the Wall at Potsdamer Platz in the presence of the mayors of East and West Berlin.

The breach of the Wall at Potsdamer Platz opened not only a new crossing point between the two cities, but also the question of the future of the place. Once again it became the focus of intense architectural and political debate, bringing together conflicting images of how to build the political future not only of Berlin, but also of a re-unified Germany and its place in Europe and the world.

THE FUTURES OF POTSDAMER PLATZ

> For them metal and stone
> Grew together.
> So short was time
> That between morning and evening
> There was no noon
> And already on the old familiar ground
> Stood mountains of concrete.
> (Brecht, 'Of the Crushing Impact of Cities')

Standing on Potsdamer Platz on 12 April 1990, the West Berlin Mayor Walter Momper declared that the 'heart of Berlin would beat again'. But the first signs of the resurrection were intense differences about the architectural and political future of the place. The months after the opening of the Wall were characterized by a severe crisis of architectural and political judgement, one that involved not only different imaginations of the future but also of how to judge and decide between them.

By the spring of 1990 the most obvious sign of the re-occupation of Potsdamer Platz was the arrival of squatters with their goats and chickens. They constructed bivouac-like dwellings out of urban refuse, and created a pattern of settlement which evoked both an archaic past and the months immediately after the war when the bombed-out land was used to grow vegetables. By the summer the area was cleared and all trace of the unofficial occupation and its buildings removed. They nevertheless represented one possible future of the place, the occupation of the border territory by alternative, anarchic communities who refused to participate in the political structures of the Republic and who constructed for themselves a provisional anarchitectural environment.

During this period considerable differences emerged in official quarters about the political and architectural futures of Potsdamer Platz. This was particularly evident in the West Berlin Senate, which at this time was governed by a Red/Green coalition of the Social Democratic Party (SPD) and the 'Alternative Liste' (AL). The East Berlin administration in the Magistrature was effectively subordinated to the West Berlin Senate, a development which was intensified after the SPD's victory in the East Berlin municipal elections on 6 May 1990. Within the Senate itself the ruling 'Red/Green' coalition of the SPD and the AL began to disintegrate, a disintegration staged in terms of public differences over the future of Potsdamer Platz.

The debate within the ruling coalition on this issue was taken by many to signify the end of the Berlin experiment of combining the SPD's bureaucratic-corporatist tradition of decision-making with the local 'grass roots democratic' culture of the green Alternative Liste.[7] It presaged the Berlin SPD's turn to a 'Red/Black' coalition with the CDU (Christian Democratic Union), one which promised efficiently to manage the social market economy. The Red/Green coalition buckled under the irreconcilable pressures of the local accountability of the AL and renewed national and international political aspirations of the SPD following the revolution in the GDR.

The West Berlin elections to the Abgeordnetenhaus (House of Representatives) of 29 January 1989 marked the end of Eberhard Diepgen's CDU administration, but left the SPD without a working majority. In order to assume power the SPD faction opened negotiations with the AL which resulted on 16 March in a 'Red/Green' coalition administration in the Senate led by Walter Momper. This comprised eight female and five male Senators, with ten departments occupied by SDP and three by AL Senators, namely 'Education and Sport' (Sybille Volkholz), 'Women's Affairs' (Anne Klein), and 'Urban Development and Environmental Protection' (Michaele Schreyer).

The new regime's statement of intent entitled 'Berlin's New Start' (*Regierungserklärung: 'Berlin im Aufbruch'*) of 13 April undertook to promote the 'democratization of all spheres of life', the 'ecological re-development of the city' and measures to alleviate unemployment, poverty and the housing shortage. In a review of the coalition's first year in office, Momper claimed that

> The political climate in the city has changed for the better. Things were protested about, discussed, disputed, reconciled. Instead of the state being distanced from or even opposed to the citizens as had previously been the case, it was now once again close to them.

The new Red/Green style of municipal government was reflected in decisions to review the adversarial culture of the West Berlin Police Force, and to extend and re-organize public transport. In Momper's public statements, Berlin's new start offered a model for coalition politics in which the partners worked together in spite of their differences. Few believed that Momper's rhetoric was much more than a virtue made of necessity. Yet in spite of widespread cynicism, the coalition represented a possible re-direction of German democracy, and not only at the city, but also at the state, and perhaps even federal levels of government.

It was this uneasy, experimental coalition that was in power when the Wall came down, and it was this regime, this potential now model German democracy, that came to grief on Potsdamer Platz. The differences within the regime were focused on the Department of Urban Development and Environmental Protection which was the responsibility of the AL Senator Michaele Schreyer. The reason for the controversy around Schreyer and her Department lay in its central role in the formulation and execution of planning policy for Berlin. Since 1981 the Senate had divided the responsibility for Berlin's built environment between the Senator for Urban Development and the Senator for Building. Their respective responsibilities seem not to have been precisely demarcated, although generally speaking the Senator for Urban Development was responsible for general urban policy, the Senator for Building for specific architectural projects.

While the AL Senator Schreyer was responsible for broadly defined Urban Development, immediate architectural decisions were in the hands of the SPD Senator Wolfgang Nagel. In this way the SPD maintained power over short-term decisions, clearly significant in a coalition of expediency. But with the end of the Wall and the *de facto* re-unification of the city on 9 November, the formulation of Berlin's medium and long-term urban development policy became a matter of national and international significance. The Senator for Urban Development was suddenly an extremely significant and powerful local and national politician. Yet through an accident of local coalition politics, it now appeared as if the fundamental decisions about the redevelopment of the potential capital city of the new German Federal Republic would be in the hands of a Green politician accountable to a radical and local constituency.

The AL's vision of the future of central Berlin and how it might be attained predictably differed from those of the Berlin SPD and the reigning Federal CDU/CSU coalition. The fundamental values of the AL were grassroots democracy, local accountability and sensitivity to the environment. The SPD, however, quickly rediscovered its corporatist style of decision-making, and began systematically to undermine its AL coalition partner, sabotaging its attempts to institute a democratic debate on the future of Potsdamer Platz. The conflict between the two styles and their two constituencies led to several open conflicts between Red and Green in the Spring of 1990. Their attempts to outmanoeuvre each other led first to an acrimonious stalemate, and then to a unsatisfactory compromise. The compromise was to aestheticize the political problem by proclaiming and agreeing on the terms of an architectural competition. This only succeeded in transferring the unresolved political differences into conflicts over the brief, framework, pace and procedure of the competition.

The differences between Red and Green were summed up in their approaches to the decision to build on Potsdamer Platz. Early in 1990 Senator Schreyer initiated a public discussion of her department's proposals while the SPD conducted secret negotiations with Daimler Benz for the sale of municipally owned land in the area. Schreyer's proposed 'Structural Plan' for a 'green heart' of the City was announced in March 1990 (9/3/1990) and published as a 'Discussion Paper' in April. Her department's recommendations were presented as the outcome of a 'Working Party for the Central Area' which began work in May 1989 and in the 'months following the opening of the border' and proceeded in consultation with East Berlin planners. The Discussion Paper was intended to form the basis 'for public discussion in the entire city and for clarifying discussions with specialists as well as for further negotiations with the Magistrature in East Berlin'.

The key points of Schreyer's proposals were a 'green heart' to the city stretching from the Tiergarten through Potsdamer Platz, and the closure of the city centre to through traffic. Furthermore, the development of the site would combine responsibility for the traces of the past, and considerations of what would be proper for the future capital of a democratic state. Schreyer's proposal called for a 'revitalization' which respected the historical ground plan but which did not necessarily rule out considerable building development on the site. Schreyer concluded with an offer to the citizens of Berlin: 'The Senate Department for Urban Development and Environmental Protection presents its proposals with this plan. I am certain that you too have proposals for the 'heart' of your city, and thus invite you to take part in the process of discussion.'

At the same time as the Alternative Liste's proposals were being formulated and presented to the citizens of Berlin, rumours began to emerge of Daimler-Benz's interest in the site (i.e. *Berliner Zeitung*, 22/2/1990 – 'Daimler Benz intends to build skyscrapers on Potsdamer Platz'). As the rumours became certainties Schreyer warned (9/3/1990) that 'The investor's cheques should not influence the decision.' At this stage the SPD pressed for the immediate announcement of an architectural competition, while Schreyer urged delay; Daimler-Benz meanwhile was 'rumoured' to be threatening to withdraw from negotiations. After the announcement of her Department's proposals, the SPD led by the Building and Traffic senators declared themselves opposed to Schreyer's plan, and called for her resignation (13/3/1990). On 5 April the SPD in the persons of Momper and Nagel repeated their opposition to Schreyer's plans, and on the following day effectively overrode her authority and declared their support for Daimler-Benz's plans to build a service centre on Potsdamer Platz.

With this decision the initiative passed to the SPD, who began to plead pressure from the investor to accelerate proceedings and effectively exclude the kind of local democratic consultation envisaged by the AL. The SPD declared the decision to be 'an investment in Berlin's future' which would bring 8,000 jobs and, with an investment in excess of DM750 million, would add up, in Momper's words, to 'a lot more than flyshit'. With this *fait accompli* the differences within the coalition focused on the terms and pace of the architectural competition, and the inclusion of Daimler-Benz at the planning stage. After a twelve-hour sitting the Senate agreed to prepare an 'urban development competition for the area Potsdamer/Leipziger Platz' (Senate Resolution No.959/90). The day after gaining this compromise the SPD once again trumped the AL by moving to close an option contract with Daimler-Benz as early as May. The AL, on the contrary, wished to delay closing the contract until after the announcement of the results of the competition, thus ensuring that potential investors would be bound by the result.

The Senate authorized the SPD Finance Senator Norbert Meisner to proceed to complete negotiations with Daimler-Benz. The result was a sale of public land which quickly provoked a scandal. 61,710 square metres situated behind the state library were sold for DM92.9 million, a price per square metre of DM 1,505. The estimated open market price for the land was estimated at DM10,000 per square metre; the then current price for land on Kurfurstendamm was in excess of DM7,000 and in Berlin suburbs such as Wedding and Wilmersdorff it was DM3,500. Berliners were acquainted with these invidious comparisons by means of graffiti, what they weren't told was that Daimler-Benz would allegedly not have to pay for the land before summer 1992. Furthermore, in January 1991, it was claimed that Daimler-Benz paid nine times this amount for a neighbouring piece of land. The original sale was subsequently referred to the European Commission under Article 92 of the EEC treaty regarding public subsidies which undermine competition, thus giving a European dimension to the events around Potsdamer Platz.[8]

In spite of Schreyer's authority being consistently undermined within the Senate, a few local, grassroots democratic actions were mounted by the AL and Citizens Initiative groups against developments on Potsdamer Platz. On the last day of April the area was occupied in protest against 'DM Nationalism' by representatives of the AL and the Independent Women's Association. In the same month 'Citizens Initiative West Tangent' (founded in protest against a planned 'West Tangent' road) issued a call for a 'Car-Free City Centre' and a 'Green Tangent contra Daimler-Benz'. They called for citizens' protests against Daimler-Benz's plans. In June the residents' association Stadtteilverein Tiergarten called a meeting to discuss the impact of the proposed developments on local residents under the title 'The Plans on Potsdamer Platz – Chance or Catastrophe?'. The Stadtteilverein considered that local views were not being properly considered. Nevertheless, such actions were largely reactive, did not form part of a broader democratic planning process and consequently had little impact.

The events around Potsdamer Platz contributed considerably to the instability of the Red/Green coalition, which lurched from crisis to crisis until the violent eviction of squatters in the autumn of 1990 caused the AL to leave the coalition on 19 November. The coalition had lasted 20 months (610 days), which was a record for Red/Green coalitions, and ended 17 days before the first post-unification Berlin elections (2/12/1990). These saw the SPD's proportion of the vote fall to an historic low of 30.4 per cent, and its subsequent coalition in Senate with the CDU. Schreyer's post was taken over by Volker Hassemer (CDU) a reformist on the left of the party who had held this post under the previous CDU administration and had been responsible for IBA (Internationale Bauausstellung Berlin – International Building Exhibition). The SPD Nagel, however, kept his post as Senator for Building.

The shift to a Red/Black coalition led to a change in the style of decision-making from the previous unhappy combination of grassroots democracy [*Basisdemokratie*] and backroom intrigue to the technocratic 'democracy of experts'. In February 1991 Hassemer convened a 'City Forum' of experts and interested parties to debate the future of the city, in particular Potsdamer Platz, and to participate in the competition process. The exercise was widely criticized as one of expert navel-gazing, although Hassemer presented it as a collection of 'critical objections and exchange of viewpoints' (interview in *Der Spiegel*, 8/7/1991). He clarified his views on the 'democratic form of architecture' in a debate with architects and historians. Architectural decisions belonged to the people and not to the bureaucracy, but the people were to be guided by experts:

> Openness and democracy in planning do not signify that suddenly everybody becomes architects and city planners. But it is necessary for the public to debate and offer alternative views on to what experts take to be quality.
>
> (Meyer 1991: 20)

Democracy in architecture consists in the people responding to proposals made by experts with approval or disapproval; they are to be consulted, but not to be involved in the actual decision-making. This conservative populism differs radically from the grassroots democracy of the AL since it makes the built environment the gift of the bureaucracy and its experts.

In the midst of the political debates around the future of Potsdamer Platz, the architectural profession was itself divided. This was especially discouraging given the increasing tendency of the politicians to seek an architectural solution to the site's political problems. The division in the profession internationally between 'local' or 'critical regionalist' and 'international style' architectural practices was already well known to Berlin from the IBA. This was quite accurately perceived by Berlin architects and critics overriding the prevailing critical pseudo-distinction between the competing international styles of 'modern' and 'postmodern' architecture.

Potsdamer Platz provoked a rehearsal of debates over the politics of architecture which had already divided the profession at the time of the IBA (1987). The unresolved tension between the *Neubau* and *Altbau* (New Building/Old Building renovation) sections of the celebrated Internationale Bauausstellung of 1987 returned with a vengeance.[9] The IBA's ambition of achieving a 'critical reconstruction of the city' led to architectural schizophrenia. On the one hand, its *Altbau* section addressed itself to local architects working alongside tenants, helping them renovate their own dwellings, and emphasized the role of the process of building in democratically empowering local communities such as Kreuzberg. On the other hand, *Neubau* addressed itself to the international architectural community, and was concerned above all with showpiece finished buildings which were often imposed on communities with the legal minimum of democratic consultation.

The architectural profession split on the issue of whether the 'critical reconstruction' of Potsdamer Platz should proceed by the methods of *Altbau* or *Neubau*, or by a fusion of both. Their disputes paralleled those taking place between the SPD and the AL. Daimler-Benz's proposals to invest on Potsdamer Platz attracted the international architectural avant-garde who proceeded to disseminate increasingly extravagant and indulgent proposals for the redevelopment of central Berlin. These were informed by much of state-of-the-art architectural imagination, but very little sensitivity to local democracy. Indeed, they placed themselves in succession to Gilly's proposal, addressed more to the history, past and future, of architecture than to the immediate problems of building on Potsdamer Platz. The local architects associated with *Altbau*, on the contrary, called for greater consultation and direct participation of the city's population in deciding the future of Potsdamer Platz.

In a widely cited article in *Bauwelt* (4/5/1990) Dieter Hoffmann-Axthelm criticized the haste with which both the Senate and certain sections of the architectural profession were moving towards an architectural solution. Accusing the Senate of 'lackeying' to Daimler-Benz, the author warned against the 'misuse of architecture', which he saw developing in the tendency to put 'architecture between us and our problems', and the willingness of the profession to lend itself to such abuse:

> We know from painful experience what is meant by the announcement of an international competition: it means that we spare ourselves the difficulty of trying to solve thankless problems along with the tedious public debates and efforts to convince the public, and simply let the architects go ahead and prepare the forms for [Daimler-Benz's] new service centre.

43

The author called for considered public discussion of the political and architectural issues posed by Potsdamer Platz, a 'political and an aesthetic process' which would be a 'matter for the entire city'. The architectural decision must emerge from this process of consultation, not anticipate it; it must at the very least follow the work of the city planning and building authorities, the one 'concerned with political and economic issues', the other with 'the grammar of city growth, how a city organizes itself spatially'. To move immediately to the architectural decision would mean the surrender of democratic process and the violent imposition of undesirable 'monuments to world trade'.

Hoffmann-Axthelm's fears were prescient, as was his view that the press and media would exploit the potential for spectacle provided by Potsdamer Platz. Newspapers and magazines competed to commission plans for central Berlin from the architectural avant-garde, who duly supplied hastily drawn projects or even shamelessly recycled old ones. The most significant example of the spectacular monumentalism of world architecture was the exhibition of seventeen proposals at the German architectural museum at the end of January 1991 under the sponsorship of the *Frankfurter Allgemeine Zeitung*. The newspaper's campaign was consummately timed to maximize excitement: a series of articles on Berlin's planning history prepared the way in the autumn of 1990 (collected in Monninger 1991), followed by the publication just before the opening of the exhibition, of the proposals in the *FAZ* on 5 and 23 January. Similar and derivative projects were then further recycled in other magazines (for example *Geo Special – Hauptstadt Berlin*, 'Eight Visions for the Coming Century' from August 1991).

These visions of aestheticised politics almost uniformly treat the site as if it were cut off from its place in the city. Even Kleihues, the erstwhile director of IBA and promoter of its 'critical reconstruction of the city', offered a bizarre project seemingly stuck onto the site with glue (perhaps it was ironic?). In a sardonic review of the exhibition Eberhard von Einem, also a leading participant in the IBA (*Altbau*), saw in these architectural fantasies a desire to turn away from 'grassroots democratic' planning procedures, and to 'wait for Schinkel' or the advent of the omnipotent architect with all the answers.

Von Eimer used his experience of working with the IBA to criticize the 'gigantomania' of the architectural profession which he saw revealed in the exhibition:

> With every stroke of the pen not only are millions put into bad building, but more importantly, and put precisely, thousands of people's lives will be disturbed, homes will have to be given up, houses demolished, traffic jammed. Who gives to urban designers their mandate to reshape Berlin with mega-structures, and to do so without taking the trouble to study the local conditions in detail?
>
> (1991: 57)

He compares this procedure with that of the IBA, which offered specific proposals for local debate according to the principle of preservation: this 'may be less spectacular, but is much more appropriate. Cities develop themselves out of the deposits left by several strata. Planning means staying open to later options.' Like Hoffmann-Axthelm, von Eimem distrusts the international avant-garde architectural profession, fearing that it has not learnt from the experiences of trying to implement the Charter of Athens. It seems to be falling back into the distinction between the 'architectural visionary' and the 'engineers', those responsible for assessing 'technical, ecological, social and economic implications'. In their abstraction from the history of the site and the demands of the local community, the architects' designs seem to be guided by a desire for a monumental present which would effectively abolish the future of the site.

The division in the architectural profession mirrored that which prevailed at the level of the ruling coalition. It involved the question of whether politics was to be aestheticized from above through showpiece architecture by internationally renowned architects, or whether it was to be politicized from below through democratic discussion between competing local, national and international interests. Potsdamer Platz once again provided a place to reflect and dispute the nature of the political, its past, present and future, and its relation to architecture. The resort to an architectural competition served only to displace these fundamental questions into a continuous and symptomatic dispute over the terms and the conduct of the competition. The displacement on to the competition of differences within politics and architecture ensured that the competition would prove an extremely unhappy and unsatisfactory experience.

THE ARCHITECTURAL COMPETITION

> The pilgrimage began before dawn at Potsdamer Platz. Bare, dirty clay. No-mans-land: if there were vultures in Germany, this is where they'd circle.
>
> (Stefan Schonmann)

The architectural competition is becoming an increasingly discredited means of decision-making. It developed as the favoured means of promoting 'modern' architectural solutions to the social and political problems of urbanization. It inevitably favours an 'architectural solution' to these problems, and is usually conducted within the framework of an authoritarian or at best technocratic process of decision-making. The architectural competition may often adopt a facade of 'democratic consultation' but the parameters and the procedures of architectural judgement, as well as the decision itself, are established by professional and political elites working under the direct or indirect pressure of the investor.

The exhaustion of this form of decision-making – with its attendant forms of modern administrative democracy and architectural avant-gardism – is exemplified by the case of Potsdamer Platz. The competition process went through several phases, beginning with the differences within the Red/Green coalition on the desirability of a competition itself, which led eventually to the agreement on the competition framework and brief in April 1990. This seems subsequently to have been undermined by the manoeuvres of the SPD and the investor Daimler-Benz. The competition process fell into disarray in the summer and autumn of 1990, and was re-constituted under the Red/Black coalition at the beginning of 1991. The brief and the scope for participation in the competition were narrowed in the course of 1991, and the final judgement in October 1991 was attended by acrimony and scandal. Meanwhile the investors commissioned another architect to produce a plan outside of the competition, and this became the preferred option of both press and professional public. The scene after the competition in December 1991 was one of confusion, with proposals on the table for an eclectic fusion of aspects of several of the plans.

The Red/Green coalition was widely criticized for its alleged inactivity in the months following the Revolution in the GDR. It was argued that its lack of a concept for the development of central Berlin allowed Daimler-Benz to step into a planning vacuum and to set the pace for its own development. However, this was not the case; what lay behind the events was a clear difference of approach within the coalition. Already in late autumn 1989 the AL was encouraging and attending a series of public debates, while the SPD was negotiating in confidence with Daimler-Benz. The SPD negotiated according to the established parameters of the West Berlin 'subsidy mentality', that is, it behaved as if it had to encourage and persuade the investor to bring jobs and money to the island of West Berlin. This obsolete approach made the SPD and the coalition unnecessarily vulnerable to potential pressure from the investor.

The main principle behind the AL's approach at the Department for Urban Development and Environmental Protection was wide public consultation on the basis of the public ownership of most of the site. It felt able to consider central Berlin as a whole, as more an issue of public urban development than of private architecture. The SPD, however, was anxious to pursue the classic neo-corporatist strategies of the 'social market economy', which in this case involved selling plots of land to investors who would then build under the control and regulative supervision of the Senate. The main means of control was to be the architectural competition. The AL, however, did not wish to proceed to an architectural competition before fundamental questions of the urban environment and ecology had been publicly debated. It pursued an holistic strategy in which architecture was but one of several social and political considerations such as transport, urban ecology and respect for the historic nature of the site.

The first sign of differences within the coalition involved the desirability of an architectural competition itself. When it became clear in early spring 1990 that negotiations between the SPD faction and Daimler-Benz were already far advanced, the dispute between the coalition partners changed to one of establishing the terms of the competition. It was clear to planners at the Department for Urban Development as early as 8 April that 'As soon as the comrades [SPD] saw the chequebook . . . they began to act as the building office for Daimler-Benz' (*Frankfurter Rundschau*, 9/4/1990). On 10 April the coalition partners negotiated the terms of the competition, the first stage of which was to be completed before the end of the year.

The result – '*Stadtebaulicher Wettbewerb Potsdamer/Leipziger Platz*' – was a document in nine sections which attempted to combine the irreconcilable aims and procedures of the coalition partners' approaches in a fragile and what was to prove an unviable compromise. The competition was divided into two stages – the first was an 'Urban Development Competition' for the area around Potsdamer Platz, the second an 'Architectural Competition' for the westerly part of the site dedicated to the Daimler-Benz development (Section VIII). The two stages correspond to the two, diverging approaches to planning decisions: the focus of the AL upon the relationship of locality and city, and that of the SPD on architecture in abstraction. The document is split between broad programmatic statements for the area, and repeated, specific references to the Daimler-Benz project, as if this was already a reality. The first mention of Daimler-Benz in the first section on the 'Basic Urban Development Idea' makes its accommodation within the general plan an 'urgent task for urban development'. Furthermore, in Section V on the proposed provision of parks for the area, it is assumed that this will be determined by the position of Daimler-Benz's 'service and office centre'.

The details of Daimler-Benz's requirements were spelt out in Section IV on 'Daimler-Benz AG', which revealed the advanced stage that negotiations for the ownership of the site had already reached. The area envisaged for the Daimler-Benz development is described, as is its purpose and scale (floor space of 180,000 to 240,000 m^2). It is also revealed that the investor would be prepared to offer an (relatively ungenerous) additional 10 per cent for subsidiary uses. The document makes some vague recommendation about height restrictions and respect for the preservation of historical features of the site, but these appear almost as afterthoughts.

The presence of Daimler-Benz in the document as a *fait accompli* may have served to distort the broader aims of the development. It was as if the planning objectives for central Berlin were to be accommodated to the interests of the investor rather than the other way round. And in the following month, control over the investor became the focus of debate, eventually to the detriment of the broader planning process. As mentioned above, immediately after agreeing to this compromise document, the SPD announced that it would proceed to sell the land to Daimler-Benz with the stipulation that the company respect the outcome of the competition. The AL and other critics wished to postpone the sale until after the competition in order to ensure that the presence of an investor already in possession of the land would not influence the shape of the decision.

The following months intensified these anxieties, for although in May (7/5/1990) Daimler-Benz claimed to set no conditions on the size of its buildings, stipulations regarding building density and price were written into the contract. As a result of two hearings in the Berlin Abgeordnetenhaus it was announced that 'The imminent sale of six hectares of building land to Daimler-Benz AG makes a qualified contest of ideas for the central area around Potsdamer Platz impossible, and burdens the competition jury in an intolerable way.' A group of architects and planners writing to *Bauwelt* in July (20/7/1990) to protest against the announcement of the immediate sale of the land asked

> What should participants in the competition be looking for? For the best solution for binding together the two halves of the city, or the best solution for a major investor? Since we hold such conflicts to be insoluble, we demand that the Senate postpone the planned sale until the conclusion of a consensual planning process.

It was precisely such a conflict between the demands of local democratic city planning and those of a large corporate investor which were to undermine the competition, but not in the way envisaged by the critics.

The terms of the competition did not survive the collapse of the Red/Green coalition. The new CDU Senator for City Development Hassemer instituted a 'City Forum' to review the terms of the competition agreed in April 1990 and to establish new ones. The 'City Forum' was also instructed to take into account the views of the investors with Daimler-Benz now joined by Sony, Hertie and Asea Brown (Boveri). As the proceedings of the 'City Forum' approached their conclusion in April several interesting developments took place. The investors suddenly commissioned the British architectural firm Richard Rogers Partnership to assist them:

> in formulating a statement to the Stadtforum with the objective of ensuring that the investor's views would be properly taken into account in the proceedings leading to the International Master Plan competition for Potsdamer/Leipziger Platz.
>
> (Statement posted in the Competition Exhibition,
> Hotel Esplanade, Berlin, November 1991)

They had not previously shown much anxiety about ensuring that their views were heard, and their sudden decision in April could not have been motivated by the anodyne 'discussion points' proposed by the 'City Forum'. Perhaps the most likely cause for their concern was the change in the procedure of the competition which was publicly announced on 3 May 1990.

Under the new procedure architectural offices were invited to submit applications from among which a limited number would be chosen to discuss and develop their proposals within the framework of the 'City Forum'. The chosen firms would subsequently submit anonymous projects to be judged by a jury comprising of 50 per cent experts, 50 per cent Berlin local politicians. Subsequently seventy-five offices applied to participate, and sixteen were chosen. The Berlin Chamber of Architecture publicly protested against the limited competition and called for a 'genuinely democratic' and 'open competition'. The CDU model of decision making by experts in combination with elected politicians differed from the previous Red/Green combination of grassroots democratic openness and behind-the-scenes negotiation. It excluded both extensive democratic consultation and the informal pressure from investors, but in so doing alienated both the proponents of democratic planning and the investors. While the former busied themselves with the proclamation of charters and manifestos for democratic planning[10] the investors commissioned the Richard Rogers Partnership to produce their own masterplan for the development of the site. Their choice was extremely shrewd, because in the Richard Rogers Partnership they received the benefit of not only an innovative architectural practice, but also one with a populist profile who would embellish their corporate plans with a façade of commitment to grassroots democracy. Richard Rogers Partnership's initial commission of presenting the investors' views to the 'City Forum' 'was subsequently extended to one of assisting in the formulation of the investors' brief for the competition and in developing the investors' own masterplan framework for the development of the site.

The tension within the original Red/Green competition brief between the official competition and the intentions of the investor now manifested itself in the guise of a double competition. The first competition took place between the sixteen official participants, the second between them and the Richard Rogers Partnership's proposal on behalf of the investors. The Richard Rogers Partnership's report was intended not only to help the investors formulate the organizational needs for the development, but also 'to provide a basis to assist the Senate in evaluating how the crowning Stadtforum competition entry may adapt to the technical realities of the site'. However, the Richard Rogers Partnership's proposal served to disrupt if not the procedure then certainly the outcome of the competition. It was exhibited in a room off the main exhibition in the Hotel Esplanade and attracted most media and professional attention, properly detracting from the winning entry. The Richard Rogers Partnership's *hors concours* project without doubt won the competition with the competition.

The official competition would have been a fiasco even without the intervention of the project commissioned by the investors. The composition of the jury led to conflicts between the experts and the politicians, with one of the experts, Rem Koolhaas, walking out or, in the bland words of the

Ergebnisprotokoll, 'Of the voting expert judges Mr Koolhaas was as of 1600 hours on the 2/10/91 no longer present.' In a protest letter Koolhaas described the experience as a 'conscious massacre of architectural intelligence' and the 'most painful experience of his professional life'. The responsibility was attributed both to the 'loud, tactless, and narrow-minded' interventions of a particular politician and the 'brutal form of selection'. Koolhaas's description of the latter is certainly borne out by the published protocols of the decision.

The competition structured the exercise of architectural judgement in terms of a bureaucratic process of selection by means of elimination. The committee met, judged, and came to its decision in less than two days. In the first round the entries were categorized, and criteria for selection established: as a result, three of the proposals were immediately eliminated. In the second round votes were taken on whether the remaining entries should be excluded or passed through to the next round. Four entries passed through to the next round. Thus ended the first day.

On reconvening the following day, the committee reconsidered the previously excluded entries, and added a fifth competitor to the final round. At this stage the jury split into three working groups to produce written reports on the proposals with respect to Urban Environment, Use and Traffic. The proposals were then ranked according to a somewhat occult set of criteria, and the first prize awarded to the proposal from the Hilmer and Sattler practice. Even though this proposal had been considered the least offensive in the first round (being the only one not to have a vote cast for its exclusion) its victory was by no means unanimous, nor did it visibly impress either the investors or the media.

In the aftermath of the exhibition the investors publicly criticized the winning proposal, preferring their own, while the media, and the public who felt moved to contribute their views in the visitors' book, began the game of combining aspects of Richard Rogers' and the other proposals. The judgement of the competition jury began to unstick, and in its place arose a barely regulated architectural *laissez-faire*.

At first the responsible senators Nagel and Hassemer declared themselves in support of the winning proposal, and reminded Daimler-Benz of its contractual obligation to respect the outcome of the competition. For Nagel, the outcome was 'obligatory' for the investors because it had been selected 'in a democratic manner, by a jury', while Hassemer initially praised the proposal, but subsequently declared himself only 'prepared to work with it'. In December further confusion was introduced by the widespread critical opposition to both Richard Rogers' and the official proposals. An attempt was made by the Mayor Diepgen to call for flexibility, but this was met by Daimler-Benz's decision to integrate aspects of the competition entries with the investors' commissioned project. The criteria for choosing between the schemes were not revealed, but what became clear was that these would be largely set by the investors. In response the Mayor called for a further workshop of experts, politicians and investors to meet in January 1992 to discuss the situation.[11]

The competition resulted in a fiasco in which the interests of local politicians, investors, and architects and other experts seemed to cancel each other out. There seemed to be no place where the contending parties could meet and agree criteria of judgement. In this little drama the population of Berlin had become 'noises off', contributing very little to the debate, and cultivating a cynical relish as they watched grandiose plans come to nothing on Potsdamer Platz. What began as an attempt by the AL to integrate direct democracy and environmentally sensitive planning had ended in what seemed to be yet another in a long line of Berlin building scandals. As a result, the historical specificity of the site and the interest of those who will have to live in and with it has become a matter of negotiation between corporate interests and a technocratic local state. The site is once again called upon to embody the future of Germany, but this time in the guise of a global economic power.

DEMOCRACY AND ARCHITECTURAL JUDGEMENT

Welcome to the lone star state!
(graffiti on Potsdamer Platz, 1991)

In October 1991 Berlin's leading department store, the KAdeWE, was selling T-shirts with a picture of Potsdamer Platz and the bilingual motto '*Wir Wiederbauen*/Lets build again'. But the events around Potsdamer Platz have called into question quite who we are, and what we are to build. Who is building on Potsdamer Platz? Is it 'the Germans' or 'the Berliners' or the 'Berlin Senate', the experts, those who bought the T-shirts, the 'architects', the builders, or 'Capital' in the guise of Daimler-Benz, Sony *et al.*? Are any of these fictional collectives engaged in the building, or are all of them, none of them; is anything happening on Potsdamer Platz, will anything have happened?

In some senses, since 1991 a great deal has happened on Potsdamer Platz. A flurry of individual competitions within the Masterplan have been fought, won and lost producing designs for the corporate centres of Daimler-Benz, Asea Brown (Boverei) and Sony. These were duly passed down to the public through a concert of press releases and the extremely attractive, subsidized journals produced by the City Forum and the Senate Building and Housing Development.[12] In accord with the procedure of the competitions, the public are kept informed but their participation limited. The list of winning architectural prices reads as a roll call of the emerging contemporary 'international style': Helmut Jahn (Chicago): Sony Centre, building to commence 1995/96;

Figure 2.6 Project Potsdamer Platz
Source: Author's photograph

Arata Isozaki (Tokyo): Office Block for Daimler-Benz, due to be completed late 1996; Richard Rogers Partnership (London): Housing and Offices for Daimler-Benz, proposed completion date 1998; Renzo Piano (Milan): Service Centre for Daimler-Benz, completion date 1997; Hans Kollhoff (Berlin): Offices and Housing, due 1998 . . . Yet all this building is taking place in the middle of an anxious, even hysterical orchestration of historical amnesia.

On a hot July morning in 1995 I walked from Bahnhof Zoo through the Tierpark on my way to the Bauhaus Archive Museum for Design to visit the exhibition 'Ein Stuck Großstadt als Experiment: Planung am Potsdamer Platz in Berlin' [A Piece of Metropolis as Experiment: Planning on Potsdamer Platz in Berlin]. The exhibition had transferred from the German Architectural Museum in Frankfurt (where it was held from December to March). The exhibition reviewed the leading designs of the competitions of the competition campaign of 1991–3, presenting an aestheticized unfolding of architectural logic. There was barely an echo of the events I have described above, no place for the defeated.[13] The political disputes surrounding the establishment, terms and procedures of the competitions have been silenced, and in their place is a set of gleaming, unstained architectural futures. The exhibition seemed to bear testimony to the erasure of the past and the triumph of a particular vision of the future: the noise of democracy seemed faint and distant.

Leaving the Bauhaus Archive I walked past the half-unwrapped Reichstag, through the crowds and then along the trace of the Wall towards Potsdamer

Platz. There I found what looked like a circus tent inviting me to visit the future of Potsdamer Platz: it was a Panorama, one of five sponsored by *Stern Magazine* showing how 'The Capital would become a Metropolis'.[14] After paying my entrance fee I walked into the ring, climbed up a gantry (which reminded of another gantry from another time, but in the same place) and stared at the phantasmal future of Potsdamer Platz. Outside, Potsdamer Platz was sunny, parched grass and sand – inside the future looked like a scene spliced together from *Blade Runner* and Schinkel's Memorial Arch. Small figures scurry across plazas, with Schinkel's King replaced by the giant structures of Daimler-Benz and the others. No hint of the past, instead a hygienic environment policed by corporate capital. This could have been anywhere – Potsdamer Platz's *genii loci* apparently absorbed by these monuments to a global marketplace.

Yet, this, of course, was but another in a long line of phantasmal, controlled futures to which the masters of Potsdamer Platz have always aspired. It remains to be seen whether this future of the site will fail as did its predecessors, because, as before, it is when everything here seems most secure that the unexpected happens.

NOTES

1 Gilly's 'Kurze Erlauterung der in der Zeichnung ausgefuhrten Idee eines Denkmals Friedrichs der Grossen' is reprinted in Knieper *et al.* 1990: 8. See also Werner Oechslin's essay 'Friedrich Gillys kurzes Leben – sein Friedrichsdenkmal und die Philosophie der Architektur' in the Berlin Museum Catalogue 1984.

2 The relationship between the past, present and future citizens of a city is discussed subtly by Aldo Rossi, 1981 and 1982. For a stimulating and well-illustrated analysis of Potsdamer Platz as a landscape of mourning and desire, see Balfour 1990.

3 See Betthausen 1983: 24–25 for reproductions of the plan and painting.

4 See Helmer 1985 for a detailed reconstruction of the Speer project, one which continues to haunt the contemporary reconstruction of Berlin.

5 See Mauter *et al.* 1993: 92–8 for photographs.

6 See the cartoon from 1988 reproduced in Müller 1990: 110.

7 For an analysis of the political culture of the AL, see Heinrich 1993, especially Chapter 1.

8 Heinrich (1993: 48) reports that the EC Commission subsequently judged that the land had indeed been sold too cheaply.

9 For an analysis of the divisions in IBA see Caygill 1990.

10 These include the 'Charta für die Mitte von Berlin' by the Gruppe 9. Dezember, Dieter Hoffmann-Axthelm's critical commentary 'Hinweise zur Entwicklung einer beschadigten Grossstadt' and Hartmut E. Arras and Eberhard v. Einem 'Metropole Berlin: Mehr als Markt', all in *Bauwelt*, 12, 1991. It could be argued that these texts, reflecting on the failure of the Potsdamer Platz development, nevertheless begin to open the theoretical space for a democratic architecture.

11 For subsequent developments see Thies Schröder's 'Die Chance des Potsdamer Platzes? Ein Platz im Spiegel der Wettbewerbe' in Mauter *et al.* 1993: 151–63.

12 These extremely attractive and beautifully produced journals are important resources for the study of the redevelopment of Berlin, but are set in a top-down context of public information. See, for example, the article by Martin Kieran on the 'realization phase' of the Potsdamer Platz project, 1994.

13 The solitary echo is to be found on p. 20 of the exhibition catalogue, in an essay by Gerwin Zoler, 1994.

14 See the special issue of *Stern Magazine*, no. 24, 8 June 1995, 'Berlin 2005: Die Wilde Schöne'.

3

THE GLOBAL COMMON

The global, local and personal dynamics of the women's peace movement in the 1980s

Sasha Roseneil

INTRODUCTION

Back in the first half of the 1980s, with the new Cold War at its height and relations between the superpowers at an all time low, the eyes of the world focused for a time on a small piece of ancient common land in the county of Berkshire, in England. The Women's Peace Camp outside the United States Airforce Base at Greenham Common came to symbolize the intense contestation which was being played out in many hundreds of places and in numerous different ways, between the forces of global militarization and movements for peace and nuclear disarmament. Greenham, although located physically and in the public mind in this particular place, was more than its physical manifestation as an encampment of women, and its impact spread far beyond the immediate environment in which it was situated. But the camp was also just the most visible manifestation of a global women's peace movement, which stretched across several continents and mobilized many hundreds of thousands of women during this period of geopolitical crisis.[1]

As a transnational social movement with global concerns and acting on a global stage, the women's peace movement exemplifies the development of a 'global feminism' (Bunch 1987). It is important to draw attention to the movement's 'planetary dimension' (Melucci 1989), because social movements research has underestimated the significance of the global connections within and between movements. There has been a tendency to conceptualize movements as bounded by the nation states in which they appear to operate, and individual movements have largely been studied either within the context of national societies, or through cross-national comparisons. However, the global aspects of social movements cannot be studied in isolation from their local and personal dimensions. As is suggested by a number of writers on globalization, the contemporary world should be understood as produced through the dialectical relationship of the global and the local (e.g. Giddens 1990, 1991; Friedman 1994a; Lash and Urry 1994), and the global, the local and the personal (Giddens 1991; Friedman 1994a; Robertson 1992b).

55

Thus the subject matter of this chapter is the global, the local and the personal dynamics of Greenham. I do not just look at the impact of global political and military power on a particular locale and on the women who constituted Greenham. Rather I am concerned with the dialectical dynamics whereby local and personal actions impact upon the global, as well as vice versa. Greenham was enmeshed in the globalizing processes of the late twentieth century, yet it was also firmly located within its specific locality and within a particular national tradition of political protest. Its global potency as a symbol of protest against nuclear weapons was derived, in part, from its very location, outside a Cruise missile base, and in the heart of pro-nuclear, pro-NATO Tory England.

THE GLOBAL–LOCAL–PERSONAL CONTEXT OF GREENHAM

The women's peace movement in Britain, and more specifically the Women's Peace Camp at Greenham Common, can be seen as having emerged in the early 1980s at the nexus of the global–local–personal dynamic of nuclear militarism. The movement coalesced and the camp was formed at the point at which geo-politics touched the consciousness of hundreds of individual women, and when these women each made personal decisions to get involved. This happened within global, national, local and personal contexts.

The long-term global context of Greenham was the globalization of military power in the twentieth century, particularly from the Second World War onwards (Giddens 1990). The division of almost the whole world into two spheres of political influence and military alliance, dominated by the United States and the Soviet Union, and the development of a 'baroque arsenal' (Kaldor 1982) of nuclear weapons, with their potential for global destruction, formed the backdrop to the specific developments of the late 1970s and early 1980s. The immediate global context of Greenham was the collapse of détente between the superpowers and the beginning of a new Cold War.[2] Although Carter's presidency had begun in 1977 with the stated aim of eliminating nuclear weapons, during his term of office the arms race intensified greatly. His exertion of pressure on NATO to deploy the neutron bomb, and the stalling and eventual non-ratification of the Strategic Arms Limitation Treaty (SALT II) signalled the deterioration of relations between West and East. Meanwhile, the Soviet Union began to deploy SS-20s and the backfire bomber in Eastern Europe, and then, on 12 December 1979 Carter persuaded NATO to take the 'twin track' decision. This constituted an offer to enter into negotiations with the Warsaw Pact about reductions in intermediate nuclear forces (INF) in Europe, whilst at the same time 'modernizing' NATO's intermediate nuclear forces by introducing ground launched cruise missiles and Pershing II missiles. The plan was to deploy 464 Cruise missiles in Britain, Belgium,

The Netherlands and Italy, and 108 Pershing II launchers in West Germany, beginning in 1983.[3]

These missiles were part of a new 'generation' of 'theatre', or tactical, nuclear weapons. Unlike earlier intercontinental 'strategic' nuclear weapons which could travel between the USA and the USSR, 'theatre' nuclear weapons were designed for use on a nuclear battlefield within Europe. So whilst Cruise, Pershing and SS-20s were weapons of the global superpowers, their range and possible use was spatially bound: they were, in effect, regional weapons, 'euromissiles'. Moreover, the NATO decision constituted the formal enactment of a change in US nuclear doctrine. Schlesinger's new 'counter-force doctrine' said that US nuclear forces were henceforth to be aimed primarily at military targets, particularly command, control, communications and intelligence centres and nuclear storage facilities, rather than at centres of population. The implication of this was that NATO had moved from a strategy of deterrence to one which aimed to fight and win a nuclear war in Europe by means of a preemptive first strike. The vehemently anti-Communist rhetoric of the new Reagan administration and the US boycott of the 1980 Moscow Olympics underlined the deterioration of US/Soviet relations, and made it seem all the more likely that Europe would be their nuclear battleground.

Within this context the announcement that Cruise missiles were to be sited in Britain was the spark for the re-emergence of the anti-nuclear/peace movement, largely dormant since the mid-1960s. The identification of the United States Airforce Base at Greenham Common as the first site for Cruise made tangible and highly specific the intensification of the global arms race and the otherwise diffuse and generalized global risk pertaining to the 'overkill' potential of the world's nuclear weaponry. Suddenly first strike nuclear weapons were to be based in Berkshire, less than seventy miles from London, and close to many of the largest towns and cities in Britain, bringing the probable site of any preemptive Soviet nuclear strike, or of a nuclear accident, within range of much of the population of England and Wales. The women's peace movement of the 1980s opposed all nuclear weapons and was not solely concerned with Cruise missiles, but the plan to install Cruise at Greenham provided a clear focus for campaigning and a specific target and place at which to direct attention.

The global context of Greenham had a gendered dimension, which contributed to the creation of Greenham as a *women's* peace movement. The state elites and transnational blocs which make foreign and defence policy, and the defence intellectuals and nuclear scientists who have developed nuclear strategy and weaponry are not only largely outside democratic control (Elworthy 1989; Kaplan 1984; Mann 1987), they are also over-whelmingly male. As political decision-making moves from the local, through the national, to the transnational level, women are more and more excluded, and power is ever more exercised by men only. After a century of struggle by feminists for access for women to these political and scientific elites, decisions of far greater potential significance to the fate of the whole planet than had ever before been taken were still almost exclusively the preserve of men. The NATO/US decision to site Cruise at Greenham seemed to many of the women who formed Greenham, and to those who later got involved, to represent the power of distant, unaccountable military men over the lives and deaths of themselves, their friends and families. The 'nuclear fear' which characterizes the 'risk society' of the late twentieth century (Beck 1992) was experienced by many women in a highly personal way, for instance in nightmares of nuclear war in which they or their children suffered terrible injuries.[4]

That this nuclear fear was translated into collective action, rather than just existing as individualized despair and depression, is to be explained by reference to the collective histories and traditions of protest, both transnational and specifically British, from within which these women came. There was a long history of anti-militarism amongst women in Britain (Liddington 1989) and the feminist internationalism and anti-militarism of the Women's International League for Peace and Freedom (Vellacott 1993) and of writers such as Virginia Woolf (1938), bequeathed an important, yet submerged, legacy of ideas on which the activists of the 1980s were able to draw in order to frame their critique of the nuclear politics of the superpowers.

More overtly, the intellectual resources with which Greenham and the women's peace movement of this decade were created came in part from a transnational, and particularly transatlantic, body of radical feminist and ecofeminist thinking. The work of American writers such as Mary Daly (1979) and Susan Griffin (1978), and the ecofeminist activism of the Spinsters and the Women's Pentagon Action (Linton and Whitham 1982; King 1983) were important sources of inspiration for Greenham. Not only were American feminist actions reported in British feminist newsletters and magazines, but individual women travelling between the US and Britain brought news of their own involvement in, for example, the Spinsters weaving of a web to blockade the Vermont Yankee Power Station and the Women's Pentagon Action's encircling of the Pentagon.

The British context of Greenham rests in the particular configuration of traditions of political action and political discourses, both feminist and not, in the post-war period. Greenham's transformation from a small, mixed peace camp in its first six months (albeit mostly women), into a large, open women's community of protest can only be understood in the light of critiques and practices developed within the British women's liberation movement from the late 1960s until the early 1980s. Most importantly, the women's liberation movement articulated the necessity of women-only organization and social space, and established the women-only, locally based, autonomous, non-hierarchical small group as the paradigmatic feminist form

58

of organization. Radical and lesbian feminist strands of the movement created a women's culture in most of the major cities and a number of towns throughout Britain. This national feminist community helped to facilitate the transmission of news about Greenham through a potentially sympathetic audience.

The mixed peace movement of the late 1950s and early 1960s, in particular the Direct Action Committee against Nuclear War (DAC) and later the Committee of 100, established a precedent for non-violent direct action, and provided a nationally specific 'repertoire of action' (Tilly 1978) on which Greenham was to draw. For example, the London–Aldermaston marches of this period suggested the form of protest with which Greenham began (the Cardiff–Greenham Women's Walk for Life, September 1981): the long-distance walk connecting a centre of population with a nuclear installation along the route of which public meetings were held and the issue publicized. Sit-downs organized by the DAC at military bases and attempts to board the supply ship for the Polaris submarine fleet at the Holy Loch were similar actions to the blockades, occupations and incursions in which women engaged at Greenham. The Committee of 100 spearheaded mass civil disobedience in 1961–2, including sit-downs in London and blockades and occupations of USAF bases around the country, and many activists were imprisoned; this too was not dissimilar to some of the actions at Greenham in the 1980s. The DAC and the Committee of 100's stress on the taking of individual responsibility for opposing nuclear weapons, and their opposition to the parliamentarian strategy of the Campaign for Nuclear Disarmament (CND) were also precursors of Greenham's ethos and mode of action in the 1980s.

A range of other movements during the 1960s and 1970s, some confined to Britain, others more transnational but strong in Britain, were also important intellectual precursors of Greenham. For instance, the Situationist movement advocated a politics of the 'spectacular' disruption, and reinvention, of everyday life (Erlich n.d.; Plant 1992), which presaged some of the more dramatic actions at Greenham. The Vietnam War called forth renewed and widespread peace protest, and directed the gaze of activists towards US imperialism in the Third World. At the beginning of the 1970s the Gay Liberation Front was formed, promoting a radical, confrontational politics of the personal. Also in the 1970s, provoked by the energy crisis of 1973, the environmental movement burst onto the political scene, challenging the post-war consensus on the desirability and possibility of continued economic growth. Environmentalists focused particularly on campaigning against the construction and extension of nuclear power plants, and large-scale non-violent direct actions were held at Torness in Scotland. Another significant precursor of Greenham was the squatters' movement, which established a large number of alternative communal households and in some cities took over whole neighbourhoods of empty houses, legitimizing within the

59

alternative culture the occupation of land which was not legally owned by those living there.

Together these movements bequeathed a legacy of anti-establishment attitudes, a strong strand of anarchist hostility to hierarchies, a critique of the materialism of industrial societies and of representative forms of democracy and the state, and a belief in the legitimacy and necessity of non-parliamentary forms of political action.

The importance of this national context of traditions of social protest can be seen by looking at the differences between Greenham and the women's peace camps which were set up, modelled on Greenham, in the USA and in Italy. The camp at Greenham was set up spontaneously at the end of the walk from Cardiff to the Cruise missile site, and was located on government controlled land directly outside the base. Some of this land had once been common land, until requisitioned by the ministries of defence and transport for military use, whilst other places around the base where women set up camps, still were 'common'. The acceptability of non-violent direct action in British traditions of collective action, the deep-seated attachment to a notion of common land in British culture which dates back to the time of the Enclosures in the sixteenth century, and the collective memory of protests such as the mass trespass of Kinder Scout in the 1930s to win access to the countryside, made this occupation of land acceptable to those who did it, and to their supporters.

In upstate New York, however, the women's peace camp which was established outside the military depot at Seneca Falls, from which Cruise missiles were to be dispatched to Europe, had no similar tradition of struggle over land access on which to draw. Women in the USA chose to buy a piece of land close to the depot and to live there legally. Moreover, the actions which were taken at Seneca were less confrontational and less disruptive of the activities of the depot than was the case at Greenham; only a few hundred arrests were ever made, compared with many thousands at Greenham. Similarly in Sicily, where laws from the Mussolini era still required foreigners visiting for more than a few days to register with the police, and where the Mafia's presence was strongly felt, women also chose to buy land close to the proposed Cruise missile base on which to set up a camp, and to keep a much lower profile than at Greenham. Neither at Seneca nor at Comiso (Sicily) did it seem possible just to 'squat' a piece of land directly outside the target of the protest. Both the illegal and the legal occupation of land had their costs in terms of the time and energy of campaigners – the former involved evictions up to three times a day for much of the life of Greenham, the latter required fundraising and the organization of shareholding. But it was undoubtedly the case that the illegal and precarious positioning of the women's peace camp outside Greenham was a more potent symbol of resistance than the tidier, legal 'camps' on small plots of privately owned land some distance away from the subject of the protest. Images of the juxtaposition of the anarchic domestic life of the camp against a back-drop of barbed wire, soldiers, watchtowers, and searchlights gave Greenham global recognition, unlike the camps at Seneca or Comiso.

THE PERSONAL–LOCAL–GLOBAL CONSTITUTION OF GREENHAM

The constitution of Greenham – the ongoing creation and re-creation of the camp and the wider women's peace movement over time – was depen dent on personal, local and global processes, and on the interactions between these processes.

Like any form of collective action, Greenham was sustained over its eleven years of existence by the individual decisions of thousands of women to get involved and to stay involved. It was concern about the global politics of nuclear militarism which provoked the initial interest in Greenham of most of the participants.[5] For many women who were mothers, this concern was focused on the future of their children or grandchildren. For example:

> I had got involved because I did feel that the world was about to end if somebody didn't do something . . . I had these terrible dreams about what would happen if my children were at school and nuclear war broke out. My whole life was absorbed in this fear that my children, not even that they might die, but that they might actually live and I might be crawling around in some half-life state.
>
> (Simone Wilkinson, aged 38)

Other women, particularly younger women without children, experienced deep psychological stress about nuclear war, and feared directly for their own future.

> I felt like the world is going to explode at any minute and why am I going to college? I mean, why go on with your life in this normal way when you feel like the world is about to blow up?
>
> (Liz Galst, aged 20)

> I remember when Reagan was elected I was still at university and we had an End of the World party because that was how we felt. I mean everybody just got roaring drunk for two days because we really felt like that was it, that none of us were going to live to see the end of our twenties.
>
> (Helen Mary Jones, aged 23)

Thus, events on the global stage precipitated action because they were experienced in a personal way.

However, it was not only the global situation which impelled women to get involved with Greenham. To understand Greenham as created only from the negative impulse of nuclear fear is to miss the centrality of the positive pull exerted by the camp as a women-only protest and community. Expressive, affective and cultural factors drew women to Greenham and sustained them in their involvement; in other words, factors local to Greenham, rooted in the social organization of the camp and the experience of being part of it, were an important motivation for involvement. For example, a sense of ownership and real participation was experienced by many women because the camp was women-only, and the opportunities provided by this women's space for developing close friendships with other women were highly valued. Other women were specifically attracted to Greenham by the large number of lesbians who were living there and the possibility this offered of being in a community in which lesbianism was the norm. But above all, women chose to live at Greenham and to continue living there or visiting because it was enjoyable, and because they found it personally satisfying.

> My reasons for going were that I thought I ought to go, because I felt that other people were doing something that I ought to be doing and I shouldn't be leaving this to other women to do . . . But when I was there it was really different because I really loved it . . . I loved all the excitement and I loved to do all the actions and all that. It was great. And mixing with a big group of women which I'd not done before. I really had a good time and liked it and enjoyed it. And that's why I stayed.
>
> (Penny Gulliver, aged 22)

Greenham was a place where women were able to engage in transforming and consolidating their self-identity.

> The women weren't the only reason I was there, but they were certainly a big attraction [laughter . . .]. For the first time in my life I felt I'd found a place where I fitted in and whatever I was OK, and the same as the others.
>
> (Jinny List, aged 20)

> A hell of a lot of women grew through Greenham, in all sorts of ways. Your awareness of your own power and abilities. It broke our images of ourselves. We went with housewives' values, the values of real narrow-minded, narrow, narrow-minded women from the Rhondha, and we broke this image of what we were. And then anything was possible.
>
> (Christine King, aged 27)

Greenham was supported and sustained by networks of people, mostly but not exclusively women, which were national, local and global. Women went to live and to stay at Greenham not primarily from the surrounding area, but from all over Britain. Greenham was located close to the M4 motorway, allowing relatively easy access for those travelling from South Wales, the West Country, London, the Home Counties and the Midlands, and even for those coming from the north and Scotland, road connections were good.[6] The choice of USAF Greenham Common as a site for Cruise missiles had been made for operational reasons within the logic of global nuclear politics: good road networks would allow the movement of convoys of missile launchers about the countryside, in order to foil pre-emptive first strikes. However, this had the effect of locating Cruise in a place easily accessible to protesters living in the most populated parts of Britain.

Supporters often travelled hundreds of miles to visit Greenham for a few hours, bringing resources such as food, clothing, building materials, firewood and money, and for several years, there were hundreds of visitors to the camp each week. These flows of people around Britain not only provided essential woman-power and resources for the continuation of the camp, but also served to embed Greenham within the consciousness of the oppositional culture of the 1980s. Information and news about Greenham was carried by individuals from the camp to places throughout the country, bypassing the news media, which consistently produced inaccurate and hostile accounts of the movement (when it was not ignoring Greenham altogether).[7] Visitors to Greenham would report to their local CND group, trade union meeting, church group, Labour Party branch or women's group, and women who lived at Greenham travelled around Britain speaking at meetings of interested audiences. Money raised by Greenham support groups, women's peace groups and other organizations through local activities such as street collections and jumble sales provided the financial resources which bought food, materials for taking action against the base (such as bolt cutters, ladders, paint), paid for petrol and camp vehicles, and supported women from overseas who were living at Greenham.

Local support for Greenham was also crucial to its survival. In the early days of the camp, it was the local anti-nuclear group, Newbury against the Missiles, which provided the tents, sleeping bags and cooking utensils which made it possible for the camp to be spontaneously set up at the end of the walk from Cardiff. Over the years a network of people who lived within ten miles of the camp opened their homes to the women who lived at Greenham, offering hot baths and a comfortable respite from the rigours of outdoor living. Some invited women to stay when they were sick, others let women store personal possessions in their homes to protect them from confiscation during evictions. The Society of Friends in Newbury gave Greenham women free access to their meeting house, which enabled meetings to be held in warmth and comfort, away from the interruptions occasioned by visitors and police at Greenham. The local Quakers also installed showers and set up a small office for the camp in their meeting house, providing an essential telephone contact point. Whilst the number of local supporters was small, their regular letters to the local papers and the constant pressure they exerted on local councillors and on the local MP destabilized the hegemony of local hostility to Greenham, and gave Greenham some roots in the locality.

Although discussions of globalization have tended to focus on cities as global places (e.g. Harvey 1989; Lash and Urry 1994), the decision to site Cruise at Greenham made this rural space, four miles from the nearest (small) town, into a global locale. The US airforce was already stationed at Greenham, and the upgrading of the base to house Cruise brought hundreds more American service personnel and their families to the area. Then as the camp organized its first large-scale actions such as the blockades of Easter 1982 and the 'Embrace the Base' demonstration of December 1982, which attracted over thirty thousand women, the world's media focused on Greenham. Reporters and television crews from Europe, the USA, the Soviet Union and beyond went to Greenham to interview the women, and to film and photograph the camp. By the time the first missiles were installed in November 1983, people in countries as remote as Nicaragua and South Africa knew about Greenham.

Greenham was outside local culture, and largely separate from the local community. Its culture was profoundly other to the conservative, small town concerns of rural Berkshire. Greenham was cosmopolitan and looked outwards to a global community of anti-nuclear campaigners and feminists. The flows of women who came to Greenham from all over Europe, from Australia, the USA, Canada, some to visit, some to live, brought to the camp their previous experiences of political action and a range of political discourses and individual histories. In an environment in which the exchanges of stories and personal experience was much valued, the praxis of Greenham was created out of these different traditions. For instance, Australian women brought information about the connection between uranium mining and aboriginal land rights, and introduced aboriginal mythology; from this grew Greenham's use of dragon and serpent imagery. Women from the USA raised concern about US intervention in Central America, which ultimately led to a number of Greenham women visiting Nicaragua, and to women from Nicaragua visiting Greenham. Women from overseas also 'carried Greenham home',[8] and spread the practices, ideas and actions of Greenham around the globe. Women's peace camps inspired by Greenham were set up in Australia, Canada, Denmark, West Germany, Italy and the USA.

THINKING GLOBALLY, ACTING LOCALLY, GLOBALLY AND PERSONALLY

The oft-quoted injunction of the environmental movement to 'think global, act local' demands that a global conscience should be enacted within a local con-text, and implicitly suggests that local actions can be of global significance.

Greenham held a similar belief. The ethos which guided action at Greenham was one of personal responsibility. It was believed that every individual has a responsibility to act according to her/his conscience, and therefore should engage in action to oppose nuclear militarism. Underlying this was a belief in the importance of individual agency in the production, reproduction and transformation of society. It was held that the cumulative power of thousands of individual, local actions could have an impact on the global situation.

The global collective conscience of Greenham produced action directed at the specific location of Cruise missiles in Britain. Blockades of the base, and many thousands of incursions into the base, as well as the constant tacit protest enacted by the camp's presence outside the base, were all local actions of resistance against global power. Reaching the point at which they felt able to break the law, cause criminal damage, and defy the police, British soldiers and armed American servicemen, was, for most women, a difficult process of internal dialogue and self-questioning, within a context of discussion with others. The taking of action at Greenham which resulted in arrest and a court case, then often further underlined the global dimension of local and personal actions. In many of the thousands of court cases tried at Newbury Magistrates Court, women, usually defending themselves without a lawyer, would use international law, such as the 1969 Genocide Act in their defence.

Greenham actions were not just located at Greenham: Greenham women roved across Britain and beyond. 'Greenham women are everywhere' was a slogan coined early in the life of the camp, to suggest that Greenham actions took place beyond that one corner of Berkshire, and were not confined to women who lived at Greenham. Whilst there was, at various times, considerable tension about the label 'Greenham woman' and over the centrifugal pull of the camp, women's peace actions inspired by Greenham, and conducted by women who identified as 'Greenham women', took place all over Britain. Some of these were the actions of women who lived at the camp, but most were those of women whose primary commitment was to working in their home communities. It was particularly in taking action beyond Greenham that the project was pursued of 'making connections' between nuclear weapons, women's oppression and other forms of global injustice. Roving actions can be divided into two main groups: those that related directly to Greenham, but which took place away from the camp; and women's peace actions in the style of Greenham, but not concerned primarily with Greenham.

The first group of actions was directly mainly at raising the profile of Greenham or at taking the protest about Cruise to other locations. For instance in January 1983 women occupied the lobby of the House of Commons to demand that the issue of Cruise be debated. Local women's peace groups throughout Britain regularly held demonstrations in town squares, set up peace camps on roundabouts and engaged in dramatic street theatre, and mass blockades were held in London and other cities to protest against and publicize the exercising of Cruise missile convoys. In 1985 there was a walk to 'reclaim Salisbury plain' from military exercises; this passed over the firing range and the area in which convoys were exercised. This spreading of women's peace actions around Britain aimed to show how the problem of nuclear weapons was not confined to Greenham, but was an issue which affected everyone, everywhere.

Perhaps the most ambitious action in this category, and the one most clearly global in scope, was the court case brought in the New York Supreme Court by a group of Greenham women, their seventeen children and two US congressmen against Ronald Reagan, Defense Secretary Caspar Weinberger and US military chiefs of staff. The aim of this case was to get an injunction against the deployment of Cruise at Greenham, using international law and the US Constitution to argue that deployment was illegal.[9] The case attracted widespread support from the wider Greenham network and from the mixed peace movement in Britain and the USA, and for twenty-four hours on 9 November 1983 camps were set up at all 102 US bases in Britain in support of the case, as well as outside the White House and the Supreme Court in New York.

The second group of actions was inspired by the distinctive ethos and style of protest of Greenham but went beyond the issue of Cruise, often aiming to draw attention to the connections between nuclear militarism and other issues, some global, others more specifically British. For instance, on the occasion of President Reagan's visit to London (7 June 1982), women from the camp and from the wider Greenham network performed a symbolic die-in outside the Stock Exchange to highlight the huge profits made by the international arms trade. In March 1984, women demonstrated outside a seminar and sales conference for missile systems and technology, throwing red paint at the building in which it was held. Making links between militarism, the exploitation of animals in research and women's oppression there was also a women's camp at Porton Down (the chemical and biological weapons research establishment). To highlight the use of uranium mined in Namibia in the production of warheads for Trident nuclear submarines, a women's action was held at the British Nuclear Fuels plant, Springfields. Greenham women, working with Women against Pit Closure groups, also organized a series of women's walks from mining villages in South Wales to Hinckley Point nuclear power station, to demonstrate the relationship between the closing of coal mines, the expansion of nuclear power and the manufacture of nuclear weapons. The other major form of action in this category was the establishment of women's peace camps at other nuclear bases. Inspired by Greenham, there were, at different times, camps at military installations at Menwith Hill, Waddington, Morwemstow, Rosyth, Capenhurst, Fylingdales and Brawdy, amongst others, and blockades, fence-cutting and incursions took place at these and other bases.

GLOBAL–LOCAL–PERSONAL OUTCOMES

Evaluating the influence of Greenham on global nuclear policy is fraught with difficulty. The impact of Greenham, in this area, is hard to disentangle from that of the wider peace movement, and, as Randle (1987) points out, commenting on non-violent direct action in the late 1950s and early 1960s, the secrecy which surrounds all government decisions, particularly about nuclear weapons, means that it is seldom possible to demonstrate beyond doubt that changes in policy may be attributed to social movements.

Obviously, Greenham did not achieve its initial aim of preventing the deployment of Cruise missiles in Britain. Unlike the Dutch and Belgian governments, the British government pushed ahead with NATO policy, unheeding of the mass protests and the opinion polls. But within four years of deployment, agreement had been reached between the superpowers to scrap Cruise, and within ten years of the establishment of the camp the last missiles were removed. Undoubtedly the most important factors which led to Gorbachev's disarmament initiatives were internal to the Soviet Union, and were primarily economic; the arms race was just not sustainable indefinitely. Commentators on the impact of the peace movement as a whole on this process are generally cautious, but argue that it contributed in a number of ways. Firstly, the peace movement heightened public consciousness about nuclear weapons, the arms race and NATO policy, galvanizing opposition to Cruise, which, according to opinion polls, ranged between 40 and 60 per cent. The movement thereby contributed to the democratization of debate about defence (Carter 1992; Wittner 1988). Its assertion that people had a right to know and form opinions in this area constituted an important attack on the geo-political privacy of state elites and transnational blocs (Shaw 1991). Secondly, in promoting debate about nuclear weapons and the implications of their use, the peace movement served to delegitimize them; Reagan's notion of a 'winnable' and limited nuclear war in Europe was publicly challenged, and its implications for Europe exposed. Wittner (1988: 287) suggests that this put a brake on the arms race and made nuclear war less likely.[10] Gleditsch (1990) concludes that the overall effect of the peace movement was to exert significant pressure on governments: 'it is questionable whether the breakthrough in the disarmament negotiations in 1986–7 would have occurred without the widespread moral revulsion against the nuclear arms race championed by the "new" peace movement' (Gleditsch 1990: 73). Shaw (1991) is more specific about how this worked, suggesting that the movement indicated to Gorbachev that Brezhnev's European policy was outdated, and that there was a significant constituency in the West which was not actively hostile to the Soviet Union. This may well have contributed to his willingness to make the substantial concessions in the arms negotiations which eventually led to the INF treaty. The strength of the peace movement meant that NATO was impelled to listen seriously to Gorbachev.

Finally, the Western peace movement stimulated the growth of the underground peace movements of Eastern Europe, contributing pressure for 'détente from below', and preparing the way for the revolutions of 1989 (Jahn 1989; Shaw 1991).

Greenham's role within the European and British peace movements was that of its most radical wing. Whilst Greenham's women-only policy was the subject of fierce debate within the peace movement, and was extremely unpopular in some sectors, Greenham undoubtedly influenced the forms of action in which other participants engaged. Mixed peace camps were set up at many other nuclear bases around Britain and in Italy and West Germany, following the model of Greenham, and gatherings and blockades and disruption of military exercises became regular types of action there. CND initiated demonstrations which sought to replicate Greenham actions, such as the Aldermaston to Burghfield human chain of Easter 1983 which imitated Greenham's Embrace the Base gathering. The peace movement as a whole was never split over the issue of non-violent direct action in the way that it had been in the 1950s (see Randle 1987), and even the cutting of fences around military bases ('snowball actions') became a widespread practice in the years after it was first done at Greenham.

It was Greenham, spotlighted by the media during 1982 and 1983 because it was women-only and because of its imaginative and unusual forms of action, which seemed to be particularly effective at raising public awareness of Cruise. In 1980, 41 per cent of those surveyed in Britain did not know that there were nuclear weapons in their country (Hastings and Hastings 1982: 330), but by 1983, only 6 per cent had never heard of Greenham (Hastings and Hastings 1984: 323). Whether Greenham made the public more or less likely to oppose the deployment of cruise is debatable. Byrd (1985) suggests that there was a 'Greenham effect' on women, citing the significant gender gap in attitudes to Cruise, and the 32 per cent of women who said that they had become more sympathetic to the campaign against Cruise as a result of Greenham, as against 50 per cent who were unaffected (*The Sunday Times*, 23 January 1983). A small non-random survey of women in *Spare Rib* also reported that 1 in 3 women had become more favourable to nuclear disarmament or more aware of the issue because of Greenham (*Spare Rib*, May 1984).

Whilst the contribution of the women's peace camp to the removal of Cruise from Greenham may be debatable, it is clear that what subsequently happened to the base and to the common has been profoundly influenced by the camp. An important strand of argument voiced by the camp highlighted the ecological destruction caused to the land of Greenham Common by the base (hundred of trees were felled, for instance), and evoked 'rural protectionist' sympathy amongst some local people who had enjoyed access to the Common in their leisure time. When in the mid-1980s the government attempted to revoke all rights of access held by 'commoners' to Greenham

Common, in an attempt to institute trespass laws which could be used against protesters entering the base, a campaign was begun by local residents to retain their rights of access to the Common. Ultimately, commoners' rights were extended rather than rescinded, when, following the closure of the base, all but a hundred acres around the missile silos were sold back to Newbury District Council and returned to common land once more. Had there been no camp at Greenham, it is unlikely that the Ministry of Defence would have given up Greenham Common, or Newbury District Council bought it back.

At the individual and collective level, women at Greenham forged new identities and consciousness. It is beyond the scope of this chapter to explore the range of ways in which identities and consciousness were transformed through involvement with Greenham; in brief these included new identities as autonomous, empowered women, and as lesbians, and consciousness of women's oppression, state and police malpractice and of the global inter-connectedness of political issues and peoples (see Roseneil 1994, 1995).

As I said earlier, although nuclear weapons are an issue of global signif-icance, many of the women who were involved with Greenham had been impelled to act against them because of personal fear and concern for them-selves and their families, rather than out of a global consciousness. Most had a fairly narrow British or western European orientation to politics when they first got involved with Greenham. This was broadened through contact with visitors to the camp from all over the world, and by the camp's growing collective interest in global issues, which was manifested both in informal discussions and in meetings and actions about connections between political struggles in different parts of the world.

As these women explain:

> Whilst you were there a lot of other issues would click. There was the miners' strike and a lot of miners' wives used to come down . . . And they'd ask us to go to the strike meetings and talk about nuclear weapons and the connection with the pits. And there was the American Indian from the Indian reservation. And he did a slide show about the uranium mines where they lived. And there were delegations from South Africa. And we were just dead ordinary working-class women from the inner cities and we were talking to people who were directly involved in struggles from all over the world.
>
> (Trisha, aged 20)

> It made me feel connected to women from other places and other countries . . . I met and spent time with women who were from other countries and had worked on connected issues.
>
> (Barbara Rawson, aged 52)

> One thing that was really historically and personally important to me was a visit of the South African Women's Theatre Troupe . . . And

they read the South African Women's Declaration of Demands and I remember that very high amongst them was the elimination of nuclear weapons from the world . . . And I remember being so touched by that, and I felt that what we were doing at Greenham was this really revolutionary thing . . . We really made a lot of connections.

(Liz Galst, aged 20)

Many women moved beyond the confines of their own personal experience, which had been forged within fairly limited local and national contexts, to identify as global actors, members of a transnational movement of women working for peace, and linked to others struggling for peace and justice. After Greenham, many women became involved in and set up political projects with a global concern: examples include transnational campaigns against violence against women and against rape in war; Women's Aid to Former Yugoslavia; and the Women's Network for a Nuclear Free and Independent Pacific.

These are highly significant outcomes. Lash and Urry (1994) express concern that women are being excluded from the information and communication structures of the contemporary globalizing world. Yet the case of Greenham and the women's peace movement, whilst it involved only a tiny proportion of the women of the world, shows that it has been possible for women to insert themselves as actors in the globalization process, and indeed to create themselves as actors of global significance with an understanding of events and politics in geographically distant places, and with connections to those engaged in similar political projects around the world.

CONCLUSION

Greenham and the women's peace movement of the 1980s were embedded within processes of globalization. They were at the same time both the product of globalization and productive of globalization. Emerging as resistance to the global threat of nuclear war and the globalization of nuclear militarism, the movement was composed of global flows of actors, ideas and images, and it contributed to the creation of global identities and consciousness and to the formation of global networks of political activists.

This discussion of the interconnections between the global, local and personal dynamics of Greenham suggests that Greenham was a movement characteristic of high modernity. In an era of ever-increasing global interdependence and high-consequence risks, in which processes of individualization mean that these changes and risks are experienced intensely personally (Giddens 1991; Beck 1994), Greenham engaged in a collective challenge to what were perceived as the negative aspects of high modernity. But this challenge was inextricably bound up in those very processes of globalization, and was dependent upon them in its operation.

My focus on a social movement highlights the importance of attention to agency and human actors when considering globalization. The global–local–personal dynamics of globalization must be understood as social processes set in train and carried out by social actors, rather than just by the structures of the world economy, the inevitable development of technology or the power play of nation states. I have shown that social movements are not just constituted through globalizing processes, but actively contribute to them. Finally, this chapter has served to insert women as actors within the global–local–personal dialectics of the contemporary world.

NOTES

1 This chapter develops my earlier work on Greenham in which issues of globalization are considered only in passing. See Roseneil 1994 and 1995.
2 For a more detailed discussion of the geopolitical context of Greenham, see Roseneil 1995.
3 The Belgian and Dutch governments later rejected the missiles, after intense peace movement opposition.
4 The source of the data referred to in this chapter is my ethnographic research on Greenham, which drew both on my own involvement and on interviews with 35 participants. For a discussion of the methodological issues involved, see Roseneil 1993 and, for fuller reports on the data, see Roseneil 1994 and 1995.
5 See note 4 above, on the source of data.
6 Lash and Urry (1994) discuss the significance of the M4 corridor to economic development in the 1980s.
7 For discussion of the media reporting of Greenham, see Young 1990.
8 'Carry Greenham Home' was a song written for Greenham by Peggy Seeger.
9 The case was eventually dismissed in 1985. See Greenham Common Women Against Cruise Missiles 1984, Hickman 1986 and Young 1990 for a more detailed discussion.
10 Randle (1987) makes a similar argument about the impact of the peace movement of the 1950s and 1960s.

Part II

HOMOGENIZED CULTURE OR ENDURING DIVERSITY?

4

'ACROSS THE UNIVERSE'
The limits of global popular culture
John Street

Charlie Chaplin, Big Bird, and Marcel Proust may have little else in common, but they are all figures in a cosmopolitan culture that, for the first time in history, embraces the globe.

(de Sola Pool 1990: 71)

Popular culture has often been used to symbolize globalization. Its icons, as Ithiel de Sola Pool observes, can be found throughout the world. Mel Gibson or Madonna are as well known in Brazil as in Belgium; Guns 'n' Roses or *Jurassic Park* draw huge audiences in Tokyo and in Toronto. The persuasiveness of popular culture, its apparently universal appeal, stands for the existence of a global culture, one that transcends or erodes national cultures. Indeed, popular culture is held to represent more than just the spread of particular stars or products. It also symbolizes the establishment of an accompanying infrastructure. The key networks of global communications (and the industries organized around them) are those of the entertainment business.

What is worrying about this version of globalization is its apolitical character. It is not just nations that are transcended but, it seems, politics too. And yet the wrangling in the last round of GATT talks, over whether film should be included in free trade agreements (and the final decision that it be exempted), suggests that politics is an inextricable part of any global order, and furthermore that things are less global, and more parochial, than they appear.

It is not hard to see why the political dimension has been ignored, especially when considering popular culture. The thought that popular culture and its market has been universalized – that the same artists, films or television programmes are consumed in London, New York and Paris, and that they are marketed by the same group of transnational corporations – leads to the view that politics is irrelevant. There are two elements to this claim. The first is that there are no effective political controls or institutions at the global level, only the corporations with their purely commercial interests.

The second is that at the level at which political controls do exist, at the national or sub-national level, the responsible organizations are powerless. Attempts to resist the intrusion of transnational corporations, in the name of local culture or economic autonomy, inevitably fail.

In this chapter, I want to look more closely at the idea of a global popular culture, to ask whether it represents accurately what is happening in the world of mass entertainment. In doing so, I want to look beyond the cultural product alone. The mere fact that a film is on 'worldwide release' is not proof of a global cultural order. Firstly, the meaning of that film may vary with time and place. And secondly, the key issue is how the product arrived there: what material and institutional interests organized its production, distribution and consumption.

Too often the analysis of popular culture is concerned only with texts and their interpretation. This approach is most typically associated with those students of cultural studies who focus upon the symbolic creativity of consumers, upon the capacity of people to make their own use of mass produced culture (Willis 1990; Fiske 1989). It is a perspective which is liable to ignore or marginalize the processes that created that product/text in the first place. To focus on the business of production is to re-introduce the political economy of popular culture, and to side with Simon Frith when he writes:

> My starting point is that what is possible for us as consumers – what is available to us, what we can do with it – is a result of decisions made in production, made by musicians, entrepreneurs and corporate bureaucrats, made according to governments' and lawyers' rulings, in response to technological opportunities. The key to 'creative consumption' remains an understanding of those decisions, the constraints under which they are made and the ideologies that account for them.
>
> (1988: 6–7)

To assess the claim that there is a globalized popular culture, therefore, we need to look more closely at the way culture is *produced*, and particularly at the political dynamics of this production. I want to draw attention to what is too often omitted from accounts of popular culture: that political institutions are involved at a variety of levels in its organization, and that as a consequence, glib talk of globalization needs to be heavily qualified. We need to begin, though, by looking carefully at what is being claimed in the name of globalization.

GLOBALIZATION

Much turns on the way the word 'globalization' is understood. Marjorie Ferguson suggests that all discussion of globalization refers to 'a more visible and powerful supernational order, a "world system" ... that shifts many former national concerns to the world geopolitical stage' (1992: 71). But to accept this definition is not automatically to accept a concomitant process of cultural unification and standardization. Mike Featherstone, for example, sees no inscribed logic which requires an inexorable movement towards 'cultural homogeneity and integration'. Indeed he is sceptical of any approach to culture that views it as either homogenizing or fragmenting, preferring instead to ask how such possibilities become 'frames of reference for comprehending culture' (Featherstone 1990: 1–2). What, then, does it mean to talk of a global culture?

One way to define global culture is to focus on the power of its producers, and to see how their interests and actions are located in some realm outside the reach of any single nation state. Another way to define global culture is in terms of the product. It is, after all, possible to have control over the methods of production and distribution without making the same product available in all places, or under the same conditions. Transnational corporations are often responsible for selling national or local culture back to the nation or the locality. French films shown in France sometimes have American distributors; African popular music is marketed in Africa by EMI or BMG. If, on the other hand, the definition of global culture focuses on the product, then globalization would be defined as the distribution of a single product across the globe. Finally, globalization can also be measured by the identity of consumer taste across the globe. The fact that the same product is made available everywhere is no guarantee that it achieves the same success or popularity (let alone acquires the same significance or meaning). So globalization in this sense refers to homogeneity of taste. In short, globalization can apply to production, distribution or consumption, and in doing so can identify quite different circumstances and supporting evidence.

Global production

The popular culture industry has changed dramatically in the last decade. One measure of this change is the way in which 'globalization' has become part of the industry's rhetoric. Keith Negus reports how, for example, Time Warner sees itself as 'feeding the [global] appetite for information and entertainment' (1992: 5), and how, in the company's own words, 'Sony is global'. Taking the record industry as one instance of this trend, we can see how consumers across the world are spending large sums on the purchase of records. In 1992, world sales of records netted $28.7 billion, of which the USA contributed 31 per cent, the EC 32 per cent and Japan 15 per cent. According to the British Phonographic Industry, 'the major areas of growth over the next ten years or so will be in the Far Eastern markets and Pacific basin territories' (BPI 1993: 55–56). In 1982, sales of music in Singapore generated $6.5 million; in 1988, they were worth $31.3 million (IFPI 1990: 85). Sales in South Korea in 1992 were worth $471 million and in Taiwan

$326 million (BPI 1993: 55). And the products upon which this money is being lavished are manufactured by a group of five corporations who together have rights in 70 per cent of all music bought (Negus 1992: 1).

These corporations are part of larger conglomerates with interests in many other forms of popular culture. Rupert Murdoch's News Corporation has stakes in satellite and terrestrial television, films, books and newspapers in the USA, the UK, Australia and Hong Kong. The Sony Corporation, owner of Columbia Records, Tri-Star and Columbia Pictures, is perhaps the most telling example of this phenomenon. With its operating headquarters in Japan and the USA, Sony not only has the rights over a vast range of sound recordings and films, it also has major interests in the production of music and films (and links them, so that Sony soundtracks accompany their cinema releases), and it is a major player in the market for the hardware that reproduces these products (CD players, video machines, etc.). It seems, therefore, that the international production of popular culture is part of a transnational corporate system (see Tunstall and Palmer 1991).

Global distribution

But the appearance of globalization does not end with the manufacturing of products. It extends into distribution. The networks that make the product available – the retailers, the cinemas, the television channels – are also part of another (often the same) transnational network. This is especially true of television, a crucial carrier of popular culture. As Annabelle Sreberny-Mohammadi observed, 'Ted Turner's Cable News Network is received by the Kremlin and the Islamic Republics, and *Dallas* enjoys an international audience in over 90 countries' (1991: 125).

As more television is transmitted by satellite, the less significance attaches to national borders and the presumption of national control. The technologies of cultural distribution seem to enhance the new global order. National governments are relatively powerless to determine what their citizens view. This was true of the old Eastern bloc, where pictures and images of Western life (and then the political uprisings in their own countries) could be seen, despite the antipathy of the Communist governments. Similarly in Britain, the government could present only a minimal barrier to the Dutch pornographic channel 'Red Hot Television'. This state of affairs engenders quite different interpretations. Ithiel de Sola Pool argues that attempts to resist are bound to fail, and indeed deserve to fail. 'Restrictions', he writes, 'are likely to be only delaying factors', which just slows progress towards a new freedom (1990: 148). By contrast, Ghita Ionescu (1993) bemoans the trend and urges action to arrest the erosion of the institutions of democracy. What both sets of critics agree upon, though, is the emergence of transnational forms of distribution.

Global consumption

Time Warner has operated under the slogan 'The World is Our Audience'. There are two ways of viewing this aspiration to global consumption. The first is to talk of a single, common culture; the second is to talk of a global multiculturalism, where consumers pick and choose from an array of cultural forms and styles. As we have seen, it does not follow automatically that because the carriers of popular culture are controlled by the same set of interests or by a small cartel, they propagate the same culture. The same corporation can own channels in Japan and the USA, but there is no necessary presumption that they will show identical programmes. There is some evidence for both versions of global consumption.

The first can be seen in the apparently universal success of certain products or artists. Performers like Julia Roberts or Whitney Houston, or film-makers like Steven Spielberg, are launched onto a global stage. U2 and Bruce Springsteen set out on *world* tours. Meanwhile, MTV's ambition is to realize its slogan of 'One Planet, One Music', echoing the theme of the global charity venture Live Aid ('We are the World'). This version of global consumption can also be detected negatively in the (usually failed) attempts by national governments to restrict the amount of 'foreign' culture being broadcast in their countries through the use of quotas or tariff barriers.

Equally, there is evidence for the second version of global consumption. It is now possible to see and experience the cultures of many different groups and societies. The spread of tourism or the fashion for 'world music' are both illustrations of this. Travel agents advertise trips to ever more 'exotic' locations. Record shops sell the music of Memphis and Mali.

In each dimension – production, distribution and consumption – it is possible to see evidence for the emergence of a global culture with an attendant political economy. It may take different forms, but it has the same essential features. It is not controlled by any one nation, nor is its access or content peculiar to any one region. It seems that, under this regime, nation states become increasingly marginal players, unable to protect local culture or to control the production and distribution of the culture their citizens consume. But does this paint an accurate picture?

THE MYTH OF GLOBALIZATION?

There are many critiques offered of globalization. My own concern is with the way in which the rhetoric of global culture has become detached from the material and institutional conditions that underlie the appearance of globalization.

The term 'global culture' itself suggests, as we have seen, two visions of the product. Either a multiplicity of forms of expression, values and experiences, deriving from across the world and with no one set taking precedence over the others. Or it refers to a single culture which is specific to no one group – an interpretation of 'We are the World', in which 'we' refers to everyone who inhabits the planet. Both these pictures of the global culture, though, are attacked by critics who argue that, in fact, there is a single, particular dominant culture (see Murphy 1983; Featherstone 1990; McGrew and Lewis 1992). The culture being touted across the globe often emerges from one bit of the world – America – and carries with it American experiences and perspectives.

While it is true that Anglo-American products are modified to appeal to their international audience, the product itself still retains the hallmarks of its origins. There may be concessions, ways of 'tailoring' an original design, to suit certain markets, but these are small compromises within the main framework. It is not just that English is the language of much popular culture; it is also that the images and concerns of the Anglo-American region are most prevalent. The film *Black Rain* may have been shot in Japan and used Japanese actors to star alongside the American Michael Douglas, but it was fear of Japanese economic success that fuelled the plot.

A similar criticism can be directed at 'global multiculturalism'. The diverse cultures do not just emerge into the global airwaves. They are selected. Tour operators choose particular resorts because of what their wealthy clients expect. 'World music' is defined by Anglo-American record companies according to marketing strategies that particular audiences represent or require (Frith 1989; Redhead and Street 1989).

So the first challenge to the notion of the global culture is that no such culture exists, in either its unitary or its multicultural form. This is not to deny that the world is increasingly connected up, that there is greater interaction between cultures, only that the net effect is not a plurality of equal cultures, or a harmonious synthesis of them in one global culture. Cultures form part of a struggle for power, in which resources (both cultural and financial) are not evenly distributed (Jayaweera 1987).

Another line of criticism is less concerned with the product itself, and more with the use to which it is put, the way it is interpreted. Even if there is a global culture, it would be wrong to see it as meaning the same to everyone. This is amply demonstrated by the way jazz was used and abused in the Soviet Union. At one time it was banned as a product of capitalist decadence; at another it was fêted as the authentic voice of an oppressed people (Starr 1983). And both readings of jazz are at odds with its interpretation elsewhere. Culture does not simply impose itself upon peoples. While, as Ferguson notes, Canada imports 90 per cent of its Anglophone TV drama, 'there is considerable evidence that Canada continues to maintain a value system and way of life distinctive from the US' (Ferguson 1992: 81). Writers about Britain also warn of the danger of seeing American culture as a synonym for 'Americanization' (Webster 1988; Strinati 1992). The myth of America takes on different meanings in different contexts. In other words, the argument that there is a global culture may also be vulnerable to the argument that there is not a global process of cultural interpretation. The same artefact docs not elicit the same response wherever it is seen or heard. In popular culture, context is vital. 'We may all hear each other's sounds these days', writes Frith, 'but we still read them differently' (1991: 281). This is not just a theoretical point about how culture is understood, it is one about the *organization* of culture and about relations of power.

If the 'global culture' is in fact the culture of a particular part of the globe, then we may be suspicious of the claim that we are now dealing with global industries. Rather, we are dealing with multinational corporations who need to expand their market or their product base. This means discovering, or organizing, new audiences; it also means finding 'new' products. The phenomenon of 'global' companies can, in fact, be a mistaken description of 'corporate trans-nationalization at a higher level of magnitude' (Ferguson 1992: 75). The appearance of global companies may disguise a reality in which corporate structure is forced to change to adapt to new markets or technologies.

Furthermore, the picture of a global industry operating unconstrained also omits the possibility of national and local mediating interests. It is important to notice that the actually delivery of popular culture depends on processes which are peculiar to particular national (and sub-national) structures. This process is most apparent in the organization of broadcasting, and is clearly exemplified in the contrast between Britain and the USA. The degree of regulation both of the airwaves and of the organizations allowed to inhabit them have an impact upon what can be heard/seen (Malm and Wallis 1993; McQuail and Siune 1986). The same can be claimed for popular music (Street 1993).

The dominant political ideology of the 1980s, the voice of the market liberal, held that culture was best managed by the market – that culture was in fact, or ought in principle to be, free from political interference. The empirical claim that underpinned this argument has, however, to be treated with some scepticism. On a number of fronts, political actors have considerable influence over the form and content of popular culture. It is only necessary to review the work of *Reporters Sans Frontières* (1993), on the censorship and regulation of national systems of communications, to realize the extent of the national political management of culture.

'Global culture' is also subject to the effects of other agencies besides the broadcasters. Government – at various levels – can have an impact on what is available and what access is allowed to it. Writing of the interaction of government and the music industry, Malm and Wallis observe: 'Laws can be made, taxes can be introduced and exempted, cultural and media policies can be formulated, subsidies can be constructed aimed at increasing the music industry's activities with national and local music (as opposed to international imports)' (1993: 26). It does not follow from this, of course, that national governments succeed in their ambitions. It is a long path from policy intent to policy implementation. None the less, the way nation states organize culture involves a process of negotiation and struggle. And what Malm and Wallis reveal, with a series of detailed case studies, is that there are many different results to these relationships, results that can be measured by the music making and consuming that any one country enjoys. Much, too, may depend on the structure of interests within a nation state. Governments may be able to regulate some aspects of broadcasting better than others. In Tanzania, the radio carries a high proportion of nationally produced music. Television cannot match this because there is no national film industry to supply videos. Thus, the TV stations make use of imported videos, courtesy of MTV. In other words, there is no unitary process of globalization, and the extent of it is dependent upon political structures and forces which are specific to national and local states.

But it is not just that states differ between themselves in the ways in which they try to manage popular culture. Within each state, the form of infrastructure has an effect upon what is being consumed and how. Though there is a pervasive impression that the world has been 'wired up', it is not altogether accurate. While it is true that in Britain and America there is a high penetration of radio and television (in 1989, 98 per cent of households had at least one TV set [PSI 1992: 2]), other nations have much lower levels of access. And in Britain, the cable network has developed more slowly than in other European countries (Dyson and Humphreys 1986). Furthermore, the access and use of communications technology is not uniformly spread. British Asian and Afro-Caribbean groups are more likely to have a satellite dish than other groups; they also show a greater willingness to subscribe to cable (PSI 1993: 3 and 19).

To summarize: there are many obstacles to the global culture thesis. My concern here has been to highlight the ways in which political processes and distributions of power qualify the notion of globalization. My approach has, though, been negative, to see what is wrong with the argument. This in itself does not tell us what is actually happening. If it makes little sense to think of global culture, what constitutes a more accurate perception? If political processes and relations of power are indeed important to the form taken by popular culture, then what are the consequences of these forces? We need, therefore, to generate a more coherent, overarching thesis about the way in which popular culture becomes part of a political network. We have so far only listed a number of the possible ways in which 'global culture' becomes subject to other countervailing forces and interests.

In trying to develop a fuller account of the political structuring of popular culture, I want to concentrate (albeit not exclusively) on music, because, as Malm and Wallis observe (1993: 7), 'the music industry is . . . at the forefront of a move towards global standardization of cultural products'. This observation is not, though, a prologue to the announcement of the industry's triumph. Malm and Wallis reject such fatalism. Similarly, Deanna Robinson and her colleagues conclude that 'even though information-age economic forces are building an international consumership for centrally produced and distributed popular music, other factors are pulling in the opposite direction' (1991: 4). They too focus on the processes of mediation that stand between global intentions and global effects. Their discussion suggests three basic categories: the *institutions* with the power to affect culture, the *policies* that are pursued, and the *levels* at which they operate.

It is too easy to talk about government or the state, without differentiating between the different agencies involved. This is compounded by the degree to which the state extends its grasp. But the obvious contenders include the institutions for the supply and regulation of broadcasting. Less obvious, but no less important, are industrial and economic institutions, and their relationship to both the economy and the polity. Finally, there are the educational institutions (which again have links with political and economic interests). Together these institutions find themselves embroiled in a variety of policy issues. In the case of popular music, Robinson *et al.* identify three major policy areas: broadcasting, copyright, taxation/subsidy. These policies derive from, and affect, different levels of society. They are not confined to the national level. The local, though often ignored, plays an important role in organizing the production and consumption of culture. There are also international-level actors, who also get overlooked. These include UNESCO and the agencies of the European Union, as well as the record business's International Federation of the Phonographic Industry (see Malm and Wallis 1993: 221–9; Frith 1994). The powers of these institutions may be compromised by the rival forces of the media industries, but they remain part of the policy network which delivers and shapes the culture.

Malm and Wallis's *Media Policy and Music Activity* represents the most detailed attempt to map the way these elements are linked in the world of popular music. Their focus, as with their previous work *Big Sounds from Small Peoples* (1983), is upon countries outside the Anglo-American mainstream. Their sample includes Jamaica, Trinidad, Kenya, Tanzania, Wales and Sweden. Though each country enjoys very different circumstances, they all are engaged on a similar project: managing the making, distribution and consumption of music. In their survey, Malm and Wallis emphasize that there is a *policy process* that affects popular culture. Music does not just leap from the artist's imagination into the audience's heart. While it is true that the policy tends to lag behind technological and economic change, coping rather than leading it, this does not detract from the fact that policy alters the final outcome (Malm and Wallis 1993: 197). For example, local radio stations may operate in a state of relative autonomy, or they may simply use programmes bought from satellite suppliers, and inject only a minimal amount of genuinely local material – weather, traffic, news reports (Malm and Wallis 1993: 202). Whether this happens depends on the county's media policy, itself a consequence of principle, pragmatism and power. Its impact can be felt directly in the range of music available. Following the granting of a commercial TV franchise, Malm and Wallis observe that 'Swedish media policy makers virtually abdicated any ability or duty to force operators to observe obligations regarding music activity in the output of a national commercial TV channel' (1993: 206). Decisions to deregulate broadcasting can lead to greater similarity in content, not greater diversity – which adds further weight to the earlier argument that it is not *globalization* that generates this effect, but the introduction of a policy of *deregulation by individual states* (see Alan Scott's introduction to this volume).

What, however, is disappointing about the work done by Malm and Wallis, is that while they are good at describing the processes, and at identifying particular arrangements and their consequences, their analysis remains largely untheorized. We are left unclear as to how, say, the local and national interact, or why particular agencies adopt one policy rather than another. I want, therefore, to end this chapter by considering how the relationship between policy and popular culture might be given a firmer grounding.

MAKING CULTURAL POLICY

Political science has had little to say about cultural policy in particular, but a great deal about policy-making in general. There are many reasons for this state of affairs, but one that is worth noting is that many Western countries do not actually have a single, explicit cultural policy. They have many policies which affect the form of culture, but there is no unified deliberative strategy. This is certainly true of Britain and the USA (see Chevigny 1991); it is less true of France (Wachtel 1987; Rigby 1991). But to acknowledge this is not to close off analysis. It is instead to require that we think of cultural policy as a variety of practices, which stand in many different relationships to global, national and local power.

I want to draw attention to three dimensions that seem essential to any coherent account of the character – and hence the impact – of cultural policy. These are *institutional practices*, *policy process* and *ideology*. In considering each, I want also to draw comparisons between British and French cultural policy. The contrast is a stark one. In 1985, France spent 1,450 million ECUs (0.98 per cent of the state budget) on cultural activities; while Britain spent only 201 million ECUs (0.2 per cent of the state budget) (Commission of the European Communities 1987). This difference in spending does not just reflect differences of priority; it also marks differences of political structure, practice and ideology. Most importantly, the contrasting strategies are revealed in the degree to which each country is incorporated within the politics of globalization.

Institutional practices

The institutions which organize cultural policy are part of established patterns of behaviour, and their own specific characteristics – the way their remit is defined, the policy instruments available to them – are crucial to determining the outcome. It would be hopeless to try and understand British cultural policy without reference to the Arts Council. In its links with the government, it has played a crucial part in, among other things, defining 'culture' in largely elitist and consumerist terms. But while this policy may be the result of a particular set of circumstances and particular key actors, it is also a result of the Arts Council's origins in the creation of the Council for the Encouragement of Music and the Arts (CEMA), established during the Second World War. Its remit and approach was also established in the division created between CEMA and the 'light entertainment' supplied by the Entertainment National Service Association (ENSA). These origins both established a status outside direct government control (as a 'quango') and also perpetuated the split between 'high' and 'low' culture (C. Gray 1993: 4). The fact that cultural policy was, in the early 1990s, assigned to a *Heritage* ministry gives further clues as to the kinds of institutional interests being established. The weakness of the cultural sector effectively posed no counter-balance to globalizing tendencies.

In France, by comparison, the institutional history of cultural policy is mapped by important political shifts. The 1960s – and particularly the events of 1968 – marked the fragmentation of the elitist, Gaullist institutions of culture. The particular targets were the *Maisons de la Culture*, established after de Gaulle's accession to power in 1959. Their aim was to supply the best of international and national culture, providing culture *for* the regions, not *from* the regions (Rigby 1991: ch. 5). The combination of the institutions and their goal created a framework which facilitated globalization. After 1968, however, the institutional structure appeared to alter under the guise of *action culturelle*. Now the rhetoric was decentralization and democratization. In fact, the distribution of power remained at the centre, but what did change was its distribution within the core. The Ministry of Culture began to emerge as a key actor in the political system, a process that was to reach its peak under Jacques Lang in the 1980s. Under Lang, the Ministry of Culture struggled ideologically and practically to maintain French culture against globalizing forces (Hayward 1993: 27ff).

Policy process

The practices and predispositions of the key institutions are, however, only part of the story. It matters how these institutions relate to each other, and how, as a consequence, cultural policy is made. There is, of course, a formal political account of how these institutions represent some sort of constitutional or legitimate process. This, though, paints only a partial picture. An equally partial picture emerges if one concentrates exclusively upon the plethora of groups around cultural policy and draws the conclusion that an informal pluralism operates. Both presumptions need to be avoided. Clive Gray argues that British cultural policy is 'characterised by the twin features of organisational diversity and value limitation, which lead to an institutional pluralism but a behavioural elitism' (1993: 9–10). This arrangement is maintained by the existence of an 'issue network' (Rhodes 1988), which is typified by an unstable coalition of a large number of groups acting with limited autonomy. The contrast is with other networks (policy community, professional-, inter-governmental- and producer-networks), differentiated by inner structure, cohesiveness and membership. The combination of devolved control, market mechanisms and elitist leadership is apparent in the recent history of government policy on the British film industry (Hill 1993). It is also evident in the development of deregulation and cross-media ownership in Britain. Here the policy process was driven by the particular symbiosis of Thatcherite practices and Rupert Murdoch's (News Corporation) business interests. The impact of the Thatcher–Murdoch nexus underlines the thought that globalization is less an inevitable process and more a political project.

The fact that the British model seems to fit best with the notion of the 'issue network' is no guarantee that this will be true for all systems. This point is reinforced by the French experience. It is noticeable how France's cultural policies, particularly in relation to its film industry, have been directed at resisting aspects of globalization, and have been formulated within a much more deliberative, politicized policy system. France was a leading (and successful) campaigner against a free trade in film under the 1993 GATT agreement. These efforts were not simply the product of individual political will. They were the product of a policy process which is much less permeable to the pressures to which Britain succumbed. The post-1968 cultural policy network in France was, according to Wachtel (1987: 23), formed by a powerful alliance of middle-class interests in the cultural realm. These interests captured the key institutions within the elite policy process, and under the guise of decentralization were able to establish a powerful political presence for culture. This bore fruit in the period 1981–6 when Lang focused cultural policy on the 'three principles: education, creation and research' (Wachtel 1987: 45). Lang was able to control and coordinate cultural policy, sustaining local/national culture and fighting off globalization (Hayward 1993: 46ff).

Ideology

Policy analysis, like institutional practices, does not provide a comprehensive account. It too requires further supplementing. In particular, some allowance has to be made for the role of ideology (C. Gray 1993: 16). Even the view

86

that cultural choice and provision should be left to the market is itself informed by a set of value judgements and political assumptions. More subtly, it lies in the way the 'public' and the public sphere are regarded: whether culture is a matter for private consumption or public expression. At its simplest, the conventional range of ideologies – liberalism, conservatism, socialism – can be applied to the development of cultural policy. In France in the 1980s, socialism was linked directly to culture: the development and deployment of cultural resources were integral to the creation of an alternative social order. In Britain, Thatcherism imposed a new right liberalism upon the issue network. While in the recent past, Labour may have made little attempt to develop a consistent socialist perspective on culture, there have been times when it sought to establish a distinct cultural policy that accorded with its political presuppositions (see Waters 1990; Labour Party 1993).

New right arguments tend to mix pragmatism and principle in their attitudes towards the arts. These are forged in the tension between a general distrust of public subsidy, a recognition that culture constitutes a potential source of revenue (particularly through tourism) and employment, and a desire to promote a particular vision of 'Great Britain'. As one commentator observed, 'Thatcher espoused a right-liberal populism whose new right ideology regarded art as a commodity to be bought in the market place by customers' (Beck 1993: 12). In the 1980s, this led to a reordering of the issue network around cultural policy, in favour of business sponsorship and tax breaks to encourage it; it also led to attacks upon perceived 'elitism' within the arts establishment and an emphasis on art as heritage – art as consumption of the past, not as production for the future (Beck 1993). The suspicion of bureaucracy, characteristic of new right ideology, gave further impetus to a desire to reduce arts administration and to hamper its ability to promote new activities (Beck 1993: 19). Its most explicit formulation was in the deregulation of broadcasting and in the auctioning of ITV franchises as part of the 1990 Broadcasting Act.

Ideology is not exclusive to new right cultural policy. In Britain, the Greater London Council tied its socialism to a version of 'culture' and to policy instruments intended to sustain it. Socialist administrations in France and Italy also operated with cultural policies that were marked by their ideologies (Bianchini and Parkinson 1993). In France, the Socialist Party's policy of *action culturelle* was an attempt to animate popular participation in the conduct of community life (Wachtel 1987).

But to appreciate the full impact of ideology on cultural policy, it is important to move beyond the conventional political categories. This means refining and separating out the categories within the traditional camps and it also means introducing new ones. Ian Henry, for example, distinguishes between versions of the left (urban-left, structuralist) and insists too on the need to introduce feminist and anti-feminist dimensions to the ideological spectrum (Henry 1993: ch. 2). In a similar spirit, Nicholas Garnham writes of the way in which ideas about culture map onto ideas about politics. Some views of art give 'special and central status . . . to the "creative artists" whose aspirations and values [are] seen as stemming from some unfathomable and unquestionable source of genius, inspiration or talent' (Garnham 1990: 154). This perspective inevitably places the artists at the centre of cultural policy, and sees the key question as being how audience might be delivered to the creator. By contrast, a focus on the audience poses a different question: what kind of art/artists should be supplied? The first favours a policy of cultural elitism, the latter one of cultural populism. And each inevitably generates a different position and attitude to the prospects of globalization.

By separating institutional practices, policy processes and ideologies, I do not mean to give the impression of discrete elements interacting within confined limits. In the first instance, the elements of the policy-making are never settled; indeed this is particularly true of issue networks (and only marginally less true of policy communities). This is not just a consequence of the changing environment in which policy has to operate; nor is it simply a result of shifts in political relations and ideas. It is also because there are no clear boundaries between these. One of the problems with globalization theories is their tendency to ignore lower level activity. Equally, those who focus on policy tend to be concerned only with the national or the local level. Such demarcation fails to reflect the reality of a world where no such neat distinctions exist. After all, the global may affect the local, but be resisted at the national – or vice versa (see McGrew and Lewis 1992).

CONCLUSION: BRINGING THE GLOBAL BACK IN

This chapter began with grand talk of globalization and has ended in the rather mundane realm of policy analysis. It seems that – literally and figuratively – we have come down in the world. It is important, therefore, to recall what led us on this path and to try to reconcile briefly these two apparently diverse habitats.

My intention throughout has been to focus on the way popular culture is organized and distributed. This concern stems from the view that understanding the role and importance of culture cannot be disassociated from the means of its production. From within this general position, I have narrowed the focus yet further. Firstly, I began by looking at the idea that cultural production, distribution and consumption has been globalized. Though there is evidence of a process that resembles 'globalization', it is not an especially helpful label. The actual developments in the culture industry are more confused, and pull in a variety of directions. My second move was, therefore, to focus on the sites of these conflicting pulls, to see how cultural policy was negotiated by political actors and agencies.

We were then left with the question as to how to comprehend the process by which these political processes operated. While there was much evidence about *what* or *who* was involved, there was less about *how* they interacted. It was for this reason that I turned to the way institutional practices, policy processes and ideologies featured in the making of cultural policy. But given the general trajectory and concerns of this chapter, we cannot leave the story here. The reason for dwelling upon the details of cultural policy was to qualify the claims of the globalists. It was not, though, to dismiss their arguments completely. Rather it was to advocate a more subtle understanding of how the various levels and dimensions of cultural policy interact, to see a proliferation of cross-cutting interests and boundaries. Just as globalization does not exist independently of the states and regions upon whom it acts, so no state exists in hermetic isolation. And within these states, there are no discrete boundaries to be drawn between the formally or geographically acknowledged areas of responsibility. This, though, is not an invitation to see everything as purely contingent, and to see policy as the product of serendipity. It is, I hope, to suggest a more finely meshed approach to comprehending how popular culture, like globalization itself, is a result of political acts and intentions.

5

AN ASIAN ORIENTALISM?

Libas and the textures of postcolonialism

Rajika Jalan

☯ INTRO/AB-DUCTION
That which leads to a *knowledge* or understanding
of something/the separation of different parts
causing the *gaping* of a wound . . .

How many times have you found yourself in a conflict – in situations, with others, with yourself? In Barthes' work *A Lover's Discourse*, the lover finds himself in such a position: 'I am caught up in a double discourse, from which I cannot escape' (Barthes 1978: 73). The lover attempts to conceal this tension and anxiety with verbal signs. However, he discovers that what he hides by his *language*, is uttered by his *body*.

This idea of conflict makes the fashion magazine *Libas* a fascinating topic to explore. It was first published in 1989 and the quarterly issues aim to create a link between Eastern and Western cultures. This link, however, is also a point of conflict – how is the interaction of two cultures staged? Is there a combination of East and West, or is there an ongoing conflict?

In an interview held on 18 May 1994, at the *Libas* shop in Mayfair, London, the General Manager, Yousaf Baig Mirza, stated that the magazine intends to have an Asian content presented in a Western style. This immediately creates a dichotomy of form and content, and such a binary opposition has been considered a defining characteristic of Orientalism – but what exactly is 'Orientalism'? Said summarizes it as the following: 'Orientalism is a Western style for dominating, restructuring, and having authority over the Orient' (1991: 85).

Implicit in this desire to control is the suggestion that Orientalism has a repressive function, as a distinct body of information is *fashioned* by a controlling force. The desire for multiplicity is curbed by the Orientalist need for totalization, and the elimination of certain elements which do not fit the image required – for what could be more threatening to the Orientalist than a plurality of voices, attitudes and media?

What this suggests about identity is that it is whole, unique, intrinsic, like Descartes' *cogito*. Emphasizing the subject, from which all principles extend, expresses a need for stable foundations and resolution. Here identities do not clash – they remain within a secure enclosure, and do not suffer the anxiety of Barthes' lover. Descartes' need for the 'real' stems from the need for security, just as Orientalism must preserve an image of the East in order to control it. Descartes wishes to strengthen himself and desire nothing that is unobtainable or uncertain – how unlike the lover who craves what he cannot have!

Habermas suggests an alternative to the *cogito* in *The Philosophical Discourse of Modernity* (1987b). His aim is to revise the Enlightenment on the basis of dialogue and a plural subject. Yet the idea of plurality is undermined, since his theory focuses upon the necessity of an 'ideal' speech situation. The importance given to speech by Habermas always takes us back to the *cogito*, for it depends upon the presence of a single speaker, thus if we only consider the lexical aspect of meaning, we cannot escape the tyranny of direct reference. This sets up a hierarchy of speech over writing, text over image.

Let us broaden the spectrum of traditional criticism to include texture, voice, relationships of shape and colour – all of which dissolve the lexical element of the text, and disseminate the division of form and content set up by an Orientalist critique. Post-structuralists Foucault and Derrida encourage us to overcome the fears within which Descartes and Habermas remained locked – let us embrace uncertainty, and become open to the suggestion that not everything needs to be – nor can be – caught up in the net of a totalizing vision.

The issues of identity, cultural authenticity and knowledge are explored by focusing on three articles/adverts in *Libas* which have been chosen for their contrasting use of text and image. The aim is to dissemble the rigid distinction between text and image, and to see what this implies for identity, authenticity, power and knowledge. By using images as well as texts, we can attempt to perform a piece of art history as well as literary criticism – thereby deconstructing the polarization of the two. Instead of looking at an article under a single discipline, the bringing together of different areas enables identity to take on multiple aspects. Rather than performing a metaphysical search for an origin or truth, we would like to respond to the question posed by Homi Bhaba: 'How can the human world live its difference? How can a human being live Other-wise?' (Bhaba 1993: 122).

☯ ODE TO VELVETS
Ask yourself as you read: are you seduced by *wholeness* or *holes*?

> the magazine's phraseology constitutes a connotative message, aimed at transmitting a certain vision of the world
>
> (Barthes 1985a: 7)

it is not easy to say something new; it is not enough for us to
open our eyes, to pay attention, or to be aware for new objects
to light up and emerge out of the ground.

(Foucault 1972: 44)

What we wish to do is to break free from the transmitted vision of the world,
and find the *new*. Is this what *Libas* does? We can answer this question by
examining two images from the magazine which have been chosen for their
contrasting use of figures and typography. We shall name the first one 'Ode
to Velvets' and the second one 'Something in the way they move'. They
will be explored in relation to *power*, in order to discover where or in whom
it lies. From this we can decide whether *Libas* succeeds in being liberatory,
that is, if the kind of power discovered *releases* energy, or whether it remains
fixed in a certain vision of the world exerting a repressive power, and what
this vision may be.

Yousaf Baig Mirza describes *Libas* as a 'serious magazine for intellectual
readers', which aims to be objectively informative rather than judgemental.
The magazine covers a wide range of articles: fashion, beauty, health,
features, profiles, art, books, palmistry, etc., and as Mirza says, it aims for
the cosmopolitan reader who travels a lot, and is mobile and open-minded
in attitude. Coupled with this objectivity is the aim for a balance of Eastern
and Western cultures. However, we can unfold certain elements which make
this Pakistani magazine project a fundamentally *Western* point of view in
'Ode to Velvets'. A betrayal of the magazine's intention to consistently maintain a balance of Eastern and Western cultures consequently occurs.

One of the reasons for using the fashion spread 'Ode to Velvets' is the
word 'Ode'. This immediately strikes us as being incongruous in a Pakistani
magazine (one thinks a *ghazal* might be more appropriate) since it is predom-
inantly associated with the period of English Romantic poetry. From this
we can make certain assumptions about what kind of cultural values the
magazine espouses, and what type of reader it is aimed at. A word such as
'ode' would most likely strike only the reader educated in English poetry.
Think of all the Asian readers who would not be familiar with it, thus we
could suggest that the culture which the article emerges from and appeals
to is ultimately an academic one. This undermines the intention to be neutral
and objective, which was suggested by Mirza.

Libas is called, and calls itself the 'Asian Vogue', and the style of the article
clearly manifests this connection. The implication is that the West produces
and codifies knowledge about non-metropolitan areas and cultures, especially those under colonial control. Instead of releasing the potential energy
of its own culture, the article relies on the knowledge and images of the
West. According to Mirza, *Libas* has discovered a niche in the market, and
offers itself as a family and society magazine. It caters for a new generation
of wealthy Asians who are interested in being educated and adopting the

FASHION

Ode to Velvets

The definition of chic this season is velvet. The Libas interpretation is soft, sensuously clinging velvet that shimmers with every graceful movement. Encrusted with gold zardozi, velvets get their due in delicately entwined gold beads and thread. Dressed for the traditional wedding or the special evening, velvets are regal. Sleek and structured velvet suits - slim, long jackets and wide cut salwars - sheathed in heavily worked, matching shawls.

Figure 5.1 'Ode to Velvets'
Source: Libas International (1993) 6, 3: 11

exotic lifestyle explored by the magazine. For the readers, images projected by the magazine become reality, and by desiring these images a demand is created for them. Like the regressive listeners described by Adorno, the reader Mirza refers to wants only what s/he has already tasted: 'Regressive listeners behave like children. Again and again with stubborn malice, they demand the one dish they have once been served' (Adorno 1987: 95). Thus images are perpetuated rather than challenged, altered or considered differently. As a consequence the *rhetorical* system, or the images, become more real than the terminological system. The reader is divested of his/her power to *act*, and can only *re-act*. The relationship of East and West is parallel to the relationship of reader and writer – one hierarchical pattern leads to another.

We can see the effect this has if we look at 'Ode to Velvets' typographically. The writing seems to lie in the foreground, while the figure lies beneath it, and the movement and energy created by the italicized '*Velvets*' takes the attention away from the still uprightness of the figure. There is no sense of interaction between image and text, and our eyes follow quickly down the page, overlooking the figure and seeking reassurance and explanation in the text. This is because it holds a position of dominance, most strongly in the way it goes over the half-curled hand of the woman, as if to stop her from reaching out to the reader. The writing obscures the lower part of the figure, and acts as a form of censorship, like a concealing *veil*. It is as if we are only permitted to see certain parts of the woman's body – her hands and her face – and the rest must remain under wraps.

The desire to be in control is reiterated in the notion of sexuality. Velvet clings 'sensuously', which hints towards a sense of eroticism for the male gaze. This is enhanced by the adjectives employed, which seek to convey a physical impression of the material, describing its size, shape, and weight: 'wide cut salwars', 'slim, long jackets', 'heavily worked, matching shawls'. Yet the physicality of the description is constantly undercut by the pervading need for control. Any eroticism is tempered by *gracefulness* – being 'civilized' is the crucial pose to maintain. The photographs of the fashion spread produce this effect. The model looks away from the camera modestly, and her long hair is tightly coiled up. Her make-up is thick and heavy. The camera angle almost captures her features in a profile, and since she does not look back, the relationship between the two recalls Foucault's panoptican. The fairly bright lighting intensifies this effect, for it gives her no dark, mysterious places in which to hide. All these elements combine to render her a mannequin. Her individuality is repressed and made into the image that the magazine wishes to convey. The notion of 'control' becomes a sign in Barthes' *Fashion System* (1985a), suggesting maturity, sophistication and elegance, as opposed to youthfulness and impulsive rashness. This also relates to the idea of 'velvet' as a sign for elegance and femininity. The projected vision of the world is one of luxury, which is encapsulated by the use of the words 'graceful movement'. Instead of asking questions or opening up doubts about what femininity may be, here statements are made and confirmed. In this view, we can categorize *Libas* as an Asian Orientalism, for the images it uses manifest the colonial desire to be in control. Rather than questioning stereotypes and opening out contradictory attitudes, it seeks to perpetuate them, and this is the reading which emerges from an analysis of 'Ode to Velvets'.

When the article tries to emulate the West, it becomes repressive. However, if we look at other articles and adverts in the magazine, we can discover glimpses of different textual strategies that become liberatory since they do not attempt imitation. The advert for India Emporium named 'Something in the way they move' makes use of adventurous typography by emphasizing contrast in both the size and kind of typeface used. A large, elaborate letter in italics underlies a sentence in a small sans serif typeface. An illusion of depth gives way to a play of surfaces – in contrast with 'Ode to Velvets' which holds firmly onto a feeling of depth. The large letter, even though it lies underneath the smaller letters, appears to be on top of them by virtue of its dominating size. The reader oscillates between these two viewpoints, but cannot fix upon either one, for a point of reference has not been given. The advert aims at an effect of incompletion, suggested by the paint brushstrokes, which show the image to be in a state of process or becoming. The idea of incompletion is emphasized by the address of the company, since it is written in a split circle rather than a joined one. Arrows appear to lead the two halves in separate directions, suggesting an essential division, one that cannot be resolved.

Mirza states that *Libas* intends to be Asian in content, yet deliberately Western in layout. However, when the text breaks out of the wish to be Vogue-like, as with the article explored above, it gains dynamism and aspires to the new. The page of the advert has a strong sense of movement that contrasts the pervading air of repression in 'Ode to Velvets'. In the advert the lettering stalks across the forehead of the model in an irreverent fashion, and one figure is superimposed upon another. This contrasts the artificial, composed appearance of the figure in 'Ode to Velvets'. Here the model is contained within a frame, rather than allowed some sort of existence outside the picture/image/page. In the advert both models are obscured in some way, and the effect aimed at is one of constant change and movement, rather than completion and stasis. Our eyes seem to follow the brushstrokes endlessly around the page, and even the words aim to defer meaning and resolution by deliberately remaining elusive: 'Something in the way they move'. The advert refuses to articulate what exactly this 'something' is, thereby instilling the reader with the desire to know more.

We can look at the advert from another angle – as a transformation of popular culture – for the words are sung in a song by the Orientalist George Harrison. The words are therefore reinscribed in another context, that of

Something in the way they move.

Figure 5.2 'Something in the way they move'
Source: *Libas International* (1993) 6, 3: 79

popular culture as opposed to the high culture of 'Ode to Velvets'. This provides another contrast with 'Ode to Velvets', where the assurance of the writer leaves the reader passively accepting the knowledge offered as sufficient, rather than considering new connections and equivalencies. We can link the dynamics of the advert with Mishra and Hodge's view of post-colonialism. They state that to write in the language of the colonizer is to write from within death itself (Mishra and Hodge 1993: 277–9). This is clear in the contrast between the fashion spread and the advert 'Ode to Velvets' deadens the life and energy of the new by imitating an already established image, while 'Something in the way they move' explodes with fresh audacity and vibrancy, just as the eye of the model stares defiantly into the reader.

☯ BRUSHING AGAINST THE PILE OF 'ODE TO VELVETS'
Self-examination leaves one *gaping* at a *gap* where there is no self to examine

The captivated image becomes captivating when it liberates asso-
ciative energies that generate new images.
(Taylor and Saarinen 1994)

What you have done here is not quite what you intended. Although claiming to do away with oppositions you are resolutely hanging on to an oppositional structure, particularly in the way only contrasts *are found between the two images – there are* parallels *too. As a result there is not enough interaction between 'Ode to Velvets' and 'Something in the way they move'. The trouble with this is that it leaves you with oppositions such as good/bad, empire/colony, repression/liberation, and what you do is to simply invert Orientalist notions.*

The first section of the chapter does, however, contain certain seismic shifts, which do hint towards possible ways out of the bipolar structure. Think about the way in which you have suggested that the woman in 'Ode to Velvets' is for the pleasure of the male gaze. Can you think of her in another way given that you use the word 'invoke' rather than 'evoke' in the following sentence: 'Its purpose is to invoke a mood of Romanticism in order to make the clothing adhere to an image of femininity and sensuality'?

The word 'invoke' suggests it is the woman creating the atmosphere, as opposed to 'evoke' which gives the agency to the male gaze. I see what you are saying – we are shifting the relations of power. The controlled now becomes the controller. I suppose you could say the same about the notion of female passivity, and what I have referred to as 'feminine softness'. Rather than being seen as a way of being controlled by stereotypes, this passivity can be viewed as a form of power itself. The soft, sensuality of the velvet is for the pleasure of the woman. She can feel it clinging sensuously to her body – but the male gaze can only look from a distance. Compare this with the advert. The emphasis on bodily movements transfers the pleasure into a sphere where the male gaze can appropriate and enjoy it in a kind of vampirism. The energy of the woman is sucked out, for the male gaze can feed hungrily on the curve of her lips, and the directness of her eyes. She offers herself to him, thus it is *she* who becomes the mannequin rather than the woman in 'Ode to Velvets' for she seems to be dancing to the tune of the male gaze. Consequently the reticence of the woman in 'Ode to Velvets' seems to be a weapon. A touch of sexuality is hinted at in the exposed wrist, an indication of hidden delights. But this is precisely the point – it remains hidden, and therefore cannot be sucked up by the male. Her eyes are directed away from the viewer, and therefore we cannot see her, know her, or possess her. The embroidery around her wrist seems to ensnare her like handcuffs, yet this also points to a source of energy which needs to be controlled and which we cannot see. Just think of the vibrancy wrapped up with the plaits in her hair. We could not gauge it because we cannot see the extent of its potential. Compare this with the advert where the woman lays herself open to be absorbed.

Yes, I can see what you mean – by wanting to brush the pile of the fabric in one direction only I failed to consider an entire range of possible meanings. But haven't I just made the same mistake? Doesn't this create yet another oppositional structure? Haven't I just simply reversed the argument?

That depends on how you treat what you have done. Are you coming to a conclusion here? Are you simply deciding that your second argument is more cogent, and therefore supersedes the former argument?

I suppose I must be. Well, hmm . . . not really. I mean, I've ended up with the second argument, but it doesn't necessarily mean that I believe it is the definitive one.

Well, what point are you making? Do you think that you can just leave it at that? Do you not think that at some point a decision between the two must be made?

I'm not really sure . . . No, actually, I don't think that is what I'm trying to say anyway. For instance, what if we consider what it means when 'Orientalism' is appropriated by the Orient? We could see the imitation of the Western style as a challenge to the presumption of origin and authenticity. What if it emulates Orientalism so well that one couldn't tell the difference? Who is to say which one is more real than the other? Alternatively, the Orient's version could create a difference to Orientalism's Orientalism by inscribing it in a different context, thereby creating a gap between the two styles, for example if the method of Orientalism is used to advertise *Eastern* rather than *Western* clothes. As a result under the same name a disjuncture can be found. For instance, how does the fact of using Eastern clothing create a subtle but crucial change?

Can you see this at work in the article/advert?

Yes, I can *now*. I couldn't before because I wasn't able to see beyond my own desire to form the articles into a specific viewpoint – although this viewpoint was undermined anyway. Now that I have noticed the erotic element of the exposed wrist in 'Ode to Velvets', which was brought out in my second reading, I can compare it with the notion that the woman is deprived of any sexuality, which was suggested in my first reading. Rather than wasting time arguing which one has authority, I could explore the tension created by the difference, or stress the fact that there is a tension and difference. Indeed, the pressure lies *within* each article/advert as well as in the difference between the two. The exposed wrist in 'Ode to Velvets' figures as what Foucault calls a boundary transgressing experience. It exceeds the limit which is set by the view of woman as controlled and ordered. Perhaps, paradoxically, those boundaries have more charge in a repressive economy of signification.

Since differing elements can be found in the same frame, this could be a way of linking the two frames. Each of them has an element of the other in itself, and neither is self-contained or self-sufficient. In fact it would seem that until the differences can be recognized, the frame lies dormant, waiting its awakening. Looking at the woman in 'Ode to Velvets' as a one-dimensional mannequin, divested of any power, is to be dead yourself – you have to awaken yourself to the Other. This changes power relations, for it does not concern a model of domination based upon repression. This hierarchy is undermined if one can see the strength of the Other, and how it operates in different ways. It is more about recognizing the existence of a plurality of power strategies, and taking *pleasure* in this plurality.

What is it you are saying about power, then? Where or in whom does it lie?

I think to consider this I would have to return to the beginnings of modernity, and the principle of subjectivity that determines the forms of modern culture.

Descartes' *cogito* radiates an inner light, and here the subject is the principle from which everything extends. It is not a being dependent on others; the being is the source of consequences, not vice versa. We can relate this to the reading strategy of the first section of the chapter, where I attempted to master the text and come to a definitive solution. The *cogito* would say, 'I read therefore I am right.'

Yet as I discovered, this conclusion was constantly undermined. I had to make brutal choices, cut into the text and image in order to make it say what I wanted it to. And my desire to be right, I suppose, came from fear of insecurity; fear of losing control.

Habermas wishes to replace such a relation-to-self of a subject knowing and acting in isolation with the 'paradigm of mutual understanding, that is, of the intersubjective relationship between individuals who are socialized through communication and reciprocally recognize one another' (1987b: 55). Habermas wishes to suggest a mode of interaction without a subject having the power to assimilate the whole. He sees this as being possible within an ideal speech situation, which can only arise if one does away with the idea of a subject-centred reason. Instead of the *cogito* possessing a unique, authentic self, with which it approaches the world, a self is constructed by linguistic interaction. What results, according to Habermas, is a *procedural* concept of rationality rather than a *purposive* rationality. However, Habermas does not escape from the speaking/hearing circle of auto-affection, and even his procedural concept of rationality becomes a kind of refined Cartesianism – after all, Descartes, like me, is in dialogue with himself: he tells himself *cogito ergo sum*.

So what do you make of the emphasis on speech in this section, considering that we are in the middle of a dialogue, and it is proving to be fruitful? It seems we are working something out, coming to an agreement – why should this be such a bad thing? The alternative is that we disagree and achieve nothing.

But do we necessarily have to agree or disagree? If one accepts the existence of a different opinion this is neither agreement nor disagreement. It is also not necessarily an *understanding* of an other, but more of an acknowledgement – and perhaps even an acknowledgement that the other is totally unrecognizable. Compare this with the *cogito* that insists on understanding the other. The *cogito* wishes to examine the self and see wholeness rather than holes. Our objective is to find a way of knowing and respecting the other, of producing knowledge of an other in a way that does not stereotype or dominate.

Habermas believes it is possible to be an individual, to retain a difference within a collectivity:

*With the system of personal pronouns, a relentless pressure toward individ-
uation is built into the use of language orientated toward mutual
understanding that is proper to socializing interaction. At the same time, the
force of an intersubjectivity pressing toward socialization comes to the fore
through the same linguistic medium.*

*Do you see this 'mutual understanding' as a means of knowing and respecting the
Other?*

In some ways I do, for both must interact rather than each one closing
itself off from the other. The intersubjectivity allows participating
subjects to come to an agreement. But in a sense this involves the
dissolving of differences, and manifests a desire to arrive at a kind of
truth. Indeed, Habermas links this communicative rationality with the
idea of logos 'inasmuch as it brings along with it the connotations
of a noncoercively unifying, consensus-building force of a discourse in
which the participants overcome their at first subjectively biased views
in favour of a rationally motivated agreement' (1987b: 347). But I don't
see how this intersubjectivity replaces the idea of hierarchy. Instead of
either one of the two holding the power, it is a third – the institution
which establishes the linguistic rules in which the participants come to
an understanding (see Habermas 1987b: 39).

Again, the emphasis on linguistic construction is placed – but is it
possible for men, within the same discursive practice, to speak of
different objects, to have contrary opinions and to make contradictory
choices? I think to discuss this, we must further explore the problem
of origin and subjectivity. By going into greater detail about the
changing relationship between text and image, we can find ways of
erasing the referent, thereby questioning the notion of depth – and all
the logocentric paraphanelia that goes with it.

☯ BOOM SHACK A LACK!! – TAKE ONE
Not an *image* or a *text*, but a text that is an
image and an image that is a text.

As soon as it begins to speak and convey meaning, the bird has
flown, the rain has evaporated.

(Foucault 1983: 19)

When we look at an image coupled with a text, we automatically make
assumptions about the relationship between the two. In colonial discourse
one fashions the other, and here the writing 'explains' the image, thereby
narrowing the possibilities which the image may hold. What results is a closing

down of the gap between signifier and signified, for the aim is to follow the shortest route to an understanding of the image. This sets up one of the oldest oppositions of our alphabetical civilization: to show and to name, to shape and to say, to imitate and to signify, to look and to read (Foucault 1983: 21). Yet how can this traditional bond between text and image be ruptured? Perhaps a start would be to recognize its intrinsic immutability.

Foucault tells us to listen to Magritte: 'Between words and objects one can create new relations and specify characteristics of language and objects generally ignored in everyday life' (Foucault 1983: 38). Taking this as a starting point, we can look at an example of image and text interacting in *Libas* – the article which will be referred to as 'Boom Shack A Lack!!' The writing goes over the body of the figure, and because of this we are doubly tempted to rely on the writing as something explanatory. Our initial assumption sees the writing stamped authoritatively upon the image, thereby closing down the suggestiveness of the figure's body language. Here the relationship takes on an unequal aspect – the writing seeks to appropriate the image, moulding it into its own viewpoint. The two systems can neither merge nor intersect – subordination is required. Either text is ruled by image, or image is ruled by text. In *Discipline and Punish* (1977) Foucault suggests that power operates on the body, attempting to master its forces. But power doesn't only say 'no', and we need to be able to see a power that is not simply repressive.

The prison of this hierarchical ordering begins to disintegrate when we notice how the *image* affects the *text*. As it goes off the body, the text changes colour from white to black, thus illustrating the impact of the image upon the text. This kind of relationship differs from the previous kind described. We are now looking at a spatial relationship – the effect of different elements interacting, merging and dissecting, rather than looking for any unifying meaning that ties image and text.

The supremacy of the text diminishes when we begin to consider the writing as the image itself (not merely as a *part*) by virtue of the interaction described above. The writing could be seen as graphic signs reduced to fragments and dispersed over the surface of the image. The words are themselves drawn. This calls into question the notion of depth – for why must we assume that beneath the letters lies a completed figure? The figure could well be fragmented too: 'In a painting, words are of the same cloth as images. Rather one sees images and words differently in a painting' (Foucault 1983: 39). The reference to cloth implies texture and interweaving, which relates back to the wayward route of postcolonialism. Again we can question the emphasis Habermas places on speech via Nietzsche: 'Is language the adequate expression of all realities?' (Nietzsche 1979: 81). Clearly the removal of a hierarchical relationship between image and text is just as liberatory for text as for image. Words are no longer confined to meaning, but enter a different sphere where relationships of words on the page become

Boom Shack A Lack!

Apache Indian vanguard o bhangramuffii and first Asia to make it ii UK's top te charts

By Tahira Rana

Apache Indian became the first Asian to feature on the UK top ten singles chart when his third hit single 'The Nuff Vibes EP' smashed into the No. 8 slot. His debut album 'No Reservations' has already won the prestigious Murcury Award for best album of the year, making the Asian super- ▶

Figure 5.3 'Boom Shack A Lack!!'
Source: Libas International (1993) 6, 3: 93

important. For instance we begin to notice the peculiar typography which combines the circular with the angular. Instead of immediately ascribing a meaning to these shapes we enjoy the unusual coupling, and see how they intersect other shapes. We linger on the postcolonial pathway, and begin to desire *desire* rather than *satisfaction*.

The pleasure lies in the way they change each other and create an opposition dynamic. The harsh angularity is tempered by the fluid curves, and vice versa. This exploration of calligraphy leads us in a direction of reading which is largely neglected in traditional criticism, and here we can see the influence of Descartes. In the *Third Meditation* he states that 'light, colour, sound, smell, taste, heat, cold, and the other tactile qualities, they are to be found in my thought with such obscurity and confusion that I do not know even whether they are true or false' (Descartes 1968: 122). These different thoughts are considered confusing because *certainty* is desired. However, once this is no longer the principle criteria of criticism, other elements become equally important. The confusion and ambiguity become desirable – perhaps the postcolonial route is less of a *pathway* than a *labyrinth*.

These multiplying ambiguities also operate in the notions of space and frame. The gesture of the figure's hands seems to reach out forcefully to the reader, thereby transgressing the boundary of a possible frame. This is emphasized by the hand and the writing transgressing the limit of the page, for they go over it. The feeling that something else is going on beyond the page leaves the reader guessing – equivocation excites desire. This is different from the tantalization described in the first section of the chapter. There our desire was under the power of the writer, and our desire expired in the discovery of a solution to the enigma. Here we can see a different type of eroticism emerging – an eroticism concerning texture and *concealment*, as opposed to an eroticism which is about *revealing*. Desire is always maintained, while satisfaction is never gained. The reader is given a dare by the text, and perhaps this dare is perceived through solicitation – an earnest request to go on guessing. This is different to our second reading of 'Ode to Velvets', where the concealment of the body gave the figure power. When power lies in a specific figure, writer or reader, if they conceal something this suggests that there is something concrete to reveal. If, however, power doesn't lie in a particular figure, this suggests there is no 'truth' to find, thus the path taken does not lead to a signified, but into a labyrinthine web.

☯ BOOM SHACK A LACK!! – TAKE TWO
The telescopic desire for *clarity* is seduced by the kaleidoscopic desire for *collision*

Is not the most erotic portion of a body *where the garment gapes?*
(Barthes 1990: 9)

Dissolving identities of image and text create the conditions in which we can move further into the postcolonial web by looking at topological variations. Let's make the letters *perform* rather than stand still:

The tip of the 'c' could unhinge itself. It could pivot around, thus losing its identity as a recognizable letter. Not only the tip, but the bottom curve could come undone and gently swing around. Both could pivot at the same time or alternate. This process enables us to alter our perception of the letter. The solidity of the 'c', and its meaning as a letter disintegrates, and we think of the 'c' as a shape or pattern, which makes us consider the *production* of the letter rather than its *function*.

We could say, then, that the term 'c' is put under erasure. We still call it a 'c', but no longer look at it solely as a particular letter of the alphabet – we have taken it out of this structure, whilst part of it still remains within it.

We can explore this further by looking at the intricacies of typography, and slowing down the process of cognition. Take the following enlarged 'B' from 'Boom Shack A Lack' as an example:

On closer inspection the uniform letter has various interferences, such as the little black triangle at the top, and the uneven boxes. Due to this unevenness the letter seems to be shifting, as the boxes slant in opposite directions. A tension within the letter occurs – one which is not resolved. The tension arises because the shapes are similar, but at the same time different. They also move in different directions. The relationship between the two becomes

105

rhythmical, as the reader dances between the uniform term 'box', and the fact that these shapes do not fully correspond to the term. Wittgenstein warns us that the uniform appearance of words is deceptive, and this applies to letters too. Again, the notion of naming is put under erasure. A systematic 'other message' is inscribed within or through what is said.

Western discourse has always determined Being as presence. However, this poses serious limits upon the reader: 'The temptation to seek a meaning is so strong that it often smothers any sensitivity to the conditions under which meaning is produced' (Caygill 1993: 29). We can disrupt this presupposition by encouraging dispersal rather than unity. Consider the following letters from 'Boom Shack A Lack':

They are both the letter 'a', but are still entirely different. The black letter apparently floats in a white background, but gains solidity since it is in one colour. However, we can perceive unevenness within the letter. The square shape of the top half of the letter is not in line with the box in the bottom half. This occurs in the other 'a' too, but this letter is made different by the various interferences around the letter. It is altered by the tonal changes in the waistcoat, and the little black triangle which creates an extra edge to the letter. Since the first 'a' is black, we could see black as being a part of the letter 'a'. Consequently we see the black triangle as being a part of the white letter. Similarly, if white is a component of the second 'a', then the white around the black letter is also a part of the letter. How, then, is identity constructed? Does the letter consist of the black shape or the white around it? This creates a point of indefinite pivoting, as the reader cannot decide which one is the 'right' answer.

Because there is no origin or point of reference, one is freed from the need to distinguish the false from the authentic. The identity of the letter does not consist of the centre as a presence, but is in a state of constant change by the friction of surrounding elements. Here we do not search for an origin or essence. Instead we dissemble and deconstruct.

The problem lies in the fact that in a 'semantically saturated culture we are insensitive to the latter kind of transformations; we very quickly read them as distortions of meaning' (Caygill 1993: 29). We could, however, see the transformations described above differently. The lack of depth and origin offers us a sense of *liberation*, as it opens us up to the idea of endless permutations and contradictions.

The text begins to seduce us when we no longer see 'Boom Shack A Lack!!' as a figure with writing on top of it. The figure can be seen as a vertical shape across which cuts horizontal writing. The lines dissect each other, and the writing seems to sever the figure, which, however, possesses horizontal lines too – the eyebrows and the headband, that consequently have something in common with the writing. Similarly, the writing is upright, so perhaps it is not so different from the figure. The lines are constantly shifting and alternating. Horizontal lines thus become the same as vertical lines – but also not the same. This kind of reading results in the illegibility of the image, and our initial response to this is one of frustration. Irigaray acknowledges the difficulty of breaking out of this: 'a long history has taught you to seek out and desire only clarity, the clear perception of (fixed) ideas' (1985: 55) but urges us to take this *risk*. The traditional way of interpreting works of art is informed by a series of oppositions: meaning/form, inside/outside, content/container, signifier/signified. But here we have a process of *interweaving*: 'it is precisely toward the notion of the thread and the interlacing that I should like to lead you' (Derrida 1987: 20).

We can enact this interweaving by seeing various parallels and equivalencies in the picture. A link between the eyes of the figure and the double 'o' is created. Such an equivalence is possible only because the notion of a unique 'o' with a single purpose has been questioned. Suddenly all sorts of similarities crop up and disappear: Letters can be made out in the figure, for instance, the button on the pocket becomes an 'o', and the net material becomes a mass of 'o's. The gesture of the hand is like the letter 'v'. Similarly we see figures in the letters, for the shape of the 'o' is like the shape of the head and the eyes. Such equivalencies create links which are not usually associated, thereby challenging habitual perception. The picture suddenly becomes charged with new images, making energy explode, with no possibility of returning to a single origin: 'one could say that the site of textual pleasure is not the relation of mimic and model (imitative relation) but solely that of dupe and mimic (relation of desire, of production)' (Barthes 1990: 55). The idea of being 'duped' links in with the notion of interweaving, for the thread appears, then disappears as it goes under, only to appear again. Compare this with the idea of deception and the mask (but a mask that conceals nothing) with Habermas's model of linguistic communication in the theory of Universal Pragmatics, where one criteria is that a participant 'claims truthfulness for the intentions expressed' (1984: 2). The thread is a process of *appearance-as-disappearance*, and relates to the disintegration of the subject:

> the generative idea that the text is made, is worked out in a perpetual interweaving; lost in this tissue – this texture – the subject unmakes himself, like a spider dissolving in the constructive secretions of its web.
>
> (Barthes 1990: 64)

Another way of describing interweaving is intertextuality, as elements become part of each other. Take the following:

Once we no longer see the black as the most important part, instead of a 'C' we can perceive a 'T' rotated anti-clockwise by 90° in a circle. Such a topology of the text enables us to see the letters as intertextual, for one refers to another, just as texts refer to other texts. The uniqueness of a text is questioned, the reader is discomforted; and his/her historical, cultural and psychological assumptions are shattered at the same time as his/her identity: 'We must imagine not the synthesizing-synthesized subject, but an uncrossable fissure' (Foucault 1977b: 172). This fissure, gape or cut, relates to texture, and we can begin to see texture as a feeling of fissures – not a smooth, harmonious resolution of different elements.

The fabric is rough – almost painful to the touch, but Habermas refuses this contact. He has the desire to single out explicit speech actions from other forms of communicative action: 'I shall ignore nonverbalized actions and bodily expressions' (1984a: 1).

What we wish to do, however, is to seek a kind of vocal writing which is nothing like speech: 'If it were possible to imagine an aesthetic of textual pleasure, it would have to include: *writing aloud*' (Barthes 1985: 66). This kind of writing aloud does not aim for the clarity of messages, but for the *pulsional* incidents, those moments of fissure, that is, an acknowledgement of the various interferences that occur in communication. Habermas aims to eradicate these differences, and calls them systematically distorted communication. We, however, would like to unleash them in all their vibrancy: '(that the voice, that writing, be as fresh, supple, lubricated, delicately granular and vibrant as an animal's muzzle)' (Barthes 1985a: 67).

This erotic pleasure is achieved by *cutting*, and the creation of more than one edge, as in the typography under scrutiny. Returning to the exclamation marks, we can see how they function as shapes. They are a combination of uneven lines and perfect circles, and therefore are not symmetrical. This combination of a geometrical shape with an unnamed shape creates an energy and rhythm of the recognizable and the unrecognizable. The way this operates is to put the reader in a state of flux – we try to put the unrecognizable into the recognizable, and vice versa. The shapes are reinscribed 'otherwise and elsewhere than they are expected, in *ellipses* and *eclipses* that deconstruct the logical grid of the reader-writer, drive him out of his mind, trouble his vision' (Foucault 1970: xviii). We search for a Utopia – a fantastic, untroubled region in which differences are resolved, but find ourselves in a Heterotopia. This region shatters or tangles common names, and does not offer the consolation of resolution or transcendence. This unresolved state is fundamental to textual pleasure: 'Neither culture nor its destruction is erotic; it is the seam between them, the fault, the flaw, which becomes so' (Barthes 1990: 7).

Returning to the 'c' at the beginning of this section, we can explore the tension in the eroticism of the cut. The letter could unhinge itself and be a free floating element. Indeed its various parts could dissemble and float away, for as already suggested, it is not a solid. But at the same time the edges of the letter parts are fused together, and there is a pleasure in this intersection, in this cut. The desire to float free creates a tension with the desire for the edges to clutch at each other. It is the energy produced in the seam between the two that we could consider, rather than imagining what is beyond. As a result, a different power structure arises: instead of 'A is opposed to B' we have 'B is both added to and replaces A' (Derrida 1987: 37). A and B are no longer opposed to or equivalent, therefore the notion of their identities is put into question. The desire to float free and the desire to stay fast is yet another point of indefinite pivoting, thus the claim to unequivocal domination of one over the other is destroyed. Domination becomes impossible because there is always an excess, a difference which cannot be sublated and which has an essential role in desire.

This rich uncertainty of disorder which occurs in the gap is what prevents domination, for this kind of energy operates without intentionality: 'to describe a group of statements not with reference to the interiority of an intention, a thought, or a subject, but in accordance with the dispersion of an exteriority' (Foucault 1983: 125). Fundamental to this is the disappearance of the subject – Foucault's search is for a 'power' that does not belong to a human agent.

As we witness the ruin of the myth of man an end in himself, we can turn to Levinas, who sees this as more than a way of overcoming domination. Levinas discusses the way that this relinquishing of the subject leads to the 'pre-original', which is prior to the ego, and more importantly prior to its freedom and its non-freedom. Within a binary opposition, passivity always ends up dominated, but Levinas points to an 'unassumable passivity which is not *named*' (1987: 133). This is crucial to the issue of colonialism, for it suggests the possibility of a passivity that cannot be appropriated. In terms of East/West relations, this could be the erasure of the term 'the Orient', which would remove all the preconceptions that go with it, thus making it impossible to be appropriated.

This becomes possible because the subject is a *responsibility* before being an *intentionality*. Levinas recognizes the problem in this, for how can responsibility avoid becoming *servitude*? This depends on how we see responsibility, and Levinas suggests it starts with a radical passivity of the subjectivity, which leads to a 'responsibility overflowing freedom'. This passivity is taken out of the opposition responsibility/freedom, or rather it occurs *before* the formation of bipolarities that have been constructed by a cogito claiming a superlative objectivity: 'The pure passivity that precedes freedom is responsibility. But it is a responsibility that owes nothing to my freedom; it is my responsibility for the freedom of others' (Levinas 1987: 136). What this freedom entails, is making room for the virility of the other – passivity lets go of the desire to reduce the other to the same. Thus we can suggest ways of moving from the colonial to the postcolonial, which sets up an entirely different kind of relationship between East and West, speech and writing, image and text. Responsibility for others effaces *Eros*, which is a possession in which the difference between the possessor and the possessed disappears. Levinas acknowledges our fear of this pre-original, and therefore urges us to *enjoy* recovering this difference which has been lost in history and order: 'Pleasure alone is capable of forgetting the tragic-comedy of being; it is perhaps defined by this forgetting' (Levinas 1987: 138).

It is through pleasure that we can learn to enjoy the other without wishing to possess it. As a result, instead of *fearing* the other we begin to *desire* it. In this *desire* we can find Foucault's agency and power that is not in a human subject, and rather than constantly imposing repressive structures, this is a power that is able to say '*yes*'.

☯ POSTCOLONIAL TEXTURES
The expectation of solidification is *exploded* by variation, generation, copulation, adoration, anticipation . . . ad infinitum

> colonisation almost invariably implies a relation of structural domination, and a discursive or political suppression of the heterogeneity of the subject(s) in question.
>
> (Mohanty 1993: 196)

Our task is to discover a way of breaking free from this relation of structural domination, and to release heterogeneity. As we have seen, a way of achieving this is by questioning the viability of 'the subject' as the ultimate candidate for representation or liberation – one can no longer assume the ontological integrity of the subject.

The reason for this is that a subject is produced in accordance with the requirements of the structure, which results in a juridical formation of language and polities. According to Butler, juridical subjects are invariably produced through certain exclusionary practices that do not 'show' once the juridical structure of politics has been established. This relates to Barthes' naturalization of myth, and the attempt to pose the artificial as the 'real':

'Juridical power inevitably "produces" what it claims merely to represent' (Butler 1990: 2).

The project of authenticity suggests the mutual implication of power and knowledge: 'the enlightenment's universalizing will to knowledge ... feeds Orientalism's will to power' (Introduction to Williams and Chrisman 1993: 8).

We have suggested that Habermas's version of communicative rationality is implicated in this universalizing will to knowledge. He, too, suppresses heterogeneity, for he aspires towards unity in promoting the *framework* of a community which allows us to communicate. The framework of an ideal speech situation, however, is always a strategy for control, for differences are resolved in a higher unity. Thus, what we wish to do is to open up differential structures, to offer a new way of looking at cultural identity.

By erasing the referent and the notion of a pre-given identity, any cultural identity which is put forward can be seen as one that is constructed by outside forces wishing to gain and maintain control. We can look at Orientalist discourse in this light: 'taking the immense fecundity of the Orient and making it systematically, even alphabetically, knowable by Western laymen' (Said 1991: 65). The Western alphabet over the Oriental body in 'Boom Shack A Lack!!' seeks to codify the East in its own words in order to make it knowable in Western terms – the Oriental is reduced to a symbol.

It is not only the 'West' which is responsible for perpetuating binary oppositions and power structure, for the East also legitimizes the use of cultural images. We must remember that 'Every regime of representation is a regime of power formed, as Foucault reminds us, by the fatal couplet 'power/knowledge'" (Hall 1993: 394). Colonial discourse is not simply an invasion from the outside, but a danger from the inside, too.

An example of a discourse that merely inverts Orientalism is the kind discussed by Amilcar Cabral in 'National Liberation and Culture'. He promotes the value of culture as a factor of resistance to foreign domination, suggesting that it is easy for a foreigner to impose his domination on a people, but the material aspects of this domination can only be maintained by the permanent, organized repression of the cultural life of the people concerned. Yet this suggests that the cultural life of the people is unique only to their people, and this again leads us back to origin and authenticity. Like colonialism, it refuses to open itself up to other cultures, and remains closed, denying the possibility of change. Cabral suggests that, 'national liberation takes place when, and only when, national productive forces are completely free of all kinds of foreign domination' (1993: 56). This kind of resistance takes place in one's own country, but it can also happen in another, which the article following 'Boom Shack A Lack!!' explores.

The figure in the image is a singer called Apache Indian, and interestingly enough his music has been received by some with hostility, for it aims to combine Western and Eastern influences. The article states,

Although Apache is popular with younger Asians, he has had his share of criticism from the older members. Labelled a 'Coconut' (someone who is brown on the outside but white on the inside), he is blamed for undermining the traditional codes of minority Asian communities.

(*Libas International* 1993: 135)

The older members remain within the binary opposition of inside/outside, and thus hold on to the idea that the metaphors described by Nietzsche still have a sensuous force. They continue to believe that inside and outside must unify, that signifier must lead to signified. The problem with this is that it restricts a person's identity to one culture only, and suggests that to explore others constitutes a betrayal. The desire to anchor the self to one culture suggests not simply a fear of the other, but a sense of one's *superiority* over the other. This betrayal, then, becomes necessary if we want to explore the other without wanting to dominate it.

Apache approaches the problem of parents refusing to allow their children to mix with those of another culture: 'A lot of parents don't want their kids to come to my shows . . . They just want them to go to temples and come home from school and not mix' (*Libas International* 1993: 135). Such an attitude reveals the desire to keep a firm hold over the children, and this grip is maintained by telling them that their culture is unique to them only. He suggests that such restrictions cause these children problems. Living and mixing with people in another culture inevitably results in an identity crisis, as a stable point of reference is taken away. But this crisis could be considered productive. Apache's desire to interact provides the conditions under which the hierarchy of one over the other can be exploded.

Thus we can relate the previous discussion of the erotic pleasure of the cut to the issue of colonialism. The singer Apache Indian creates fissures via his style of music, called bhangramuffin, which is a mixture of Afro-Caribbean reggae and Punjabi bhangra. This new musical genre questions the idea that reggae should be the sole property of Afro-Caribbeans, and that bhangra ought to be the style played best by Punjabis. Interestingly enough, Apache himself grew up in Birmingham – in neither of the two regions which the two styles are associated with.

Again we can question authenticity as we did via Nietzsche in the third section of this chapter: 'What is surprising is not that the real has become questionable but that it went unquestioned for . . . so long' (Taylor and Saarinen 1994: 'Interstanding', 8). *Imagologies* asks if there been a fundamental change in our world that makes it different from other epochs, or if we have finally realized what has always been so. This question remains unanswered, but *Imagologies* does celebrate the growing role of images as opposed to mythologies, and suggests this is due to the media: 'In the media, the autonomous cogito is torn to pieces' (Taylor and Saarinen 1994: 'Interstanding', 1). A magazine such as *Libas* encourages this by being 'international'.

What occurs is a process of deterritorialization, which links back to the erasure of the referent and the shaking of foundations. Arjun Appadurai suggests that such global interaction leads to a tension between cultural homogenization and cultural heterogenization. Remember the fragmented 'c' from 'Boom Shack A Lack', and the tension between a section of the 'c' wishing to break free, yet wanting to hold on at the same time? The 'c' has the desire to move from the centre to the periphery, from a state of homogenization to heteroge-nization. But as Appadurai points out, perhaps we must reject existing centre/periphery models and think of the new global economy as a complex, overlapping, disjunctive order – which relates back to Barthes' interweaving. Appadurai suggests that as rapidly as forces from various metropolises are brought into new societies they tend to become *indigenized* in one way or another. We can certainly see this at work in *Libas* as the various clothes advertised show influences from various cultures to the point where one is unsure where they come from:

> The critical point is that both sides of the coin of global cultural process today are products of the infinitely varied mutual contest of sameness and difference on a stage characterized by radical disjunctures between different sons of global flows and the uncertain landscapes created in and through these disjunctures.
>
> (Appadurai 1990: 308)

In this we can perhaps move on from colonialism to postcolonialism, which is not a homogeneous category either across all postcolonial societies or even within a single one. Instead it refers to a typical configuration which is never consistent within itself, but is always in the process of change. This enables desire to be fired endlessly, and one always has the urge to seek dis-closures rather than en-closures.

The implications of this for cultural identity is that it is always a '*production*', never complete, and always in process. As well as points of similarity, there are always points of *difference* which constitute what we are. Thus we must acknowledge the discontinuities of identities. Cultural identity, then, is a matter of *becoming* as well as of *being*, belonging to the future as much as the past.

☯ CONCLUSION
A conclusion is not a conclusion when *nothing* can be concluded – we can put the word under erasure.

The pleasure of the text is its dissemination – not its consolidation. What we have attempted to do is to transgress the boundaries of traditional criticism by exploding language and identity and taking them into a kaleidoscopic zone where the fragments rearrange – only to be dispersed again . . . and again. The experience of postcolonialism is thus defined not by essence or purity, but by the recognition of a necessary heterogeneity and diversity. This is integral in forming new relations between cultures that seek to know and respect the other without being locked in the power/knowledge couplet: 'Abandoning essentialist notions would be a serious challenge to racism' (Hooks 1993: 425).

By relinquishing notions of origin and authenticity we can move from hierarchical to lateral relations, and this is necessary to enable us to find both parallels and differences, to see a constant interchange between different cultures. This breaks away from the repressive fear of the parents in 'Boom Shack A Lack!!', who seek to cling resolutely to their own culture rather than open themselves up to change.

Certainly, this leads to an identity crisis, but perhaps identity is *always* in crisis. What is at stake is the way in which this is dealt with. The *cogito* is one way, but we have found this always takes the linear path to domination in the desire to aspire higher than the other. There are alternatives: we could acknowledge the differences and ruptures in ourselves, thereby cutting this path and entering a web where a constant change of direction is required. Such a route provides the conditions for *accepting* the other without the necessity of *knowing* and *possessing* the other. Thus we can see how the state of emergency is also a state of emergence, and the pressure of different cultures proves to be productive. A magazine such as *Libas*, since it openly addresses East/West relations, manifests this pressure clearly – but *all* texts contain contradictory elements.

The opening of this chapter sought to criticize *Libas's* desire to emulate Western culture in 'Ode to Velvets', but this led us to consider whether or not *Libas's* version was 'less real' than a Western one, thus enabling us to question the idea of authenticity. Difference is already differed, and therefore cannot be thought of as a concept having an original and a copy – neither West nor East holds the position of the original. In addition, the traditional style provides a necessary contrast to the more adventurous articles in order to create an opposition dynamic. As a consequence we can see *Libas* as *more* than just an Asian Orientalism. Due to this one must reconsider what is radical and what is traditional. It is not a style itself that is radical, but the interaction, contrast and clash of styles which increases the friction and eroticism of the gap between them. This is similar to the idea of needing a frame to transgress and undercut. The frame is never stable – sometimes it takes the form of stereotypical Western culture, and sometimes Eastern culture. But it is never a final limit, just as there is no limit to the text – where should one stop? At a picture, an article, a page, a section, a magazine, a genre . . ?

What do you make of the fact that we have inserted speech and dialogue into the essay, when speech has been linked with logocentricism, presence, hierarchy and domination – in other words, the asking of questions to which one already knows the answers?

Speech certainly effaces *textuality*, and within this structure 'other' voices cannot emerge. I can talk to myself – both producing and receiving at the same time, and therefore remaining self-sufficient like Descartes uttering the *cogito* to himself and to the text – but not allowing the text itself to speak. The reader can also recite the text and swallow it whole, and this is the condition under which nothing 'new' can be said. But speech can become writing and explode through semantic horizons when the reader sees *holes* instead of wholeness. Liberation lies in the way we read, in our attitude. There is no 'real' and consequently knowable East or West. Orientalist discourse, far from being monolithic, *does* allow counter-hegemonic voices to be heard from within, for instance the play of words allows new possibilities to come through. We can return briefly to 'Ode to Velvets', and recall how our second reading allowed such unbidden voices to emerge. We dissolved our identities as readers and became writers ourselves, only to be read by others in a continuous process of folding and reinscription. But this happens only under certain conditions – and the reader's attitude is crucial to these conditions.

You have just ended on a conclusion – surely this contradicts what you have been suggesting.

Precisely! You have transformed into the reader who sees speech as writing, for you can see how discourses constantly shift and undermine themselves. Colonial discourse, then, does not exist, except when the deadened reader perpetuates these scripts and mythologies. Everything must remain inconclusive, for 'Holes in the net are openings for the imagination' (Taylor and Saarinen 1994: 'Gaping', 7).

6

ELVIS IN ZANZIBAR

Ahmed Gurnah

The Only Way to Predict the Future is to Shape it.
(A German exporter)

INTRODUCTION

The shaping of international culture implies more than the machinations of economic and political imperialism or the diffusion of 'popular' culture (Smith 1990: 179). It also involves the existence of powerful processes of exchange and competition, influences motivated by merit, curiosity and long-term perspectives. Ulf Hannerz observes that world culture 'is created through increasing interconnectedness of varied local cultures' and the development of those 'without a clear anchorage in any one territory' (1990: 237). But this is theoretically too general for my purpose. These processes need to be explained and understood; yet, talk of culture or its globalization famously invites a special kind of pedantry.

Bauman thinks the concept contains 'unyielding ambiguity' (1973: 1) and Williams that it is 'exceptionally complex', has its etymological roots in agriculture (1981: 10) and is 'one of the two or three most complicated words in the English language' (1983: 87). T. S. Eliot gloomily sets out to rescue it from the 'appearance of heresy' and misuse (1972: 3). This reaction may be due to the fact that culture is something all of us habitually are part of and express and know a lot about, but because culture is also reputed to define our character and quality of life, we are anxious that it should not be mundane. A travel guide captures the paradox I imply:

> For Westerners, *Morocco* holds an immediate and enduring fascination. Though just an hours ride on the ferry from Spain, it seems far from Europe, with a culture – Islamic and deeply traditional – that is almost wholly unfamiliar.
>
> (Ellingham *et al.* 1994: Introduction)

In fact, Ellingham *et al.* describe the context of every culture. For culture is what connects us and contrasts us from our immediate communities. Its

116

paradoxes drive us to communicate, clarify and wonder about others whose raw material we use to interact with our own and other communities.

Ambiguity in our words, like air on the wings of Kant's dove,[1] is the friction produced by the rub of social analysis which eventually lights up with meaning. Ambiguities in our concepts indicate competing values and approaches in our viewing of objects, social life and events. They also signal the gaps in our knowledge and a need to carry out different or more sustained inquiry. Arguments over the meaning of concepts at once clarify and introduce more complex puzzles so we may clarify them and confront yet more problems. Like other descriptive/analytical concepts, culture is transparent or opaque according to how we use it, or as defined by the process and the 'culture-complexes' which kick into place to shape our understanding. The question for us is, how does this understanding happen? Particularly, how does it do so when we are speaking about cultural acquisitions from other societies? (Wilson 1970). How do we overcome the linguistic and symbolic barriers that are raised by cultures clearly different from our own?

I shall respond to these problems by telling you a story about a little boy from Zanzibar and the cultures that influenced and profoundly shaped him. I shall later use Ludwig Wittgenstein, Peter Winch, Claude Lévi-Strauss and hermeneutic philosophers to show how culture finds its meaning through forms of life.

TALES FROM MALINDI

Growing up in Zanzibar in the 1950s, I was lucky from the outset to experience international culture. Zanzibar Town was then a cosmopolitan urban *entrée-port*, which for several centuries handled trade between the Mid and Far East and the eastern seaboard of Africa. From Zanzibar bazaars the smells of cloves, chillies, shark fins, perfume and red piping hot halwa, transported one through the Orient. In the nineteenth century, Sultan Said partially ruled along most of the Indian Ocean coast from Oman to Mozambique and traded with people on the coastal settlements between the two. This 'merchant prince' chose Zanzibar as the seat of his government, where several great cultures routinely mixed and exchanged goods and ways of living. If for now we leave aside how it was possible for these cultures to mix, the depth of our core learning experience in the 1950s was, therefore, shaped by African and Arabic cultures, and articulated by Indian, Western and Chinese cultures.

The first sounds I wriggled to as a toddler I heard on Radio Cairo. Every local café tuned into Arabic love songs by Mohammed Abdul-Wahab and Farid El-Atrash before evening prayers. As cups of strong and bitter Arabic coffee were consumed, these singers eulogized about the moon's ability to mend their broken hearts or rescue them from drowning in their own bitter tears. Sometimes men at the cafés became sufficiently moved by a particular taunting phrase to interrupt their game of dominoes or a political controversy, assume a love-pained expression and sing along with the love-bitten poet. In extreme cases, serious men disrespectfully – but maybe not intentionally – articulated their Quranic Stanza with an odd lunar phrase. Women had their sessions too, which included a little dancing, but as a nosy little boy I was dispatched on harmless errands out of the way, and I never suspected the truth.

There was no 'bookish' tradition of music in Zanzibar; sound, meaning and performance were the main ways people related to it. In this atmosphere at the age of 6 or 7 I learnt to sing Kiswahili *taarab*; though my immaturity allowed me only a partial understanding of the innuendo and fierce but highly amusing war of words hidden in the lyric of competing music clubs or writers.

As a 9-year-old in the mid-1950s, I stumbled over Harry Belafonte's version of calypso. My older cousin who wanted to go and study in Trinidad bought a record player on which we ceaselessly played and danced to 'Hold 'Em Joe'. Around the house were also records of the mellifluous Latin bands for Hollywood of Xavier Cugat playing such waist twisters as 'Mambo Jumbo', 'Linda Mujer', 'The Peanut Vendor' and 'Mambo Negro'. Rock and roll followed OK Jazz and other 'Congolese' and Kenyan bands. Elvis was king in our household in Malindi (or was it Sir Cliff?) as much as he was in Iowa or Liverpool. My brother later reneged to the Rolling Stones; unbelievable. In my late teens I listened to American jazz, especially Sutchmo, and a little swing, but mercifully held out against Bing Crosby; but at no time was even he 'foreign'. The grandson of a deposed Sultan three houses away (still in waiting for the British to allow him to resume his crown) used to sing along with Bing. We used to accompany him loudly in distorted voices, which rather provoked him into drunken abuse about us and our whole lineage.

Architecture in Zanzibar Town itself is a testimony to that cultural confluence. There were buildings of Mediterranean Arabic styles in the Stonehouse area, African bungalows in N'gambo, Anglo-Indian hybrids in official buildings and mystical Eastern courtyards for the wealthy. Historical buildings in different states of repair include Arabic, Portuguese and British fortifications from the seventeenth to the nineteenth century.

Not counting the colonial government mobile cinema showing Pathé News and the Three Stooges, I saw the big screen for the first time in 1954 at the age of 7. Delmer Daves' liberal reinterpretation of Cochise in *Broken Arrow* only left me confused about the routine racist treatment of 'Red Indians' and interrupted my sleep for months afterwards. After that I caught many glimpses of other cultures through Indian and Egyptian cinema and Hollywood. We went to the Sunday matinée at *Cine Afrique* or *Majestic* for 'one shilling all round'; when we could sit for the same price even in the exclusive boxes usually occupied by the select: the rich, the aristocrats and Europeans. English cinema was largely restricted to our huge appreciation of Terry Thomas, whom everybody inexplicably and immovably believed to be 'typically British'.

My knowledge of Shakespeare, eighteenth- and nineteenth-century English literature and Enid Blyton grew with my familiarity with the library of our English-speaking King George VI School. Mao Tse Tung, Franz Fanon, Che Guevara and Khame Nkuruma did not feature much here, but became essential reading once the anticolonial/nationalist movement got going. I was introduced to Peter Abrahams, Chinua Achebe, V. S. Naipaul and Raymond Chandler not by my white British teachers, but by a returning Zanzibari student. Of course, long before I engaged with this 'English' literature in secondary school, I had been learning Kiswahili sayings, Arabic and the Quran. Our appreciation of Islamic literature, theology and culture was organic and considerable.

Our ability to read these and other literatures in the original is the proof of the competence of many Zanzibaris in English and Arabic, in addition to Kiswahili. In some communities, people also spoke and read Hindi and Urdu. The sense of linguistic plurality was periodically increased by visits of Somali and other African traders and workers who came to Zanzibar during the monsoons for seasonal employment and trade.

This sense of linguistic plurality was topped only by the variety of cuisine easily available on the streets, in cafés and in small shops. It was possible routinely to eat Indian or Arabic food, African – local or from the mainland – or Chinese food. Indian Ocean trade brought in goods from up the coast and from the Mediterranean and the Far East.

Curiously at this time, however, I devoured the British literary material as I have never done since. The latest fashions were in our living rooms only a few months behind London. *Romeo* kept us informed about Eden Kane or Brenda Lee's hairdo, *Valentine* about Ricky Nelson or Bobby Vee. This *was* the stuff of globalization, as significant as the adoption of communism or science. Daniel Bell would have been proud of us: the American dream travelled safely through Liverpool to the tropics. The European teachers in my school in Zanzibar were not so sure. Pleased about the 'modernization' (Westernization), they were rather alarmed by our voracious consumption of the rebellious pop and youth culture, particularly when juxtaposed to our growing nationalist views. I guess they must have felt rather like Deborah Kerr did in *The King and I*, when she was seeking to transform a 'native boy' (the king) into a colonial parody. Our teachers probably viewed our enthusiasm for rock and roll as part of their 'burden'.

Equally alarmed were the politicized older Zanzibari folk stuffing snout up their noses. They shuddered in disbelief at the sight of our stiff and curly hair sculptured into teddy styles, but not so very silently. They were equally mystified by our imitations of Yul Bryner (arm extended) saying, 'etc., etc.,

etc.' or Marlon Brando nasally muttering 'You scum-sucking pig' from *One Eyed Jacks*. Viewing us as spoilt brats seduced by foreign (Western) glitter, they loudly prayed to the amusement of the whole neighbourhood that our deviation from our organic culture was only temporary. A sentiment which no doubt increased their hostility to living under colonialism and strengthened their nationalist resolve. On a visit back to Zanzibar in 1994, dressed and perfumed like an Arab Sheikh, one of these old folks, not having seen me for thirty odd years, sidled up to me at a funeral and checked if I had eventually returned to my culture! They were not so worried about Egyptian or Indian 'foreign' cultures because they shared them. Some did later turn against these too as the nationalist struggle hotted up.

I was always in trouble with our copper-moustachioed Welsh headteacher for wearing tan terylene 'drain pipes' instead of the stipulated large khaki shorts which he too sported, along with brown leather shoes, woollen leggings and a ribbon! I was on firmer ground here. As a Muslim adult I could legitimately count on common sense and my long suffering parents' support for the need to cover my knees; as it were, cultural manipulation for personal liberty.

The question here is, how was all this possible? It would seem odd that little African girls and boys should get so excited and involved with the image of Elvis in the way we did; yet, from this description it was the most natural thing in the world for us to do. My problems increase if you reject, as I do, essentialist explanations of human communication put forward by Kant, Lévi-Strauss and Habermas (see Gurnah and Scott 1992). Clearly African children in the 1950s were able to acquire other cultures from a very wide range of sources – some old standing and some new. But by what mechanisms were they able to do this? How do we explain the fascination and alienation of our traveller to Morocco? Pointing at colonial influence and imperialism or at the power of popular culture is not sufficient. For that only describes the political background within which all of this takes place and the fact that it happens widely, but does not identify the sociological processes which enable or incline Africans to acquire and later also express effectively through such 'foreign' cultures or why these processes succeed at all.

INTERNATIONALISM OR MISSPENT YOUTH?

What this proves is that there is a sophisticated selection process going on that brings about intercultural exchange and influences and that cultures around the world are much more open-ended and complex than politicized or functionalist accounts might imply. This also shows that while identifying 'communal', 'group' or 'national' culture, we cannot ignore the individual cultural modalities. My teachers and the old folk in Zanzibar could not both be right. For if we were parodists, culturally we were still Zanzibaris. But if Westernized, we were no longer parodying. In fact, the foreign experiences –

Egyptian, Western, Caribbean, Yemeni, Omani, Indian – were all partial, but never superficial: they rarely replaced our organic culture, but they also significantly contributed to our developing world view. I got into fights equally to defend my father's honour, as I did to proclaim Elvis supreme. This is the point. In fact 'foreign' contact with our culture was formative and transformative and somehow real to our organic experience. Foreigners must have had substantive communicative devices, and counted upon and found a translation route with which to engage with our understanding. This is a rather different form of explanation from those offered by either diffusionist or cultural imperialist theorists. But why did this cultural contact happen?

It is also obvious that engagement with trivial teenage culture did not drive us away from our communities, then or later. Quite the contrary, it offered us a looking-glass through which we viewed those cultures more closely and compared them to our own. It is doubtful in any case that our sculptured teddy hairdos meant the same thing to us or were even the same act as when a white Manchester lad or Eden Kane did it. Most likely, once past the trivia, engagement with 'foreign' cultures introduced us to arguments and literature that we later used to explore further and defend those distinctive and valuable aspects of our organic culture while learning from other cultures in the same way as it had complicated lives of prominent people like Fanon or Cabral. It gave us the language with which to promote those elements in our culture we recognized as unique because we compared them and focused on what was enduring about them and against imperialism. We partly absorbed or 'indigenized' (Appadurai 1990: 295) this foreign culture because instinctively and experientially we knew this. However, once absorbed, aspects of the processed 'foreign' cultures became ours, as much as they once were located elsewhere. Indeed despite my sculptured hairdo, I followed my mother around to anticolonial meetings (and picnics). But the teachers and the old folk failed to recognize the existence of a generational divide or the need to cope with new challenges and times, which demanded new engagements.

Using Ien Ang (1985) and Katz and Tamar (1985), Tomlinson (1991) underlines this paradoxical thinking by questioning the argument that the American media exploit and manipulate audiences. Watching *Dallas*, Arabs confirmed rather than abandoned their conventional views (1991: 48), a Moroccan Jew rejected Western decadence (1991: 49) and the material obviated underlying universal values. From which Tomlinson concludes that audiences are more active, critical, complex and responsive than media theorists think:

> their cultural values more resistant to manipulation and 'invasion'
> ... [with] a gap between how people rehearse their views of a text
> in public ... and how they might 'live' that experience of that text in
> the undisturbed and unmonitored flow of mundane existence.
>
> (1991: 49–50)

But this does not quite clinch it. Young Zanzibaris did more than 'watch' European cultural icons and products, which in fact transformed their lives. They used them like so much change in their pockets to purchase extra excitement and power and maybe also like all other teenagers, to get up their parents' noses a little. Indeed, many people who watched *Dallas* were sufficiently influenced by it to copy its style in clothes. I think it would actually be fair to say that European culture profoundly affected my life and influenced my tastes. The point is, what does that actually mean? Furthermore, cannot the same now be said of young people in Britain with regard to African culture?

The tongue-in-cheek account and Tomlinson's comments raise important issues about the globalization of culture. Clearly the prima-facie evidence from our tale implies culture is exported. The point, however, is how can culture export be explained in terms of context, sharing of meaning, recovery of meaning and the internationalization of culture; how can we, in short, explain the pedagogic and formative properties of culture? (See also Giroux and McLauren 1994; Moharty 1994; and Gurnah, forthcoming.) Indeed, how do we explain cultural nationalism and imperialism in this context?

The fundamental tension in contemporary discussions about these problems lies between those who view the acquisition of a 'foreign' culture as beneficial when shared 'naturally' and willingly, and those who are watching out for bewitchment and domination. There is much literature under the banner of 'modernization' and 'popular culture' which fits in the first category (Gellner 1964; Tomlinson 1991), while the second category begins from the assumption that the introduction of foreign culture can only be achieved through manipulation, market penetration and imperial domination (de Kadt and Williams 1974; Nelson and Grossberg 1988). Culture here is used cynically by the powerful to reinforce and impose personal and class, national and imperial interest on other people, so they can exploit them economically and politically. The tension between the two positions probably represents the analytical separation of parallel processes, both of which are likely to happen concurrently, in sympathy, or in opposition.

While these are parallel and continuous processes tied together in a tense and complex relationship, they cannot be the only means of explaining the export of culture: the example of the young Zanzibari boy I described points to other possibilities. The export and import of culture cannot uncomplicatedly depend on 'exchange' or 'sharing', 'domination' or 'imperialism'. Both sets of processes presume for their possibility, the pre-existence of profound social, cultural and especially linguistic common denominators, what Wittgenstein refers to as 'finding one's feet with' (1953: 263), which can hardly be claimed to have existed in any significant way in the 1950s between the Indian Ocean and Anglo-American countries. Clearly, 400 years of colonization have left their mark on world relations (Frank 1969). But for these common denominators to drive this exchange or cultural imperialism they need to be deep and all consuming – they also need to be continuous and fragmented throughout the said culture and very difficult to isolate and remove by analytical surgery.

The third explanatory possibility must address the *nature* of the exchange itself and not concentrate simply on the agents or pressures which bring it about. We must also examine the *working* of that exchange both from the point of view of the subject – whether it is an individual or a group – and how that exchange affects subjective cultural modalities.

What made young Zanzibaris vulnerable to and participants in foreign cultures was, of course, partly the educational and commercial exposure they received from European tutors and partly the rationale of the colonial infra-structure and the glitz of dominant ideologies and lifestyles. But all could have been resisted and aspects were readily rejected by close adherence to local social life, especially in the heated nationalist context of Africa in the 1950s. What in my view made African people engage so enthusiastically with selected 'imperialist' and other cultures, was an active desire to *construct* particular current and powerful cultural common denominators with the West and elsewhere. In our case, we were motivated to develop and be part of the young people's global culture. Taking an example from music and youth culture, the phenomenon started emerging in a really big way in the 1950s with Frank Sinatra, Marlon Brando and the Everly Brothers and took off with Elvis, the Beatles, Jim Reeves and Ray Charles. The next question then is, why did Africans choose to be part of this global culture and so passionately love – of all people – Jim Reeves? In order to be 'modernized'? Hardly.

BACKGROUND TO A CULTURE-COMPLEX

Five considerations immediately spring to mind regarding the problem in Zanzibar. First, the commercialization and therefore internationalization of regional music through the radio – calypso or rhythm and blues or Congo jazz – and culture, in the 1950s and 1960s, and cheaper technology, which made access to them easier all round the world. With this appeared young people's assumptions that it was a 'hoot' to imitate the 'beautiful people'; so we did! Second, led by Ghana in 1957, many African countries gained their independence then or soon after. The experience of mounting campaigns and winning elections and/or armed struggles was immeasurably significant in the development of this African self-confidence. It increased people's willingness and desire to explore other cultures themselves, and not just accidentally bump into them. Third, many young people from the Third World were becoming highly politicized at a very early age and were moti-vated to seek better knowledge of imperialists and to learn arguments that contended against their ideologies, especially from radicals and those who were colonized themselves. The youth rebellions in imperialist countries were both amusing and appealing to them. Many sought, found and used effectively their political alliances with radical metropolitan intellectuals. Fourth, increased immigration to London, Paris and New York by young people from the colonies and ex-colonies increased their familiarity of the imperialist, but their presence there equally had a profound cultural and social impact on Western countries, which inclined young Third World intellectuals to absorb more from the West. Fifth, and most importantly, the politicized African middle classes and workers actively sought to create a knowledge-bridge and technology transfer from the West, in the belief that this would also bring them more excitement, wealth and political power. But they also worked just as hard to create effective barriers against Western economic and political exploitation. It proved to be a hopeless economic and political defence strategy, but a very powerful and productive cultural fusion. In short, they sought cultural exchange to enhance their lives, which was hardly the same as the search for 'modernization' or 'modernity' with its built-in evolutionary hierarchy. These factors together stimulated a powerful dynamic that enabled people to construct a new culture-complex with approaches that cannot be explained by diffusionist or imperialist models.

A foreign culture in this context is neither taken at face value nor mindlessly imposed. The processes that make up this culture-complex squeeze it for benefits, sieve it for relevance and partly reconstitute it before absorbing it. Geertz, dealing with very similar issues, talks of 'control mechanisms – plans, recipes, rules, instructions (what computer engineers call 'programs') – for the governing of behaviour ... [man is] most desperately dependent upon such extragenetic, outside-the-skin control mechanisms, such cultural programs, for ordering his behaviour' (1973: 44) and notes: 'undirected by culture patterns – organized systems of significant symbols – man's behaviour would be virtually ungovernable, a mere chaos of pointless acts and exploding emotions, his experience virtually shapeless' (46) and people 'would be unworkable monstrosities with very few useful instincts, fewer sentiments, and no intellect: mental basket cases' (49).

I shall return to this idea later when I discuss culture-complex in greater detail. For now I would simply point out that Geertz's 'control mechanisms' fail to explain even what he is describing, which is dynamic and constantly moving.

The integration of a foreign Western culture into the body culture of the importing African communities, therefore, involves the reconstruction of the former, for in such an exchange there is an expectation that concessions have to be made by the exporting cultures too.

A political example from the 1950s and 1960s will clarify the point. The powerful impact of Western communism significantly transformed most Third World cultures and political ideas and institutions, regardless of whether they aspired to socialism or capitalism. Third World radical reformation of these ideas into 'the Long March', 'the Cultural Revolution', 'Guerrilla Wars', 'Ujamaa Villages and African Socialism' and so on, transformed Marx's and Engels' original ideas out of recognition, not least because these new ideas reflected much more the working of Chinese or Cuban or Tanzanian struggles and not nineteenth-century European working-class ones. And yet, powerfully though Marx's and Engels' influence on Third World people had been, the writings and thought of Mao Tse Tung, Ho Chi Minh, Fidel Castro, Che Guevara, Franz Fanon and Julius Nyerere too colonized the minds of young socialists and liberals in the West (and in the Third World); some adhered to the original just as strongly as the developments. The absorption of these new ideas by the thinking and seeking young intellectuals in Britain, France, Italy, Germany and the USA, made it possible for Third World intellectuals then to accept more ideas from Western communists.

These comments must not be taken to mean that there were not attempts by colonial governments or the USA to *impose* cultural (as well as economic and political) systems. Nor do I want to leave the impression that Africans did not parody Westerners in unhelpful ways which undermined emancipatory efforts of others. The point is, first, there is a tendency to read trivial parody into profound influences, such as sculptured hairdos or woollen socks in the tropics. Second, we must always try and remember that despite the colonial and imperial agenda, force and complete cynicism, African nationalists have wrestled considerable political and some economic freedom from colonial and resident white settlers and their agents. These comments, therefore, are not meant to make light of colonial/imperialist determination to continue to exploit and dominate. Rather, they are meant to point out what is too easily forgotten in radical rhetoric, that Africans were neither simply passively taking it all nor being influenced from a status of a deficit culture. The organic African cultures were and are as powerful as any others and as capable of selection and absorption as easily as they were of rejection. I shall return to some of these issues later.

In short, in the process of influencing other cultures, exporting cultures too make themselves comprehensible in order to *be understood*. Their signs and symbols become transparent, explicit and *charged*, to *read* and couple with those they aim to influence. Failure to do both reduces their ability immediately to connect with and influence the importer. But for the exporter to be more transparent the exporter also has to import ideas and thus understand the needs of importers. Unless the exporter also imports, the lines of communication dry up. Paradoxically, because good communication tends to be two-way it also in this case deletes the very *directional* distinction between importer and exporter. This is the fascinating context in which lie the processes of globalization and I hope my argument. And it is this aspect which diffusionist and cultural imperialist arguments neglect. Cultural stock inherited from parents, previous contacts, new contacts, all offer the *conductivity* for the development of an appropriate culture-complex. Of course the power carrying capacity of this new culture-complex signals both hope and danger. Individual or group cultural 'recklessness' may lead to new findings, but it is also likely to trigger in other communities the need for caution and conservatism. The processes therein, which help to create new cultures, work in a continual paradoxical nexus: hermeneutic and educative, reassuring and challenging, at the same time familial and community developmental. But in the same way as Wittgenstein's 'language games' do not, there is no reason to believe that these processes lead to 'sameness' or cloning. Changing patterns in different cultures can *never* reproduce each other, for they are made up of different cultural raw materials forged in variant histories.

My description is not meant to replace the diffusionist and cultural imperialist explanations, but significantly to add to them. It does, however, emphasize aspects other than the viewing of culture as 'custom' – something to be followed or passed on mindlessly – or as a symbolic given – a gift from nowhere – that we merely seek to interpret. It recognizes that an appropriation of own or other cultures is an active and intellectually intensive and demanding exercise which mobilizes rational and sensual faculties, always. But more importantly, our approach helps to explain *how* culture is in fact exported and 'absorbed' and what motivates that in terms other than greed and trend. It calls for a *sociological* and *analytical* level of explanation, to what was previously mainly a descriptive (diffusionist) or political economic (cultural imperialist) explanation for globalization.

In the next part of this chapter I shall examine more closely the notion of culture-complex, i.e. the processes of 'cultural games', 'cultural recovery' and 'cultural pedagogy', which make the export and globalization of culture possible. In the final part, I shall comment on diffusionist and cultural imperialist models and explain how I think they fit in with what I describe as the process of culture-complex models. We should then have a clearer view of how culture is exported and what effects its globalization has on the importers.

THE CULTURE-COMPLEX

Culture is a repository of symbolic forms and social and individual experiences. It is the medium for personal, interpersonal and group exchange, expression and reception of ideas. Its mesh ties together personal ambitions and desires to a legitimate moral order and political action, authority and the economic system. Through culture, people create moral and epistemic parameters to control, yes, but also enhance their social and personal lives, in a way they can come close to and accept them as their own. It is a medium for the construction of meaning in those lives and a channel for transmitting and exchanging that meaning and knowledge – it is a 'form of life', yes, but also a process for creating new lives and meanings and cultures. The culture-complex is the means for exchange, education and change. It

126

is in this sense that it differs from Geertz's computer program, which is about control, not freeing of energy and creativity. I suspect Geertz would not disagree with this; his description of people's development attests to that (1973: 47–8). It is just that his nomenclature is out of step with those views.

When symbols representing individual and group experiences re-emerge or are imported from other cultures for our use and communication, they are always 'screened' by us before reuse. To be *people* means precisely that every day, everyone of us, even the most confused and least informed amongst us, *never* accepts any representations, not even those constructed by ourselves, simply as naive copies of 'reality' or as evidence of settled and agreed symbolic interactions without first personally screening them, regardless of whether we get it right or what we actually say theoretically. In this sense, to be a person is to be cultured. To be cultured is to stop playing a passive role in nature, or remain a cog in a regulated social machine. It is instead to be an active contributor in social interaction, change and development and to play a keen, active and integral part in social development, nature or in some of its parts. If there is a characteristic which is universally human then it is this need to check before use. Indeed, it is common to encounter non-professionals grappling with and forcefully forwarding *their* explanations for complex social and political events and representations. It makes no difference really whether their analysis is right or wrong to the reaffirmation of their humanity, that is confirmed by their participation in social life and their unwillingness to take anything for granted. This learning merely gives them tools to do it better – maybe. The idea of culture-complex provides the mechanism for this intellectual 'testing', and 'squeezing', this screening and selection process.

As I see it, the sole and integrative task of this culture-complex after selection is *to construct common cultural denominators within and between cultures*. Culture-complex works quite unlike the way formalists and philosophers conceive of social relations. In *The Uncertain Science* (1992) Alan Scott and I argued that social analysts fail effectively to carry out their radical investigation when the influences of formalism and philosophy prompt them to seek security for our knowledge from the outside and thus ignore what is actually happening on the ground. We were sceptical of the epistemological solutions put forward by Habermas and Lévi-Strauss, because we thought their work contained such formalist assumptions.

With regard to Lévi-Strauss particularly, the formalism reduces the effectiveness of his highly original concept of 'binary opposites', because by linking the concept to the workings of the savage mind he does eventually ground it in philosophical anthropology. But should the Lévi-Straussian technique for gathering knowledge internationally be viewed sociologically/culturally with the aid of such ideas as culture-complex, I believe we shall once again have a powerful analytical tool. So what is this culture-complex? It is a group of processes all of which motivate and cajole us to work with processes which screen, order, sieve, select and activate signs and symbols so that we make cultural encounters productive, meaningful and therefore possible. These processes are of cultural games, cultural recovery, cultural contrasting, cultural exchange, and cultural pedagogy and developments. Metaphorically speaking, these processes act through the concepts and cultural icons in such a way that later they may act rather like charged electrons in a chemical reaction. The 'charge' then enables exchange between two or more fairly 'stable' cultures when they make contact or 'touch' each other. That is to say the charging processes – which are always there in every culture – stimulate communication between cultures by 'energizing' their symbols and signs and 'sensitize' their users to inter-action. Put prosaically, the contact raises people's curiosity to examine closely each other's mores and cultural products. The curiosity locks the people of the two cultures close together, encourages them to dig out permanent tunnels of communication between them, so that they can test and share each other's meanings, words, language and juxtapose their myths and histories. In short, this culture-complex makes it possible for cultural *common denominators to be constructed between cultures* by following specific rules.

But what stimulates the appearance of this cultural 'charge' to energize cultural representations in encounters and ensure that all cultures involved are working from the same assumptions? Where do these processes in fact come from? I think the answer to the first question has to be that each instance is shaped by different stimuli which can only be isolated *a posteriori* through analysis similar to what we observed in the context of Africa. In that context I suggested there were at least five different reasons for the development of the stimuli, most of which were connected with change and a desire for a better life. If that is how the charge appears, what about the processes? I believe them to be implicit and practically immanent to an honest effort to create communication channels, but let me hasten to add there is nothing transcendental about them. And while better quality communications improves exchange, contra Habermas, there are no guarantees of emancipation here, though when that is induced it is always welcome.

Thus the acquisition of culture, even within one's own community, is neither a straightforward act of imitation, nor is it, as some will have it regarding language, merely a matter of training and usage. Training, usage and imitation are important aspects in the development of language and these are common denominators, especially at the beginning of the process. But more importantly, the acquisition of culture becomes possible when the culture-complex also comes into play. Following the stimulus, the culture-complex enables individuals and groups to play an active, forceful and permanent role in the continual construction of the common denominators, as an aspect of their routine participation in *any* cultural activities or framework.

The drive to construct these denominators comes from the impassioned human curiosity and obsession to experience and make sense and meaning, and maybe when people are in search of a little fun too. It is also to do with the character of aesthetic rationality (Gurnah and Scott 1992, ch. 6) and the implicit nature of the communication process itself, as Habermas would put it, truthfulness is implied in validity claims (1984). This said, however, it is precisely because the culture-complex can never work in a natural environment that we need to keep using it to get back to something like a 'fairer' or less interest-bound interpretation of reality. In other words, though the culture-complex results from the sociological context, human curiosity and the process of communication, it is not due to some spontaneity – it is an active political act and interest-bound too. I shall return to the workings of the culture-complex as a whole after looking at its individual components.

'CULTURAL GAMES' AND RULES FOR CULTURAL COMMON DENOMINATORS

As I envisage them, 'cultural games', like language games, make exchange possible. They create movement in the system and make it possible for people to use their cultural products and experiences to specify their meaning as they relate and change their placement in different parts of the system or as they take up cultural products and experiences of new partners. Meaning emerges at each point of a continuous social movement: each point of inter-action can be frozen into an image of the system's kaleidoscope in space and time, as it tumbles round to create new images and meanings.

Cultural games

In his later philosophy Wittgenstein suggests a device for viewing the status of language and its acquisition, which here I shall blend with the work of Lévi-Strauss to make sense of the process of cultural acquisition. Wittgenstein identifies the not unproblematic but still highly productive notion of language games to show how people acquire language and communicate. For him words are meaningful in their use in a social context where they become part of a language game (Kenny 1973: 14). They assume shared meaning and trigger people to recall their previous experiences. Thus, words and their behavioural surround make up language games. Thus by placing language games within the forms of life he sets up an internal association between linguistic competence, sociability and communication. Indeed, much of what Wittgenstein claims about language already has a respectable pedigree in sociology and anthropology (Nisbet 1976: x) and increases our understanding of how cultures work and how people use them to interrelate. But what Wittgenstein particularly offers me in this work is an analogy for viewing cultural acquisition and use in terms of cultural games. Here cultural practice and products too are internally linked to human association and cognition. Signs and symbols represent community meanings and values in a complex network that offers individuals the medium for self-expression and self-realization and, of course, self-correction and improvement.

For Wittgenstein, language is about *signs* and *symbols* learnt not only intellectually, but also through use (1972). Culture being symbolic too, I would argue, its use constitutes the social fabric and evidence for social analysis. For Durkheim (1995 [1912]) the study of religion (and therefore of culture) is not about internal and external *things*, but 'rather, in what it does for the believer in his relation to the world, society and self' (Nisbet 1976: ix). Cassirer (1953, 1955, 1957) distinguishes people from animals by the fact that we live in the *symbolic* dimension of reality by our engagement with language, myth, art and religion as part of our universe: 'They are the varied threads which weave the symbolic net, the tangled web of human experience. Instead of dealing with the things themselves man is in a sense constantly conversing with himself' (Cassirer 1944: 25). Then he observes, 'instead of defining man as an *animal rationale*, we should define him as an *animal symbolicum* and assume that people are profoundly tied up in cultural forms' (25).

Working with something akin to the concept of '*animal symbolicum*', Lévi-Strauss (1966) develops his highly original anthropology which links the mind to cultural products and human communication, indeed, humanity itself (see Gurnah and Scott 1992, ch. 3). These arguments significantly tell us something about culture, its meaning for people and in short the use they make of it in order *to be* people. Culture is reality *sui generis*, thought Malinowski (see also Winch 1958:15).

In *Philosophical Investigations* Wittgenstein brings together language, rule following and a game, but does not distinguish any specific features of the 'game' (1972, paragraphs 65–7). Rather, he points to 'a complicated network of similarities and relationships overlapping and criss-crossing'. He stresses that the way rules work in a game, is similar to how they work in a language. A language 'is part of a communal activity, a way of living in a society a "form of life". It is through sharing in the playing of language-games that language is connected with our life' (Kenny 1973: 163). The games clarify meaning and define what makes sense. In games, words connect with other words and find purpose.

The way that cultures connect is rather similar. In a symbolic network, particular cultural products assume different meanings depending upon their placement in the system at a specific time and space and justification for their being there. In other words, the same cultural product will mean different things to the same person in varying contexts and to different people in the same context within the overall frame. This constitutes the general pattern of the 'cultural game', shaped by aesthetic rationality – perspective of ordering – which defines use and meaning and conveys that to other participants in the system. When cultures which are foreign to each other come in contact, the energizing of cultural products and sensitizing of the people involved tentatively create the initial system for communication. The culture-complex then does its work here, and the initial fabric develops into a system of communication – a system of common denominators. Invariably this is a complex interaction whether it happens slowly or rapidly. Also inevitably, it is informed interaction whether recognized as such or not. People in all cultures habitually create these communication bridges within the narrow familial or community culture and expand them more widely to the nation and eventually the global systems.

Modalities of culture

In the example of the Zanzibari boy, cultural icons of rock and roll, foreign literature and music all formed part of the exciting mixture that brought enjoyment, instigated critical evaluation of home culture and helped to promote the search for liberty against colonial occupation. The motivation for the whole of the culture-complex here was also to dispose of colonialism, and that became the group focus, the modality of its culture. The motivation was powerful, successful and progressive. The raw material for that challenge came from both greater political awareness of and increasing familiarity with foreign cultures. What was internalized and used depended on individual experiences and interests, intelligence and also on luck; depending upon where and how individuals or groups entered the cultural game and what they took from it and chose to express by it. That combination for each individual that shared a 'family resemblance' within the group modality, also expressed an individual modality or combination that distinguished her or his cultural preferences from the group.

To put it another way, regarding group cultural modality, our experience of Elvis was real, organic and selective. No doubt a point can be made about the black (African) influence in Elvis and rock 'n' roll, but, although quite valid, such an argument misses my present point. It is not fanciful to claim that rock and roll signified for us:

- collectively a link to the international youth movement, Western struggles and new heroes and at that time were as significant for us as Jesse Owen, Gamal Abdul Nasser or Che Guevara;
- our political distance from both the white colonial teachers and our parents and the development of our own political and cultural platform;
- emerging cultural common denominators that linked us to the knowledge in the West and paradoxically anti-imperialist struggles elsewhere;
- our opportunities culturally to manipulate situations for personal liberties that later linked us to the search for political liberties. (The same people who read about Elvis later also read about Mao and Lenin. The ones who did not probably also continued to sing along in cafés);

131

- the absurdity of our situation, like nausea, highlighted our awareness of the liberties we took and offered a looking-glass that led to critical thinking.

The way the bits fit together is complex and requires much more detailed study and analysis. Furthermore, each individual version is influenced in different degrees and with variant subsequent identifications, leading to individual cultural modalities. This is an important issue, one which has in some ways motivated the writing of this piece. The idea of individual cultural modality explains why two members of the same family, with only a year or two difference in age, having received pretty much similar upbringing, should have in some ways quite different perceptions of their cultural identities. Such examples are pervasive in Zanzibar. Some see themselves as Westernized Afro-Arabs, while their brothers or sisters see themselves as Westernized Arabized Africans. Some see themselves as Africans pure and simple, with foreign origins and influences. Others still hang on to their origins – Arabic, African, etc. – and view the influences as 'interferences' caused by the misfortune of growing up in a foreign country or one contaminated by foreign influences. The permutations of identity are endless but their general experience, knowledge and expression of their culture has a family resemblance. This describes a very complex framework for moral legitimacy – all have the right to be Zanzibaris – and creates room, liberty and emancipation from group tyranny. Indeed, it creates this very desirable creative tension that *charges* the local community for internal communication and makes it available for communication with other cultures.

The general point made here is that such was a nexus for change and progressive thought. People are not led by their noses into other cultures' agendas, not even within the same culture group or family. If they enter these worlds in that fashion it is mainly out of choice – something there attracts them and becomes the most challenging world of learning and experimenting. This does not mean for the learners that they always make the right choices. I am sure the sculptured hair was on the margin of good taste, but great fun at the time.

Following a rule

For Wittgenstein, the notion of following a rule or grammar should not be taken literally, but works on 'family resemblances' (1972: paragraph 67); 'covering many different but related things: what we call a rule in a game, or language-game, may have very different roles in the game' (Kenny 1973: 171). Wittgenstein's greatest insight here is apparent in the view that the study of the nature of rules is best done by examining their expression, in the same way as we do with sensations and thoughts. To interpret a rule, therefore, 'is rather to substitute one expression of a rule for another' (Kenny 1973: 173, P1: 1, 201). Rules are applied repeatedly. A very important principal is involved here. Taking the example of learning natural numbers, Winch (1958: 59) summarizes following a rule thus:

> Learning the series of natural numbers is not just learning to copy down a finite series of figures in the order which one has been shown. It involves *being able to go on* writing down figures that have not been shown one. In one sense, that is, it involves doing something *different* from what one was originally shown; but *in relation to the rule* that is being followed, this counts as 'going in the *same* way' as one was shown.

Winch takes this insight to the organization of culture, and not without difficulties. Following rules has the curse of functionalism, but the above and his opposition to following *formulated* rules and adherence to the notion that such following is to be judgemental and can be mistaken, maintains a theory of action in his outline and therefore in the notion of cultural games. This ability to go on doing culture in relation to the rule with diversity is what creates the freedom for the group that absorbs a foreign culture and allows an individual freedom within the group culture. In that scenario, the processes of binary oppositions, cultural recovery and so on combine to give us the culture-complex.

THE SYSTEM, BINARY OPPOSITES AND CULTURAL EXCHANGE

The sociological working of binary opposites originates with de Saussure and Lévi-Strauss. Using this technique in his anthropology, Lévi-Strauss takes us a long way towards explaining how culture is globalized. He shows that in the same way that culture countersigns itself symbolically with nature, it does so with other cultures too through taxonomy and the contrastive method. His method depends on international sociological raw material and leads to the stance of 'humanity without frontiers', in a reversal of philosophical anthropology.

To construct this sociological humanism, Lévi-Strauss follows Durkheim in recognizing the importance of a system. Human experience and meaning is symbolized within a system that as Mauss showed in *The Gift* (1990 [1950]) communicates through implicit logic and reciprocity (Badcock 1975: 49). Within this system, taxonomy or aesthetic ordering classifies and analyses discrete symbolized aspects of our experience, but, most importantly, it *connects them up* to the system's implicit logic, communication and reciprocal arrangements (Lévi-Strauss 1967: 21) and, of course, meaning. It is organized according to its laws of involvement and exclusion, which can perhaps be compared to Wittgenstein's rules of family resemblance or the context of culture-complex. This system connects up the natural to the sociological

(Lévi-Strauss 1966: 93) and makes communication possible between cultures and at different levels in the same culture. Lévi-Strauss argues that the system becomes *a language* that links the structural to the historical elements of a culture to enlighten insiders and outsiders, making culture diverse, protective and projective, and then increases social integration and intercultural communication.

Another step in this argument is to do with the status of this 'heterogeneous and arbitrary classification'. For Lévi-Strauss this forms the 'memory bank' with which to 'assail nature' (1966: 16), by means of 'bricolage' or work of a handy person or for the culturally active person. Nature offers culture an example to follow or reject: other cultures do the same. By juxtaposing the formal characteristic of cultural products – music, language, myths, signs, etc. – they become able at that formal level to offer their meanings for translation within the system. An important aspect of this formal communication is made possible by the technique of binary opposition and, for my argument, the cultural games contained within it.

Culture imposes on the world a series of 'contrasts' and 'oppositions' by means of analogical thought. Distinctions and contrasts can help communities to add to their perceptions or meaningfully to distinguish themselves from others (Lévi-Strauss 1966: 170). Thus in this binary opposition we learn not only to preserve what is ours, but most importantly to do so *only* by linking our selves to a larger world system, and work within its broader logic (Lévi-Strauss 1966: 161–2), thus creating a wider overlap. The logic is 'definable by the number and nature of the axes employed, by the rules of transformation making it possible to pass from one to another; and finally by the relative inertia of the system'. So far so good. The difficulty we need to overcome in Lévi-Strauss is when he seeks universality no longer by the method of cultural confederation as was implied by his substantive argument, but once again turns to philosophical abstractions of the savage mind.

Thence, Lévi-Strauss views the working of this technique of binary opposites as formal and universal and appears not to need content for its operation. The technique then assumes the transcultural and transhistorical character which he believes makes translation possible and offers a common denominator between contrastive historical and sociological entities. He is thus satisfied that the formal level of culture transcends its functionalism and relativism. What makes this identification of contrasts possible is the 'savage mind', the shaping mind.

An odd conflict then appears in Lévi-Strauss's work. He recognizes that in sociological bunching we create an international context for exchange and he turns to Kantian philosophical anthropology to *justify* that bunching. Contained in this is ambiguity of the concept of the unconscious as developed by Freud (1968: 22–5) and the murky formalism of Kant's transcendentalism. It is then that problems start. Expecting security from that source he shifts his ground from *practical* notions of aesthetic ordering to occult considerations and thus denies us a powerful tool for analysing the sociological processes which lead to the globalization of culture. In this formalism, common denominators are philosophically assumed rather than culturally constructed by games and oppositions. The insertion of the notion of cultural games here helps us in our determination to avoid the need to introduce Freudian or Kantian transcendence. That in turn helps to rescue binary opposites from ideas of the unconscious and transhistorical universality in order to present the whole process sociologically and aesthetically

CULTURAL RECOVERY: HERMENEUTICS AND POLITICAL ECONOMY

Another process of the culture-complex is the consideration of hermeneutics and political economy – recovery of meaning. Both are about truth and fairness: the former is about recovering an interpretation of culture that accords with the views of the subject and the latter is about doing so within a broadly objective world of comparative standards that takes into account the existence of interest and exploitation. Weber was acutely aware of the first and Marx of the second. Our explanation for globalization of culture requires an appropriate consideration of both, in order to incorporate notions of imperialism and diffusion.

Hermeneutics

To guard against the too common 'tourist' methods of acquiring knowledge of other cultures, we turn to a variety of methods: the collection of objective information about it, interrogation of its organizations and the view of the subject group and its symbols. The recovery of knowledge from the subject group will be via hermeneutics. Zygmunt Bauman (1978: 7) derives the word from Greek '"related to explaining" . . . "clarifying", . . . rendering the obscure plain, the unclear clear', to authenticate the 'true version versus distorted ones'.

   This will do for our purposes. The versions of symbols and signs we wish to authenticate for export or import are the subjective ones of individuals and groups. Given my comments on modalities of culture, this recovery of subjective meaning becomes most crucial for sound communication or the views and signs exchanged will remain stereotypical and fail to reflect the actual constitutive cultural core of those individuals or groups. In other words, as part of the globalization of culture, the culture-complex 'checks out' meanings hermeneutically as part of its selection process. I have already argued that this is almost an automatic process for most of us, brought about by our genuine curiosity and the drive to understand others. But I don't suppose we can expect this natural curiosity to survive the scientific inclinations of social scientists. This form of 'authentication', nevertheless, will

135

enhance the processes of the cultural game and the contrastive method in their forms of life. Clearly, no curiosity or drive to understand remains pure and untainted. People always seek answers which accord to their inclinations and interest. That is where Marx's political economy also comes into scientific analysis.

Political economy

Cultural 'exchange' has been a common feature of world history since the empires of Ancient Egypt, Mesopotamia, Ancient Greece, Rome, the Muslim Empire, the Renaissance, nineteenth-century colonialism and imperialism and so on. In these periods have been diffusion and counter-diffusion and developments of music, literature, technology, knowledge, religion and philosophies in unequal and unpredictable ways. On the island of Pemba in Zanzibar when I left thirty years ago, people still congregated for a 'bloodless' bull fight in the afternoon and once a year for the Nairooz-Zoorastran Festival; legacies of the Portuguese and Persians from the sixteenth and ninth centuries respectively. These examples show that cultural exchanges take place as direct (sometimes forceful) inputs by colonizers, as translations of visitors' contributions, distillations of remembered contacts or they are second-hand simplifications.

Tomlinson observes that claims to universality 'nearly always relate to some project of domination: it is very rare that the model of essential humanity is taken from an alien culture' (1991: 54). Therefore regardless of uniqueness or specificity of individual cultures, set in a long-term world history it is clearly nonsense to talk of endogamy of cultures as Europhiles tried to do in the nineteenth century with regard to the Ancient Greek culture, effectively labelled as an Aryan model by Bernal (1987). Our problem here then is within the workings of the culture-complex to recognize what needs to be recovered from 'cultural imperialism'.

Marx's main discovery against false analysis is that it must be based on 'non-contaminated' biased (interest-bound) perspectives. By deriving meanings about other cultures based not purely on our own one-sided understanding, but from reviewing objective factors and interest that motivates the exporter (and maybe importer too), we can reach something like a fairer or representative analysis of social life. This approach is against formalism and foundationalism and accumulates meaning against our natural socioscientific tendency to review our navels. It is also here where arguments about cultural imperialism come into full force, as part of recovery of cultural knowledge.

Comment on imperialism

My starting point is to reject all attempts to view culture as universal if by that people wish to imply an anthropological foundation. That is what for me constitutes a cultural imperialism. Cultural representations *become* universal, *after* they have been politically and sociologically so constructed, using the process discussed here. Tomlinson astutely discusses the appeal of Charlie Chaplin in South America and rejects this universal argument by suggesting:

> Quite obviously, if his [Chaplin's] films had never been distributed outside America, he would never have been a candidate. The force of this argument is seen when we think that no Mongolian or Balinese comedian has been suggested, by Western critics, as striking the chord of common humanity.
>
> (Tomlinson 1991: 52–3)

While not doubting that imperialism of culture and other social relations exist, I do, however, believe that, first, in culture its context is ambiguous. Marx realized this by insisting that imperialism and capitalism was a nasty 'stage' towards transition to socialism. There is a sense of this in our description of the Zanzibari boy who obviously lived under various economic and cultural imperialisms, but from them he also found liberating international opportunities. Though organically African, he learnt easily and meaningfully to relate to cultural products and attitudes of different parts of the world, and perhaps also to use them to defend personal integrity and develop ideas about defending social and economic infrastructures of Zanzibar. It is arguable that such a person stands a better chance of being successful in both cases from his knowledge of imperialists than one who is ignorant of them. The cost to him is he does not so much lose his distinctiveness, but increases it, for his personal cultural modality sets him aside from his group, as he is obliged to absorb and learn from other cultures and has a duty to sell his own to the foreigners and his own group. There is something morally defensible and attractive about this, so long as we continue to oppose force as a means of introduction of culture, not only because then the culture acquired becomes tainted, but because it is wrong politically and economically to impose and exploit, and on the longer term universally inefficient.

Second, as I have indicated earlier, I am fully aware of the violence of imperialism on the Third World, I just do not accept that after violation Africans actually 'lose' their culture. What I think confuses people is the ability of the West to control the image of world relations through its economic and political dominance and control of advertising. The fact is while there is imperialism of culture, there are equal counter influences which tend to be ignored, e.g. the influence of African music on Western society through the development of jazz, swing, rock, tango, to name a few.

Third, by living within this ambiguity and economic and cultural clientship, the African obviously in some ways becomes possibly more vulnerable to

137

cultural manipulation, but also as we have seen, the African becomes wiser about imperialist operations and knowledge and more experienced of the wider world. This is crucial; only then is the African in a position to be an international player and also seek cultural recovery. It can be said that what was 'organic' to the Zanzibari boy's culture (what is that – Bantu? Egyptian? Indian?) is valuable to him because it was organic. What is material is that some combinations of what *he* recognizes as such will then be preserved and communicated, to be linked within other people's 'organic' cultures to combine in some notions of universalism.

There is a real danger in such arguments of disappearing in a puff of smoke, but treated sympathetically these observations do carry some understanding. Imperialism is morally indefensible but it is a social reality that will continue to be with us in its political, economic and cultural forms. Its presence, however, does contribute to the widening exchange and more importantly does not denote cultural slavery for weaker nations or communities. It is part of the cunning of culture that even under occupation, people can exert counter influences. Unfortunately, much of our social scientific analysis is not geared up to deal with problems in this complex dialectical way because its formalism is itself framed from a Western imperialist perspective.

In this regard, I differ from Roland Robertson's project to analyse (following Wallerstein) from a global frame (1992b: 8–31, 51–60). He puts it this way:

> The world could, in principle, have been rendered a 'singular system' via the imperial hegemony of a single nation or a 'grand alliance' between two or more dynasties or nations; the victory of 'the universal proliferate' . . . religion . . . 'free trade' . . . world-federalist movement.
>
> (1992b: 54)

The point is that none of these historical events have been representative enough to hold cultures together in that way and even if so successful, the banding cannot last if my views about culture-complex hold. International culture then is better represented by a kaleidoscope; it tumbles, it is complex, it changes, and its unity is achieved by the constant interactions. The search for a general frame of an essentially given and static world is pure platonic formalism and indicates a greater desire for analytical neatness than for the understanding of social interactions between different cultures. For understanding most assuredly does not come from one vantage point, but emerges from a constant learning and reviewing of the obvious and the apparently incomprehensible.

In this context, then, imperialism becomes one more barrier which communities have to scale. Like friction on Kant's dove or ambiguities in concepts, the additional difficulty offers imperialized people an unpleasant, but a given reality against which to struggle and discover progress and liberty.

COMMUNAL, NATIONAL AND
INTERNATIONAL CULTURES

In *The Uncertain Science* (ch. 6) Alan Scott and I described three standards of rationality – historical, comparative and aesthetic – as means of judging international sociological materials. These standards are appropriate in our subject of globalization. Failure to construct meaning with such a frame takes us back to formalism or relativism.

There, we represented *historical standards* as engaging with conventional knowledge of our culture, institutionalized cognition. The *comparative standards* refer to the accumulation of awareness and a willingness to communicate with other cultures. *Aesthetic standards* denote the process of learning symbols, concepts, arguments and compromises, so that others outside and inside your culture understand them. Third World children have become masterly in all these three regards (Gurnah and Scott 1992: 172).

Buried somewhere deep in this understanding is the Hobbesian social contract, which also helps to remove a suspicion that what we are describing is 'natural'. People accept such standards for moral reasons, 'he that is to govern a whole nation, must read in himself, not this or that particular man; but mankind' (Hobbes 1972: 60). But even for Hobbes this was not enough, for self-preservation is a law of nature:

> A covenant not to defend myself from force, by force, is always void . . .
> No man can transfer, or lay down his right to save himself from death, wounds, and imprisonment . . . where there is no commonwealth, there nothing is unjust . . . justice consisteth in keeping of valid covenants: but the validity of covenants begins not but with the constitution of a civil power.
>
> (1972: 153, 157)

Cultural games and the workings of the culture-complex in general reduce the need to take up arms to defend ourselves and increase our ease to communicate freely and correct misrepresentations. These are additional motivations for a civilized society.

CULTURE AS A MEDIUM OF SOCIAL EDUCATION

An internationalized culture is the most powerful covenant for world peace. It comes about by the institutionalization and internationalization of cultural knowledge. Specific cultural contributions are mostly made common not by force or imperialism but over a very long period by the selective process of rational aesthetics through the frame of culture-complex. The method of dispersal of processed cultural knowledge is institutionalized through the learning process. Cultural pedagogy thus becomes another process of the culture-complex. Culture is pedagogic in the sense that it provides the raw

139

material which creates movement in history. Giroux talks of the mythic and symbolic deconstruction especially of modern forms – cinema, TV, etc. This may be part of it, but it is not what I mean by pedagogy of culture.

For me culture has a capacity for continuous organization and social continuity that leads to complex developments, progress and globalization. The motivation for that capacity is deep. Joao Veiga Continho observes 'the characteristic of the human species is its repeatedly demonstrated capacity for transcending what is merely given' (1974: 9). In my view this characteristic is not realized through some anthropological magic, but by cultural action and transference of ordinary people's ideas from generation to generation through their learning processes. This takes me to the final and most important aspect of the culture-complex.

By its nature culture offers human societies the means and the total opportunity for preserving and passing on accumulated learning and skills. Cultural acquisition, then, is the best and the most comprehensive school for human communities. Culture offers a sophisticated and all-consuming medium for transporting ideas and technology, morality and ways of living. Its greatest success, therefore, is not so much connected with its sophistication, but its most mundane and routine functions. Through routine engagement with culture everybody learns a language or languages, acquires complex social and technical information and prepares for culturally specific information. If you imagine how easy it is to spot a 'foreigner' despite his or her great familiarity with our culture, it gives one an idea about the treasury of learning ordinary people accumulate through culture, in both its general and specific guises.

What is important to remember here is that any reconstruction of cultural knowledge that becomes necessary to achieve effective knowledge and skills that lead to emancipation is not so much the outcome of reading Foucault or Derrida. Clearly any form of enlightenment is good for personal development, but it does not play a great part here in the pedagogy of culture as I understand it. The emancipatory stimulus is in the processes of this culture-complex itself: in the curiosity we show about others, the use we make of cultural combinations that we put together, in the long-term culture instincts and cunning that we inherit, the aims that lie behind our motivations to understand fully others' perceptions of what they think they have to offer us and the comparison we make between what is culturally familiar and what is not so familiar. Pedagogy lies in the steps that are taken in communities to ensure packages of cultural knowledge are passed on and are celebrated, especially to make the most mundane part of the important feature of ordinary exchange. The simple attachment to what is culturally yours and a powerful passion about what is not, makes this exchange balanced and dynamic. It is these activities which add up to the pedagogy of culture. It is the transfer and explication of this mundane but crucial knowledge for social continuity and development, expression and growth which makes culture a medium of education. In this way, culture assumes a super-highway status for educating the population, becoming both the most effective and routine way of transporting very complex social knowledge and skills literally to everybody in the community. It is also the means by which each individual and group learn what is relevant *for them*.

CONCLUSION

So, where does all this talk about Zanzibar, cultural games, binary opposites and recovery get us? I believe it takes us a long way from many of the current discussions; if I may list a few:

- Culture is globalized and it is not entirely or even mainly a negative experience. When Zanzibaris sing rock and roll or South Americans laugh at a Chaplin film we should be glad, particularly when we notice also English people are eating curries and reading African and Indian writers. This connotes a widening of human experiences and wisdom.
- The existence of group and individual cultural modalities ensures the confirmed existence and the workings of 'family cultural resemblances' and individual choices. It helps to explain the internal struggles and accommodations within cultures (e.g. the old folk in Zanzibar and the young people). It also explains the meaning of 'organic' culture, not as a collection of ossified traditions, but what a group or individuals come to construct and recognize as theirs and as life enhancing.
- Through this discussion I have in any case gained a greater understanding of how culture is shared and spread essentially not even mainly through brutality and mindless copying, but for positive reasons connected with human curiosity and the desire to improve and enrich our lives; it is the super highway for life-sustaining social knowledge and change.
- Cultural imperialism is often shorthand for identification of other struggles rather than clear explanation of cultural slavery. The cultural process is far too complex to be viewed in such a limited fashion. In cultural exchange both sides are affected for better or worse in the short term. Almost all imperializing nations end up civilizing and culturally broadening their own people through their attempts to occupy others.
- Imperialism of culture is a real enough experience, but not one which either lasts long or has a lasting *harmful* impact. For example the imposition of the English language on African people and Americanism on the Japanese both show the diabolical taking of liberties by imperialists. However, the people whose liberties were so grossly violated soon learnt to find ways to benefit from both.

The point is, a better understanding of cultural processes should pave the way for more intelligent cultural action and allow the processes of culture-complex to provide an efficient interrogation of cultural exchanges for greater knowledge and for obviating and keeping at bay mystifying immoralities.

As much as culture-complexes work between nations, they do so between classes, community groups and gender groups in the same nation. The working class and women are not passive receivers of ruling-class or high-culture domination. They do not, any more than do 'immigrant' workers in European countries, merely *fight* and *resist* such cultural imperialism, but also play an important role in shaping and reshaping the dominant culture around them, and create new syntheses. These are some of the questions and issues that now require greater extrapolations via the culture-complex model.

NOTES

I have many people to thank for the development of the ideas in this piece including especially Gill Simmonite and Molly Neville, Abdul-Razak Gurnah, Tom Steele, Angela Martin, Rosie Betterton and Peter Ashworth. Not least, I am grateful that Clifford Geertz writes so beautifully.

1 'The light dove, cleaving the air in her free flight, and feeling its resistance, might imagine that its flight would be still easier in empty space', Kant (1929) *Critique of Pure Reason* (trans. N. Kemp Smith, London: Macmillan), p. 47.

7

CHINESE ENTREPRENEURSHIP

Culture, structure and economic actors

Julia Tao and Wai-Nang Ho

INTRODUCTION

This chapter intends to analyse the development of entrepreneurship and the emergence of private entrepreneurs as part of the private economy in China under economic reform. The analysis seeks to explore four basic questions: 'Who are the private entrepreneurs?', 'What are their characteristics?', 'How do they venture into entrepreneurial activities?' and 'What are the forces that shape Chinese Entrepreneurship?' The analysis argues that notwithstanding the thesis of globalization, the development of Chinese entrepreneurship suggests that there is no single growth model. It draws attention to the cultural context which shapes economic behaviours, the institutional context which structures economic opportunities, and the social embeddedness of economic actors which influences the strategies and success of economic action. The interplay and relationship between culture, structure and action are crucial for understanding the choice of economic strategies and the availability of economic options in different societies for attaining the goals of economic growth and modernization. The analysis also suggests that in the Chinese experience, private entrepreneurs are not just self-interested abstract individualists who seek maximization of personal preferences through capitalist markets. It lends support to Berger's thesis that there is no intrinsic or inevitable relationship between individualism, capitalism and modernity (1988: 4–6). Notwithstanding the assumption among many Western modernization theorists (e.g. Parsons and Smelser 1956) about the importance of Western individualism for the development of modernity and capitalist entrepreneurs, China's modernization and entrepreneurial development are intimately linked to traditional values and corporatist structures deeply embedded in family, kinship and lineage groups all of which are important forces shaping the spirit of China's modernity.

143

CHINESE ENTREPRENEURSHIP:
THE ECONOMIC CONTEXT

Revitalization of the private economy:
emergence of the *getihu*

The revitalization of the private economy and the development of private entrepreneurs are partly a response of the Chinese state to meet the challenge of globalizing forces which have been on the ascendant, in order to enhance its competitiveness and participation in the converging world order of capitalism. For the purpose of this chapter, private entrepreneurs are defined narrowly as those who are inclined towards setting up their own businesses. They are those who own private enterprises employing eight or more employees in the People's Republic of China (PRC) today. They differ from '*getihu*' who are 'self-responsible, individual-based or family-based economic units'. But both *getihu* and entrepreneurs are key economic actors in China's developing private economy.[1] The development of *getihu* in China in the 1970s was to meet a threefold objective. First it was to supplement the centrally planned economic system; second to provide jobs for surplus labour in the transformation of the rural population to non-agricultural productivity; and third to improve overall living standards. This led to the well-known household contract responsibility system in the rural areas which started the economic metamorphosis.[2] The intention was to encourage rural people to move from agricultural production to non-agricultural production without leaving their locality and to develop uncomplicated and small-scale private economic units with high mobility. It led to the abolition of the commune system, followed by a series of regulations passed in the mid 1980s in response to the rising need for a 'market' for the many products and services which developed. Licensed private business began to be revived under these new regulations.

Nowadays the term *getihu* in Chinese refers to two different modes of production: individual artisans such as carpenters; and petty peddlers and those who work in the tertiary sector of the economy. However, they can only employ up to seven workers and are less formalized in scale (e.g. in terms of formal accounting and auditing systems), unlike the private enterprises which developed in the late 1980s. They are also limited to non-mechanized forms of production and transport in a narrow range of businesses. These lead some scholars to hold the view that the term *getihu* is more closely related to the meaning of 'self-employment'. At the same time, the achievements of the *getihu* during the period between the late 1970s and mid-1980s have been highly impressive in terms of its accessibility, market-orientated production and customer-orientated services when compared with its counterparts from the state side. The role the *getihu* played in providing more channels for economic activities, facilitating the country's economic development by allowing contracting-out production at home or in a backyard factory to make use of cheaper factors of production, in raising personal income as well as in raising the level of personal savings among *getihu* practitioners was highly significant.

At the same time, the loosening of economic policy created new opportunities open to competition and mobility in the social structure. Society became more open and fluid. The economic structure also provided people with more opportunities for entrepreneurship by moving up from being self-employed to the status of employers. The expansion of the economy gave rise to many new forms of economic activities open to entrepreneurial ventures. The changing economic structure was conducive to the setting up of private businesses with small structures, both in terms of assets and size of establishment.

Revitalization of the private economy: emergence of private entrepreneurs

The emergence of private entrepreneurs in China was associated with the development of private enterprises in the 1980s, following the decision of the state to further expand the economy under economic reforms. It was the first time the PRC government had permitted this kind of enterprise to reappear since the early 1950s after it had completely transformed China's economy and successfully eliminated private enterprises. To justify the reform programme, and to argue for pragmatic economic policies, Deng Xiaoping openly proclaimed that it did not really matter whether it was a black cat (capitalism) or white cat (socialism), but that it was good as long as it caught the mice (economic development). He reiterated the ideal that 'socialism means eliminating poverty. Pauperism is not socialism, still less communism. The superiority of the socialist system lies in its ability to improve the people's material and cultural life' (Department of Research on Party Literature 1987: 37). Government policies were issued in 1987 which formally allowed private enterprises to exist and put them under state administration. The 1988 Provisional Regulation of the People's Republic of China on Privately-owned Businesses further removed the limit on employees of private enterprises. In 1988 also the legal status of private enterprises was written into the state's supreme law, the Constitution of the People's Republic of China. In China, 'private enterprise' is now a special legal concept, meaning a privately owned profit-making economic organization, employing eight or more people.

Private enterprises in China received further support when the Rules for Implementation of the Provisional Regulation on Privately-owned Businesses of the People's Republic of China were promulgated by the State Administration of Industry and Commerce of China in 1989. At the same time, Procedures for Registration of Privately-owned Business were set up.

The status of the private enterprise in China was given further recognition when the resolution of the Central Committee of the Communist Party of China (CPC) concerning the establishment of a socialist market economy received approval at the Third Plenary Session of the Fourteenth CPC Central Committee on 14 November 1993. Private enterprises are now assured equality of opportunity and policy in competition with state-owned enterprises by the Chinese government. Under the existing regulations, they are entitled to apply for bank loans; to use registered trademarks to the stipulated extent; to make decisions as to the running of the business; to decide on the organizational structure of the enterprise and the hiring and firing of personnel, with no limit on the number of working staff; to determine the wage system and division of profit; to set the standards for prices of products and services; and to sign contracts, apply for patents and register trademarks. By the end of 1989, 90,000 private enterprises had been registered. By the end of 1992, the figure reached 140,000 and in 1993, it rose close to 240,000. In 1989, private enterprises employed 1.64 million workers; in 1992, this figure rose to 2.32 million; and in 1993 it was 3.73 million. Their registered capital in 1989 was RMB84 millions; in 1992, it was RMB2.21 billion; and in 1993, it was RMB6.81 billion (see Table 7.1).[3] In the 15 years between 1980 and 1995, the distribution between the public sector economy and the private sector economy in China changed from 99.5 per cent and 0.5 per cent respectively in 1980 to 80 per cent and 20 per cent respectively in 1995, with state-owned enterprises occupying 77.6 per cent of the public economy in 1980 and 42.8 per cent in 1995 (*Ming Pao* newspaper, 15 March 1996).

Beginning in the 1980s, state policies also allowed groups of four or more unemployed individuals to pool private capital to set up collective enterprises which were later termed cooperatives. These privately run collective enterprises are formally classified as publicly 'owned' in the effort to further stimulate the economy. Their 'public' status enabled entrepreneurs to bypass state restrictions and to enjoy public enterprise advantages such as lower taxes and easier access to bank loans. At the same time, many collective enterprises were also set up by local governments and administrations or by state-run companies. As pointed out by Wank (1995: 154–5), these enterprises to a great extent reflected an 'interest convergence' between officials and entrepreneurs and were systematically favoured by political bodies in every aspect of economic life. On the other hand, they did not have to carry the burden of the state sector. Thus, innovation in state policies also led to the rapid development of the collective sector in the Chinese economy, which now comprises three major components: the state, the collective and the private sectors. However, the actual number of private businesses in China today is probably much greater than what appears in official statistics and the reason for underestimation is that many cooperatives are counted as part of the collective rather than the private sector.[4]

146

Table 7.1 Development of private enterprises in China, 1989–93

Year	Units		Personnel		Registered capital		Output value		Retail value	
	Units	Growth in % (with last year)	People (in 10,000)	Growth in % (with last year)	Value (in RMB million)	Growth in % (with last year)	Value (in RMB million)	Growth in % (with last year)	Value (in RMB million)	Growth in % (with last year)
1989	90,581		164		84		97		34	
1990	98,141	8.35	170	3.66	95	13.10	122	25.77	43	26.47
1991	107,843	9.89	184	8.24	123	29.47	147	20.49	57	32.56
1992	139,633	29.48	232	29.09	221	79.67	205	39.46	91	59.65
1993	237,919	70.39	373	60.78	681	208.14	422	105.85	190	109.90
Average growth rates		27.30		22.81		68.47		44.27		15.15

Source: Statistical Data of the Bureau of The Administration of Industry and Commerce

Table 7.2 Year of commencement of private enterprises

	Before 1988	1988	1989	1990	1991	1992	Total
Units (%)	51.9	12.2	11.7	7.9	7.4	9.0	100.0

Source: Research Report on Private Entrepreneurs in the survey carried out by All-China Society of Private Economy

Table 7.3 Start-up capital of private enterprises

	Registered capital (in RMB 10,000)							
	Below 2	2–5	5–10	10–20	20–50	50–100	100 or above	Total
Units (%)	23.1	18.4	15.2	16.1	15.2	8.0	4.0	100.0

Source: as Table 7.2

CHINESE ENTREPRENEURS: THE SOCIAL CONTEXT

Capital and resources

The first national survey on privately owned businesses was conducted in China under the auspices of and coordinated by the All-China Society of Private Economy Research.[5] The survey reported that among the 1,440 private business respondents, 51.9 per cent of them had been in operation since 1988 (see Table 7.2). Their average life history up to the end of 1992 was 5.8 years, their median history being 5.1 years. Their median registered start-up capital was RMB52 thousand, with over 40 per cent having an initial registered capital of less than RMB50 thousand, and 4 per cent having over RMB one million as their start-up capital (see Table 7.3).

For the majority, accumulation from previous economic activity was one of the primary sources of the start-up capital. Loans from relatives and friends was the other important source. Resources pooling through forming partnerships was third, loans from banks and credit unions ranked fourth and fifth respectively. Only one-third of the businesses relied on the banks and credit cooperatives for financial assistance when setting up their businesses (see Table 7.4). This confirmed the importance of the earlier reform of the communes under the contract responsibility system in facilitating the accumulation of capital for re-investment in private enterprises. It also confirmed the observation made by many scholars that kinship connections and local loyalties are an important driving force behind both China's

148

Table 7.4 Sources of start-up capital of private enterprises (in RMB10,000)

	Inherited from family estate	*Accumulated from economic activities*	*Pooled from partners*	*Loans from relatives/ friends*	*Loans from banks*	*Loans from credit co-operatives*
Main source	7.8	45.3	12.1	16.2	5.5	5.2
Second source	1.8	16.6	11.0	22.3	8.3	5.5
Third source	2.1	6.5	1.6	10.0	6.5	5.0

	Loans from collective	*Loans from private*	*Overseas investment*	*Others*	*No answer*	*Total*
Main source	1.0	1.4	3.0	1.0	1.6	100.0
Second Source	1.6	3.4	1.7	0.8	27.0	100.0
Third Source	1.7	7.7	1.1	0.8	53.2	100.0

Source: as Table 7.2

economic transformation in general, and local development initiatives in particular (see e.g., Wong 1994; Johnson 1993).

Entrepreneurial activities

The survey also showed that the principal factors which affected the business choice of private entrepreneurs when setting up their business were market demand, personal skills and expertise, social connections, and state policy in order of priority. Social connections, although not the most important factor, were rated a very significant factor by many of the entrepreneurs surveyed (see Table 7.5). Their activities covered industry, commerce, construction, transportation, catering, service, technology consultancy, repair and maintenance. The highest concentration was in industry and commerce but the fastest growth in recent years has been in the tertiary or service sector.

The major cities where private enterprises have experienced the fastest growth in the recent two to three years are in the provinces such as Guangdong, Zhejiang, Shandong, Liaoning, Jiangsu and Fujian located in the eastern part of the country, in more or less that order of priority in terms of number of enterprises, number of employees and registered capital. The largest private enterprise covered by the survey employed 1,250 employees, had an annual net profit of RMB6,650 million and a business volume of RMB83,000 million. Also in 1993, there were a total of 76,000 private enterprises in the tertiary sector, representing a growth of 130 per cent on the previous year, as well as a growth from 30 per cent to 41 per cent in the total number of private enterprises.

149

Table 7.5 Factors considered in making business decisions

	Personal skills and expertise	Market demands	Social connections	State policy support	Others	No answer	Total
Most important	54.5	29.8	6.4	4.7	1.7	0.8	100.0
Second important	10.8	35.3	12.3	9.6	0.9	29.1	100.0
Least important	4.3	8.6	15.2	18.1	1.7	49.9	100.0

Source: as Table 7.2

Social characteristics

The survey indicated a distribution ratio of 900:100 between male and female entrepreneurs in the country. In the cities, it was 857:100; in the rural areas, it was 1463:100. As for age distribution, 43 per cent of the private entrepreneurs were found to be in the age group 35–45. Those in the age group 45–55 constituted the next largest group among the respondents, occupying 23.6 per cent. Those who were under 25 constituted the smallest group at only 1.6 per cent. The next smallest group was among those over 55 which took up 11.3 per cent. Those in the age range 25–35 made up about one-fifth of the total at 20.5 per cent (see Table 7.6).

The average age of the Chinese entrepreneur covered by the survey was 42.9 years old. Compared with statistics from the 1990 Population Census for the whole country, which showed an average age of 33.1 for the country's working population within the age range of 15 to 64, the profile of the Chinese private entrepreneurs revealed in the survey was on average 10 years older than the average age of the country's working population. The majority of them were entrepreneurs in their middle age; with those in the eastern part of the country showing a relatively younger age structure.[6] These

Table 7.6 Age of private entrepreneurs

Age	%
Below 25	1.6
25–35	20.5
35–45	43.0
45–55	23.6
55 or above	11.3
Total	100.0

Source: as Table 7.2

were also the areas which in recent years have experienced a faster rate of growth in private entrepreneurship.

In general, the educational level of the entrepreneurs surveyed was also relatively higher than that of the rest of the country's working population. Only 1 per cent of entrepreneurs were illiterate, but about 36.1 per cent had completed junior secondary school, 29 per cent had attained senior secondary or senior technical school, and 18.6 per cent had received special- ized secondary or college education. For the country's working population as a whole, the corresponding figures were 32.3 per cent, 9 per cent and 3.3 per cent only (see Table 7.7). Education level among entrepreneurs in the rural area was generally lower, with the majority at lower than junior middle level. On the whole, education level was higher among private entrepreneurs in the eastern part of the country, and among those who were younger in age. The age group with the highest education level was those aged between 25 and 35 years old. The trend seems to be that the younger the age of the private entrepreneurs, the higher the education level. These younger, better-educated private entrepreneurs also tend to concentrate in the tertiary sector in the eastern part of the country. All in all, it is not unreasonable to assume that Chinese private entrepreneurs are generally older in age and better educated than the average worker in China today.

Previous employment

Among the owners of private enterprises in the cities and towns, the survey found that 7.95 per cent of them had been cadres in charge of sections of government departments or state enterprises; 21.9 per cent had held super- visory positions in enterprises; 4.2 per cent had been village cadres.[7] As for occupational status, 25.2 per cent were manual workers; 22.1 per cent were cadres; 17.2 per cent were peasants; technicians and professionals took up 12.1 per cent; self-employed *getihu* occupied 9.2 per cent; military, service and other business personnel made up the rest. In the rural areas, peasants and cadres made up the majority of the owners of private enter- prises, occupying 53.5 per cent and 17 per cent respectively. Over 18 per cent of them had experience in supervisory positions in township enterprises and over 2 per cent of them had been cadres serving as section heads in state departments or state enterprises (see Table 7.8).

All in all, the survey findings seem to suggest that quite a sizable propor- tion of the private entrepreneurs in China had been cadres with experience as section heads of government departments or supervisors in state enter- prises. Technicians, professionals and self-employed *getihu* made up another significant proportion of the original occupation of the private entrepreneurs. Furthermore, the largest single group, 36.4 per cent, were previously employees of the state sector. The next largest group came from the collective sector in the cities (19.3 per cent). In the rural areas, half of the private

151

Table 7.7 Comparison between educational level of private entrepreneurs and those in employment within the general population (%)

	Illiterate	Primary	Junior secondary	Senior secondary	Senior technical	Specialized secondary	Polytechnic/ university	University undergraduate	Research students	Total
Private entrepreneurs being surveyed	1.0	9.9	36.1	26.3	2.7	6.9	11.7	4.9	0.6	100.0
Those in employment within the general population	16.9	37.8	32.3	9.0		2.1	1.2	0.7		100.0

Source: as Table 7.2

Table 7.8 Occupational distribution of private entrepreneurs before setting up their business (%)

	Professional /technician	Cadre at different management levels	Manual worker	Business/ services	Military forces	Peasant	Self-employed getihu	Others	Total
Private entrepreneurs in cities and towns	12.1	22.1	25.2	7.6	1.2	17.2	9.2	5.5	100.0
Private entrepreneurs in rural area	4.1	17.0	11.6	2.7	0.7	53.5	6.1	4.1	100.0

Source: as Table 7.2

entrepreneurs came from rural households and village collectives. Only 3.2 per cent of the entrepreneurs in the cities and only 2 per cent in the rural areas were unemployed before they set up their private enterprises. In the cities, entrepreneurs who came from the private sector accounted for 9.5 per cent; in the rural areas they accounted for 6.8 per cent.

Motivation for private entrepreneurship

For most entrepreneurs who left their original occupation to set up their own private enterprises, the main reason given was that the original 'danwei' (work unit) was unable to allow them to fully develop their potential (56.8 per cent). This reason was particularly pronounced among those who came from the state-owned enterprises (74 per cent). For those who came from the non-state owned sector or who were peasants or who had no jobs, the aim to secure stable employment was the more important reason, their percentage being 43.8 per cent and 66 per cent respectively (see Table 7.9). The majority of them resigned from their jobs to become private entrepreneurs. Only a small percentage were retirees or took early retirement to leave their original employment. Autonomy and wealth for self-development were the primary motivating factors for private entrepreneurship.

Social network

For urban entrepreneurs, the survey found that around 35 per cent came from a family where the father was a peasant. Cadre constituted the second largest category; manual worker took up 17.4 per cent; technician and professional 9.4 per cent; self-employed *getihu* 3.1 per cent. For rural entrepreneurs, 68.9 per cent came from a family where the father was a peasant. Cadre and manual worker made up the second largest categories, each being 7.9 per cent (see Table 7.10). Regarding the occupational distribution of the spouses of the private entrepreneurs, cadre constituted the highest percentage (44.1 per cent for both sexes), followed by manual worker (32.7 per cent), and self-employed *getihu* (30 per cent) (see Table 7.11). In so far as the occupational distribution of children was concerned, cadre (23.9 per cent), technician and professional (18.9 per cent), manual worker (15.8 per cent) and self-employed *getihu* (11.8 per cent) constituted the major categories for those in the cities. In the rural areas, the major categories were peasant (24 per cent), manual worker (18.3 per cent), cadre and self-employed *getihu*, each of which took up 15.5 per cent of the total. (see Table 7.12). For close relatives, 37.9 per cent of the urban entrepreneurs had close relatives who were cadres whereas for rural entrepreneurs, the figure was 31.2 per cent. Peasant was the second largest category, the distribution for urban and rural being 16.5 per cent and 49.6 per cent respectively (see Table 7.13). A large proportion of the friends they associated with were

153

Table 7.9 Motivation for setting up private enterprises (%)

	No opportunities for self-development in original work unit	Earn more money	Seek a stable job	Poor relationship with their original work unit leader	Total
Head count (%)	56.8	19.9	18.0	5.3	100.0
State-owned enterprises	74.0	16.6	3.9	5.5	100.0
Township collective enterprises	58.4	25.9	10.7	5.1	100.0
Rural collective enterprises	48.9	20.5	23.9	6.8	100.0
Private enterprises	23.8	27.5	43.8	5.0	100.0
Unemployed peasants	21.8	10.9	66.0	1.7	100.0

Source: as Table 7.2

Table 7.10 Occupational distribution of the fathers of private entrepreneurs (%)

	Professional technician	Cadre at different management levels	Manual worker	Business services	Military forces	Peasant	Self-employed getihu	Others	Total
Entrepreneurs in cities and towns	9.4	19.4	17.4	10.1	1.6	36.2	3.1	3.8	100.0
Entrepreneurs in rural areas	3.3	7.9	7.9	6.0	2.6	68.9	2.0	1.3	100.0

Source: as Table 7.2

Table 7.11 Occupational distribution of the spouses of private entrepreneurs (%)

	Professional technician	Cadre at different management levels	Manual worker	Business services	Military forces	Peasant	Self-employed getihu	Others	Total
Wives of entrepreneurs	7.0	17.0	20.0	9.6	0.1	18.9	13.1	14.2	100.0
Husband of entrepreneurs	14.4	27.1	12.7	4.2	0.0	11.9	16.9	12.7	100.0
Spouse of entrepreneurs in cities and towns	8.2	18.8	20.1	10.0	0.1	14.3	14.2	14.3	100.0
Spouse of entrepreneurs in rural areas	3.6	10.1	13.7	2.9	0.0	49.6	7.2	12.9	100.0

Source: as Table 7.2

Table 7.12 Occupational distribution of the children of private entrepreneurs (%)

	Professional technician	Cadre at different management levels	Manual worker	Business services	Military forces	Peasant	Self-employed getihu	Others	Total
Children of entrepreneurs in cities and towns	18.9	23.9	15.8	9.3	3.2	10.3	11.8	6.7	100.0
Children of entrepreneurs in rural areas	8.5	15.5	18.3	1.4	1.4	24.0	15.5	15.5	100.0

Source: as Table 7.2

Table 7.13 Occupational distribution of relatives and friends of entrepreneurs (%)

	Professional /technician	Cadre at different management levels	Manual worker	Business/ services	Military forces	Peasant	Self-employed getihu	Others	Total
Relatives of entrepreneurs in cities and towns	13.2	37.9	11.5	2.8	8.3	16.5	7.1	2.8	100.0
Relatives of entrepreneurs in rural areas	6.4	31.2	7.2	1.6	0.8	49.6	3.2	0.0	100.0
Friends of entrepreneurs in cities and towns	17.5	42.4	8.9	9.8	1.4	7.9	9.4	2.9	100.0
Friends of entrepreneurs in rural areas	12.9	39.4	3.0	6.1	0.8	28.8	6.8	2.3	100.0

Source: as Table 7.2

also reported to be cadres, the percentages being 42.2 per cent and 39.4 per cent respectively for urban and rural. Technician and professional were the second largest category (17.5 per cent) in the former case, and in the latter case, it was peasant (28.8 per cent) which ranked second.

It seems therefore that cadres and technicians provide the largest source of entrepreneurship in China nowadays. In the cities, the percentage was as high as one-third and in the rural areas, it was one-fifth of the total. The other important sources in the cities were manual workers, business and service personnel. Peasants are another important source of private entrepreneurs in China, forming as high as close to 50 per cent of the total in the rural areas. This could be a direct consequence of the success of the implementation of the household responsibility contract system in the village communes at the beginning of the economic reform, resulting in higher productivity, improved income, increased savings among the peasants and thus increased availability of capital for re-investment in the establishment of new enterprises. The proportion of joint spouse ownership of private enterprises is not high among those being surveyed. Furthermore, both in the cities and in the villages, cadres constituted an important part of the social network of the private entrepreneurs, with approximately half of them working in government departments and the other half in the management of state enterprises. Such a social network was the result of the deliberate and conscious cultivation of the private entrepreneurs. It reflects also the extent to which the development of private enterprises in China today is determined by the tripartite relationship and interaction between the state, the public enterprises and the private enterprises. The demand for and the emphasis on technical expertise and management skills in the private enterprises explain why technical experts and professionals form the second most important set of social relationships within the social network of the private entrepreneurs.

Private entrepreneurs in China are active 'socialists' with a wide social network and extensive social experience, ample social knowledge and alertness and a highly pragmatic and this-worldly outlook. Much of their activities and efforts have evolved around the expansion and consolidation of their social network and their personal ties with those in authority. This is not at all surprising given the particular economic contexts and the structural factors which shape Chinese entrepreneurship. These include a highly vulnerable social status, anxiety about unpredictable state policies and the predominant economic opportunities in manufacturing processing, which profits from a highly versatile and adaptable subcontracting network. It is therefore important that entrepreneurs are able to form business networks and subcontracting systems to enhance flexibility and to coordinate production. They have to maintain close kinship and regional ties, particularistic relationships and social connections for economic use to raise funds, to acquire industrial know-how, to gain access to supply of raw materials and to secure an abundant and reliable supply of cheap labour. It is no coincidence that many of these private entrepreneurs had been cadres with experience either as section heads in government departments or managers in state enterprises, and that they are relatively well educated, technically strong, and well versed in the mode of operation of the state bureaucracy.

External and internal linkages

A family-based, corporate management structure seems to be the prevalent pattern among the private enterprises in China. The family, interpreted in a broad sense, is not only an important source of financial capital for Chinese entrepreneurship; it is also an important source of human capital, in terms of both labour supply and management function. In the sample surveyed, about half of the employees at management level of private enterprises found their way there through family or blood ties, personal connections, or particularistic relations based on land or locality. Those who got the job through open recruitment made up about 46.6 per cent (see Table 7.14). For enterprise employees, open recruitment from society was rated by about 48.5 per cent as the primary source. In the rural private enterprises, about 36.5 per cent of the employees were in one way or another related to the owners; 14.4 per cent were the owners' neighbours or friends. In the urban enterprises covered by the survey, these two categories constituted one-third of the employees. In other studies, such as the study of Bin Sha in the western district of Chengdu city conducted by Ole Bruun (1995: 189), it was reported that the recruitment of labour in private businesses did not create a new open job market in the area but largely followed the extension of kinship relations and private networks, *'guanxi'* (personal connections).

At the same time, the survey also found that in over one-third of cases, private enterprises had to make use of non-market channels and transactions to obtain the supply of raw materials required for their businesses. These included personal connections and using all kinds of strategies and connections to lubricate the system of supply. The important role played by social

Table 7.14 Channels for management personnel to join private enterprises (%)

Channels	Personal relationship with the owner or investor friends of		Introduced by relatives/ friends of owners	Open recruitment	Others	Total
	Related through lineage	Related through marriage				
Management personnel (%)	19.2	10.2	15.7	46.6	8.3	100.0

Source: as Table 7.2

networks and personal relations has been highly instrumental to China's entrepreneurs during the present stage of transition from a command economy to a socialist market economy where the market is neither completely free nor visible (see Table 7.15).

Maintaining good local relations is another important concern for the private entrepreneur who wishes to gain status, acceptance and community support. Such relations are fostered through donations to various kinds of community building projects, such as roads and bridges, water and electricity installation, schools and welfare relief for the poor. The survey revealed that about 62 per cent of the private entrepreneurs had been involved in making such kinds of donations, the median donation was around RMB 11 thousand annually. Among the reasons given for the donations, contribution to society was rated by 78.8 per cent as the primary factor; gratitude to the state was second most important (6.2 per cent); and assistance to the local community was third (4.5 per cent) (see Table 7.16).

CHINESE ENTREPRENEURSHIP: THE CULTURAL CONTEXT

The recent phenomenal economic growth achieved by the Chinese population in Taiwan and Hong Kong and by overseas Chinese in various parts of the world has led many researchers to suggest that there is an entrepreneurial ethic shared by the Chinese which underlies Chinese economic culture and behaviour (Wong 1994). It is an ethic that places high value on running one's own business and therefore constitutes an important driving force behind the spectacular growth and economic success of Taiwan, Hong Kong and the overseas Chinese communities.

As a set of cultural values and normative orientations, Chinese entrepreneurship provides the motivation for starting one's business and self-employment, and promotes an orientation towards autonomy and proprietorship. It is identified by many scholars to be closely related to the ethical teaching and norms of Low Confucianism (Wang 1988) or Popular Confucianism (Wong 1994) in the Chinese culture. This is the secularized version of Confucianism – the 'Confucian derived values in the lives of ordinary people' (Berger 1988), the Confucian ethic operative in the secular world of everyday life among the general populace, or the Confucian 'habits of the heart' (Tu 1989a: 15). It has been viewed by many researchers as the spiritual or ideological source of inspiration or impetus for successful indigenous transformation to capitalist development in the initial state of East Asian modernization. (Wong 1994; Wang 1988; Berger 1988; Tu 1989a). It is an ethic characterized by first, a generally this-worldly humanism, including a positive and non-fatalistic attitude towards the affairs of the world; belief in our natural equality and intrinsic value; and acceptance of and receptiveness toward the notions of meritocracy and mobility. Second,

Table 7.15 Main channels for the purchase of raw materials and goods by private enterprises

		Through state plan	Through market	Through personal relationships	Through all kinds of connections and influences	Total
Units (%)		1.8	63.4	17.3	17.5	100.0
By regions:	Eastern	1.3	63.2	19.3	16.1	100.0
	Central	3.2	64.4	9.9	22.5	100.0
	Western	2.1	63.3	18.1	16.5	100.0
By business:	Industry	1.7	61.7	19.3	17.3	100.0
	Construction	2.9	60.0	11.4	25.7	100.0
	Transportation	4.0	64.0	8.0	24.0	100.0
	Business	1.6	59.8	19.3	19.3	100.0
	Catering	1.1	83.9	6.9	8.0	100.0
	Services	7.8	62.5	10.9	18.8	100.0
	Repair	0.0	63.4	22.0	14.6	100.0
	Consultancy	0.0	72.0	10.0	18.0	100.0
	Others	1.6	68.8	12.5	17.2	100.0

Source: as Table 7.2

Table 7.16 Reasons for donations by private enterprise (%)

	Contribute to society	Gratitude to state	Reciprocation to kin group	Promote community relationships	Raise prestige	As a kind of levy	Others
Primary	78.8	6.2	4.5	3.3	3.1	3.0	1.1
Secondary	7.6	36.5	16.7	14.5	17.9	5.4	1.5
Tertiary	6.0	10.9	20.5	16.7	27.1	17.8	1.0
Total	92.4	53.6	41.7	34.5	48.1	26.2	3.5

Source: as Table 7.2

it supports a conception of the self as being socially embedded and being partly or largely constituted by relations and obligations. It has a central belief in human connectedness and an overriding concern for the family based upon a relational ethic. Third, it emphasizes duty consciousness, respect for authority and public accountability of authority; and acceptance of the political order as a moral community (Tu 1989b: 16). These values of natural equality, meritocracy, human connectedness and reciprocity have been dominant in structuring society and shaping social interaction in Chinese society. At the same time, these values are particularly supportive of the development of entrepreneurship in China. According to Wong, they underpin the strong desire for autonomy and self-reliance in matters relating to work and economic activities. In fact, Wong (1994) has argued that until the 1980s, Chinese entrepreneurship thrived in 'external China' where risk-takers abound in Hong Kong, Taiwan and other overseas Chinese communities, seeking profit and autonomy. Their collective strength was derived from their private initiative. Within the People's Republic of China itself, entrepreneurship had hitherto been both restrictive and diffused under the practice of central planning and control. However, Wong argued that economic reforms in the PRC in the late 1970s altered the situation drastically as a consequence of which there was a rapid intermingling of the two patterns of entrepreneurship in external China and the PRC. Wong suggested that what had made this intermingling possible was in part due to the shared entrepreneurial ethic embedded in the Chinese culture of the 'little dragons' and mainland China (Wong 1994). Under the influence of these value orientations, the development of entrepreneurship in China can be characterized by *pragmatism, collectivism, moralism* and *familism*.

Pragmatism

As explained earlier, popular Confucianism is characterized by its pragmatism and a this-worldly humanism. Confucians hold that people are born equal although by practice they can become very different. Notwithstanding the natural equality thesis, Confucianism emphasizes the virtues of bettering oneself and the reward of social advancement by individual efforts. Although we possess common attributes at birth, social inequalities are inevitable because some people can better utilize their potential through their own efforts. Self-development and self-advancement are the primary responsibilities of oneself. Such an ethos provides an important moral grounding for the revitalization in socialist China of private entrepreneurial activities. This is borne out in the survey findings which showed that it was the lack of opportunity to develop one's potential which provided the major impetus to resign from the Iron Rice Bowl and the One Big Pot of state enterprises to initiate entrepreneurial ventures. In other words, it was the desire to search for opportunities for self-development which propelled these individuals to become entrepreneurs. The

164

largest source of entrepreneurs came from those employed in the state sector; not the unemployed, or the retirees, or recent school leavers. Business ownership and self-employment were the means to free themselves from the constraints of bureaucratic subjugation and state control. They provide an alternative channel for social advancement other than cadrefication. Autonomy and wealth were closely intertwined and provided the incentive to break out from the strait-jacket of the state industrial bureaucracy. As Wong pointed out (1994: 130), this craving for autonomy and wealth is often associated with the tradition of the 'small man' and the marketplace in Popular Confucianism which extols the virtues of individual daring and nonconformity. It is counterposed to the tradition of the gentleman and High Confucianism which stresses the quest for personal cultivation and moral order. It represents the subculture of non-conformity and innovative deviance. But it is non-conformity and innovative deviance tempered by pragmatism – a pragmatism kept alive by Deng Xiaoping's famous motto of 'No matter whether the cat is black or white, it is good as long as it catches mice.' The pragmatic and innovative outlook of the Chinese entrepreneurs also facilitated the assimilation of foreign technology, the synthesis of foreign investment, and an overall orientation towards the maintenance of a patron–client relation between owners of private enterprises and state cadres and government officials, notwithstanding the urge to break out from the bureaucratic hierarchy. It has also helped to ease some of the tensions and conflicts engendered with the demands of authority.

Collectivism

Despite recent Chinese propaganda honouring individual entrepreneurs, Chinese thinking and practice has always been somewhat collective. Chinese entrepreneurship is less propelled by a doctrine of 'ethical egoism' (Lukes 1973: 99) than by a doctrine of 'ethical collectivism' (Ware 1992: 128). The doctrine of ethical egoism is an ethic of self-interest according to which 'the sole moral object of the individual's action is his own benefit' (Lukes, ibid.); the pursuit of the individual's self-interest is therefore a moral obligation. Ethical collectivism is the attribution of interests to groups or collectives. In ethical collectivism, attention is being given to the benefits for the family, group or society. Ware has argued that ethical collectivism is a way of thinking that has been thoroughly Chinese since the time of Confucius. As he explains, Chinese philosophy is pervaded by ideas of the family and the society. In Chinese philosophy, the individual is sustained in the group to which he or she belongs, at least the family, the neighbourhood, the village and the society. Private entrepreneurship was and still is a very much collective, group or familial effort in China as evidenced by the family-based or lineage-based corporate management structure, the reliance on kinship or lineage groups and social networks for the factors of production, and the emphasis on the harmonization of personal interests and social utility as the ideal of entrepreneurship in all official documents and public publications. To some extent, it could be said that entrepreneurial development and private enterprises in China are propelled by a strong sense of identity with the family kinship group, or the locality of origin, as an interest group. In general the basis of loyalty are the much smaller, limited units of collectivity rather than the nation state itself. The achievement motive was driven and sustained by a kind of 'family egoism' or community/regional self-interest.

Graham Johnson (1993) has analysed the success story of the Pearl River Delta in Guangdong province showing how rapid economic growth and transformation were made possible partly by the Delta's ability to mobilize the extensive links it possessed with its expatriate kinsmen who live in Hong Kong, Macao and overseas. From the mid-nineteenth century onwards, the Delta has long been an area of out-migration and has provided the greatest majority of Americans and Canadians of Chinese origin. In the 1980s, the entrepreneurial skills and capital of these emigrants were actively sought to provide the motor of development of many of the private enterprises in China.

However, the major transformation in the rural sector was not in agriculture. Rapid economic growth occurred as the rural sector shifted to non-agriculture production. The capacities of peasant households to create strategies to meet changing economic and political opportunities were determined by a set of internal and external factors which Johnson discussed in his study (Johnson 1993: 121). Internally, the size of household, in particular the number of adults, the resources it has, e.g. amount of land available, capital, social (class) status and the assumption of administrative or political roles, as cadre or party member, by household members, are all important in determining the ability of a household to respond to the changing economic and social options. Externally, political leadership available in the locality, and the ability of leaders to establish connections and create entrepreneurial opportunities are critical factors for economic diversification. At the same time, kinsmen have become important sources of investment and entrepreneurial skills. Hence, the presence or absence of kinsmen outside of the village and the broad communities that villages form have been decisive for the development process and strategies adopted.

Today many of the village-run enterprises in the Delta reflect the extensive involvement of Hong Kong-based expatriates in the village economy. For example, in Fucheng, Johnson's study showed that there is often a much greater proportion of the indigenous labour engaged in enterprises, the bulk of which are run by the village as collective units. They are either lineage-based villages or villages characterized by intense local loyalty. This led Johnson to conclude that the consequence of local economic transformation is a strengthening of the corporate kinship structures of the Delta. Kinship

166

connections and local loyalties have become a central part of local development initiatives while community led responses have succeeded in warding off the threat from global forces of disruption of the delicate social fabric of rural areas. In the Pearl River Delta region, 'The patrilineally structured rural household has not merely maintained its corporate character, but has also used its intrinsic flexibility to meet new possibilities in the 1980s' (Johnson 1993: 119). At the same time, as Johnson observed, 'it is the loyalty to ancestral points of origin on the part of expatriates that calls forth a willingness on the part of overseas Chinese, even after decades abroad, to donate to homeland projects.' (127) It is therefore not surprising that the involvement of expatriate Chinese in local economic development has also resulted in the revival of lineage in the region (131). Thus local history and local tradition, economic advances and upward mobility are mutually complementary and reinforcing forces of modernization in China's rapidly changing social and economic realities. The Pearl River Delta example shows how dramatic economic developments have been in harmony with a local cultural base that is firmly rooted in kinship. It confirms Helen Siu's observation that throughout Chinese history, 'lineage membership was at once proof of cultural identity and a shrewd strategy for strengths in numbers for social mobility and political legitimacy' (1992: 5).

Moralism

Chinese entrepreneurship, like the market, is a creation of the state in China. Often state officials and political leaders urged support for Chinese entrepreneurs on grounds of their economic and social utility as well as their contribution to nation-building through entrepreneurial activities and wealth creation. In many instances, they were also portrayed as exemplars of China's long-standing traditional values of social responsibility, philanthropy, reciprocation to society and deference to authority. In a series of twenty-seven biographies of distinguished private entrepreneurs compiled in their honour by the All-China Society of Private Economy Research published in 1993 under the aegis of the All-China Federation of Industry and Commerce, the virtuous character and moral behaviours of the entrepreneurs were portrayed almost as a criterion or a standard of Chinese entrepreneurship. They were full of praises for the generous donations to local community development projects and to nation-wide infrastructure building, to poverty relief, to care and honouring of the elderly, to welfare of the handicapped and to other general charity work. The entrepreneurs' concern for the collective interests of the locality or community to which they belonged constituted an important motif in almost all their success stories, and came across almost as a requisite moral quality of private entrepreneurs in China. Other traditional values that were glorified in the personal success stories of the entrepreneurs were diligence, self-discipline, frugality and self-reliance. In each of the twenty-seven accounts, details were given regarding the increasing amount of tax they were paying to the state authority each year to reciprocate the state and society for the wealth-creating opportunities from which they had benefited. Successful private entrepreneurs were portrayed as people of high moral standards and virtues. Thus, despite the dramatic shift to meritocracy under economic reform that supports occupational selection according to professional or intellectual ability rather than political ideology, a person's moral righteousness is reaffirmed in China today as a criterion of social advancement under a system of 'virtuocracy'. The Chinese seem to be still devoted to a form of moral economy in which economic activity must be bound to the principle of collective redistribution, although redistribution does not necessarily mean economic equality. The legitimacy of economic success still depends on social status and moral righteousness and not the opposite. In almost all official and semi-official reports and publications, entrepreneurs were characterized as honest and modest businessmen who attained economic success through diligence and self-discipline. Far from being self-interested egoistic individualists, they were glorified as people who were altruistic and cared about the public interest, infused with a strong sense of social responsibility, community solidarity and a deep regard for the collective good. (See for example issues no. 3, 5, 7, 9 and 12 of the bi-weekly newsletter published between February to April 1993 by the Zhongshan Self-employed Labourers Association, *Zhongshan Geti Laodongzhe Xiehui*.) As has been pointed out in the national survey, 'To contribute to society' was the primary reason given by 78.8 per cent of the private entrepreneurs for their donations to local charity and other development projects.

Familism

Chinese entrepreneurship is also characterized by an ethos of entrepreneurial familism which emphasizes corporate family interest and involves the family as the basic unit of economic competition. At the same time, the Chinese have always emphasized personal resources and claims of particularistic relationships over state aid and impersonal relationships where assistance or support is called for. Notwithstanding that in Chinese philosophy superiors have certain responsibilities for looking after the needs of the people, there is a lack of an instrumental conception of the state as the guardian of individual interests among the Chinese. There is no conception of a contractual relation between the people and the state, nor is there any notion of the state as the ultimate insurer or guarantor of the welfare of its citizens. Reciprocal duties and obligations, family ties and traditional values still form the basis of justified moral claims to assistance in times of need and distress in modern China under socialism. Despite serious assaults on the family during the Great Leap Forward and the Cultural Revolution, studies have shown the persistence of norms of filial piety and economic reciprocity between parents and children (see e.g., Goldstein and Ku 1993; Chu and Ju 1993). In reciprocation for loyalty to the family, the family provides its members with the impetus to innovate and take risks. It is not surprising that large numbers of private entrepreneurs emerged with initial capital provided by family members and relatives.

Ole Bruun's study of Bin Shen in Chengdu, Sichuan, during parts of 1987, 1988, 1989 and 1991, is a good illustration of how new market opportunities have provided the Chinese household further impetus to aggregate its individual members' social and economic capital to optimize resources under a strong sense of family corporatist interest for collective gain (1995). His study revealed that many households, in order to maintain the status and security of the household, frequently started business with only one household member registered, the wife or an employed son. Such a strategy of having one household member placed in a secure state job, particularly the household head, is certainly quite a common practice in China nowadays. The strategy successfully grants 'social esteem to the entire household', enables 'households to benefit from the opportunities offered by private business for increasing material welfare and also for some more freedom, and to retain at the same time the basic services, security and social respectability provided by official employment' (Bruun 1995: 101).

CHINESE ENTREPRENEURSHIP: THE STRUCTURAL CONTEXT

The positive role played by parts of the Chinese tradition in facilitating economic development has received much attention among scholars who argue that the emergence of entrepreneurship as a type of new and creative behaviour is grounded in traditional and conservative values. At the same time, other scholars have drawn attention to the embeddedness of economic actions and argued for the need to relate the economic actions of the entrepreneurs to their structural positions as well as to the economic context wherein their actions are undertaken. They argue that Chinese entrepreneurship is a good illustration of the significance of structural positions as well as social context in the structuring of economic action. They further point out that 'While recognizing the autonomy of culture, the ways culture constitutes our strategies of actions are by no means random. We need to identify the structural and contextual factors which are shaping the economic concerns of the actors' (Lui 1994 and Wong 1994: 11).

Data derived from the national survey show that those who became private entrepreneurs were those who possessed a particular set of resources which made them competitive in the partially reformed economy. As we saw earlier, in 1993, the average age of the entrepreneurs in China was 10 years older than the average age of the working population. The majority were in their

169

middle age. While they were older than the national average, they were also better educated. The older age structure and higher education attainment of the entrepreneurs suggest the importance of social experience and professional knowledge or technical know-how as attributes in the self-recruitment process of entrepreneurship in China at the present stage of development.

The desire for entrepreneurship, however, is not entirely related to the level of education of prospective entrepreneurs. As pointed out by one commentator, 'To have good connections in the bureaucratic fields and to come from a family with good face (i.e. good reputation)' (Rocca 1994: 16.4) also constitute important factors in economic decisions and actions regarding entrepreneurship in China. Social contacts with those in the same business, social connections with those in power and authority in the government bureaucracy and social recognition by the local community are essential to the survival of Chinese entrepreneurs. They have to possess the necessary personal resources to build intricate webs of personalized business relations. Such a particularistic orientation puts an exceptional emphasis on *guanxi* (personal connections). As explained by a Chinese sociologist, *guanxi* as a socio-cultural concept is 'deeply embedded in Confucian social theory and has its own logic in forming and in constituting the social structure of Chinese society' (A.Y. King 1991: 79). One strategy is to devote much of their energies to the cultivation of personal connections with local public units. Another is to hire recently retired officials to work in private firms. During their long service, these officials have accumulated strong personal ties with the bureaucracy, which are still fresh. These sponsoring public units of local private enterprises are often called 'popo' or 'mother-in-law'.

Private entrepreneurs in China are obviously a very varied group of people in terms of their social background, their social network and their social resources. Their social position and social status are highly critical in determining their autonomy, wealth and success in their entrepreneurship. For the sake of analysis, we might attempt to divide the emerging private entrepreneurs in China into three main categories on the basis of their wealth, standing and autonomy. These three categories are marginal entrepreneurs, corporatist entrepreneurs and elitist entrepreneurs.

Marginal entrepreneurs

The first category of entrepreneurs were largely migrants or those with weak social ties or social roots. They were individuals who were able to take advantage of the country's rapid urbanization and more open policy on internal migration to improve their material well-being. They tended to be rootless individuals who did not have a foothold in danwei which provided secure employment. They were a varied group including surplus village labour, youths seeking occupational openings, school leavers, ex-state employees, servicemen and technicians, etc. Some of them might have worked as a *getihu* before. They were the direct products of an economic reform which reduced the scope of state planning and permitted individual business activities to flourish. Their main activities tended to be in trade and services, which were relatively less demanding in terms of start-off capital and technological know-how, with only a small proportion in industrial production. They were mostly weak in educational and technical expertise but were seeking occupational openings or a means of livelihood. As pointed out by one commentator, these migrant entrepreneurs were tolerated because they were involved in technical services (repair, tailoring, plumbing, painting, etc.) and commerce (clothing, restaurants, etc.) which met the aspirations of the urban population for sharp improvement in daily life; these two sectors had been grossly neglected by the authorities since 1949 (Rocca 1994). They might have acquired their capital and entrepreneurial opportunities through the assistance of family members and relatives, but very often they were socially rootless, isolated and vulnerable. They constitute a type of transitory entrepreneurship. Their rootlessness and lack of social status and community ties have put them at a distinct disadvantage when competing with the corporatist entrepreneurs and the elitist entrepreneurs in China's evolving market economy. They were the most insecure, the least protected and frequent victims of bureaucratic harassment. Even those who were economically successful often remained a disparaged sector of 'wealth without social standing'. In a sense, many of them represented the traditional spirit of classic entrepreneurs: breaking out to do independently what they had done for someone else, using their own skills and talents. In many ways, they were also the traditional non-confromists, the real risk-takers.

Corporatist entrepreneurs

Corporatist entrepreneurs were those who engaged in a kind of lineage-based or family-based entrepreneurship. They were often head of a kinship or family group in the cities or were once leaders in charge of collective enterprises in the rural communities, or village leaders of traditional lineage. They might have come from a background of either manual workers or peasants. In particular, peasant entrepreneurs, with collective backing from kinsmen and fellow villagers, were one of the main sources of corporatist entrepreneurs who became the thriving capitalist entrepreneurs under socialism. They were found in the countryside for example, in Guangdong and Fujian, where there was often already a long history and a high concentration of lineage functioning as corporate groups. When economic reform was introduced, many of these kin groups were revived in support of industrial development. The experience of these traditional leaders in management and business provided support for launching a private entrepreneurial career. Their close kinship or regional ties provided the basis for forming the necessary industrial subcontracting networks. They were motivated to seek economic betterment and to foster solidarity through striving for autonomy and competing for wealth and status on a collective basis, with the huge pool of rural residents providing an abundant and reliable supply of cheap labour. Many of them also possessed close links with expatriate overseas Chinese which enabled them to tap overseas capital and skills for the setting up of these local collective enterprises. Family-centred patterns form the roots of many of these new developments. As Johnson observers (1993), analogues between the group characteristics of modern enterprises and both family and rural community organizational traits in China are not uncommon. For example, concern for family and community means that individuals work hard in these coporate units to satisfy the expectations of the group. At the same time, these kinship-based or lineage-based groups can also make broad claims on their members without worrying about contractual agreements that require members to perform only specified tasks. In reciprocation, these corporatist entrepreneurs are not just working for their own private gain. They are also dedicated to the kin or lineage groups. All in all, corporatist entrepreneurs that had cultural roots firmly based upon traditional corporate structures of lineage, kinship or the family constituted an important economic force in China's modernization.

Elitist entrepreneurs

Elitist entrepreneurs were previously local bureaucrats or bureaucrats of administrative bureaux. They included the princelings – young relatives of high rank officials or party members, '*taizi dang*'. Generally speaking, they were relatively well educated, technically proficient or experienced in the management of enterprises or in trade and services, well groomed by the state and well connected with those in power and authority in the government bureaucracy. Nowadays, the Chinese economy is characterized by the coexistence of three main kinds of ownership (collective, private and state ownership) and by the gradual decrease of the proportion of state-owned enterprises in the industrial sector. But the absence of state control does not mean total freedom, and neither is the Chinese economy ruled mainly by the market. This is because most of the raw materials, most of the means of transport and most of the energy products are distributed along the bureaucratic networks and do not follow the principle of demand and supply. To procure necessary means of production, to transport products, to find customers and to obtain loans from the banks, enterprises must use informal connections inside bureaucratic fields. Most of the power over employment, finance, production, investment, and supply and demand surrendered by Beijing was intercepted by local governments and local administrations. Many private entrepreneurs were able to influence local politics through the power of money. At the same time, their social network and bureaucratic links allowed them privileged access to official thinking, information and raw materials. They are in many ways the economic elite in China today because of the bureaucratic entrepreneurship which they have developed and the influence they were able to command over the local bureaucrats and the official hierarchy through their wealth and activities.

CHINESE ENTREPRENEURSHIP:
THE STATE CONTEXT

China's present economic system is still far from being a market economy and the process of developing a market economy in China is very different from that in the Western experience. Unlike in the West, the idea of the socialist market economy was invented by the state and propelled and promoted by the state and its officials. In the West, the bourgeoisie and civil society were the main driving forces behind marketization and corresponding legal changes. But in late twentieth-century China, the state has been the dominant actor in the move towards the market economy. Nearly all the major steps in the post-1978 economic reform were initiated by policy instruments issued by the Party and the State. Thus it can be said that the state in China has been instrumental in establishing the market and market parameters. The establishment of a socialist market economy is the declared objective of the State as written in the constitution of the Communist Party of China in late 1992 and in the Constitution of the People's Republic of China itself in early 1993, following Deng Xiaoping's declaration that socialism does not equal the planned economy nor is the market economy intrinsically the meaning of capitalism.

Unlike the case in the planned economy, actors in the socialist market economy are believed to be autonomous subjects who enter into exchange relationships with one another, exercising their free will. The market therefore symbolizes or is the embodiment of freedom, autonomy, equality and democracy. But as pointed out earlier, China's present economic system is still far from being a market economy. The market which has been created so far is still largely neither free nor visible. Non-market channels and transactions still exist and are playing an important role in China's economic system.

China's private entrepreneurs are a symbol of modernity. They represent the new values of the reform era: freedom, innovation, wealth, equality of opportunity and autonomy. The market and entrepreneurial behaviour are seen as challenging and re-making the old tradition of China. But whether as marginal, corporatist or elitist entrepreneurs, there are no signs that China's private entrepreneurs are a potent democratizing force, or that their emergence has engendered any fundamental changes in the political order. Many *getihu* and private entrepreneurs have shown a strong interest in politics and sought government positions. They have tried to apply for Party membership, and some have been offered official posts, e.g. as city mayors and as members of the Chinese People's Political Consultative Conference.

But because of the CPC's firm intention to sustain its monopoly on power, most private entrepreneurs can only hope to gain some honorary positions in the CPC or in the People's Congress. Politics still dominates the economy through local bureaucrats. There is increased economic openness and social participation but no enhanced political autonomy. The Chinese government also openly declared in September 1995 that Party membership would not be granted to private entrepreneurs in the country (*Hong Kong Economic Journal*, 28 September 1995). This means that their political participation is limited to consultative political organizations and not decision-making political organizations. They are either too scattered and diverse, too conforming to traditional values or too intimately connected with the state apparatus or hierarchy to pose any real challenge to state authority, to contest power or to create fundamental political changes. Here one finds no contradictions between economic development and political conservatism. As the case of the Chinese entrepreneurs indicates, prosperity and development do not necessarily entail a full free market system and democracy.

CHINESE ENTREPRENEURS IN CONTEXT

China's experience of development raises questions about the applicability of much of the central thesis about the importance of 'civil society' in Western literature on modernization – in which an emerging autonomous society is attributed the potential for the creation of a new kind of democratic state. Equally being questioned is the crucial antagonism so often asserted between 'state' and 'society'. In the Chinese case, as pointed out by Bruun, 'modernization and development seem to have taken place alongside a strong continuity in fundamental ideologies, values and orientations among the social groups within the locality, all of whom seek to establish and utilize connections to the bureaucracy' (1995: 185). It is true that economic reform and the emergence of private entrepreneurship have weakened the socialist rank-order society, and brought about the coexistence of a market-based economic social order in society and an undemocratic, totalitarian polity. It is also clear that because of the reforms, there have arisen, or have been revived, a large variety of groups within Chinese society that are at least partially autonomous from the state, whether these be commercial associations, professional associations or clan associations. But at the same time, Chinese entrepreneurship also appears to have served to bind the individual closer to his family, group or lineage through its practice of a corporatist or familial entrepreneurship, rather than to liberate the individual totally from larger collectives.

Chinese entrepreneurship is a synthesis of new and traditional values. One of the most important driving forces behind the entrepreneurial decision is the desire to break away from the strait-jacket of state control and bureaucratic hierarchy. But at the same time, there is a strong orientation towards the maintenance of a patron–client relationship between owners of private enterprises and state cadres and government officials. The move towards a socialist market economy and the emergence of private entrepreneurship are to a large extent a response to the need to modernize to meet the challenge of globalization forces in order to be able to compete in the new world order and to preserve political stability via growth. But marketization has not led to a complete Westernization of the local culture nor has modernization resulted in a complete marginalization of traditional values in the Chinese experience of development.

On one level of interpretation, it could be argued that the development of the private economy, the emergence of private entrepreneurs and the spread of the market have created new values and ideologies, supporting new social space and institutional forms in many domains of public life in China. This has aroused much concern about the possible contradictions which may arise between these new ideas and practices on the one hand, and 'traditional' values, behaviours and institutions on the other hand. For example, the emphasis on equality and democracy brought about by economic development towards marketization and the increasing recognition of the values of autonomy and individual interests underlying privatization and the emergence of private entrepreneurs are potentially disruptive. These may all be seen as posing a challenge to the traditional value of the family, the collective orientation of the Chinese and the deeply entrenched norms and hierarchy of Chinese society. On a different level of interpretation, however, it can be also argued that 'traditional' values, institutions and orientations are in fact re-created and re-affirmed in present changes and current developments, not despite the new institutions, but because of them. As in the case of private entrepreneurs, Chinese traditional values are not only used to lend support and legitimacy to entrepreneurial activities, they are in turn further reinforced and re-affirmed by Chinese entrepreneurship under the socialist market economy. On this understanding, private entrepreneurs are cultural conformists. They are driven by traditional values and vindicated by them. The pursuit of private wealth and autonomy is thus made safe within the framework of traditional values and behaviours, instead of being opposed to them.

Chinese entrepreneurs are firmly embedded in social relationships and particularistic ties, unlike their Western counterparts. They are deeply rooted and firmly based on locality, kinship, lineage and tradition. They thrive on local loyalty, family solidarity and a symbiotic relationship with state bureaucracy. Contrary to the view of Western scholars such as Marion Levy (1949), Max Weber (1951) and Clark Kerr et al. (1960), the traditional Chinese family, although a highly particularistic structure, is not a major obstacle to industrialization or economic development. The Chinese family, although providing shelter and food for all its members, regardless of their individual contributions, has not diluted the individual incentive to work, save and invest. The Chinese 'sib' relationship, which in Weber's eyes was the embodiment of the strong force of traditionalism that blocked rationalism, has not weakened 'work discipline' nor thwarted the 'free market selection of labour'. Instead, the family has provided the main impetus for innovation and support for risk-taking in China's modernization and development process.

It is not our intention here to argue for a monocausal mode of economic development but to suggest that the determinants of economic growth and social development are inevitably complex, multiple and interconnected. As Berger has pointed out (1986: 5), modernity in the West began with individualism. This has led to an assumption that modernity is inevitably and intrinsically linked to individualism. Individualism in turn is conceived to be intrinsic to capitalist entrepreneurs, an important element of modernity in the West. The Chinese experience of capitalist development, whether in its socialist version within the People's Republic of China, or in its non-socialist version outside the People's Republic of China, such as in Hong Kong or Taiwan, suggests a non-individualist model of capitalist modernity. Here experience and strategies challenge the thesis that the linkage between modernity, capitalism and individualism is inevitable and intrinsic. It also reopens the questions about the relation of modern capitalism and culture which is at the heart of many current debates in globalization theories.

China's experience has confirmed the positive role of the Chinese tradition in facilitating economic development. It is a tradition with a cultural base firmly rooted in family and kinship. But culture does not inform or determine who should launch into an entrepreneurial career. Chinese entrepreneurship is a good illustration of the significance of structural position as well as social context in the structuring of economic actors. The Chinese experience fully illustrates the contradictory and competitive drives and forces which underlie the actions and choices of various economic actors. These include the conflicting and contradictory forces of market and plan, autonomy and community, local loyalty and national identity, traditional values and global culture. The rise of the market and the emergence of private entrepreneurs have not completely undermined traditional networks nor destroyed social ties and cohesion in China. Neither are market forces certainly or completely released from political constraint. Creation of the socialist market economy in China has not brought about the liberation of a new social class of private entrepreneurs from traditional social ties and cultural norms, nor the full independence of the merchant class from state intervention and control. Instead, it has strengthened the symbiotic relationship between merchants and the official class, and the greater interpenetration between political and economic elites in the country. The emergence of private entrepreneurship in China illustrates the contradictory character of social change and economic development which have to be understood in terms of their historicity and specificity, rather than merely as an inevitable outcome of the unstoppable forces of global capitalism.

ACKNOWLEDGEMENT

The authors wish to thank Professors Paul Wilding, Glenn Drover and Graham Johnson for their comments on earlier drafts of this chapter.

NOTES

1 In employment terms, *getihu* and private enterprises in urban China employed 15.6 million employees at the end of 1994. They made up 67.2% of the total numbers of participants employed in the country's different economic ownership systems which include the state-owned and the collectively owned systems (China Statistical Publishing House 1995, Table 4-2: 84–85).

2 The rural contract responsibility system was initiated in the 1950s (the system of 'contract household production' or in Chinese *baochan daohu*) and revitalized in the late 1970s. The main purpose of this system was to separate economic organization and activities from the political system embedded in communes. Individual families were recognized as independent economic production units which were allowed greater flexibility and initiative in production.

3 RMB or Renminbi is the official monetary unit in Mainland China. On 27/10/1995, the official exchange rate was US$1 to RMB8.295, or £1 to RMB13.087.

4 See, for example, Zhang and Shi (1992: 66) for a discussion of such a case of 'pseudo-collective' enterprise in Shantou Shi, Guangdong province, that employed 1,100 workers with a turnover at RMB15.12 million in 1989.

5 Data on the social characteristics of Chinese private entrepreneurs tend to be scattered and incomplete. It was only in 1993 that a first national questionnaire survey was conducted on privately owned business in China. A sample of 1,700 private business from all over the country based upon distribution, production and scale of operation was covered by the survey. The report, based on 1,440 returned questionnaires, was published in 1994.

6 The eastern part of China refers to the coastal areas including Hainan, Guangdong, Fujian, Zhejiang, Jiangsu, Shanghai, Shangdong, Tientsin and Beijing. Relatively, the central part includes Heilongjian, Jilin, Nei Menggu, Henan, Hubei, Jiangxi and Anhui. The western part refers to Yunan, Sichuan, Shenxi, Xizang, Qinghai and Guizhou. This definition appeared in the State Statistical Bureau (1990) and was used in the survey conducted by the All-China Society of Private Economy Research in 1993.

7 Cadre or '*gangbu*' generally refers to staff in state-related units. Broadly speaking, there are six main groups of state cadres who hold public office: (1) cadres in state organizations; (2) cadres in all levels of the Communist Party of China as well as in other political parties; (3) servicemen at the rank of platoon leader or above in the People's Liberation Army; (4) management staff at different levels of the People's Political Consultative Conference, trade unions, Communist Youth League, Women's Federation and other social organizations; (5) cadres with professional skills; and (6) professional management staff in business and enterprise units (Luo 1993: 201; our translation).

Part III

THE NATIONAL,
THE INTERNATIONAL
AND THE GLOBAL

8

GLOBALIZATION, URBAN CHANGE AND URBAN POLICIES IN BRITAIN AND FRANCE

Alan Harding and Patrick Le Galès

CITIES, SUB-NATIONAL DECISION-MAKING AND THE GLOBAL–LOCAL DEBATE

The diversity amongst the chapters of this book suggests the process of globalization is proving difficult to pin down conceptually and to demonstrate empirically. One theme nevertheless stands out. Questions are increasingly being posed about the appropriateness of 'the nation' as the level of aggregation at which the most important governing decisions are made and, consequently, as the predominant unit in social scientific analysis. Academics from the many disciplines which have long taken nations, (national) societies and national governments as their frames of reference have become more interested in supra-national *and* sub-national issues and analyses not only for the light they shed on national ones but as important variables in their own right. The interplay between global and local forces, in addition to or independently of national ones, has thus attracted more attention. It is clearly a critical issue for this volume. In this context, urban/locality studies have experienced a resurgence. Urban geographers, sociologists and political scientists still tend to plough their own furrows. A lively debate has none the less begun to develop within, and occasionally across, disciplines about the extent to which sub-national levels of analysis – and the economic, political and cultural processes that operate sub-nationally – have become more or less important in a period of increased globalization.

Debate about the autonomy of urban entities, processes and institutions *vis-à-vis* national ones is not new. Cities often fit uneasily into national frameworks. Inter-city tensions, especially between capitals and provincial centres, are common. This is unsurprising if viewed in historical perspective. As Weber (1958) argued, European cities in the pre-nation state era were unique for their political autonomy, economic power and social structures. City states and the networks for trade and cultural exchange that linked them (e.g. the Hanseatic League) were the primary mechanisms for territorial governance and economic regulation. Nation-building in Western Europe can be seen, at least in part, as a history of the subordination of cities and their often reluctant absorption into national urban hierarchies (Hohenberg and Lees 1985; Tilly 1992). National governments reduced the fiscal autonomy and privileges of urban ruling elites (Braudel 1986), thereby weakening 'international' political and economic linkages between cities and replacing them with networks of influence largely flowing outward from national capitals to provincial centres. In the process, cities lost much of their independence as economic, social and political actors, along with their utility as units of social scientific analysis.

The question now being posed, of course, is what happens in an age when nation states appear to be losing their pre-eminence? Will cities re-emerge as key actors? Will the unified Europe eventually be dominated by strong city regions as some ambitious city leaders hope (Freche 1990)? Or do the globalizing processes which cause such problems for national decision-making also effectively destroy local social systems and erode the distinctiveness of place? There are almost as many positions as there are commentators on these questions but, to oversimplify, there are two main arguments about the contemporary place of 'the local within the global'. Both adjudge economic globalization to have posed economic, political, social and environmental challenges that individual nation states, and nation-specific methods of governance, are unable to cope with. Both see a deepening trend toward greater global, or at least transnational, decision-making as the most obvious result. They come to different conclusions, though, on whether contemporary economic and political change also privileges sub-national decision-making. One variant of the global–local thesis suggests a measure of balance; the other, global-level domination.

One argument is that sub-national as well as supra-national levels of action and problem-resolution inevitably grow in importance as the relevance of national boundaries and nation-specific decision-making declines. Under this scenario, the economic and political roles of big cities, in particular, are set to expand. The reconcentration of economic command and control functions into major urban areas and the much-trumpeted 'resurgence' of urban-regional economies will make established metropoli the critical points at which regions and nations are wired into circuits of global business (Ohmae 1993). At the same time it is argued that national governments will increasingly see the economic contributions of urban regions as being decisive for national economic fortunes. As country-specific macro-economic management proves less and less effective, national governments will find that it is only by enhancing the comparative strength and competitiveness of cities/urban regions – through customized, decentralized and place-specific interventions – that they will be able to boost national economies. Indeed the phrase 'national economy' will have no meaning other than as shorthand for the collective power of various sub-national production complexes in world markets (Reich 1991).

A quite different argument is that globalizing processes erode the autonomy and distinctiveness of places at an ever-increasing rate (Harvey 1989). This view dismisses the notion of resurgent urban-regional economies and any possibility that sub-national levels of governance will increase in importance. On the contrary, economic globalization means the decisions which have most impact on local labour, land and capital markets are increasingly taken at distances ever further removed, psychologically and geographically, from the locality and on the basis of what suits transnational organizations, not what benefits local workers, firms or consumers. At the same time, even if national governments are becoming less autonomous and less effective problem-solvers it does not follow that sub-national authorities become more autonomous and more effective. National governments might choose to decentralize – or off-load – responsibilities to sub-national authorities. But this will only force localities to face up to some harsh realities which national welfare systems, the other major casualties of globalization, once cushioned them from. Additional sub national powers will count for little in an increasingly desperate, US style competition between localities. Transnational organizations hold all the major cards in this game and can play sub-national authorities off against each other to the ultimate advantage of none.

These two scenarios are overdrawn for the sake of argument. They might seem like stark alternatives at first glance but they do not have to be. The situations they describe might occur simultaneously but in different places, or in the same place at different times, depending upon criteria such as location, stage of economic development, industrial mix, range of institutions, the nature of intergovernmental relations and so on. It might be better to refer to 'glocalization' (Swyngedouw 1992) in which a dialectical dynamic between globalization and localization is resolved in different ways in different space-times. The problem in pushing this analysis further is that it quickly leaves current theorization and empirical evidence behind and enters the speculative realm of science fiction or the bland public relations world of the 'city booster'. Since this chapter is not an exercise in futurology or urban marketing, it does not take either of these paths. It sticks instead to what is known, or at least to what commentators think they know.

The remainder of the chapter poses two very general questions. What changes in the nature and functioning of cities are ascribed to globalizing processes? And what practical difference have such changes made to the way decisions are made within, for and on behalf of cities? The questions are examined in three sections. The first searches for evidence that cities are becoming more important economic and political decision-making centres as a result of globalization. The focus then moves to the French and British experiences. The second section asks if a new urban agenda has really developed in response to globalizing pressures. The underlying hypothesis is that if globalizing forces are paramount, there should have been significant convergence between the two countries in terms of decisions in urban and related policies and institutional change. The final section looks for countervailing evidence about the lack of impact of globalization before asking whether policy-making can only be understood within particular national frames of reference or, alternatively, whether globalization so reduces freedom of manoeuvre that differences between nations and localities are dwindling.

GLOBALIZATION AND CITIES: ELEMENTS OF THE DEBATE

Globalization, though an underdefined term, is associated with a number of supra-national economic, political, social and cultural processes which are usually dealt with in separate literatures. This section comments upon those conceptual accounts which seem most relevant to the present discussion. By drawing out the urban implications of globalization identified or hinted at by others it is possible to assess which, if either, of the crude scenarios presented above command most support and to specify some institutional and policy changes that might be expected to occur *if* adaptation to globalizing tendencies is really driving policy agendas. For the sake of neatness, what are here referred to as the economic geography and the politics of globalization are dealt with separately but clearly the two are interlinked.

Changing urban development patterns: the economic geography of globalization

Economic globalization is generally argued to have a number of basic features:[1]

- The growing spatial 'reach' and centrality of the international finance system and its ability to organize complex and rapid transactions on a global scale.
- The growth and expanding influence of transnational corporations, able to maximize potential returns by switching investments between a vast range of localities.
- The growing importance of less traditional economic factors of production, not least the productive value of the storage, generation and retrieval of knowledge and information.
- The capacity, afforded by innovations in information technology, to organize production on a global scale and to transmit information instantaneously across the globe.
- The constant expansion of international, compared to domestic, trade in goods, services and labour.

There has been substantial commentary, if less detailed research, on the effects these factors have on the economic map of urban Europe. Much of the debate in the 1970s and early 1980s stressed the de-industrializing effects of growing competition and the new international division of labour, triggered by transnationals developing new capacity in previously undeveloped regions of the globe, on Europe's older metropolitan areas. Britain's experience of inner metropolitan decline and the deconcentration of population and 'new' economic activity to small, free-standing cities and semi-rural areas was echoed elsewhere in Europe's traditional industrial core (the Ruhr, northern France, southern Belgium, the Mediterranean industrial areas around Genoa/Turin and Bilbao). The older metropoli stood for economic decline, environmental degradation and social stress whereas smaller urban centres were considered less congested, cleaner, more economically dynamic and able to offer a higher quality of life to residents. Although urban areas that had industrialized earliest experienced deep-rooted problems, it was often argued that the short-range decentralization of economic activity still held out the possibility of regional economic equilibrium (Planque 1982).

Later accounts concentrated more on inter-regional than on intra-regional differences and attempted to account for and map, at least partially, the broad spatial consequences of a 'post-industrial' system of production, distribution and exchange (Amin and Goddard 1986; Aydalot and Keeble 1988; Brotchie *et al.* 1987; Hall and Markusen 1985; Hall *et al.* 1987; Henderson and Castells 1987; Keeble and Wever 1986; Muegge and Stohr 1987). Whilst some commentators felt the importance of local economic linkages had grown sufficiently to talk of the 're-emergence' of urban-regional economies (Sabel 1988; Scott 1988; Storper and Walker 1989), others argued that such a change, if it existed, was more symbolic than substantive (Amin and Robins 1990). Urban-regional economies are clearly no more autonomous or self-contained than national ones (Lovering 1988). City regions are none the less the sites where global processes and interconnections are grounded and they are also differentially advantaged by new location factors relevant to the information age (Amin and Thrift 1993). They are important without being determinate in any sense.

One strand of the recent work in urban-regional economic geography concentrates upon the potential freedom of locational choice opened up by new information technologies and greater capital mobility. Here, it is generally assumed that the technological revolution and the move toward an information society represents a new paradigm in the evolution of capitalism (Lash and Urry 1987). Castells (1985 and 1989) pushes this analysis furthest, and gives it the most explicit urban focus, in arguing that the revolutionary 'informational mode of development' carries with it a distinctive set of requirements for inputs into the production process and highly selective spatial implications. He illustrates the emergence of the 'informational city' mainly with reference to the research and development-intensive, military contract-driven growth of the US sunbelt up to the mid-1980s. Whether the productive dynamism identified by Castells *had* to have these particular technological origins, and whether rapid development was found in areas other than the 'edge city' suburbs and metropolitan fringes of the USA is open to debate (Storper 1993; Le Galès 1993). A more convincing argument would demand examination of a larger number of cases, drawn from more places.

Less technologically determinist accounts ask what it is about 'local social relations of production' – local institutions, cultures and interfirm linkages – which enable some places to find profitable niches within the global economy whilst others cannot. The literature on 'new industrial districts' charts the rise of a limited number of localized systems of production into global markets and the factors that facilitate it. The rapid economic and population growth enjoyed by small urban centres in Veneto, Emilia-Romagna, Umbria and Tuscany – the 'Third Italy' (Bagnasco 1977; Bagnasco and Trigilia 1993; Beccatini and Sengenberger 1990; Brusco 1994) – provides the model. Here, dense networks of small, craft-based firms and supporting institutions were able to organize themselves flexibly and react quickly to better quality market information in responding to world demand for 'niche' consumer goods. Some analysts suggest that new industrial districts teach important lessons about the role of cooperative local social relations of production (Piore and Sabel 1984; Hirst and Zeitlin 1988; Sengenberger 1993). Others argue that the areas which are usually studied[2] are interesting but very limited spatial forms of accumulation not found, or easily replicated, elsewhere (Amin, Robins and Schoenberger 1992) and that very different local social relations of production can produce similar sorts of economic dynamism (Storper 1993).

These two recent literatures essentially identify *new and emergent* sites of rapid economic growth and assess the factors underpinning their develop-ment. They point to *deconcentration* of economic activity, with established urban centres the relative losers. Looking specifically at Europe, such decon-centration occurred at two levels in the two decades to the mid-1980s. At the micro level, population and economic activity within suburbs and small towns grew, albeit at slower rates over time, whilst more urbanized areas declined or stagnated. At the macro level, a decisive shift of economic gravity away from the traditional economic core of northern Europe and toward the historically less industrialized Alpine and Mediterranean regions seemed to be developing at one time. Just as the 'sunbelt–rustbelt' distinction failed to hold in the USA, however, so arguments about deconcentration do not tell the whole European urban story. From the mid-1980s on, there was significant economic and demographic resurgence amongst some established metropolitan centres in the old European core (Parkinson *et al.* 1993). Economic *reconcentration* in Europe's old core cities, particularly within higher order services, suggested that the power of new technologies to open up locational choices had its limits and that the cooperative social relations of production of certain craft-dominated, small urban centres were not the only sources of innovation and economic growth.

Why should globalization lead to enhanced agglomeration effects in and around certain cities when the information revolution supposedly enables dispersal and deconcentration? Several reasons have been identified. First, cities enable firms to reduce risks, limit uncertainties and maximize opportunities. In the words of Pierre Veltz (1993), the city is 'une assurance flexibilité'. Globalization generates increased competitive pressures which firms have answered, as ever, by competing on product cost, quality and reliability but also through the creation of new markets (segmentation and differentiation). The weakening of national economic regulation deepens market instability and multiplies risks for firms (Porter 1990). Faced with volatile business environments, corporations have increasingly tended to decentralize and externalize functions they once performed in-house. They also need to be able to guarantee rapid inputs to evermore complex projects. Only cities contain the range of resources (partners, information, infra-structures, qualified staff, finances, services, networks, innovations) that firms now need at the appropriate level of sophistication.

Second, cities facilitate innovation. The conditions for innovation and its transfer to firms are more likely to occur in cities, where there are high densities of research centres and larger clusters of innovative small firms. The new conditions of economic development and competitiveness require sophisticated combinations of various inputs which are not traditional factors of economic development and again tend to be located in cities. Globalization and post-industrial economies therefore tend to favour agglomeration.

Third, globalization intensifies exchange and networking – the rapid, reliable movement of goods, people and information. This inevitably favours areas which earlier periods of agglomeration have left well served by communication infrastructures. Core European cities again hold the advantage. The sheer concentration of market and political power in these centres means that it is within and between them that innovations are applied, and infrastructural improvements made, first and most extensively.[3] As global communication deepens, the need for major infrastructures, including interconnections between different modes, prove evermore important for firms, and reinforce agglomeration tendencies. Increased exchange and networking triggers investment in quicker, more powerful, technologically advanced and more expensive infrastructures whose costs are only justified if they link major cities first.[4]

Fourth, differentiation of markets and just-in-time production and delivery methods encourage firms to locate closer to consumer markets, and hence to densely populated, highly urbanized areas. Transnational corporations investing in Europe, especially in services and consumer goods sectors, would at one time have looked to open up undifferentiated national markets. Now, they tend to follow a strategy of 'global localization' which means locating in areas that can serve denser but more spatially differentiated markets, often straddling national borders. Fifth, the sheer clout of transnational firms and corporations increases the concentration of economic power in selected cities. More than two-thirds of European transnationals, for example, are located in London or Paris. Sassen (1991), assessing the urban consequences of recent changes in the financial services sector, argues that 'global cities' at least

> now function in four new ways: first, as highly concentrated command points in the organization of the world economy; second, as locations for finance and for specialized service firms, which have replaced manufacturing as the leading economic sector; third, as sites of production, including production of innovations, in these leading industries; and fourth, as markets for the products and innovations produced.
>
> (Sassen 1991: 3–4)

Sassen describes the selective logic of urban economic reconcentration. She also makes pertinent points about who and what big (post-)modern cities function for in suggesting that the spin-off effects associated with living or trading in or near the most powerful cities are dwindling even as their international influence grows. For example, it is no longer possible to assume that the parallel processes of concentration within certain economic sectors and deconcentration in others breed complementarity and that different local functional specializations will lead to greater overall economic strength and coherence at the urban-regional level. Sassen suggests that, on the contrary, a new and original form of urban economy may be developing in which there is growing disjuncture between cities and their regions. Many major cities, she argues, have become centres of production for a range of services which are traded globally and are at best only tenuously linked to, and hence supportive of, regional economic specialisms.

Sassen also looks at the implications of urban labour market change for various groups of city-dwellers when raising some key concerns about growing social polarization and its particularly high incidence in internationally orientated cities. Globalization is associated with an international division of labour in which the comparative advantage of advanced nations (Europe's included) resides, if anywhere, in the knowledge and skill of the labour force rather than its low cost. The processes of sectoral change brought about by globalization have led to middle-income jobs in manufacturing being lost in large numbers. Employment growth, meanwhile, has been in better-rewarded technical, professional and managerial employment, primarily in services but also in manufacturing, and in poorly rewarded, low-skilled work in consumer and personal services. The result has been the creation of 'dual labour markets' in which there are growing income differences between people in work.

And of course not everyone *is* in work. High rates of structural unemployment are now common in 'successful' and 'unsuccessful' cities alike. Entitlement to welfare payments has generally become more stringent in the last decade and benefit levels have often dwindled relative to general income levels. Urban household composition has also changed markedly, with double-income and no-income households becoming far more common. Taken together, these factors generate very strong pressures for a growing gap between the haves and the have-nots. There are reasons to believe that 'the divided city' (Fainstein *et al.* 1992) which can result from these changes is very much associated with economic reconcentration and the 'new' agglomeration. Recent research, for example, suggests that the locational preferences of the 'service class' of well-qualified, well-paid professionals is the most important factor influencing business locations in France. Since the generation of a great deal of secondary, low paid employment for the poorly qualified is intimately related to the growth of the service class, its influence on local labour markets is much greater than rough employment figures suggest.

In centralized countries like France or Britain a social, as well as economic, logic to agglomeration is particularly apparent. In both countries, the higher one rises in career terms, the more likely one is to (have to) work in the 'primate' cities of Paris and London. Increased female participation in the labour force, at increasingly high levels of qualification, intensifies this pattern when the relevant decision-making unit is the double-income household. Young, highly qualified professional couples naturally look for two jobs in the same place. Their chances of finding them – not once but several times during their careers – are far higher in the capital city than in major provincial centres. If they think purely in career terms, then, the rational choice is to remain in the capital whatever conditions of life it offers them.

The social logic of agglomeration is further reinforced by professionals desiring retention of class status by their children. Prestigious schools and universities, offering well-connected young people the chance to mix with their peers, are generally found in major cities. To ensure the right sort of environment for their children, service class families prefer to stay in or move to major cities. In most of Western society, there is an element of social prestige to living and working in major cities. Globalization, by reinforcing the superior level of the urban hierarchy and by opening up national spaces, makes it essential for service class families to strive to be part of the European urban space; to belong to the right sorts of network. Social reproduction therefore reinforces labour market logic in that it reinforces concentration and agglomeration, particularly in dominant city regions such as those surrounding London and Paris.

Changing forms of governance: the politics of globalization

If globalization in some senses makes cities more important economically, is the same true of their role in governance and regulation? Most of the literature on the politics of globalization deals with the challenges facing nation states. This is unsurprising, since the most talked-about consequence

global interdependency has been to force nation states to surrender some
ereignty and cooperate in the development of supra-national institutions
to manage problems that do not respect national boundaries (Luard 1990).
For Held and McGrew globalization produces 'a "re-articulation of international space" in which the notions of sovereignty and democracy are being
prised away from the traditional rootedness in the national community and
the territorially bounded nation-state' (1993: 263–4). Their comments echo
those from other disciplines (Appadurai 1990; Featherstone 1990, 1993;
Robertson 1992b; Sklair 1991) which suggest ever-stronger cross-national
flows of people, money, information, images, products and pollutants make
nations, nationality and national boundaries less important to people's lives.
It is barely disputed that globalization has forced nation states to surrender
powers and responsibilities upwards in recognition of the fact that national
fates are intricately intertwined. But does globalization also result in the
downward surrender of sovereignty? Is there any clear pattern to the restructuring of sub-national administration or to shifts in policies applied at
sub-national level?

Recent attempts to trace links between global economic change and institutional restructuring at the *national* level have probably been pursued most
rigorously in regulation theory (Aglietta 1979; Boyer 1986; Jessop 1988,
1990). Regulation theory argues that in capitalist societies there is always
an interdependent relationship between the dominant regime of accumulation – the way in which production is organized – and the mode of regulation
– the way in which (principally) the state supports a particular system of
production through its many economic, political and social regulatory functions. There is broad agreement that the processes represented here as
globalization have substantially weakened previously dominant, nationally
based regimes of accumulation. In so doing, they have called into question
the mode of regulation – based on nation-specific Keynesian welfare states
– which accompanied and supported them. 'National economies', to the
extent they can be said to exist, are now so dependent on international
trade flows that demand management strategies practised in one country
cannot be effective. Such strategies have slowly been abandoned, along with
attempts to guide productivity through various forms of national accord
between labour and capital.

Jessop (1992, 1994) suggests there are signs of cross-national convergence
in the development of new modes of regulation, although it is too early to
say whether they will prove stable. He argues that national governments
have responded to intensive global economic competition and the effects of
economic restructuring within their boundaries in two main ways. First, they
have gradually abandoned the instruments of the Keynesian welfare state
and are replacing them with others that he collectively characterizes as the
'Schumpeterian workfare state'. Here, emphasis is placed on supra-national
coordination of macro-economic policy and nation-specific supply-side

strategies which aim to strengthen the structural competitiveness of national economies, through sectoral or area-based interventions, and 'to subordinate welfare policy to the demands of flexibility' (Jessop 1992: 12). Second, there has been a 'hollowing out' of the nation state as the principal locus of social and economic intervention. This involves powers and responsibilities passing upward, to supra-national level and downward, to sub-national authorities. Jessop might also have mentioned that they have passed outward, to market and quasi market delivery agencies (Bennett 1990).

These changes, the results of adjustment by nation states to globalization, have very significant implications for the direction and type of programmes delivered by local, decentralized agencies and for the form these agencies take. It is therefore surprising that more attention is not devoted to the sub-national implications of regulation theory.[5] If Jessop is right, the development of localized supply-side programmes will increasingly emphasize economic objectives geared to international competitiveness. Urban areas will everywhere be seen as potential assets to national economies and national urban policies will be rejigged to downgrade welfare considerations. Competitive, fine-grained development initiatives will be promoted by national governments at the urban-regional level, replacing more traditional regional policies which attempted to redistribute economic activity in a nationally equitable way. They also have institutional implications that help explain the growing interest in new forms of local governance. The hollowing out of the nation state is associated with the selective decentralization of responsibilities to sub-national agencies (though not always to elected ones). At the same time, the fragmentation of local programme delivery and the re-orientation of national policies toward developmental goals increases the non-local pressures for quasi-market or partnership-based agencies for service delivery in many policy areas.

It is important to recognize that pressures do not emanate only from the national level. At the sub-national level, too, cross-national similarities in urban-regional problems and opportunities encourages greater mobilization around urban-regional issues, particularly with regard to new developmental programmes. If national governments can see the value of transferring certain responsibilities to sub-national agencies, these agencies can be just as tempted to welcome such changes, even to lobby for them, in order to strengthen urban-regional autonomy. It is no coincidence that resurgent regionalist movements often support a case for decentralization with economic arguments for greater sub-national autonomy, for example that national governments unjustifiably favour richer over poorer areas or, in contrast, drain richer areas of 'their' resources.

Sub-national mobilization has responded to various problems and opportunities (Harding *et al.* 1994). Local public, private and voluntary sector interests have had little choice but to react, if only symbolically, to a widely perceived local need to respond to the effects of economic restructuring, rationalization and job loss. They have had to do so in a policy climate wherein national governments rarely offer the sort of cushion to urban areas – in terms of intergovernmental financing and the absorption of the costs of economic change – that they did at the peak of Keynesian welfarism. 'Successful' cities face pressures too. Even strong local growth, in that it is often accompanied by labour market polarization and the physical and psychological segregation of marginalized groups from mainstream city life, has triggered local responses. A more positive side to local agenda reflects the potential opened up by 'new' location factors like efficient air, road and rail connections, advanced telecommunications systems, excellence in higher education and good quality cultural, residential and physical environments. These characteristics all have one thing in common: they are more amenable to public policy influence than traditional, 'natural' factors of production, particularly if the necessary intergovernmental agreements to finance improvements can be secured.

Regulation theorists generally assume, paradoxically, that the transition to a new mode of regulation will be led from the national level even though national governments will ultimately need to share or surrender much of the governing capacity they have traditionally held. In one of the few regulation analyses starting from the sub-national perspective, however, Mayer (1994) makes some strong claims about the implications of globalization for local governance. She rehearses familiar arguments about there having been (a) greatly increased mobilization around urban economic development issues, and (b) a pronounced tendency toward partnerships and coalitions between local actors and agencies in this field given a context of fragmented service delivery responsibilities, constrained public sector resources and more ambitious economic development strategies. She also echoes Jessop in suggesting that as local entrepreneurialism in economic development has become more important, so social policy concerns have been linked more firmly to economic and labour market considerations.

Most important, she argues that local governance has a vital role to play in whatever new mode of regulation develops out of current uncertainties. Global economic change, she argues, has 'made it increasingly impossible for particular (re)production conditions to be organized/coordinated by the central state' (Mayer 1994: 2). In another variant of the global–local thesis, she suggests nation states can no longer guarantee the conditions of production and reproduction

> required locally by globally mobile capital ... hence local political systems, with their skills in negotiating with supraregional and multi-national capital, in the effectiveness with which they tailor the particular set of local conditions of production, have become decisive factors in shaping a city's profile as well as its place in the international urban hierarchy.

GLOBALIZATION IN BRITAIN AND FRANCE: TOWARDS ENTREPRENEURIAL CITIES?

We can hypothesize from previous sections that attempts to help cities cope with and benefit from globalization, rather than shelter them from its effects, would demand three things. Decision-making for urban areas would need to become more 'entrepreneurial' and attempts would be needed to make urban regions more competitive in global markets whilst at the same time encouraging deeper local economic linkages so that the benefits of growth were spread throughout urban regions but also internalized within them as far as possible. Clearly there are limits to what public policy initiatives can achieve within this broad agenda but in institutional and cultural terms there would need to be a move from nationally based, process-orientated governing arrangements to ones that are locally based and product-orientated.

Whereas the former stress vertical integration, standardized rules, clear lines of authority, accountability and national equity, the latter would put a greater premium on horizontal integration, flexibility, networking, problem-solving and realization of potential through strategic competition and collaboration. The motivation for change would be to encourage cities – or rather the key interest groups acting within and on behalf of them – to act cooperatively, coherently and strategically and to develop greater awareness of the way social and environmental goals interact with economic ones. At the national level, one would expect clear evidence that cities were viewed as national economic assets and not as liabilities. Efforts to release urban economic potential, particularly through targeted national infrastructural investments, would be concentrated on those areas perceived as having greatest potential.

Given that there is 'no one way, no one model' (Murray 1991: 6) for improved innovation and growth, and that flexibility and experimentation is therefore essential, the design and delivery of policy initiatives would need to be left to sub-national institutions and interests who know localities best. One would expect national governments to use various sanctions and incentives to improve mobilization and capacity-building at sub-national level whilst playing a supportive role in intergovernmental development efforts through their various departments and agencies. The themes guiding institutional and policy change, whether top-down or bottom-up, would probably include the decentralization of responsibilities to more responsive sub-national layers of government; the development of local institutional capacity – public, private and public–private – in production-related fields; ensuring closer local trade-offs between welfare and growth, rather than perpetuating individual, service-specific bargains between national departments and sub-national authorities; re-orientating welfare programmes so that they are sensitive to economic ends and vice versa; encouraging 'business-like' methods geared more to achievements than processes; and promoting partnerships between

193

the wide range of urban 'players' whose efforts are needed to effect change at a scale which makes economic sense.

The French and British experiences in the last ten to fifteen years suggest there has been considerable movement on many items of the above agenda. The massive growth in local economic policies in the two countries indicates the growing salience of sub-national development issues and a shifting balance between the local politics of consumption/welfare and those of production (Le Galès 1993, 1995; Teissenc 1994; Young and Mason 1983; Hausner 1986, 1987, 1988; Mackintosh and Wainwright 1989; Brindley et al. 1989; Campbell 1990; Eisenschitz and Gough 1994). Initially, the emphasis in both countries was on practical actions to reduce unemployment, support firms in crisis, create and sustain small enterprises and provide better land and buildings for economic activity. These reactive priorities were replaced by others focused more on changing the wider economic environment as a new orthodoxy of interventions developed after the mid-1980s. The dominant themes in the later approach were a rhetorical commitment to compete with other cities, often internationally, and a desire to capture rare resources that maximize potential and minimize problems – middle-class households, 'clean' firms and finance from higher levels of government.

Inter-urban competition encourages a somewhat schizophrenic approach amongst local authorities who need to be innovative and distinctive on one hand but to imitate their domestic and international 'rivals' on the other. A typical economic package might now include the promotion of prestigious cultural events and spectacles,[6] collective transport systems (metros, tramways, airport expansions), prestigious architectural flagships, science parks and links between technologically advanced higher education and local business, high-tech office centres, image-creation and place marketing, new public buildings (research centres, opera houses, theatres, museums, sports stadia, TGV railway stations) and exhibition/conference centres. Much less priority is now attached to creating firms or assisting those in crisis. The broad mobilization against unemployment hoped for by left-wing urban local authorities in the early 1980s did not transpire. Whilst the 'fight' against unemployment remains in muted form, the means to achieve it are increasingly indirect and long-term. An implicit ideology more redolent of US growth coalitions (Logan and Molotch 1987) – that economic growth of any kind benefits all (eventually) – has tended to bind together local economic programmes whose capacity to 'reach' the poorest urban residents quickly are often extremely limited (Deakin and Edwards 1993).

National governments have encouraged inter-city competition in various ways. Whilst the experience of the two countries differs markedly, in neither case has there been an overt national strategy to encourage competitive behaviour. Rather, individual government departments have taken isolated decisions which have encouraged competition directly or indirectly. One clear change has been in the expenditure environment. Central financial support for urban investments declined from their high 1970s levels in both countries. Whereas relatively resource-rich French city authorities were able to take on extra investment responsibilities, tightening government controls over local spending in Britain meant central cuts translated more directly into declining local investment. In both cases, though, change triggered greater local mobilization in the form of more sophisticated lobbying for non-local resources – which meant arguing that localities had special potential rather than general needs – and more joint-financing (intergovernmental and public–private) of capital projects. In both countries, the number of partners able and willing to strike deals with local authorities has grown.

Whereas the governance of urban areas in both countries was long structured by the relationship between central and local governments, the 1980s saw new players enter the scene. In France, the key newcomers were the corporations that now control water, the building industry, waste disposal, cable TV, transport and certain privatized hospitals and health services. Lorrain (1991 and 1995) perceives a 'silent revolution' in the privatization of urban utilities. Their functions and power grew as they diversified and adopted internationalization strategies which saw them, for example, buy up an increasing proportion of private utility capacity in the UK. They have become indispensable partners in major investments in French cities, not just because they are able to plug gaps in public funding and hence limit the proportion of project costs falling on rate-payers but because they range over sectors central to urban life and are able to offer considerable technical and financial muscle. Relations between the utilities and city authorities have blossomed on the basis of mutual benefit. The corporations are able to secure large, complex and expensive contracts whilst the authorities can, for example, retain ownership of water provision but have the service run independently or gain public goods such as sports stadia, community centres or social housing at reduced cost.[7]

The number of partners in urban development efforts in the UK has also grown. To a limited extent this stems from businesses, particularly in the property sector, diversifying and becoming adept at using a growing range of discretionary public subsidies (Harding 1991). But more importantly it reflects significant government restructuring of the machinery of local governance. The approach to local government by post-1979 Conservative governments has been centralist and constraining (Stewart and Stoker 1989 and 1994) but it would be wrong to argue that no decentralization has occurred. In fact local institutional capacity, particularly in development-related fields, has grown significantly with the creation of new, government-appointed/-sanctioned agencies. The new 'quangos', usually dominated at board level by business representatives, account for a rapidly growing proportion of public expenditures in fields like area planning, land reclamation, physical redevelopment, training and housing. As a result, policy initiatives in British cities, particularly but not only in economic development, are increasingly characterized by complex partnerships between local authorities, regional offices of government, national departments, local and national quangos, business interests and voluntary sector bodies (Harding and Garside 1994).

In France, where fundamental reform of the hugely fragmented communal system has long proven impossible, the promotion of partnership in urban governance is also a key issue (Lorrain 1991; Borraz 1994; Lefebvre 1994; Novarina 1993; Le Galès 1994). Governing capacity in French cities is divided between a host of state agencies, their external field services, various local quangos, a growing range of public–private bodies, the complex world of 'associations',[8] a plethora of communes and agencies for intercommunal cooperation which attempt to ameliorate fragmentation and the limited executive capacity of many communes. As the politics of economic development grew in salience, key urban interest groups became more concerned with strategic socio-economic planning.[9] New strategic plans in major cities were often based on public–private collaboration, and closer inter-sectoral relations were also seen in attempts to promote the city externally or to strengthen political integration within the urban area. Local Chambers of Commerce, for instance, have lobbied for unified local governments in large urban areas in order that they can compete with their equivalents elsewhere in Europe.

Despite these efforts, fragmentation within sub-national government persists, even deepens, in both countries. In both cases it seems that tinkering with institutions, though it is tried sporadically, will ultimately prove less effective than encouraging networking between institutions. If there is one clear difference between the two national experiences it is that decentralization in France has at least seen a genuine shift of power and responsibility from national government. The French decentralization reforms, along with initiatives like regional *contrats de plan*, signalled the end of the centralist, *dirigiste* Jacobin state. They also paved the way for different forms of intergovernmental relations in which there is more open competition between local authorities to attract state investments, for example in research, education, public services, culture, transport infrastructure and urban renovation (Balme 1994).

In this competition, the most powerful actors within the French politico-administrative system – the *grands maires* of the larger cities – have been able to capture a growing proportion of public investment for their projects at the expense of weaker players in small and middle-sized towns. The extension of joint-planning and co-financing between the state and local authorities will deepen this trend and increase the power of the larger cities and the rich departments.[10] In Britain the traditionally weak position of local authority leaders in national politics (Bulpitt 1983) has been further eroded in recent years. Here, government re-enforcement of inter-urban competition has been spurred, not by strengthening the competitive capacity of sub-national authorities, but by making them compete for resources they would once have been allocated as of right according to needs-based criteria.

A recent move to integrate and strengthen certain production-related government functions at the regional level suggests a measure of administrative deconcentration in Britain. The new Regional Government Offices, with their oversight of competitive bidding programmes, seem set to play the prefectorial role that is being downgraded in France.

French governments have been more active than their British counterparts in encouraging cities to compete at the European scale. DATAR, the French regional policy agency, was instrumental during the 1980s in arguing that major state investments in urban research, culture and public utilities could underpin the competitive position of French cities in single market Europe. Under DATAR's *Chartes d'objectifs* initiative in the late 1980s (Le Galès and Mawson 1994), French regional capitals were asked to develop twenty-year strategic plans and a series of actions and investments which could drive urban economic development and establish them as specialized places of excellence in the new Europe.[11] The scheme, though ineffective thus far, further boosted the status and ambitions of *les grands maires*. Attaining European status became a key, albeit vague, objective in most French cities in the late 1980s. British cities also claimed 'Europeanness', particularly when marketing themselves and building links with foreign cities, but more in opposition to national government than at its behest. On one hand, self-appointed European status helped British cities distance themselves, symbolically, from the Euro-scepticism of national governments. On the other, it formed part of a highly pragmatic attempt to attract EU resources and to escape government spending restrictions.

Research on other aspects of the Europeanization or internationalization of sub-national government is still in its infancy (Benington *et al.* 1992; Martin and Pearce 1992; Goldsmith 1993; John 1994). It is clear, though, that French mayors and urban authorities, along with rather fewer of their British counterparts, have embraced inter-city networking enthusiastically, not least because it provides them with an international profile which, paradoxically, supports national ambitions. This has led them to play leading roles in sub-national network organizations like Eurocities, develop bilateral links with cities in Europe and beyond, and maintain close ties with the Directorates General of the EU. This internationalization, yet another facet of supranational–local linkage, contributes to a political representation of the world in which national governments have the status of one partner among many. It also helps diffuse models and norms of European cities and understandings of what competition (and collaboration) between cities means beyond sloganeering (Balme and Le Galès 1997).

GLOBALIZATION: IS THERE ANY CHOICE?

Our brief review provides firm evidence of growing urban entrepreneurialism, selective strengthening of urban-regional institutions, particularly in development-related fields, limited cross-sectoral mobilization for economic growth and enhanced inter-urban competition. However, the situation it describes stops far short of fulfilling the wider hypothetical agenda specified in the previous section and it certainly does not suggest that a new economic and political golden age for putative city states is imminent. It would be a big mistake, for at least five sets of reasons, to read recent change as evidence that limited room for independent policy manoeuvre by nation states is creating a vacuum that can only be filled by sub-national authorities or that all governing structures below the supra-national level are constrained to carry out the same, narrow 'globalization agenda'.

First, as even those regulation theory accounts which flirt with economic determinism accept, national responses to globalization take various pathways,[12] which have different implications for approaches to sub-national policies and institutions. France and Britain may be fellow travellers in a global journey but they did not arrive at their current, only roughly comparable, positions via the same road of reform, nor did they set off from the same point. Although the ostensible causes of change may have been similar – sluggish growth rates, perceived public expenditure crises, burgeoning welfare expenditures, loss of economic sovereignty and so on – national responses remain sufficiently different for globalization to be interpreted as a key influence rather than an overriding constraint on institutional and policy change.

Second, the constitutional, legislative and financial power of national governments continues to give them a decisive role in central–local government relations and in determining the structures and modes of operation of subordinate tiers and agencies of the state. This confers a great deal of power upon dominant governing parties which, in turn, means that national politics continues to dominate those at sub-national level. Political change at national level therefore remains critical in mediating between global pressure and local response.[13] Central government also continues to be the one mechanism through which meaningful redistribution of resources can take place.[14] Whilst sub-national forces grumble about particular patterns of redistribution, very few express any willingness to take on the job of redistributing resources themselves. Sub-national agitation for greater autonomy concentrates almost exclusively on decisions linked to productive investment. The financing (but not the delivery) of social welfare, in contrast, is generally seen as a national responsibility. This suggests that a war of position about sub-national autonomy may be going on between levels of government but there are few signs of a revolutionary groundswell for fundamental change in which sub-national tiers take on responsibility for balancing investment as between production and socialized consumption.

Third, city and urban-regional economic development has simply not been accorded the importance within government policy that our hypothetical agenda suggested. Neither have specific urban policies, a subset of the fields covered in this chapter, aimed unambiguously and consistently at picking potential winners in the global marketplace. One or two modest initiatives apart, French and British governments have been reluctant to break with a post-war commitment to the 'fair' distribution of resources and to 'back winners' instead. Neither have they undertaken, or else acted upon, the sort of economic analysis that might underpin such favouritism.[15] Specific urban policies in both countries have gone through a number of experimental incarnations but, hyperbole about 'urban potential' aside, they have primarily been driven by a concern to ameliorate urban problems. Recent British urban policy initiatives retain a strong economic orientation but specifically as a means of solving social problems in areas which currently lack economic strength. In France, initiatives like *Contrat de ville* have an even more explicit social focus; they essentially aim to improve the machinery of the welfare state in 'neighbourhoods in crisis'. By comparison, overt concern with the international economic competitiveness of urban areas rarely figures on the urban policy agenda.

Fourth, and related to the previous point, whilst recent urban policies have aimed at better horizontal integration between policy areas, policy-making at all levels still remains dominated by sectoral rather than spatial considerations. This is not to argue that changes within different policy sectors do not have significant, differential impacts on urban areas and social groups but it would be wrong to view government as a unified entity pursuing non-contradictory strategies. In reality, isolated policy reforms have invariably been driven by perceived answers to sector-specific problems or by Treasury-dominated agenda about effectiveness and value for money. The welfare state is changing in both countries in different ways which can still be situated within Jessop's analysis. Such changes have not, however, been motivated by a wish to achieve better synergy between policies at sub-national level or to create multi-purpose, autonomous governing arrangements below the national level. New sub-national partnerships often reflect a desire to *overcome* fragmentation rather than evidence that reform of the machinery of government has managed to achieve coordination and coherence.

Fifth, the power of our hypothetical, competitive, globalization agenda is called into question by signs of backlash against the 'growth at all costs' agenda followed in many cities during the 1980s and early 1990s (Harding 1994).[16] In both national urban policy[17] and local economic development policy fields the growth ideology, as promulgated by the more entrepreneurial French mayors and practised at the height of Thatcherite urban policy, is losing ground. Urban leaders have become increasingly cautious and worried about the contradictory logic of competition, social exclusion and spatial polarization. In place of the simple economic boosterism of recent years, a new desire to understand the causes and patterns of urban social polarization[18] and to do something about them before ghettos of American proportions develop is beginning to grow. There is no evidence that anyone thinks this can be achieved without a strong role for national government.

Overall, the evidence from Britain and France suggests that some cities – probably far fewer than benefited from previous industrial revolutions – are enjoying a limited, if socially problematic, resurgence as a result of globalization. The wide array of governing agencies in urban areas more generally are also facing up to new responsibilities and pressures which result from the hollowing out of the nation state. The idea that the nation state has therefore reached crisis point and is slowly being supplanted by new structures of governance at the city or urban-regional level, however, is a crude exaggeration. Even the somewhat weaker claim, that the welfare state is on the point of collapse and that future prosperity can only lie in a competitive free-for-all between urban regions, finds remarkably little political expression or empirical support. The trends identified in this chapter may presage 'the end of the state' in both senses in the very long term but this outcome is but one, rather less likely, possible pathway out of current uncertainties. Ultimately we have to agree with the sceptics (e.g. Peck and Tickell 1994) that the current phase of experimentation in sub-national policies and institutional restructuring is a 'search for a fix' which so far falls short of any decisive shift or resolution.

NOTES

Alan Harding's contribution to this chapter forms part of a research project entitled 'Coalition-formation and urban redevelopment: A cross-national study', financed through the UK Economic and Social Research Council's *Local Governance Programme* (Project Reference: L311253002). He wishes to thank the ESRC for its support.

1 For a sceptical account, see Hirst and Thompson 1992 and 1996.
2 The empirical material for this debate comes mainly from the Third Italy, with Baden-Württemburg (Germany) and Jutland (Denmark) following at some distance. The conceptual inspiration is Alfred Marshall's analysis of local economic development in nineteenth-century England. See Marshall 1919.
3 EU traffic liberalization, for example, is re-creating the US hub and spoke model of air transport in Europe, with increased concentrations of traffic in London, Paris, Frankfurt and Amsterdam (cf. Kassim in this volume). Figures on road and rail transport and electronic infrastructures tell similar tales of concentration in and around the major cities between southern England and northern Italy.
4 The race to install fibre-optic cable systems or attract a 'stop' on the growing European high-speed train network illustrate this process.
5 Partial exceptions include Duncan *et al.* 1993, Hay 1993, Peck and Tickell 1992, 1994. See also Pickvance and Preteceille 1991 for a non-regulationist analysis.
6 Cultural activity now accounts for 15 per cent of French city budgets. Although local authority financing responsibilities are fewer, it has assumed greater importance in British cities too. See Bianchini and Parkinson 1993.

7 The relationship between *grands maires* and major utility companies has a darker side. Recent corruption scandals suggest the distinction between public good and private profit has become blurred and state officials have found the new system of partnership and mutual favours difficult to police.

8 A legal term covering a variety of organizations more-or-less linked to local authorities.

9 The *projets de ville* of the later 1980s are a good example. See Demesteere and Padioleau 1992.

10 Under the 'plan Université 2000' programme to develop universities, for example, local authorities have, for the first time, to take over 50 per cent of investment responsibilities from the state. The richer, more dynamic local authorities in the big cities gain most because they can find matching funding more easily.

11 A similar, more limited British government initiative – City Pride – pointedly lacks the explicit European focus.

12 Jessop 1994, for example, mentions neo-liberal, neo-statist and neo-corporatist variations of national response.

13 The rehabilitation of the local government role in economic development programmes which occurred after the Thatcher years is an example, as is the 1993 Balladur government's less city-friendly approach to regional policy.

14 Resource redistribution across national borders by the EU is trivial in comparison.

15 An interesting contrast is the shift in Denmark to an industrial policy based overtly on Porter's analysis of the sub-national bases of national competitiveness. See Porter 1990.

16 This agenda was never entirely dominant. It was not shared, for example, by the British 'new urban left' authorities, the Communist communes outside Paris and the conservationist right-wing authorities in both countries.

17 Examples include the British City Challenge programme and *Politique de la ville* in France.

18 For the French and British experiences, see Chenus and Tabard 1994, Veiellard-Baron 1994, Lapeyronnie 1993, Joseph Rowntree Foundation Inquiry Group 1995 and Green 1994.

9

AIR TRANSPORT AND GLOBALIZATION

A sceptical view[1]

Hussein Kassim

The dramatic developments that have taken place in air transport in the recent past at the regulatory level and the level of the firm have been interpreted as evidence that the industry is experiencing globalization. Louis Gialloreto of Canadian Airlines gave notice in 1988 that 'the global war begins', while Daniel Kasper, an airline analyst, predicted in the same year that:

> By the year 2000, and perhaps sooner, most of the free world's air services are likely to be provided by a score of large multinational airlines competing on a global scale ... [C]areful analysis will show that the emergence of a global airline industry by the turn of the century is neither far-fetched nor unrealistic but rather the natural and, I believe, predictable result of fundamental economic and political forces now at work in the world economy.
>
> (1988: 1)

However, although it is true that the changes, which include deregulation and privatization, the hybridization of ownership, the proliferation of transnational partnerships and alliances (many involving equity holdings), the creation of a single European market in air services, and the transformation of public enterprises into commercial companies, have been nothing short of spectacular in an industry historically characterized by the pursuit of protectionist policies of patriotic interventionism, by collusive relationships between airlines and governments, and by fundamentally anti-competitive practices, it is far from certain either that the globalization of the sector has taken place or that the industry is moving inexorably in this direction.

This chapter argues that there are strong reasons for contesting the claim that the industry is being globalized. In the first place, states retain important powers which impact significantly upon the commercial freedoms of the airlines and maintain a strong interest in the well-being of the aviation industry, even if most are less willing to subsidize their companies than previously.

Second, airlines remain largely dependent on their governments for their commercial opportunities in the international domain, while their performance can be profoundly affected by government policy in aviation and other areas. Third, even if airlines have increasingly entered into transnational alliances and partnerships, they have not lost their national identities. The era of the 'stateless firm' has not yet dawned in the air transport industry. Fourth, the spread of developments in aviation has not been truly global. Changes have been limited to certain regions and particular markets, many governments remain unsympathetic to current trends in the industry and have the power to resist them, and considerable differences in income between and within regions mean that there is no genuinely global market. Fifth, transnational alliances which are regarded by global theorists as the principal vehicles of globalization have not yet become stable features of the industry. There are few instances of durable partnerships and many examples of cross-cutting partnerships, where the airlines belonging to the same computer reservation system (CRS) consortium do not necessarily cooperate with each other in other areas. Sixth, global theorists predict that labour will become increasingly powerless as globalization proceeds. In air transport, however, trade unions have not ceased to be significant actors. Finally, there are important constraints which threaten rapid growth of the industry. There are physical constraints on airport capacity, political constraints deriving from increased concern about environmental protection, and financial constraints reflecting the industry's low profitability and its limited attraction to private investors in many parts of the world.

In the first section below, the concept of globalization is discussed, and the forces and processes that global theorists argue bring it about are outlined. The fundamental features of the regime that has historically governed air transport are considered in the second section. It looks at the powers enjoyed by the state, the policies traditionally pursued by governments and the position of the airlines within a tightly regulated system. The third section considers the developments in air transport in the recent past. It considers the implementation of liberalization and privatization programmes, the creation of the single European market in air services, and the transformation of airline strategies under the new regulatory environment. The argument that these developments do not amount to globalization is presented in the fourth section.

GLOBALIZATION

Theorists of globalization contend that the world economy is moving into, or in fact has entered, a new phase. As the authors of a recent book observe:

> It is widely asserted that we live in an era in which the greater part of social life is determined by global processes, in which national cultures, national economies and national borders are dissolving.

Central to this perception is the notion of a rapid and recent process of economic globalization ... The world economy has been internationalized in its basic dynamics, it is dominated by uncontrollable market forces, and has as its principal economic actors and major agents of change truly transnational corporations, that owe allegiance to no nation state and locate wherever in the globe market advantage dictates.

(Hirst and Thompson 1996: 1)

Global theorists contrast the globalized economy with the (literally) *international* post-war world order. This old world was an aggregate of essentially national economies, linked by trade, where companies produced primarily for domestic markets and only secondarily for export, where the production process took place within national frontiers, and where governments protected, supported and championed home industries and national firms, and devised rules for international trade within intergovernmental forums, principally the GATT (General Agreement on Tariffs and Trade). This system, it is argued, has been, or is being, transformed by a number of processes (Ohmae 1991). Technological developments have brought about revolutions in communications and information provision, diffusion and storage, thereby altering fundamentally the logistics, structures and relationships which previously characterized industry, creating new commercial opportunities and strategic possibilities, and undermining previously existing rationales for state intervention and regulation. Thus, the application of new communications technologies has facilitated the internationalization of capital markets, and enabled energy suppliers, broadcasters and telecommunications operators to extend beyond their national borders. Technological advance has also made possible competition in these industries where the existence of natural monopolies previously was used to justify public ownership and strict regulation. It has also had other effects. It has, for example, raised the premium and the cost of research and development, which has increasingly led companies keen to keep their fixed costs at tolerable levels to collaborate both within and across national frontiers, and it has made possible the rapid transfer of capital across the globe.

Trade between countries has increasingly been replaced by foreign direct investment, as companies have become internationalized in production, management and marketing, and as they seek new markets and cheap labour, and 'regime shop'. Growing larger and larger, as they reap economies of scale and scope, these internationalized firms become transnational corporations (TNCs), genuinely 'stateless firms', which can shift their activities around the globe effortlessly (Ohmae 1991, 1993, 1995; Julius 1990). The emergence and growth of TNCs, perhaps developing out of multinational corporations (MNCs), are facilitated by the globalization of consumer tastes, the internationalization of financial markets and the explosion of foreign currency

204

markets – developments which have been made possible by the spread of new advanced communications systems. Governments have become increasingly powerless in the face of these changes. Whereas previously they controlled and managed their home economies, the internationalization of economic activity has rendered them impotent and any attempted intervention is inevitably to the detriment of the consumer. In the words of Kenichi Ohmae:

> The globalization of consumer tastes, the rapid dispersion of technology, and the explosive growth of FX empire has changed landscapes familiar to corporate strategists, so that if we look closely at the world Triad [US, EU and Japanese] companies inhabit, national borders have effectively disappeared and, along with them, the economic logic that made them useful lines of demarcation in the first place. Not everyone, however, has noticed.
>
> (1991: 214)

> The interlinked economy of the Triad is so powerful that it has swallowed most consumers and corporations, made traditional national borders almost disappear, and pushed bureaucrats, politicians and military towards the status of declining industries.
>
> (1991: xii)

Although, as Hirst and Thompson note, '[g]lobalization has become a fashionable concept in the social sciences, a core dictum in the prescriptions of management gurus, and a catch phrase for journalists and politicians of every stripe' (1996: 1), it has remained 'weakly specified' (Hirst and Thompson 1994). Various global theorists have identified various dynamics of the process, but none have formulated a satisfactory conceptualization. Hirst and Thompson in their sceptical appraisal of globalization have elaborated an ideal-type, however, identifying four elements (Hirst and Thompson 1992, 1996).[2] The first is a truly globalized economy where distinct national economies are subsumed, and national economic actors, governments and firms alike, find themselves confronting an international economic system which has become 'autonomized' and 'socially disembedded' (1996: 10–11). TNCs are the 'major players' in the world economy – the second element – and are 'genuine footloose capital, without specific national identification and with an internationalized management, and . . . willing to locate and relocate anywhere in the globe to obtain either the most secure or the highest returns' (1996: 11). A third element is the 'further decline in the political influence and the economic bargaining power of organized labour' (1996: 12–13). The growth in 'fundamental multipolarity in the international political system' (1996: 13) is the final element. 'The hitherto hegemonic national power could no longer impose its own distinct regulatory objective in either its own territories or elsewhere . . . A variety of bodies from international voluntary agencies to TNCs would thus gain relative power at the expense of national governments' (1996: 13). This ideal-type provides a very valuable model for judging the significance of developments in air transport and assessing the extent to which the industry has become globalized.

THE TRADITIONAL REGIME

The regime that has historically governed air transport approximates very closely to the international model described above. It was founded on the principle, originally enshrined in the Paris Convention in 1919 and re-affirmed by the Chicago Convention of 1944, that each state enjoys absolute sovereignty over the airspace above its territory. Under this regime, governments used their prerogatives to develop their air transport industries and to support their carriers, intervening extensively and building protective walls around their national aviation markets. The industry that grew up within this regulatory system has been aptly described by Kasper (1988: 1) as a 'series of local monopolies connected by a set of equally protected international routes'. Economic fragmentation into distinct national markets was matched by the division of airspace and the management of air traffic control along national lines. Governments acted independently in determining the organization of national airspace and in operating air traffic control systems.

Limited international cooperation took place within a number of global and regional aviation organizations. Signatories to the Chicago Convention became members of the International Civil Aviation Organization (ICAO), a UN-affiliated body which played a major role in developing technical standards for the industry. Regional organizations, notably, the European Civil Aviation Conference (ECAC), the African Civil Aviation Commission (AFCAC), the Arab Civil Aviation Council (ACAC) and the Latin American Civil Aviation Commission (LACAC), constituted important forums for discussing more local concerns. In addition, the European Organization for the Safety of Air Navigation (EUROCONTROL) was created by six West European nations for the purpose of strengthening cooperation in air navigation.

The regulatory system and policies of patriotic interventionism

Recognition of the principle of absolute state sovereignty at Chicago, where delegates had met to determine the post-war framework for international air transport, equipped governments with powers which they used to pursue policies of patriotic interventionism in the three principal domains of commercial aviation, namely, international scheduled services, international non-scheduled (charter services), and domestic services.[3] With respect to international scheduled air services, it proved possible to reach multilateral agreement only on the definition of the freedoms of the air (see Table 9.1) and on the availability of the non-commercial freedoms (the first and second freedoms). The commercial freedoms (the third, fourth and fifth) came to be exchanged on a bilateral basis, following the example set by the then leading aviation powers, the United Kingdom and the USA, at Bermuda in 1946. Contracting governments negotiated air services agreements under which they designated the airlines that would be permitted to operate services between the two countries and they decided how capacity should be shared between each other's airlines. Importantly, in order to safeguard against the security risks presented by flags of convenience, a nationality clause was included in the bilateral agreement, stipulating that only airlines which were 'substantially owned and controlled' by nationals of the contracting parties could be designated and thereby exercise the traffic rights exchanged. The parties also specified the routes that carriers would be authorized to follow and the points in each country that they could serve.

While retaining their ultimate authority over the authorization of fares, the contracting governments obliged the designated airlines to reach agreement on the fares to be charged for each route. In most cases, this was to be done in accordance with the relevant rate set by the International Air Transport Association (IATA), the world trade association set up in 1945 to represent international scheduled air carriers.[4] The setting of fares at its

Table 9.1 The freedoms of the air

Freedoms defined by the International Air Transport Agreement and exchanged in bilateral agreements

First freedom: the freedom to overfly the territory of another state

Second freedom: the freedom to land for technical reasons in another state

Third freedom: the freedom to carry commercial traffic from the home state to the foreign state

Fourth freedom: the freedom to carry traffic from the foreign state to the home state

Fifth freedom: the freedom for a carrier to carry commercial traffic between two foreign states on a route to or from the home state

Other freedoms

Sixth freedom: the freedom to operate commercial services between two foreign states via the home state

Seventh freedom: the freedom to operate commercial services directly between two foreign states

Cabotage (Eighth freedom): the freedom to operate commercial services between two points in a foreign state

---

Source: Based on R. Doganis (1991) *Flying off Course: The Economics of International Airlines*, London: HarperCollins.

207

regional Traffic Conferences was its principal function. In addition, the designated airlines negotiated pooling agreements which implemented the terms of the bilateral accord, set out operational procedures and often included revenue-sharing arrangements. Thus, the air services agreements negotiated intergovernmentally were complemented by multilateral and bilateral inter-airline agreements.[5]

Bilateral agreements were flexible mechanisms which enabled governments to control access to and from their aviation markets. Although some governments were more liberal than others[6] and there was some variation in the terms of bilateral agreements,[7] they were negotiated on terms that offered protection to its carrier(s).[8] Typically, each government designated one airline only ('monodesignation') – usually its flag carrier – to operate services, so that most international routes were operated by duopolies, and agreed to split capacity between the carriers of each country on a strictly fifty-fifty basis. More valuable traffic rights were exchanged by governments only if their airlines were not disadvantaged. Thus, fifth freedoms rights were rarely granted, and cabotage virtually never. Moreover, a state would protest whenever it considered that a foreign airline was combining third and fourth freedoms, thus creating the so-called sixth freedom, so diverting traffic away from its own flag carrier.

Governments enjoyed no less control over international charter and domestic services.[9] With respect to the former, strict conditions were set for operators by both governments, and the state of destination could refuse to authorize such services. Charter operations flourished only in markets serving countries whose governments followed liberal aviation policies and those wishing to develop their tourist industries. Concerning domestic services, governments unilaterally controlled market access, specified routes and determined fare levels.

With respect to all three categories of commercial aviation, governments exercised control over the freedom of establishment. All carriers had to satisfy nationally determined criteria for technical and economic fitness and fulfil the requirement that they be owned and substantially controlled by nationals of the country of registration. Moreover, aviation was typically excluded from national rules that prohibited anti-competitive practices.

Government intervention and protectionism was justified on a number of grounds.[10] First, air transport was considered to engage the state's responsibility for ensuring the nation's security. Second, commercial aviation was an infant industry, and although there were important exceptions to the rule of public ownership, including most notably the US airlines, but also Cathay Pacific, Korean Air, Canadian Pacific, UTA (France) and Varig (Brazil) (Hanlon 1996: 5), it was widely believed that carriers would not survive and the industry could not develop without the state's financial support. Third, detailed regulation was considered necessary to guarantee high safety standards and the stability of the industry. Fourth, the possession of a flag carrier came to acquire a near-mystical significance, signalling national independence and becoming an indispensable and proud symbol of sovereignty (Sampson 1984: 115–20; Sochor 1991). Finally, governments regarded their air carriers as instruments with which to pursue important non-aviation objectives in foreign policy, defence, industrial policy and employment.

With the notable exception of the USA, where the interests of its international air carriers were none the less defended in aviation diplomacy, the central pillar of national aviation policy was sponsorship and support of the flag carrier. The national airline was typically brought into being by the state, and partially or fully state-owned. It was supported from the public purse with a variety of direct and indirect subsidies, cheap loans, tax exemptions and various other dispensations. It enjoyed privileges guaranteed by statute and was insulated from competitive pressures through the grant of monopoly rights on international routes and over the domestic network, and the presence of its subsidiaries in the non-scheduled sector protected by restrictive charter policies. The flag carrier was granted dominant positions at the major national airports, privileged access to landing slots and favourable ground handling arrangements. Moreover, the flag carrier benefited from a battery of minor privileges. For example, civil servants travelling on business were obliged to fly with their national airline.

Governments, airlines and commercial strategy

Under the traditional regime, the commercial opportunities of airlines depended on their governments. The fortunes of independent carriers were determined by the willingness of governments to permit them to operate services either alongside the flag carrier or on routes not served by the national airline, their (the governments') willingness and ability to secure additional traffic rights, and the degree of leverage that could be exerted on government by a hostile flag carrier. Flag carriers, in contrast, enjoyed a protected position in many important respects. However, they were not completely free agents. Indeed, they were constrained in a number of important ways. First, strict rules governed the sale, transfer and ownership of their equity. Ceilings were typically imposed on the permissible levels of private and foreign ownership. Second, as part of the public sector, flag carriers had to compete with other state-owned companies for financial resources and, like them, the level of resources made available to them was influenced by the performance of the national economy rather than their own commercial endeavour. Third, they enjoyed little commercial freedom. Subject to the technical tutelage of the transport ministry and the financial control of the finance ministry, their top management was appointed typically on the basis of political or patronage considerations rather than managerial or commercial skills. Also, they were often subject to public service obligations. Moreover, a government's concern for employment, foreign or diplomatic considerations, or desire to support the aerospace or other industries often led it to make decisions that were costly for the company and which would not have been chosen on commercial grounds.

Air transport under the traditional system was thus characterized by protectionism, detailed regulation, collusion and anti-competitive practices. The opportunities available to independent airlines, while the flag carriers, tightly regulated and insulated from the pressures of competition, lacked the freedom to operate on a commercial basis and the incentives to improve services or increase productivity or profitability.[11]

CHANGES AND DEVELOPMENTS IN AIR TRANSPORT

Aviation has witnessed very considerable change since the late 1970s both at the level of government policy and commercial strategy. A growing number of governments have implemented more or less far-reaching programmes of liberalization, deregulation and privatization, and airlines have been forced to respond to the new regulatory environment, new imperatives and new opportunities with varying degrees of enthusiasm and success.

The new US policy and its consequences

The US government made the first breach in the traditional system in the late 1970s. Following criticisms of the costs of regulation over a number of years and the rise of an alternative economic model – contestable markets theory (Baumol 1982) – which held that competition would, contrary to conventional wisdom, be feasible in air transport, the Carter administration deregulated domestic air transport, renegotiated its air services agreements with many of its bilateral partners and challenged IATA to 'show cause' as to why it should be exempted from US anti-cartel legislation. The new policies and their consequences had a profound affect on the industry, as well as serving as a point of reference for all subsequent debates about the regulation of the industry.

Domestic deregulation has had a number of effects.[12] Passengers have generally benefited from lower fares and competition in quality of services. However, there has been some debate about whether the airlines' development of hub-and-spoke route structures, which means that passengers often have to break their journeys and change aircraft on route, has been beneficial to customers who it is assumed would prefer direct services. Another issue has been whether small towns and cities have lost air links as a result of deregulation, since, under the previous system, airlines were obliged to serve them, even if the routes were unprofitable. Finally, there has been considerable anxiety about the bankruptcy and disappearance of both old-established carriers and new entrants, and about the anti-competitive effects of the consolidation that has taken place in the US industry since the mid-1980s.

The new foreign aviation policy pursued by the USA also had very significant consequences. In the first place, the US government not only liberalized certain of its bilateral agreements, but also included some innovative concepts and practices in its revised bilateral agreements. The new accords expanded access, allowed multi-designation, granted fifth freedom rights, included and extended unlimited freedoms to non-scheduled operators, removed capacity restrictions and introduced a system of double disapproval for fares under which tariffs proposed by air carriers become operative unless both governments disapproved. Second, the US government's challenge to IATA led to the effective downgrading of the body's operations after 1979, particularly concerning routes to and from the USA. IATA could no longer require that the fares agreed at its tariff-setting conferences be enforced by its members. Third, the USA called for a non-tariff zone on the North Atlantic. It signed a Memorandum of Understanding (MOU) with twelve members of ECAC in 1982, introducing a new concept in tariff setting. Zones of flexibility were established in relation to a reference fare, and governments were not permitted to disapprove of tariffs that fell within these zones, irrespective of the conditions set down in bilateral agreements.

Finally, the new US policy led to very significant developments at the level of the firm. The consolidation of the domestic industry led to the emergence of a small number of powerful airlines – American Airlines, United Airlines, Delta, Northwest and Continental.[13] These airlines gradually acquired international traffic rights, and harnessed their domestic strength to pose a formidable challenge to their competitors, particularly European majors on the North Atlantic. Today, five of the top ten world airlines ranked by sales are US carriers, while in terms of capacity six of the top ten are American (Hanlon 1996: 4, 6).

At the level of the firm, airlines developed new strategies and techniques in order to compete in the market. One important change was the development of hub-and-spoke networks, whereby airlines collected passengers from several small settlements and carried them in small aircraft to a larger city, then in a single large aircraft transported them to another larger city, from where they would be dispersed once again in small aircraft and flown to their final destinations. This system had two main advantages over the point-to-point networks which preceded it: first, it enabled each airline to offer flights to a larger number of destinations; and second, it afforded them significant economies of scope. A second innovation was the extended use of computer reservation systems (CRSs). US airlines began to use these powerful marketing and ticket distributing tools, which provided information about services and fares to terminals located in travel agents, to devise increasingly sophisticated ticketing policies and to respond rapidly to changes in demand or a competitor's fares.

Third, airlines extended their networks through acquisition, take-over and alliance-building, and the creation of independent low-cost subsidiaries (Hanlon 1996: 92–3). In alliances between major and minor carriers, the former increased feeder traffic into its hub, while avoiding the costs that a full take-over would bring, and the latter was able to secure a guaranteed flow of traffic. Code sharing, whereby a connecting flight involving alliance partners would be advertised under a single code without necessarily indicating an on route change of planes became an increasingly widespread practice. Finally, airlines developed customer loyalty schemes, Frequent Flyer Plans (FFPs), which offered rewards on a progressive basis to passengers who accumulated air miles.

These practices, pioneered by US carriers, were emulated by other airlines as liberalization spread and the industry was opened up to competition.

The spread of deregulation and privatization

From the early 1980s, other governments, influenced by the US example, the rise of free market ideology and pressures on public spending which made them less able to support unprofitable enterprises, embarked upon liberalization and privatization programmes in aviation. The United Kingdom was the first, having for a number of years pursued a more liberal policy than its European counterparts. It partially deregulated its domestic market in 1980, then renegotiated a number of its air services agreements in Europe and took the dramatic step of privatizing its flag carrier, British Airways (BA). It also sought to multilateralize liberalization by supporting the European Commission's attempts to develop an EC aviation policy.

Liberalization and privatization programmes have also been implemented in Canada, Australia, New Zealand, the Far East, and Central and South America (Button 1991; Hanlon 1996: 4–10; Wheatcroft and Lipman 1986, 1990) and are set to continue throughout the 1990s. However, it is important to recognize that the trend is not necessarily universal. Although well-established in the Americas, Australasia and the Far East, it has yet to take hold in Africa and the Middle East. Moreover, it is sobering to reflect that BA remains the only fully privatized flag carrier in Europe (Hanlon 1996: 8).

A single European market in aviation

The creation of a single European market in air services has been one of the most important developments in aviation.[14] Involvement of the European Community had been strongly opposed for thirty years by a majority of the member states. However, the coincidence of a number of factors in the mid-1980s set in train the progressive liberalization of air transport within the EC, brought about by the adoption of three air 'packages' of measures in

1987, 1990 and 1992. While the first two built upon the bilateral system, relaxing the provisions of air services agreements relating to market access, capacity sharing and tariff fixing, the third has created a single regulatory structure. Full rights of market access for routes within the Union, including fifth freedom rights and from 1 April 1997 cabotage rights, have been extended to all carriers (scheduled and non-scheduled, home and foreign) satisfying EU licensing requirements and 'owned and substantially controlled' by EU nationals: airlines are free to set tariff levels according to their own commercial judgement without requiring approval from the regulatory authorities and restrictions on capacity have been lifted, although safeguards have been instituted in all three areas to protect against abuses and to allow action to be taken in emergency situations. Moreover, the competition rules of the EEC Treaty, covering anti-competitive agreements (Article 85), the abuse of dominant position (Article 86) and state aid (Articles 92–4), as well as the Merger Regulation, have been implemented in air transport. Finally, rules aimed at ensuring transparency and the prohibition of discrimination against EU nationals have been introduced with respect to the allocation of airport landing slots and the operation and ownership of computer reservation systems.

EU action has had radical consequences for the member states (see Table 9.2), who have been deprived of the instruments which they previously used to pursue protectionist policies (Kassim 1996a), and for European airlines, who are free to exercise not only the third and fourth freedoms, but the fifth, sixth and seventh freedoms and even cabotage rights (Hanlon 1996: 78). Moreover, a number operate subsidiaries or have taken substantial holdings in independent carriers in other member states. For example, British Airways successfully operates Deutsche BA in Germany and has a 49 per cent holding in the French carrier TAT. However, enacting and implementing the common aviation policy has not been as easy as some commentators have alleged.[15] A number of the more conservative member states, particularly those with loss-making carriers, have found it difficult to desist from intervention, remain reluctant liberalizers and privatizers, and are still unused to the idea that the financial relationship between government and flag carrier is regulated by EU competition rules and scrutinized by the European Commission's air transport directorate. Moreover, a number of companies have found the transition from public enterprise to commercial company very difficult to effect. Air France, Alitalia, Iberia and Olympic Airways have all experienced considerable difficulties in implementing restructuring programmes.

Further difficulties have been faced by the European Commission, whose role has been considerably enhanced in the area with the development of the common policy. Not only has it limited resources, both financial and in personnel terms, but it has been constrained by the prevailing scepticism about, if not hostility to, EU action in the post-Maastricht era. It has thus

Table 9.2 From the Chicago regime to the single European market in air services

Policy	Chicago regime	Third package
Fares	Agreed by both governments (double approval)	Airlines set own fares (safeguards for excessively high or predatory fares)
Licensing	National rules	EU rules for ownership, airworthiness and economic fitness
Access		
• relations between state and own airlines	Governments full discretion	Subject to EU regime
• relations with 'foreign' (i.e. EU carriers)	Negotiated bilaterally	Subject to EU rules
• multiple designation (country to country)	Negotiated bilaterally	Yes, under EU rules
• multiple designation (city pairs)	Negotiated bilaterally case by case	Full access allowed
• fifth freedom	Rarely granted	Permitted without quota restraint
• cabotage	Never granted	Full rights from 1 April 1997
Capacity	Generally shared 50:50	No limits, but safeguards can be triggered in case of catastrophic change

Source: EC/EU legislation

exercised its regulatory powers, particularly with respect to state aid, with considerable flexibility and sensitivity.[16] Moreover, it has proved very difficult for the Commission to convince the member states that air services agreements with third countries could be more profitably negotiated if the EU bargained as a collectivity rather than on an individual basis. It has been particularly disappointed that a number of member states have signed 'open skies' agreements with the US government, which it considers has followed a strategy of 'divide and conquer'. Were member states to entrust the European Commission with a wide-ranging external competence, it would perhaps facilitate the development of US–EU cooperation with respect to a number of pressing air transport issues.

Airline strategy and liberalization

Airlines in Europe and elsewhere have responded to regulatory change by following many of the practices introduced by US carriers. Hub-and-spoke networks have been developed,[17] consortia formed to operate CRSs, and FFPs introduced. Three developments have been particularly striking (see Table 9.3). The first is consolidation by which means airlines have taken control of their national competitors. Thus, British Airways has acquired British Caledonian and Dan-Air; Royal Dutch Airways (KLM) took over NLM and Transavia; Air France took a majority shareholding in UTA and thereby acquired control of Air Inter (the French domestic airline); Lufthansa gained control over Interflug (the national carrier of the former GDR); and SAS acquired a majority shareholding in the independent Scandinavian carrier, Linjeflyg.

A second significant change has been the proliferation of alliances and partnerships between airlines wanting to benefit from complementary networks.[18] These have been struck not only between airlines sharing the same nationality, but also between carriers from different countries and other regions. Thus, BA has agreements with other British carriers including Cityflyer Express, Loganair, Manx Airlines, GB Airways and Brymon European. At the European level, Swissair, SAS (Scandinavian Airways Systems), Austrian Airlines and Finnair cooperate within the 'European Quality Alliance', while a number of major international groupings have also been formed (see Table 9.4). They can involve code-sharing, joint marketing, block spacing, the pooling of FFPs and franchising.

The third noteworthy development is hybridization, taking the form either of mixed public–private ownership or home and foreign ownership. The first case has occurred with full or partial privatization; the second, when airlines in transnational alliances have decided to underpin their cooperation by purchasing a proportion of their partner's equity. The development of the latter has been striking, even though neither transnational investments nor even multinational airline consortia are altogether new (Hanlon 1996: 9, 195–6).

Table 9.3 Major partnerships of selected flag carriers

Airline	Shareholdings	Alliances	Other operations
Air France	Air Charter 80% Air Inter 76%	Air Canada[a] Aeromexico[a]	Merger with UTA Bought shareholding in CSA (Czechoslovakia), but negotiated re-sale of stake
	Air Austral 34% Air Tchad 33.7% Middle East Airlines 28.5% plus smaller stakes in various African airlines	Vietnam Airlines[b] Japan Airlines[c]	Negotiated sale of stake in Sabena
Alitalia	Avionova 45% Eurofly 45% Malev 30% Air Europe 27.6%	Malev[c] British Midland[c] Continental Airlines[c]	
British Airways	British Asia Airways 100% Brymon European 100% BA Regional 100%	Cityflyer Express[d] Maersk Air[d] Loganair[d]	Merger with British Caledonian Merger with Dan-Air Proposed alliance with American Airlines

	TAT 49.9%	Manx Airlines[d]	Holding in proposed new airline, Air Russia
	Deutsche BA 49% GB Airways 31% Air Russia 25% USAir 24.6% Qantas 21% Qantas[f]	TAT[d] Deutsche BA[d] GB Airways[d] Brymon European[c] USAir[c e g]	
Lufthansa	Condor Flugdienst 100% Lufthansa Cargo 100% Lufthansa CityLine 100% EuroBerlin 49% SunExpress 40% Lauda Air 39.7% Business Air 38.4% Cargolux 24.5% Luxair 13%	United Airlines[c e] Canada[c e] Varig[c] Thai Airways[e] Lauda Air[c] Business Air[c] Luxair[c e] Cargolux[f] Finnair[e]	

Notes: a = alliance agreement; b = equipment sharing; c = code sharing; d = franchising; e = joint sales/marketing agreement; f = joint operations; g = frequent flyer programme

Source: AEA (1995) *Yearbook 1995*, Brussels: AEA

Table 9.4 Major international alliances (ranked in order of sales)

1. United Airlines – Lufthansa – Japan Airlines – Varig – Hawaiian
2. Air France – Sabena – Alitalia – Continental – Air Canada
3. Delta – Swissair – Singapore Airlines – Varig
4. British Airways – USAir – Qantas – Air New Zealand – TAT – Deutsche BA – Air Russia
5. Northwest – KLM – Transavia – Air UK
6. American Airlines – South African Airways – British Midland
7. Iberia – Ladeco – Aerolineas Argentinas – TAP Air Portugal – Viasa

Source: Hanlon, P. (1996) *Global Airlines*, Oxford: Butterworth, Heinemann

To give four examples, BA has acquired minority holdings in Air Mauritius, Air Russia, Deutsche BA, Qantas, TAT European Airlines and USAir; KLM has acquired stakes in ALM Antillean, Air UK and Northwest; SAS has holdings in British Midland; and Iberia has acquired stakes in Aerolineas Argentinas, Ladeco and Viasa.

GLOBALIZATION OR 'CONSTRAINED INTERNATIONALIZATION'

The transformation undergone by the industry has clearly been considerable. However, there are strong reasons for believing that this does not signal globalization. Moreover, there are formidable obstacles confronting any putative globalizing tendencies. Taking the four elements of the ideal-type elaborated by Hirst and Thompson, it can be argued that air transport does not approximate to a globalized system.[19]

An autonomized world system beyond governance?

In a globalized system, the distinctively national is subsumed, subordinate and subject to the play of autonomized international processes. However, in air transport, the national retains its importance, even if deregulation, privatization and liberalization – and in the EU, the development of a common aviation policy – have marked a certain retreat on the part of the state and altered the relationship between state and flag carrier. Critically, the bilateral system, which enshrines the absolute sovereignty of the state, enabling governments to negotiate the terms of access for international air services and to pursue mercantilist policies, remains largely intact. (Only for international services within the European Union has it been superseded.) It is used by all states, including the most liberal, to promote the interests of its national industry,[20] and is still defended as a flexible mechanism for ensuring the equitable exchange of traffic rights.[21] Though multilateral and 'plurilateral' schemes have been debated, and the possibility of revising the Chicago

Convention floated, it seems unlikely that the current system will be radically modified in the near future. The unanimity that would be required for global multilateralism clearly does not obtain. Regional differences are evident, with an overwhelming majority of ICAO members and whole regions, notably, Africa and the Middle East, solidly in favour of the existing bilateral system. There are many countries who are happy to allow IATA to continue performing its traditional function (Hanlon 1996: 223–4). Moreover, there is no readily available organization or framework which could be charged with responsibility for managing a multilateral regime. It is extremely unlikely that the leading aviation powers with large domestic markets would agree to bring air transport within the scope of GATT, since the Most Favoured Nation and National Treatment principles would disadvantage their carriers, while not bringing reciprocal benefits. ICAO is considered to be too cumbersome to perform such a role.

Not only do states still have the power to intervene in the industry, they still retain an interest in so doing – the USA's recent round of aviation diplomacy and the inquiry set up by President Clinton, as well as the fact that European governments under severe financial pressure still continue to plough state aid into ailing flag carriers bear eloquent testimony to this. Airlines are not only important employers, customers, income generators and hard currency earners; their symbolic role as flag carriers shows no sign of being diminished. A considerable number, it must be remembered, remain state-owned.[22]

Although international conditions provide opportunities for air carriers and impose constraints on the power of governments, the influence of the national is still considerable and the importance and impact of an airline company's home base remains unchanged.[23] As well as depending on the capacity of governments to provide a stable environment within which to operate, airlines are profoundly affected by exchange rate policy, general macro-economic policy, the fiscal regime, competition policy and the regulation of consumer, safety and environmental matters. Also, since they raise capital, recruit labour and appoint management largely from their home state, the regulation of the labour market, and education and training policy influence air carriers.

Finally, recent developments in the industry concerning transnational alliances and the forms of cooperation between airlines do raise regulatory issues and questions about jurisdiction and territoriality. However, there is no reason to suppose that because they fall outside the jurisdiction of national authorities they lie completely beyond the scope of governance by, for instance, regional or other international authorities.

Truly trans-national corporations?

The emergence of genuinely transnational corporations, footloose organizations which owe allegiance to no particular country, is a second feature of the globalized economy. TNCs are the 'prime movers' (Hirst and Thompson

1992) of the globalized economy. Although the horizons of airlines have expanded dramatically, even the most ambitious global strategy – that of BA – does not have a global reach and has a substantial presence in only three of the world's six major markets (Hanlon 1996: 222). Despite the creation of transnational alliances, hybridization, the separation between 'producer interest' and 'the national interest', and the fact that some airlines have 'exported' segments of their operations, the era of the stateless airline has not yet emerged. As Sir Colin Marshall has noted, there is a considerable difference between being 'a global airline' and 'flying the globe' (Sochor 1991: 203). In the overwhelming majority of states, limitations on the level of foreign ownership of equity remain, and the nationality clause in air services agreements restricts traffic rights to airlines that are 'owned and substantially controlled' by nationals of the contracting parties. Moreover, the trend towards private ownership is still not universal. Perusal of the ownership structures in the annual surveys of the industry published by *Airline Business* reveals a very mixed pattern, with some states retaining a 100 per cent stake in their flag carriers.[24]

Moreover, alliances which are considered by global theorists such as Ohmae to be essential to the process of globalization have not been solidly established in air transport. There are very few examples of active partnerships with impressive longevity, but a considerable number which have experienced difficulties and even rupture. Thus, the relationship between KLM and Northwest has not always been easy, the European Quality Alliance may be threatened by SAS's partnership with Lufthansa, the Air France Group has sold its stakes in Sabena and the Czech carrier CSA, and has found integrating its parent company and the former Air Inter problematic, and BA's proposed alliance with American Airlines has reportedly led its (BA's) partner USAir to contemplate legal action.

The demise of organized labour?

Global theorists assert that the power of organized labour declines as globalization proceeds. However, in aviation, although considerable pressure has been exerted on labour as airlines have attempted to increase productivity, cut costs and restructure in order to become competitive, trade unions have not become insignificant. Indeed, in France, Greece, Italy, Spain and the UK, trade union action and industrial unrest has influenced management decisions. Moreover, in the USA, employee participation has been increasing. Northwest, United Airlines, TWA and USAir all have exchanged shares in the company for concessions, pensions and working rules (Hanlon 1996: 9).

Emerging multipolarity?

In the globalized system, hegemonic national power is superseded and authority is dispersed between actors and organizations at sub-national, regional and global levels. In air transport, however, states retain decisive powers. Only within the European Union has an alternative authority developed, and even here national governments exercise an important influence over the development of policy. Elsewhere, other organizations exist, but they are intergovernmental and so do not challenge the power of the state.

CONCLUSION

Radical changes have taken place in air transport, but they do not amount to globalization and the industry does not approximate to the model of the globalized economy defined by Hirst and Thompson. Moreover, there are strong reasons for believing that globalization is unlikely to take place in the near future. The international regime remains fundamentally intergovernmental, states are reluctant to cede their sovereignty, and the importance of nationality has not been eradicated. In addition, the global community of consumers envisaged by Ohmae has not been realized in aviation. Income is the main determinant of air transport demand, but income distribution is uneven within and between regions, so that the globalization of consumer demand is yet to take place. Also, there is no technological revolution on the horizon, analogous to advances in telecommunications. The march of globalization is not inevitable and all-embracing, contrary to the assertions of the global theorists.

NOTES

1 I should like to express my gratitude to all the officials, past and present, airline executives and interest group representatives who have generously assisted me in my research on the airline industry. I should also like to thank Sara Connolly for her encouragement and forbearance, and Alan Scott for his patience.

2 Hirst and Thompson's formulation is too long to be quoted in full here, so the description here is the author's attempt to paraphrase it.

3 For detailed discussion of the regulatory system, see Cheng 1962, Doganis 1993, Hanlon 1996, Martin *et al.* 1984, National Consumer Council 1986, and Naveau 1989. The main document signed at Chicago was the Convention on International Civil Aviation (the 'Chicago Convention'). The most important of the associated agreements were the International Air Transport Agreement, which defined the freedoms of the air, and the International Air Service Transit Agreement, which provided for the exchange of the technical freedoms of the air.

4 See Doganis 1991, Naveau 1989, and Sampson 1984 for discussions of IATA.

5 The following analogy has been suggested: 'Imagine Japan allowing Sony to be the only Japanese firm to make a product like a Walkman; and then imagine all the other world's consumer-electronics firms getting together to agree identical prices for televisions, CD players and video camcorders. If one firm happened to sell more than its share, the cartel would split the extra revenue between its members. Consumers would be in uproar. Yet that is exactly what airlines have been doing for decades' *The Economist*, ('Survey – Airlines', 12.6.93: 6).

6 For example, the UK had followed a liberal charter policy since the 1960s and attempted to secure traffic rights for a second British carrier on international routes.
7 See Doganis 1991, for discussion of the new style of bilateral agreements.
8 See Hanlon 1996: 70–88 for an excellent discussion of bilateral agreements.
9 See Doganis 1991 and Loder 1986 in National Consumer Council 1986 and Naveau 1989 for further discussion of charter and domestic regulation and services.
10 The following paragraphs draw heavily from Kassim 1996a.
11 See Attali 1994 for the views of an 'insider' and Vinçon 1991 for those of a critical outsider.
12 For detailed discussion of US deregulation and its consequences, see Naveau 1989, Doganis 1991, Morrison and Winston 1986 and 1995, Pryke 1991, and Borenstein 1992.
13 The top five carriers accounted for 57 per cent of output of the US industry in the mid-1980s, they carry more than 70 per cent ten years later. See Hanlon 1996: 188 for a survey of mergers and acquisitions in the deregulated US industry.
14 For further discussion of EC/EU liberalization and its consequences, see Comité des Sages 1994, UK Civil Aviation Authority 1993, Balfour 1994, Button and Swann 1989 and 1991, De Coninck 1992, McGowan and Seabright 1989, Wheatcroft and Lipman 1990, and Kassim 1996a and 1996b.
15 See, for example, the argument in Balfour 1994, which presents a somewhat rosy picture.
16 See Balfour 1993.
17 Though conditions in Europe are significantly less conducive to the development of hub-and-spoke networks than the USA, since the population is more evenly dispersed, distances between population centres are shorter and the competition from other modes of transport is greater.
18 See Gallacher and Odell 1994 for a comprehensive survey.
19 Though, of course, Hirst and Thompson did not elaborate their model with air transport in mind.
20 For example, the US 'open skies' policy attempts to use the bilateral agreement as a means to promote the interests of US carriers. See, for example, Shenton 1994.
21 See, for example, Espérou 1990.
22 The remarks of an anonymous official of the European Commission are worth recalling: 'The biggest barrier to air transport liberalisation in Europe is this crazy idea that every member state has to have its own airline ... People still assume that there is something glorious about flying, but airlines are just glorified bus companies', quoted in *The Financial Times*, 29.7.94: 2.
23 This paragraph draws heavily from Wright 1995: 24.
24 See also Hanlon 1996: 8.

10

GLOBALIZATION, THE COMPANY AND THE WORKPLACE

Some interim evidence from the auto industry in Britain[1]

Paul Stewart and Philip Garrahan

INTRODUCTION

The basis of the globalization thesis is that the nation state is becoming marginalized by new economic forces. However, the argument that capital is now sufficiently organized to exercise increasingly unrestrained power and influence across the industrial world needs to be applied to particular national circumstances with a great deal of caution. In fact, the state remains a major force for change in the late twentieth century and this view, at the core of critical perspectives on transformations in economic relations, necessitates placing limits on the globalization thesis. We should not ignore 'the extent to which today's globalization both is authored by states and is primarily about *reorganizing, rather than bypassing, states*' (Panitch 1994: 63; emphasis added). The political economy of change in an industrialized country like Britain cannot be adequately explained without accounting for the key role of the state operating neo-liberal economic policy.

The specific explanation of change in the British auto industry must also acknowledge the two main pressures on manufacturers which were in operation before the arrival of the Japanese transplants from the mid-1980s onwards. Firstly, vagaries in the market are shown by dramatic shifts in demand over very short periods of time: for example, between 1989 and 1992 UK auto sales fell by over 20 per cent as the recession deepened. At the same time, neo-liberal economic policies embraced by the state supported opening up the economy to foreign competition. The ideological belief in the benefits of free-ranging, deregulated market competition led to government encouragement for Japanese transplants. But, the new industrial order which they signified did not convince everyone that the playing field was level. Although the growing output of the Japanese transplants in the UK is boosting exports, the arrival of Honda, Nissan and Toyota as major manufacturers in the UK has generated an additional competitive pressure to the general recessionary forces of the last decade and a half. Management's rationale for change has thus been driven by the twin elements of recession and heightened competition from Japan *within* domestic and European Union markets.

It is in this cautionary vein that the influence of Japanese capital exercised via transplant operations needs to be seen. Japanese transplants have attracted major attention in contemporary debates about the globalization of economic relations. Within these debates, the 'Japanization' of industrial relations in Britain is held to be symptomatic of a global trend affecting manufacturing industries in general, and the British auto sector in particular. Just as the limits placed on the state's freedom to act in the face of global economic forces are often misread, so the 'Japanization' process has to be critically questioned (Elger and Smith 1994). The empirical findings in this chapter refute aspects of the globalization thesis, especially in so far as the national experience ought to conform to a standardizing effect. In the UK case employees' (largely negative) responses to change in the automotive sector are conditioned by the fact that the nature of new production arrangements arise from a different social milieu. It may be that if the social arrangements in Japan were transplanted here then employees attitudes would be more favourable. But the unlikely possibility of this becoming reality is only one further reason to doubt the efficacy of the globalization thesis: the reproduction of cultural and national differences (at the level of society and state) suggest the need for social science to account for the *re-articulation* (and possibly adaptation) to international forces for change at local (i.e. state) level as opposed to *local adoption (reproduction)* of global trends and developments. While the economic forces embraced by the term 'Japanization' are evident across many of the world's manufacturing industries, a quantum leap is required to assume that their effects will be uniform (ibid.). In this chapter we use evidence from three British car assembly plants where new management techniques said to mirror the production methods of the Japanese model have been introduced. However, their introduction does not guarantee an automatic development from old style Fordist industrial relations to predictable improvements in the experience of work. Our conclusions reinforce a general scepticism about the inevitability of local conformity, whether at state or regional level, to presumed global trends. This is not just because of the idiosyncrasy of social relations at the three plants studied. It is also justified by the critical stance which we take on the notion of globalization and the contributory role played by state policy.

The conception of globalization comes in many shapes and forms and in the automotive industry it has been represented in the canon of the Japanization school. Beginning in the UK in the late 1980s, this has been the dominant form (later evolving into the lean production paradigm at the level of technological change) within which developments in the automotive industry have been judged. Notable here in the generation of the canon are Oliver and Wilkinson (1992) and the early work of the Japanization Management Research Unit at the Cardiff Business School (see Elger and Smith's discussion of some of the discourses of Japanization 1994: 31–59). The early perception amongst the followers of the Japanization of British industry was that success demanded the adoption of actual Japanese management practices, or, failing that, their functional equivalents. This was to be the only significant change that economies should contemplate. The fragmentation of this paradigm into more or less coherent accounts of the fate of Japanese direct inward investment will not be examined here, but suffice for the present to note that the key assumption was of the convergence of industry in the West towards something approximating a Japanese model (see Stewart 1996). The model, of course drawn from the automotive sector, was largely dependent upon specific elements from one company (Toyota) and this further limitation made the model even more problematical. Nevertheless, this has allowed for something of an easy transition to the lean production model, the latest account of the progress towards globalization in the auto sector and by extension, industry as a whole. In the next section we assess the way conceptions of Japanese success in the auto sector underpin assumptions of the process of industrial restructuring and argue that the misleading character of this particular variant of globalization flattens the complexity of real differences in the sociology of manufacturing in general.

THE INTERNATIONAL AUTOMOTIVE INDUSTRY AND INDUSTRIAL RESTRUCTURING

The study of manufacturing organizations in contemporary economies has been exemplified, if not led, by the attention paid to the automobile sector. This derives from the cultural, political and social significance of the automobile for consumption and production models of life in modern capitalism. The automobile's meaning is inextricably linked to notions of modernization, and the industry which produces the automobile both generates and satisfies individual consumer demand (Williams *et al.* 1994). The auto industry in turn has become the measure for the well-being of advanced industrial societies, such that if the industry sneezes the whole economy catches a cold. Against this backcloth theories are proposed about the organizational specificities of the auto industry, especially given the Fordist model of mass production and the nature of the work organization underpinning it (Dankbaar *et al.* 1988; Wood 1989; Berggren 1993; Elger and Smith 1994). Currently, attention is focused on interpreting whether innovations in work organization represent a progressive force for change or instead are a case of old wine in new bottles (Hirst and Zeitlin 1991; Hirst and Thompson 1996). Using the auto industry as the basis of much broader explanations of societal change is also common (Piore and Sabel 1984; Williams *et al.* 1987). Here the emphasis increasingly is upon the nature of the social settlement, in which public policy's role is to ameliorate the divisions and inequalities associated with market competition (Clarke 1991; Williams *et al.* 1994). In this way, the study of the auto industry is also the study of how modern social contracts embodying the relation between the individual and the state should be set out and renewed.

These specific and general fields of inquiry are richly endowed with theoretical observations, yet there are significant lacunae in the empirical evidence. With some recent exceptions, much of the literature about the auto industry takes as given things which we would argue should be questioned (see *inter alia* Womack *et al.* 1990). There is a definite sense of apriorism discernible here. Aspects of this are raised in the critical discussion which follows of what we term 'the evangelistic school of lean production'. This school of thought holds to the view that there is just one best way forward, carrying with it the warning that any attempt at alternatives will wreak economic havoc. Such prescription does little to recognize the need for wider debates about how first to understand, and then to respond, to the complex and turbulent world of manufacturing industries, including the recognition that it is indeed possible to intervene at national and regional level with a multiplicity of policy initiatives and industrial strategies (Hines and Lang 1995). In the British case, the most important process of industrial change in the last two decades has been the trend towards de-industrialization, evidenced by the erosion of the manufacturing base.

The number of jobs in manufacturing employment declined from 8.03 million in 1970, to 4.4 million twenty years later. This period has also seen Britain becoming a net importer of manufactured goods for the first time in its history in 1982. Of course, the UK auto industry has been prominent in this decline and the consequences have been far reaching both for final assemblers and for the previously strong auto components sector. Import penetration of completed vehicles was low for a European country at around one-third of the market in 1970, but this had almost doubled by the beginning of the 1990s. The components industry has been radically restructured also, a process influenced significantly but not entirely by the relocation of assembly and local parts sourcing to Europe by UK-based multinationals (Amin and Smith 1990). In view of these currents of change, the fact of de-industrialization at a broader level and the policy of switching the location of production at the level of the firm, caution must be exercised when searching for solutions. Nevertheless, as we have indicated, a panacea is at hand for some commentators, and the deeper the economic crisis, the greater the temptation to succumb to catch-all solutions.

The pace of change in the British auto industry has been rising throughout the 1980s and 1990s. The far-reaching restructuring of the British industry is both a reflection of the internationalization of ownership and production, and of the transition in the hegemony of political ideas in Britain (Dicken 1992; Law 1991). Over and above the general trends worldwide, the specificities of the British case are notable, in that the Thatcher government elected in 1979 unleashed a radical version of liberal market economic policies (Hutton 1995). These policies signalled the demise of the post-1945 settlement which had been made around a welfare state, a mixed economy and extensive state regulation. In its place, the growing dominance of a new right ideology in British politics saw the rolling back of the state's bound aries, the deregulation of extensive areas of economic and social life, and the opening up of the economy to foreign direct investment attracted by depressed wage levels and a demoralized labour movement. Britain was not entirely alone in this, but the radical nature of the new right project pursued by the Thatcher and Major governments during the 1980s and 1990s made Britain a distinctive case at least in a European setting. The particularities of Britain's political economy serve as a reminder that the internationalization of economic relations is mediated, though not controlled, by state policies and national economic fortunes.

Three major Japanese automotive transplants have arrived in Britain during this period. They have been taken to indicate the beginning of a new phase of globalization distinguished by its fragmentation effect upon the peculiarities of the British transition from the post-1945 settlement. This new feature of change in the auto industry is the drive to greater market success on the basis of revised ways of managing the business, drawing in the main on the lessons of the Japanese auto industry since the 1950s. The perceived need to learn these lessons became pressing for management once the member states of the European Community (EC) signalled their intention in the mid-1980s to move towards creating the Single European Market (SEM). The corollary of establishing the world's single largest consumer market of 320 million people was that protectionist economic policies might ensue. The hugely successful Japanese auto firms responded to the possibility of 'fortress Europe' by transplanting production within the EC member states, choosing in the event to locate primarily in Britain. Beginning in 1986 with the greenfield site Nissan investment in Sunderland, there followed Honda's joint venture with Rover at Swindon and Toyota's greenfield sites in Derby and Shotton. By the middle of the 1990s, the three Japanese transplants in the UK reached a capacity of half a million cars a year, amounting to around one-third of the British domestic market. In the event, many of these vehicles are being exported to EC countries.

The effect of these transplants has been that it is no longer the case that competition with Japanese companies can be dealt with at arm's length. Not only have imports proved in the UK, as in North America, to be the means for increasing the market share of Japanese firms; now there is direct competition from Japanese cars made in Britain and without the disadvantage of import tariffs. Nissan and Toyota are advanced as UK examples of the move towards the Japanese model of industrial success – that 'we can do it here'.

LEAN PRODUCTION

Were change to follow the assumptions of the Japanization school of convergence the next phase of globalization in the automotive industry would be identified as lean production. This is understood to be distinct from the previous phase (that is, Japanization) in that it is not culturally specific – indeed its explanatory power is seen to reside in the fact that it has nothing whatsoever to do with *culture* in a sociological sense. In other words, the concept of the 'Japanization' of western industry is redundant. The lean production model claims universal applicability, since its protagonists regard it as a technical development without any social or cultural preconditions – one of the drawbacks to the 'Japanization' paradigm. However, we argue that the lean production school has both social and technical ambitions. The origins of the term lean production are to be found in the book *The Machine that Changed the World* by Womack, Roos and Jones (1990). According to them lean production represents a definitive break from the manufacturing idiom of mass production associated with Fordism. Lean production will allow both employers and employees to transcend the perceived drawbacks of Fordism which are characterized by the disharmony between production and consumption. Technical imperatives such as 'just-in-time' production scheduling are seen as axiomatic for this new manufacturing system. The obvious benefits to employers are that we only produce for need as defined in the rational market where the needs of the customer are understood in advance. The benefits to employees are that only necessary labour is to be expended in the process of production, thus allowing them to be more intelligently involved in the business of the planning and execution of their work. The first are beneficiaries because waste is removed from manufacturing whilst the second benefit because their skills will be enhanced in the new manufacturing paradigm. In addition, by following the prescribed pathway to success:

1 Lean production will replace mass production.
2 Under lean production, employees work smarter rather than harder. This is because, in contrast to the neo-craft relations of mass production, work is concentrated on labour process and organizational control through the dynamism of creative activity – the recombination of mental and manual labour axiomatic of Taylorism (ibid.: 102–3). Mass production cannot achieve this because slackness, an inherent part of the buffer system, allows for idle time.
3 Lean production will see the replacement of problem makers by problem solvers. By ensuring that all unnecessary activity is eradicated it becomes

possible to allow for both the creation of highly skilled/trained 'problem solvers' (ibid.) and the elimination of boring jobs.

4 The new production arrangements will give a new meaning to the concept of mutuality. Where old style industrial relations led to a dysfunctional tension between employers and employees, lean production will create a new industrial citizenry (ibid.: 103; Jones 1992).

5 The inefficiencies of all previous management regimes are essentially the fault of management.

These claims have been extended in more popular form:

● 'Lean production plants are 2–3 times better in productivity, quality, time and space' (Jones 1992: 25).

● Lean production is the foundation of a neo-capitalist solution to the problem of control and subordination of labour via responsibility which will inevitably lead to a change in the nature of capitalism (ibid.: 31).

● Lean production is not inherently Japanese (ibid.: 43).

RESEARCH FINDINGS

The research for this chapter is part of an ongoing study of responses to the introduction of new management techniques associated with lean production. Three plants have been studied, and a fourth plant is included in the disaggregated data for the completed findings (see Stewart and Garrahan 1995). A major aim of the research is to probe the extent to which lean production methods (LPMs) live up to their ambition in generating a more humane working experience. It is also intended that the research will provide insights into degrees of compliance and consent, plant by plant, as the indigenous UK auto industry undergoes changes in management styles. Central to this element are the problems of transforming an established tradition of employee relations from a conflictual to a collaborative mode. In this chapter, the evidence reported stems from taped interviews with union officials, including shop stewards, at three auto assembly plants in the UK. In addition, up to fifty detailed questionnaires were completed by shopfloor employees at the sites visited. This allowed for an analysis of worker responses to current management-initiated changes.

In the following analysis, we contend that the lean production paradigm fails to offer either a useful description of recent management changes (including the impact of these on employees) or a realistic prescription of what can be done to engineer change. As Williams *et al.* (1992) have argued, the latter is in any case a somewhat erroneous view which takes for granted the omnipotence of management in its ability to control the business environment. In the fourth section, we present the evidence which suggests that the impact of lean production is more recognizable in the terms of some of its critics, in effect, raising significant problems for the One Best Way

229

imperative with the insistence that lean production is socially benign. In short, the new management practices do not work in the way that their leading protagonists believe and certainly not in brown field sites.

The fieldwork for this research was conducted during the summer and autumn of 1992. This research concentrates on three plants already operational before the first Japanese transplant opened in 1986. The selection process encompassed one UK and one US company (two plants from the latter, one from the former) allowing us to concentrate on management practices undergoing change to mimic the lean production model (an account of the relationship between industrial relations and the new management initiatives is given in Stewart and Garrahan 1995).

The profile of our respondents reflects several significant dimensions of employment in the auto industry in Britain. In the three plants surveyed, few of our respondents were female, which was no surprise given the traditional predominance of male employment in the industry. However, another less predictable characteristic of our sample was the extensive duration of employment with the same employer. Economic recession and industrial restructuring since the 1970s have resulted in major downsizing exercises by the key auto firms. The remaining workforces are typical of our sample, where over 50 per cent had worked for their company for more than ten years. In such circumstances, such a well-experienced sample is a good sounding board for assessing the new management techniques recently introduced.

We have argued elsewhere that there is little to support the notion of a uniform trend towards the integrated factory said to typify lean production. Indeed, the evidence suggests significant local variation. This local variation is evident by the absence of a widespread transition from mass production (with its varieties of 'Fordist' rigidity and inefficiency), to lean production (with its equally varied 'Neo-Fordist' features). The argument that locale matters is thus our point of departure and is examined in some detail below where we assess the responses of employees to some aspects of the new management arrangements for change on the shopfloor.

MANAGEMENT, UNIONS AND THE EMPLOYEES' RESPONSES

Management–union relations in the UK auto industry were already stressful especially after Britain joined the European Community in 1972 and the declining competitiveness of the industry was emphasized. As exports declined and the market share of imports carried on increasing, companies inevitably sought to remove the perceived obstacles to improved productivity. As with automobile firms worldwide, automation was initially seen as a major solution. The current period of management-initiated transformations in work organization has also witnessed associated assaults on traditional demarcations within the industry. However, in the 1990s, this has less to do with the installation of new technologies. One generalization here might be that trade union responses to innovations such as team working were geared to defending skilled as against semi- or unskilled workers, but this would be to assume that skilled workers would resent the new opportunities for promotion that resulted from grouping workers in teams, in effect via a more open internal labour market. Where this has limited validity is at the intuitive level only. Our field work in the indigenous auto industry in the UK points to a more forceful division. Namely, the difference between the strategies preferred by the trade unions' national officers, and the plant-specific situations in which members and their stewards have to find immediate means of responding to the new management techniques.

Team working is theoretically a central plank in the drive towards the integrated plant necessary for lean production to be diffused. We can begin by citing a relatively less disingenuous view than that of Womack *et al.*, but one which is none the less alarming in its candour regarding the role of team working in the securing of surplus value from labour. Tyrni (1987: 32) opines that in the optimal teamwork setting,

> if some member shirks more than others, his effort is called unfair. In these circumstances, there develops pressure within the firm called ostracism, which prevents unfair effort. This does not only equalize the effort of all the members of the team but it increases their effort so that the highest possible reward is achieved. This result is called the cooperative game solution.

Such potentially damaging pressures are never alluded to in the language of the LPM literature, and there is rarely the same frankness in admitting this actual undercurrent of team working.

Restructuring the UK's auto industry has required a high level campaign on the part of all parties involved to sell the new practices. The initiatives to promote changes have included practices such as 'just-in-time operations', 'continuous improvement' regimes, 'commitment to quality', 'team working' and 'flexible working practices', amongst others. However, almost 90 per cent of our respondents interpreted new management practices in terms of team working. Clearly for employees, it is the more limited version of change, as opposed to management's grander design for a new auto industry model of regeneration, which at present prevails. This is not to pre-judge the effectiveness of plans to achieve the implementation of new working practices as broadly conceived, and indeed it can be shown that this varies substantially between plants in the UK auto industry reflecting different modes of trade union acceptance and participation in the new settlements (Stewart and Garrahan 1995). However, it does clearly highlight the divide between those who devise strategies of change, and those who are expected to deliver the results.

A significant element of the current changes for employees might be expected to be recorded in the personal experience of change to the daily

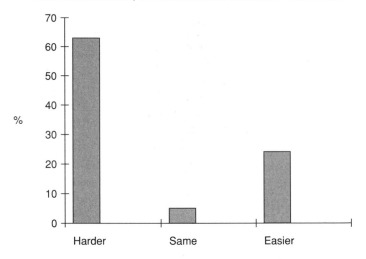

Figure 10.1 NMTs and working harder
Source: Author's survey of the UK auto industry 1993

work routine. A third of our respondents recorded that their work was varied between sections before the introduction of the new management techniques, rising to only 40 per cent thereafter. The perception in many management texts of manufacturing work becoming more varied at the individual level is thus not shared by employees in this instance. Whether individual work has also become more rewarding through this proposed variation is thus put in question. (For a full account and exploration of this theme of job enrichment, see Stewart and Garrahan 1995.) But for present purposes we focus on the issue of the positive transformation of the work place into a less arduous environment. We examined the claim of the protagonists of lean production that work will become less arduous after the change process. For 63 per cent of respondents in our sample, the new management techniques have resulted in work being made harder (see Figure 10.1).

On the issue of 'how far does lean production lead to an enhanced possibility for upskilling?', the results, represented in Figure 10.2, do not support the lean production thesis. A majority (60 per cent) of our respondents identified no difference in skills levels following the introduction of new management practices to achieve lean production. Although in a minority, over 25 per cent of employees see themselves as being more skilled under the new ways of organizing production. How might we account for this variation? Respondents who say that NMTs lead to more skilled work may be functionally distinguished within plants by the nature of their individual work, suggesting a profile of skilled/semi-skilled/unskilled employees typical of Fordist arrangements. More significantly, it could be that as capital investment in the body shop proceeds in line with lean expectations, those

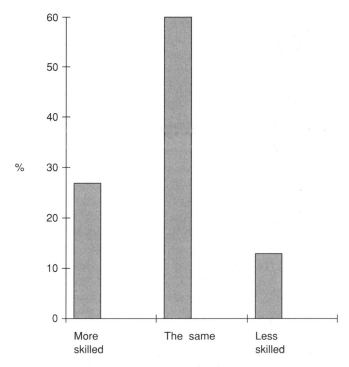

Figure 10.2 The effect of NMTs on skill
Source: as Figure 10.1

employees remaining – an increasing proportion of whom work on sub-assembly and final trim – are performing a greater number of job routines. Employees may well perceive the latter as upskilling. However, it should be said that from the size of our data set we have not been able to draw any statistically significant conclusions in respect to the differential impact upon skill of LPMs in either body shop or subassembly and final trim. But as we have said, the lean production school certainly expects employees outside the body shop to benefit from the increased level of skills required by LPMs. In addition, it may also be the case that for some, the personal involvement in the new order is a reflection of the powerful ideological pressures to conformity and commitment as is the case at Nissan, Toyota and Honda.

We now report on employees' views of three specific features of the effects of NMTs, specifically, to what extent work is perceived to be more or less physically demanding, mentally demanding and interesting. In the questions directed at the kind of mental and physical effort which is required of individuals once NMTs are introduced, employees identify a requirement for greater physical effort (Figure 10.3) and greater mental effort (Figure 10.4). In both cases, our respondents were overwhelmingly of the view that NMTs

233

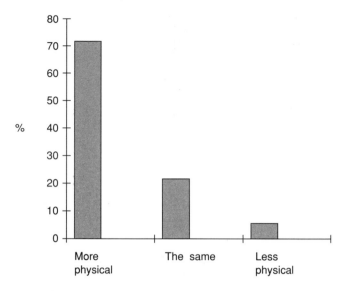

Figure 10.3 The effect of NMTs on physical effort
Source: as Figure 10.1

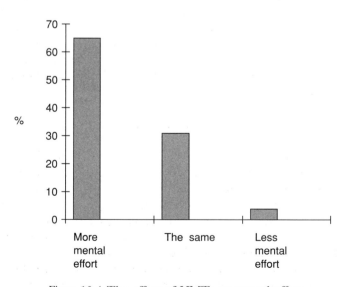

Figure 10.4 The effect of NMTs on mental effort
Source: as Figure 10.1

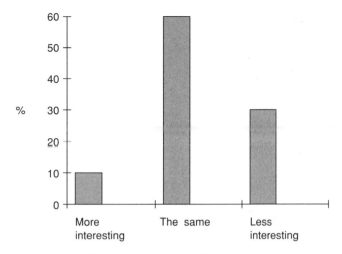

Figure 10.5 The effect of NMTs on job interest
Source: as Figure 10.1

demand more effort. Fewer than 10 per cent of respondents see the NMTs causing work to become less demanding of their effort.

Finally, the view that NMTs make work more interesting is not supported by the results as represented in Figure 10.5. Indeed, 30 per cent felt that after the introduction of NMTs their work had become less interesting.

As themes characterizing the general diagnosis of the drawbacks of mass production and as a prognosis for future success it is clear that the discourse of lean production is inherently flawed. Yet it still purveys a powerful if simple message. It is this simplicity which is so seductive and in this respect it stands in line to inherit a fairly conventional managerial tradition. We shall consider some of the implications of the project lying behind the lean production model in the final section.

CONCLUSION

The preceding assessment has been concerned to highlight the uniqueness of the social organization of production in the context of company and sector restructuring. We sought to locate this account in terms of the way employees themselves understand the change process. This is by no means a plea for an explanation of company or sector development in terms of social and economic relations *sui generis*. On the contrary, there is no question that foreign direct investment linked until recently to the hegemony of the Japanese economy has underscored profound transformations in all sectors, even if in a more obviously dramatic manner in the auto sector. Yet there is no evidence to suggest that international restructuring follows the certainties of the globalization theorists in their assumption of convergence. Internationalization is not being driven by the specificity of Japanese capital, so recently being challenged by the US as Berggren has cogently pointed out (1993). Neither is restructuring the result of the greatest of all ideological imperatives, technological innovation in the form of lean production. Quite the reverse. The process of internationalization is rather characterized by the unevenness of local adaptations, as Panitch (1994) argues in the context of particular state discourses and practices. This is true just as much of companies and in conditions and circumstances not always (and very rarely) of their own choosing. Our data is part of a wider study into the nature of contemporary social structural change in the automotive industry from the employees' standpoint. It cannot be taken to highlight the variation by company let alone by plant and so we need to be cautious on this score.

Our argument here is that changes in the operation of international capital have to be understood, in addition to their impact upon the company, from the point of view of the employee. One of the first factors this starting point allows for is the acceptance that employer intention, together with the outcome of implemented strategies, is mediated by employee predispositions, experience and personal (not to say collective) agendas. If the nature of the outcome of the strategy of the firm tells us something about the certainties and uncertainties of management and employees, we can advance the unremarkable view that the success or otherwise of the former depends upon the unevenness of social and economic development. That there can be no definitive turn in the fate of international capital towards some form of economic, social and organizational convergence is apparent. However, what is clear and distinctive today is the development of very powerful ideological prognoses which are founded on the imperative of international convergence. Prosecuting this line is wrecking the lives of many millions of employees. Lean production is the latest in a long line of management fixes, no doubt soon to be followed by Business Process Re-engineering (Grey and Mitev 1995) and is all of a piece with previous One Best Ways. As a project in the restructuring of international capital, lean production is a reasonably convincing ideology. But as Williams *et al.* have demonstrated time and again, this does not lend it greater efficacy as an analysis of the crisis of business relationships or greater weight as a recipe for business survival. Quite the contrary and as our research helps to illustrate, the nature of the changes introduced by international businesses are not easily made commensurable with the intentions of their authors quite apart from the ways in which they are received by the actors concerned.

Thus, while the sociological import of the lean production paradigm is without serious foundation, its ideological and propagandistic significance cannot be overlooked (Stewart 1996). It is now unusual to interview actors in the auto sector without being made aware of the pervasiveness of the *idea* of 'lean production'. *Pace* Williams *et al.* (1992) management, unions and employees use the term to explain the far-reaching changes occurring even though (as Williams *et al.* are indeed correct in pointing out) it is a less than adequate account of the actual processes and consequences of change. Clearly, substantive developments both to the manufacturing process and the social organization of production are influenced, not to say inspired by, institutions of success in other countries, localities and companies. Nevertheless, it is also true to say, as Ackroyd *et al.* (1988) pointed out almost a decade ago in their discussion of the concept of Japanization, that one must distinguish between management fixation with a panacea derived from emulation/copying of exogenous processes and management as retrenchment, i.e. the repackaging of old wine in the new bottles labelled Japanese, or in contemporary terms, lean production. By stating matters this way it might appear that we downplay the radical changes taking place but this is certainly not our intention. The idea of lean production is profoundly seductive for all concerned because it is so simple – it can be applied anywhere, anytime and by anyone convinced of its teleological verities. However, we need to recognize that in re-creating the new arrangements for manufacturing, companies are sometimes retreading old ones and that it is employees at the sharp end of 'change' who are often best placed to understand the difference between innovation as renovation and innovation as rhetoric. Another way of putting this is to say that it is the reality of the messiness and uncertainty of social relations themselves that will ensure the unlikely outcome which is being feverishly pursued by advocates of the notion of globalization – in all its hues.

NOTE

1 This chapter draws on material originally perpared for the American Sociological Association 88th Annual Meeting, 1993, in Florida.

11

NATIONALISM AND THE FALL OF THE USSR

Mike Bowker

INTRODUCTION

The collapse of the USSR in December 1991 is recognized as a pivotal moment in post-war history. It both ended the Cold War and brought the communist experiment in Europe to a close. Many commentaries attribute the fall of the Soviet Union to popular nationalist forces (see, for example, Diuk and Karatnycky 1993: 40). The aim of this chapter is to examine this view critically and to assess the impact of globalization on the process of fragmentation in the USSR. To do this, it is first necessary briefly to consider some relevant issues in the current academic debate on nationalism.

THE NATURE AND ORIGINS OF NATIONALISM

After a period of relative neglect, in recent times social scientists have become more interested in the ideology of nationalism and its persistence into the modern age. The central questions relate to the nature and origins of nationalism. What are the continuities and discontinuities between modern and pre-modern nationalism. How new is nationalism?

It is clear that national sentiment existed in some countries, such as England, Spain and France, in the pre-modern period, but it is accepted by scholars that the nature of nationalism has changed over the last two hundred years in a number of important ways. First, the modern nation demands a commitment and loyalty far greater than that of an earlier age. In the pre-modern age, individuals may have felt some national sentiment (although this was far from always the case), but most identified more closely with the locality, church or monarch. This changed in the modern era, however, when all competing loyalties had to be subordinated to the nation alone. Another distinctive feature of modern nationalism, linked in many ways to the above, was its politicization. Co-nationals were said, not only to share a common culture and history, but also to share common interests which, it was argued, could only be furthered within the political structure of a nation state.

Whilst few academics would deny the changing nature of nationalism, the reasons for that change have been a matter of greater controversy. This has led to an interesting debate over the origins of nationalism. The nationalist appeal to blood and soil has often given nationalism an atavistic and reactionary flavour (see, for example Kedourie 1966). Nevertheless, a growing number of scholars, for different reasons, perceive nationalism as very much a modern phenomenon.

One view, originating from J. S. Mill, sees nationalism as an emancipatory and democratizing force (1977: 547). Nationalists have argued that legitimation to rule can only come from the people. Only the people's consent gives a government the right to rule over them. Hence, the notion of national self-determination. In traditional societies, this amounted to a revolutionary ideology.

Others like Ernest Gellner (1983), whilst accepting the revolutionary potential of nationalism, view it as more of an elitist project. Developing Marxist ideas, nationalism is perceived in this, the modernist view, as a bourgeois ideology serving the interests of that class. According to Gellner, the main aim of nationalism in the modern age is to legitimize and facilitate the process of industrialization. Industrial society, based on technological innovation and the division of labour, requires an educated, well-disciplined workforce to work in and run modern enterprises, as well as a literate and efficient bureaucracy to administer an increasingly complex society. Only the state can provide the investment in education and infrastructure to produce the necessary skills. Nationalism plays the role of unifying society around this modernizing project by emphasizing a shared culture. The propagation of this view is possible in the modern age through print capitalism (Anderson 1983) and the audio and visual media.

One important implication which flows from the modernist viewpoint is that national identity is essentially a social construct. It is not, therefore, a natural and normal entity formed by historical and cultural circumstance. The uniqueness of modern nationalism is emphasized and the links with its traditional past dismissed or downplayed. Therefore, national identity is not fixed, according to this account, but constantly changing and eminently changeable. Modernist writers talk about 'imagined communities' (Anderson 1983) and 'invented traditions' (Hobsbawm and Ranger 1983).

No one would deny the importance of many of the insights of modernist theory. It provides a useful antidote to those arguing that in multi-ethnic states like the Soviet Union it is impossible to repress nationalism. However, opponents, such as Anthony D. Smith, have argued that modernists too easily dismiss the ethnic roots of nationalism (1986 and 1991). Smith claims that it is difficult to invent (or disinvent) national identity, and that the most effective and stable nationalities require an ethnic core (*ethnie*) which has real resonance beyond the intelligentsia and the power elite.

Although the nature of nationalism has clearly changed, ethnicists, such as Smith, stress continuities from the pre-modern era and argue that the ethnic core of a nationality is developed over a prolonged period of time.

The modernization process may consolidate some aspects of national identity, but national consciousness is more likely to be formed by dramatic political events, such as migration, revolution or war. When a nation comes under threat, it tends to redefine its identity often in contradistinction to its enemies. Therefore, national history tends to be recalled in the popular memory as a struggle, with the nation identified in terms of hero or victim, martyr or messiah. Such self-perception is clearly muddled with mythology, but it can affect a nation's behaviour on the international stage.

Ethnicists see nationalism as more deep-rooted amongst the people than in the modernist model. They, therefore, are rather sceptical of some modernists who perceive nationalist conflicts largely in terms of a power struggle between different elites (for this modernist view in the Soviet case, see Snyder 1993). They also perceive nationalism as less time-bound and therefore better able to survive the modern twin challenge of globalization and regionalization (Hutchinson 1994: 104). The ethnicist model provides an account which demands closer attention to particular national histories. It is, therefore, less parsimonious as a theory. It is able, however, to explain certain phenomena which modernists sometimes have difficulties with. For example, it is able to explain the emergence of nationalism in the pre-industrial age and has no problem in explaining the nationalist political agenda which often seems to have little to do with modernization. The theory is also flexible enough to allow an explanation of differences in the nature and form of nationalism both over time and across nations. This latter point was one of considerable importance in the case of the Soviet Union.

THE RISE OF NATIONALISM IN THE SOVIET UNION

For many, the explosion of nationalism in the Soviet Union was predictable. The USSR always looked an unwieldy, multi-ethnic state prone to nationalist explosion. It was the biggest country in the world, covering a sixth of the surface of the globe. Its population of 290 million was the world's third biggest, incorporating, according to an official census of 1989, no less than 128 nationalities. This picture was simplified somewhat by the fact that the Slavs made up about 75 per cent of the total population. On the other hand, about 60 million people (including 25 million Russians) lived outside their own national area, which became a major cause of ethnic unrest after the breakup of the Soviet Union in 1991.

Many of these nations (like the Slavs) were related, but at the extremes, economic, social and cultural differences were enormous. The best example of this was the contrast between the Baltic Republics – European, Christian, urbanized and well educated; and Central Asia – Asian, Muslim rural, and still largely tribal. Such differences led to one commentator, Victor Zaslavsky, referring to the USSR as being as unlikely a union as a hypothetical one between Norway and Pakistan (Bremmer and Taras 1993: xxii). This may have been an exaggeration, but it highlighted the central question for any nationality policy in the Soviet Union: what mutual interest could possibly unite the Baltic Republics and Central Asia in a single state?

A number of Western writers, such as Helene Carrère d'Encausse, identified nationalism as the Achilles heel of the Soviet political system. Carrere d'Encausse had long argued that nationalism posed a threat in the USSR not only to the union but to communism itself (1979). Since the 1960s there had been a rise in national awareness, expressed in movements to protect ancient monuments, churches and the preservation of minority languages. In 1991, she published a widely read account in which she highlighted the difficulties for Gorbachev as he attempted to democratize the country. The French academic and conservative politician was able to claim with some justification that she predicted that the Soviet Union would collapse under nationalist pressure. For such writers the problem was less explaining why nationalism exploded under Gorbachev in the late 1980s, than why it did not erupt earlier.

The most common explanation could be termed the 'pressure cooker' model. This theory accepted the arguments of the ethnicists that nationalism is deep-rooted in the psyche of humankind and is consequently very difficult to erase. To many this seemed proved in the Soviet case where an openly supra-national agenda pursued with some brutality over a prolonged period of time failed to destroy people's allegiance to the nation. Instead, Soviet nationality policy produced what Robert Conquest has called a 'frozen instability' (Bremmer and Taras 1993: xvii). Therefore, only a policy of repression throughout the Soviet period prevented explosion. Repression was harshest under Stalin – almost all national leaders were arrested and whole peoples, including the Volga Germans, the Crimean Tartars and the Chechens, were exiled from their homeland. Yet even in Brezhnev's less brutal age, about 50 per cent of all political prisoners were jailed for so-called nationalist offences (Sakwa 1989: 314). Therefore, when Gorbachev ended state repression and lifted the lid of the pressure cooker, the nations of the Soviet Union inevitably, it is argued, began to campaign for national self-determination.

There is, clearly, much truth in this explanation. Many nationalists in the Gorbachev era were able to offer an alternative vision of reality to Marxist-Leninist orthodoxy and organize around a nationalist programme. Thus, national popular fronts began to emerge from 1988 and campaign for election. In the first competitive, union-wide elections of March 1989 some nationalists were elected, but in the freer elections at republican level the following year, they did even better and popular fronts began to gain power, most notably in the Baltic Republics. By October 1990 all fifteen Union Republics in the Soviet Union had declared sovereignty. In the wake of the East European revolutions, the USSR looked in danger of total disintegration. Gorbachev, who had initiated democratic reform, seemed wholly incapable of preventing the collapse of the Soviet Union. Nationalism, it seemed, had prevailed over communism. Why was this so?

Ernest Gellner had argued that nationalism and communism were competing modernizing projects and the state in both systems had a similar role to play. Gellner, however, had consistently argued that nationalism was the more effective modernizing ideology. At least in the case of the Soviet Union, this proved to be true. By the 1960s it was already clear that the USSR was unable to compete economically with the West. Even in an area where the Soviet Union had some success – education (the USSR boasted the highest number of doctorates per capita in the world) – its success para- doxically fed nationalist instincts. For this growing group of professionals often felt alienated from a society based on a working-class ideology and tended to be attracted to the bourgeois project of nationalism.

There can be no doubt, however, that the achievements and the inter- national status of the Soviet Union won it supporters within the country. The majority of the intelligentsia were co-opted into the state by perks and privilege. The workers and peasants were largely passive. But the image of unity was a facade which was created largely through the suppression of dissent. After the defeat of the Prague Spring in 1968, any remaining public enthusiasm for the communist project throughout Eastern Europe had faded and it had ceased to be a great mobilizing force. Nationalism had greater appeal with its emphasis on a shared culture and the territorial instinct for a homeland.

However, it would be wrong to argue from the Soviet case alone that nationalism was bound to prevail over Marxism-Leninism. In many ways, the Soviet administration encouraged national awareness. On the one hand, the policy of repression only served to produce new myths and redefined national identities. On the other, for all its anti-nationalist propaganda, Moscow always held an essentially ambivalent attitude towards nationalism. All Soviet leaders argued that nationalism was a bourgeois ideology. They propounded the Marxist-Leninist case that nations would merge (*sblizhenie*) under socialism and ultimately fuse (*sliyanie*) under communism. Yet the Soviet authorities always showed themselves ready to both use and make compromises with their bourgeois enemy. The most basic compromise came in the first years of the revolution when the Union Treaty of 1922 described the USSR as a federal state divided along ethnic lines. Stalin at the time declared that the USSR was 'proletarian in culture, nationalist in form'. And even he, for all his brutality towards the nationalities, never tried to replace the federation with a unitary state. Instead, Stalin introduced a highly centralized state, held together by the majority Russians. Russia was the only republic without national institutions, such as a Russian communist party or academy of sciences. The aim was to make Russians identify with the Soviet Union rather than their nationality. At the same time, Stalin forcibly pushed a policy of Russification, promoting the Russian language and culture as a civilizing process over 'inferior nations'. Stalin had some success in reducing differences amongst the nations and creating the concept of the Soviet person (*sovetskii chelovek*) (White 1994: 152). However, by Brezhnev's time in the 1970s, there were clear signs of the policy fracturing.

Most important of all, non-Russians never lost their national awareness. All Soviet citizens also had to register their nationality in their internal passports. And whilst the majority spoke fluent Russian in the 1970s, this did not mean reduced loyalty to minor languages. Inter-ethnic marriage was also limited largely to the slav nationalities (White 1994: 153). Demographic changes led to discontent amongst the ethnic minorities. This was most visible in the policy which preferred Russians in key state and party posts at both the central and republican levels. Such a policy may have been defensible in 1922 when 70 per cent of the Soviet population was Russian, but this was far less the case in 1982 when the proportion had fallen to barely 50 per cent. This at a time when the number of non-Russians with college education had increased four-fold over the same period.

In the 1970s, local leaders were also more ready openly to argue for policies on the grounds of national interest. To a large extent, the success of a local party first secretary was judged on economic performance. Therefore, as the economy slowed in the 1970s, competition for resources grew fiercer. Shelest, First Secretary of the Ukraine in Brezhnev's time, was just one of the first to promote a distinctively nationalist line on this issue. Shelest argued that investment should be increased in the Ukraine at the expense of poorer republics, such as Central Asia, since his more skilled and disciplined workforce would provide the country with higher returns.

However, despite evidence of growing nationalist sentiment amongst both the elite and the masses, Gorbachev underestimated the extent of the problem. In 1987, he reiterated the Stalinist view that the nationality problem in the USSR had been settled (*Soviet News*, 4 November 1987: 400). It sounded a complacent statement at the time, but when nationalist violence erupted less than a year later in Nagorno-Karabakh, it made Gorbachev look rather silly. Nevertheless, there is a danger in reversing Gorbachev's view and arguing that the strength of nationalism was such that the collapse of the Soviet Union was inevitable the moment he began his reforms. As will be shown below, such a view would be equally misinformed.

DID NATIONALISM BRING DOWN THE USSR?

Nationalism undoubtedly played a part in the collapse of the Soviet Union. The outburst of nationalism in the late 1980s put pressure on the leadership and undermined both the authority and the power of the centre. Millions of Soviet people went out on to the streets to demand greater national rights and many died in the effort. It was a time of great drama and symbolic gestures. Perhaps the most remarkable of all was on 23 August 1989 – the fiftieth anniversary of the Nazi–Soviet pact – when an estimated two million people in the Baltic Republics held hands forming a human chain across the region to symbolize both their unity and determination to be free from the Soviet incubus.

Not everyone in the Soviet Union who demonstrated under a nationalist banner, however, sought secession and the breakup of the USSR. In the absence of civil society, nationalism for many was simply the most logical focus for political activism. With a natural territorial base, it was relatively easy to organize around the concept of the nation, which was, after all, one of the few recognized political divisions in the Soviet Union. As a result, nationalism meant different things to different people. Apart from the secessionists, there were at least three other groups using nationalist terminology to further a more general reform programme.

First, there were the radical reformers. In Russia, many such as Kozyrev and Starovoitova, grouped around Yeltsin from 1989. They were not Russian nationalists as such, but they tended to support secessionist movements because they believed that democracy would be unattainable unless the Soviet empire was abolished. Therefore, nationalism was perceived more as a means rather than an end in the campaign to overthrow the status quo. In June 1990, Russia declared sovereignty, and the following year Yeltsin was elected President of Russia by the people, a vote he saw as a mandate to bring down communism rather than the Soviet Union.

A second more moderate group favoured decentralization rather than abolition. No one could deny that the Soviet system was over-centralized, and it was generally agreed that this over-centralization had led to inertia and stagnation in decision-making. This, in turn, left the Soviet Union slow to respond to new challenges both internally and externally. To a large extent, these views reflected those of Gorbachev himself. He promoted decentralization and hoped that perestroika could deliver a system which was more sensitive to local opinion whilst also retaining a strong, unifying force at the centre (*Pravda*, 9 April 1986 and 14 March 1989). This proved to be a difficult balancing act, especially as a growing number of potential Gorbachev supporters saw the centre as the main obstacle to reform.

A third group may have had less clear ideas about the future than either Gorbachev or Yeltsin, but knew some kind of change was necessary. Past leaders had failed. Now it was increasingly felt that the Gorbachev administration had also failed. As the economy declined in the late 1980s, people lost faith in their leaders. A growing number of local leaders recognized public disquiet and tried to distance themselves from responsibility for the mounting crisis. One way of doing this was to seek refuge in local politics and the ideology of nationalism. For example, Leonid Kravchuk First Secretary in the Ukraine, abandoned his earlier hardline image and became a crusading nationalist. His attraction to non-secessionist voters was that he was more moderate than nationalist leaders in the Ukrainian Popular Front, Rukh, whilst also having the experience of working with the Kremlin.

These individual differences of opinion over the future of the union were paralleled by regional differences across the country. Nationalism was strongest amongst the non-Slavic Europeans – in the Baltic Republics, Moldavia and the Caucasus. Here, the growing mass movement, which pressed for greater autonomy and independence, played a key role in undermining the central authorities in Moscow. Elsewhere, this was less obvious. In Central Asia, nationalist sentiment was weak (although it grew as the Soviet Union broke up). In the Slav republics, the nationalist movement was divided and rather incoherent over its ultimate goals.

These regional differences were most graphically revealed in March 1991 in the referendum on the future of the union. Of the fifteen Union Republics, only the nine Slav and Muslim republics participated, but they voted decisively (76 per cent) in favour of keeping the union. This was a significant vote only nine months before the final demise of the USSR in December 1991. The six republics that boycotted the referendum were strategically important to Moscow but represented a comparatively small proportion – about 14 per cent – of the total Soviet population. Nevertheless, alternative polls in Georgia and the three Baltic Republics revealed the polarization of opinion on the issue of secession when overwhelming majorities there voted in favour of independence.

Nationalist opinion was most divided in Russia and the Ukraine. In the Ukraine, 70 per cent voted in favour of the union, but the west of the republic, absorbed into the USSR only as part of the Molotov–Ribbentrop pact of 1939, wanted secession. Only 25 percent in the western city of Lvov supported the union. Big cities generally, in both Russia and the Ukraine, were less union-minded. The cities were more radical and viewed their local parliaments as more reformist and the centre as bastion of conservatism. Small majorities favoured the union in Moscow and Leningrad, whilst a small majority in Kiev voted for secession. Results on parallel polls in both Slav republics only served to complicate the matter further, for Russia voted overwhelmingly for Yeltsin's proposal that direct elections should be held in June for an executive Russian President. This vote greatly increased the power of Russia vis-à-vis the centre and ultimately led to the collapse of the union. In the Ukraine meanwhile, the same electorate that voted against secession confusingly also voted overwhelmingly in favour of sovereignty. The only rational explanation for this result is that the Ukrainian people believed that sovereignty meant greater autonomy within the existing Soviet Union rather than the abolition of the union altogether. This was the way sovereignty was defined by Ruslan Khasbulatov, a Chechen, who supported Yeltsin at the time of the August coup in 1991 (Khasbulatov 1993: 222).

Why were there such differences in perception across the union? The five Muslim states had weak nationalist roots yet, despite their semi-colonial status inside the USSR, gained most economically from their membership of the union through generous central subsidies . It would be untrue to say, however, that there was no evidence of nationalism in Central Asia. One of the first cases of nationalist unrest in the Gorbachev period occurred in 1986 when Gorbachev removed the local Kazakh First Secretary, Dinmukhamed Kunayev, for corrupt practices, in favour of a Russian, Gennady Kolbin. But national allegiance was less well developed in the region and tribal and religious allegiances remained powerful alternative foci of loyalty.

It was also true that the elites of Central Asia feared the rise of populist nationalism and were less willing than other communist leaders to try to exploit it. The borders drawn up by the authorities in the 1920s and 1930s were designed to prevent the emergence of a unified Central Asian identity and paid little attention to ethnic divisions. As a result, any nationalist uprising was likely to lead to demands for border changes with violence a probable outcome. Their worst fears appeared realized when Tajikistan exploded into civil war after the collapse of the USSR in September 1992 – essentially as a result of tribal rivalries and economic collapse. Other Central Asian states feared the spread of violence, particularly to Uzbekistan where two ancient Tajik cities, Samarkand and Bukhara, are located. Although the danger of escalation still exists, the threat has been contained so far, largely due to the adoption of authoritarian policies throughout the region.

In the Slav republics, nationalism was stronger than in Central Asia, but it was also highly divisive. Was the real basis of common identity religious, racial or national? Belorussia had no experience of being a sovereign state, whilst the Russian and Ukrainian histories had been inextricably intertwined since earliest times. The cradle of the Russian nation was said to be Kiev Rus. Amongst the Russians, there existed both empire builders, such as Vladimir Zhirinovsky, and nation savers, like Alexander Solzhenitsyn. The empire builders noted that no Russian identity had existed outside the empire. Russian power rested on its dominant position in first the Tsarist Empire and then the Soviet Union. Given Moscow's strategic interests in the Soviet successor states, its imperial position, according to the empire builders, should not be given up (Frazer and Lancelle 1994). Nation savers, on the other hand, argued that Russia had suffered along with the other nations of the Soviet Union under the communist system. It may have dominated the union politically, but at a terrible economic and moral cost. Nation savers, therefore, argued that Russia should abandon its global pretensions and rediscover its nationalist past, either alone or, as Solzhenitsyn proposed, as part of a new Slav federation (Solzhenitsyn 1991).

The Baltic Republics, in contrast, had a clear national identity and a recent memory of independence in the inter-war years. National conscious-ness in the region had been raised by the brutal treatment of its people by

Moscow since its forceable integration into the USSR in 1940. Under Stalin, three-quarters of a million Balts were exiled whilst Russian emigration to the region was actively encouraged. The explicit aim was to dilute the national cultures of the Baltic peoples and Moscow had had some success in this policy. The Estonians made up 90 per cent of the population of their republic in 1940, but only 62 per cent in 1989. The number of Latvians over the same period had fallen from 77 per cent to 52 per cent. The Russian minority numbered over 30 per cent in both cases and were in the majority in some cities. Only in Lithuania did the native culture look safe – 80 per cent of the population were Lithuanians and only 9 per cent were Russians. This demographic threat to Baltic culture was bad enough, but everyone in the region looked down on Russian culture, perceiving it to be alien and oriental. The Balts, in contrast, viewed their own as Western and wholly European. They attributed the gap in living standards that had emerged since the war between themselves and their Scandinavian neighbours solely to their membership of the USSR and the neo-Stalinist system which had been imposed upon them since 1940. Baltic nationalism, therefore, was deeply anti-Russian.

In the Caucasus, anti-Russianism also existed but, with important exceptions, it was less important as a mobilizing force than in the Baltic Republics. The Caucasus was a highly volatile and ethnically mixed area which had experienced frequent population shifts which had led to a heightened national consciousness. The region was also perceived to be on the front-line in Europe dividing the Muslim and Christian religions. In those circumstances, conflict was generally intra-regional rather than directed upwards, as in the Baltic Republics, against Moscow. In fact, in Armenia, Russia was traditionally seen as an important friend and defender against the traditional enemy, the Turks.

Both Armenia and Georgia won reputations in the Soviet Union for their relative wealth and independence. There was considerable nationalist sentiment in both republics, but opinion radicalized only in response to particular events in the late 1980s. In the case of Georgia, the native population was outraged by the assault on a peaceful demonstration in Tbilisi in April 1989 when at least nineteen people were killed. Moscow, rightly or wrongly, was blamed for the bloodshed (see Ligachev 1991). Armenia, for its part, became a radical secessionist state after disillusionment set in over Moscow's unwillingness to resolve the Nagorno-Karabakh problem to its own advantage. Instead, Gorbachev argued against any change in internal borders without the consent of all interested parties. Since the collapse of the Soviet Union, both Georgia and Armenia have returned, however reluctantly, into the Russian sphere of influence within the Commonwealth of Independent of States (CIS).

In the above analysis, it has been argued that public opinion, sometimes but not always driven by nationalist sentiment, played an important role in undermining central authority in Moscow. However, it is important to note that the collapse of the Soviet Union was a result not only of revolution from below, but also revolution from above. For there is considerable evidence to show that Gorbachev's reform programme hastened the collapse of the Soviet Union.

Gorbachev introduced radical change into the sclerotic Soviet political system when he came to power in 1985. He recognized the urgent need for reform, but failed fully to recognize the weakness of the communist system itself. On the contrary, Gorbachev believed that the system was fundamentally so robust that it could survive any amount of disruptive change. As a result, Gorbachev was prepared to attack all the major institutions of the USSR. Arguably, the KGB and military were least affected institutionally, although Gorbachev's reforms were designed to undermine their authority and status. Glasnost threatened the KGB's future role, whilst the 'metal eaters' were blamed for economic slowdown and political reaction at home. Elsewhere, however, the reforms provided a more substantive challenge. The central ministries, for example, which had controlled the Soviet economy since Stalin's time, faced a massive reduction in power as a result of Gorbachev's 1988 reforms which sought a dramatic decentralization of the Soviet economic system. But most important of all, Gorbachev deliberately undermined the power of the CPSU, which the General Secretary perceived to be an obstacle to reform. From 1988, the party was sidelined as a decision-making body and it lost control over personnel appointments. Its leading institutions met less frequently, and party discipline broke down in the course of the multi-candidate elections of March 1989 (Ligachev 1993: 91 and 110). After Gorbachev set up the executive presidency the following year, the party formally abandoned its executive role in the Soviet Union. Its much publicized renunciation of its guaranteed monopoly right to rule in July 1991 became a mere formality thereafter.

Unquestionably, such policy changes aided democratization and decentralization. Unfortunately, from Gorbachev's point of view, democratization in 1988 led to ungovernability less than two years later. Gorbachev remained the master of political intrigue at the Kremlin – he was able to get his way on most matters of importance. Gorbachev also continued to have the power to make decisions, but with the party and state institutions undermined, he had no means of implementing them. As a result, Gorbachev's power extended little beyond the walls of the Kremlin.

To make matters worse, as the political system disintegrated, the economy (due in large part to Gorbachev's 1988 reforms) simultaneously began its dramatic decline. Against the backdrop of impending economic collapse, power leaked perceptibly from the centre to the regions. Republics and regions tried to protect their citizens from the results of the chaos in the rest of the country. Barriers to trade between different regions of the Soviet Union were set up to prevent the outflow of vital goods – most notably, food. Rationing was reintroduced, and some areas inaugurated a system whereby consumers had to prove local residency before they were allowed to purchase certain goods. In what has since been called the biggest tax strike on record, many regions also began to withhold tax revenues from the centre.

Gorbachev in the spring of 1991, after the March referendum, attempted to gain agreement over an amended Union Treaty. As his position weakened, Gorbachev made a series of remarkable concessions to the republics. Most important of all, he accepted the idea that the USSR (to be renamed the Union of Soviet Sovereign Republics) should become a loose confederation of sovereign states. In the final version of the treaty (which was never signed), the republics were to raise all tax revenue leaving the centre with no direct means of finance (*Pravda*, 15 August 1991). This effectively would have emasculated the centre, making any decisions impossible without the prior agreement of the republics.

The implications of the treaty enraged supporters of the union. The proposal, however, was still not enough for the six European non-Slav republics which sought nothing less than complete independence. Nevertheless, the day before the treaty was due to be signed by the remaining nine, Gorbachev was overthrown in the abortive August coup of 1991. The coup attempt was not unpopular in the Soviet Union. In one poll at the time, the state of emergency was supported by 40 per cent of the Soviet population (White *et al.* 1992: 19), and 60–70 per cent of regional governments in Russia also backed the coup (Dawisha and Parrott 1994: 347). This provided evidence that the regions in Russia were not, even at this late stage, in favour of dismantling the Soviet Union. On the day Yeltsin stood on the tank outside the White House to declare his opposition to the coup, a matter of a hundred Muscovite intellectuals were there to listen (Steele 1994: 73). Yeltsin's appeals for a general strike were largely ignored and life in Moscow and other big cities went on much as before. Only as the coup showed signs of collapse did support for the oppositionists begin to grow. Yet when the coup collapsed after three days, the whole communist system unravelled. Why?

Yeltsin, as the representative of Russia and centrifugal forces in the USSR, had won the power struggle with the centre. The pro-communist forces lay defeated and humiliated. The centre disintegrated and Yeltsin moved in to fill the political vacuum. The Baltic Republics took the opportunity to declare independence and others followed suit. Gorbachev attempted to resurrect a diluted form of his amended union treaty, but his powers had been cut from under him. The final nail in the coffin of the USSR came on 1 December 1991 when over 90 per cent in the Ukraine voted for secession. The vote represented yet another violent mood swing in the republic in those very volatile times. It was not entirely the result of a rise in nationalism since many Russians in the Ukraine also voted for secession. In fact, there seemed to be a combination of despair over the current state of affairs in the USSR and an inchoate optimism that radical change would produce a better future. On 8 December, the three Slavic republics moved to manage the disintegration of the Soviet Union by setting up the CIS, later extended to some non-Slavic republics on 21 December. Formally the Soviet Union ceased to exist at midnight on 31 December 1991. The communist experiment which began almost seventy-five years earlier had come to an end by mutual agreement of Soviet national leaders.

THE IMPACT OF GLOBALIZATION

How far does any of this relate to the debate over globalization? In one respect, not much. The Soviet Union participated at most as a semi-peripheral member of the capitalist world system (see Little 1995: 80). In part, this was due to ostracism by the West; it was also due to a conscious decision by Stalin to isolate the Soviet Union from the rest of the world. Stalin rejected Marshall Aid in 1947 for fear of the power of capitalism to absorb and dominate.

As Stalin's successors, Khrushchev and Brezhnev, adopted a more active third world policy, the Soviet Union attempted to set up an alternative, communist world system centred around Moscow. To protect this project from international capitalism, contact between the two worlds was kept to a minimum. Even in the Brezhnev period, it was possible to live in the Soviet Union and believe that the West did not exist – no McDonalds, no Hollywood and no rock and roll. Trade with the West increased in the détente period, but its aim was to fill gaps in the Soviet market rather than to introduce competition into the system. Although Soviet trade with the west grew in the 1970s it was from a very low base – in gross terms it was no greater than that of The Netherlands. Yet as a share of world trade it actually fell from 1.8 per cent in 1970 to 1.6 per cent in 1982 (Geron 1990: 28). The information-technological revolution largely passed the Soviet Union by. Even something as basic as photocopying was severely controlled whilst home computers were almost invisible in ordinary people's homes. TV, radio and the state-run media were used as means of propaganda, although a growing number had access to alternative viewpoints via Radio Liberty and Voice of America.

Overall, however, the Soviet example showed that it was possible to escape the globalization process. But this was at the cost of internal repression, high military spending and an economically weakened state. Indeed, it was the acknowledgment by Gorbachev that Moscow's alternative world system had failed which led to the adoption of his ambitious reform programme. Trade barriers could protect domestic industries, but they could not protect the Soviet economy from comparative international decline which ultimately threatened Moscow's status as a superpower. Gorbachev wanted to end the USSR's isolation and integrate the Soviet Union into the international system (Gorbachev 1987). Thus, fragmentation did not occur in the Soviet Union due to globalization, but because Moscow wanted to become a part of that process. Gorbachev recognized that this would mean radical change in Soviet policy. He was surprised, however, that it required systemic change. How far will this mean the former Soviet Union becoming like the West? Will the Soviet successor states be able to form viable liberal democratic nation states? Carrère d'Encausse has argued that nationalism in the Soviet Union should be viewed positively as a significant step towards democracy. Legitimacy now rests with the people rather than a self-appointed vanguard party. Nationalism, wrote Carrère d'Encausse, is a 'distinctive feature of civilized humanity. It represents some progress over primitive society, not a regression toward it' (Carrère d'Encausse 1991: 236). There have, indeed, been many democratic gains in the former Soviet Union. Elections and referenda are a feature of post-Soviet politics, and the media remains freer than at any time during the Soviet period. Furthermore, the command economy has been rejected as a model, and it has been accepted that the market has a role to play in any successful economy.

However, the shift to a market system has been difficult and the state is likely to retain a prominent place in the economy for some time to come. National culture affects economics as much as any other area of life, and in Russia there is little tradition of capitalism. Democratic culture is similarly primitive. The Leninist maxim *kto kogo* (who has power over whom) still applies. An ability to compromise and recognize the legitimacy of contradictory points of view remains a rarity amongst the governing class. Relations are still highly personalized. Respect for the law as an independent arbiter remains limited. All of which has led to high levels of corruption and crime, as well as an under-regulated market.

Soviet political culture has also meant that nationalism remains one based on ethnicity rather than the more liberal concept of civic rights. As a result, minority rights are frequently disregarded. For example, Russians in Estonia and Latvia face discrimination and have been denied the vote in national elections. Worse, violence, or the threat of violence, has been an ever-present reality on the southern periphery of Russia. The Caucasus, an area of comparative prosperity in Soviet times, lies devastated by war. Armenia occupies a third of neighbouring Azerbaijan; Georgia has suffered from civil war; whilst Chechnya has been destroyed by the Russian invasion of December 1994. Central Asia also faces conflict after the tribal bloodletting in Tajikistan.

All Soviet successor states are weak. Formally, they are independent, sovereign states. In practice, they have little independence or sovereignty. They may have entered the global system, but they remain largely dependent on Moscow. This dependence has been exacerbated since the West has shown little interest in the non-Russian republics. The more or less covert dominance of Russia in the Soviet period has become overt in the post-Soviet period. Russia has the largest population (149 million) amongst the Soviet successor states. It is richest both in natural resources and skilled labour. Even the Ukraine, potentially the most powerful state outside Russia, found its independence was more apparent than real. Economically, Kiev was dependent on Russian oil and gas, giving Moscow considerable influence in the Ukraine's affairs. Furthermore, its possession of nuclear weaponry turned out to be a white elephant since Kiev had neither the money nor the expertise to maintain strategic nuclear weapons, and in any case control over their launch remained in Russian hands.

Such limitations on sovereignty have brought all but the Baltic Republics into a closer relationship with Moscow inside the CIS. The CIS at least provides non-Russians with a say over the political and economic future of the Eurasian landmass. Russian troops guard many of the borders of the former Soviet Union and they are playing a role in all the conflicts currently convulsing the southern periphery of the country. Despite all these problems, few favour a return to a supra-national state. Some Russian nationalists would like to see the return of empire, but even they are reluctant to pay the price. Russians feel a natural empathy for Belorussians and Ukrainians, but they are not happy at the prospect of picking up the tab for those bankrupt economies.

The nation state remains the most popular structure in the modern world, but there is no necessary link between the nation and the state. Yet, the nation remains the most democratic legitimation of governmental authority. The pressure on state sovereignty has increased in this more interdependent world. However, the state retains a monopoly right to legislate, raise taxation and implement policy. Therefore, the individual still looks towards the state for the provision of his or her basic welfare. It is also worth bearing in mind that sovereignty has an external aspect as well. For the state has the right, in international law, to represent its citizens in the international system. The state concludes treaties with other states, and has the exclusive right to sit on international bodies, such as the UN and the EU. As a result, the state provides the best opportunity for representation on the international scale for individuals whose lives are increasingly affected by global forces. The nation state, therefore, provides a democratic barrier to the unaccountable globalization process. Thus, as the sociologist Christian Juppke has written, until the birth of a world society 'the national society remains the place in which citizenship rights are effective and guaranteed' (1994: 554).

CONCLUSION

The USSR collapsed for a variety of reasons. Nationalism was one of them. It mobilized popular opinion in the Caucasus and the Baltic Republics. In the Ukraine and Russia, on the other hand, nationalism was taken up by radicals more as a means towards democratization and economic reform. In practice, only a minority in the Soviet Union actually sought the abolition of the USSR. Only when the centre collapsed in the aftermath of the August coup did the process of state-building, in the Slavic and Central Asian republics, really start in earnest.

State-building has proved difficult throughout the former Soviet Union. The process has been bloody in the Caucasus, Tajikistan and Moldova. Economic crisis has made the situation worse, but the central problem has been a lack of a democratic political culture in the USSR. Optimists believe that nationalism is a step towards liberal democracy; others fear that, in the Soviet context, it is more likely to lead to tribalism. It is noteworthy that Central Asia has attempted to avoid the latter through abandoning democracy and adopting more authoritarian measures.

The Soviet successor states are ill-equipped to compete in the global system. But neither a return to a Soviet superstate, nor further fragmentation offers anything but civil strife. In the circumstances, the nation state represents the only chance for peace and stability in this troubled region.

Part IV

THEORETICAL REFLECTIONS: SOCIAL THEORY, CULTURAL SUBJECTIVISM AND DISEMBEDDED MARKETS

12

GLOBALIZATION AS AN EMERGENT CONCEPT

Richard Kilminster

> With the passage of time, nations, hitherto living in isolation, draw
> nearer to one another.
>
> (Turgot 1750)

INTRODUCTION

In the last decade, social scientists have become more and more aware
of the importance of transnational social processes. This book itself is
symptomatic of the flourishing interest in this level of inquiry. The term
globalization, increasingly used in the 1980s and 1990s in a number of
fields, in fact first appeared in Webster's Dictionary in 1961. This marked
the beginnings of explicit recognition in the contemporary period of the
growing significance of the worldwide connectedness of social events
and relationships. In 1972, the OED Supplement recognized the word
'global' as being in current use meaning worldwide, complementing the pre-
existing sense of pertaining to the totality of a number of items. There has
also been a transformation over the last 25 years or so in the meaning of
the word 'global' in sociology, from meaning total, as in total society, to
meaning a focus on the globe as a unit of analysis in its own right (Albrow
1992a: 5–6).

In contemporary discussions, the extending interdependency chains
between nations have been variously referred to as the 'global human
circumstance', 'the transnational scene', 'the compression of the world', 'the
global ecumene' or simply as the world 'becoming a single place'. Martin
Albrow has offered a sociological definition which rightly emphasizes that
it is the changing nature of human bonding that is implicated in the process
of globalization: 'This is the process whereby the population of the world is
increasingly bonded into a single society' (Albrow 1992b: 248). This definition has echoes of Hobhouse, who wrote in 1906 that 'humanity is rapidly
becoming, physically speaking, a single society' (cited by Robertson 1990:
21). Neither of these definitions claims that the world *is* a single society, nor

257

that it will inevitably become one. Both of them hint at a process, perhaps a trend, but without any commitment to a timescale.

The reality of the growing interdependence of nations has been further thrown into relief by detrimental environmental effects such as global warming and pollution as well as by the danger of nuclear war, the perilous consequences of both of which respect no national borders. Knowledge of the seriousness of these effects for all humans, irrespective of national allegiance or cultural identity, has heightened the awareness of the process of the growing interconnectedness of national societies which had been going on apace anyway. It has thus reinforced the growing awareness of our common human fate. The environmental effects, the threat of nuclear war and globalization are related. The more extensive and intensive people's dependence on each other becomes globally, the more it is in their mutual interests to mitigate the unintended harmful environmental effects as well as to reduce the risk of a nuclear war.

In sociology, political science, international relations, economics and applied fields such as marketing, the process of globalization is now taken for granted. The global dimension of human experience and 'global issues' generally are routinely presented in sociology textbooks (e.g. Kerbo 1989: 355–79; Brinkerhoff and White 1991: 608–34; Giddens 1993: 2–3), with perhaps Joan Ferrante's *Sociology: A Global Perspective* (1992) being the most thoroughgoing attempt at an internationalized textbook that I have seen so far.

Recent studies and discussions of globalization have been legion and I cannot do justice here to the vastness and complexity of the rapidly developing literature. However, for my purposes in this chapter, it is not incorrect to say that the recent sociological discussions of the globalizing process fall into three groupings, investigating the problem area in three different ways:

1 *The effects of the international division of labour in the generation of a structure of inequality between nations.* Research has gone ahead into global economic interdependencies using the 'world-system' model developed by Immanuel Wallerstein (1979, 1991; Chirot 1977). This influential theory has become the leader in the field, establishing a model for further research and a bench-mark for subsequent critique and theoretical development. As is well known, this neo-Marxist theory posits a developing, tripartite, interconnected world structure of nations – the core, periphery and semi-periphery – and stresses the importance of the activities of transnational companies and movements of capital across national frontiers. In this paradigm, it is the economic logic of capital accumulation in the larger capitalist world economy that is assumed largely to determine social events and political changes within nations.

2 *The role of culture, including the globalization of information and communication, in shaping the world reality.* The part played by symbolic representations, political culture, information technology, the global media and religious

counter-movements are the focus here (Robertson and Lechner 1985; Robertson 1990; Bergesen 1990; Hannerz 1990). Global communication, in particular television, has played an important part in bringing people instantaneous images of distant peoples and events, thus broadening and relativizing local experiences (Featherstone 1990). The contradictory interplay of 'particularism' and 'universalism' (Parsons) in the emerging consciousness of humankind as a whole brought about by these cultural developments has also been a prominent theme (Robertson and Chirico 1985; Garrett 1992). The argument of this tendency is that a more unified picture of the globalizing process must embrace the counter-movements and traditional-communal reactions, which are organic to the process, for which we need a concept of culture. At the same time, we must look at the level of transnational institutions and the creation of international legal norms for any observable harbingers of the emergence of a genuinely global human solidarity.

3 *The explanatory relationship between the figurational compulsion of the network of interdependent nations and international violence; the formation of We- and I-identities (and/or we- and I-self-images); and codes of interpersonal behaviour.* Following the lead of Norbert Elias (1987a, 1987b, 1991) research has proceeded into the consequences of the Cold War superpower confrontation under conditions of mutual nuclear threat (Benthem van den Bergh 1992) and into the competitive survival and status struggles between nations (Wouters 1990). This paradigm has also stressed the importance of humankind as a whole, both as an incipient reality and as a subject for empirical investigation, viewed in the long-term, as well as the related conception of social integrative levels *sui generis* (Goudsblom 1989; Mennell 1990, 1992: ch. 9; Kilminster 1994).

The work in the field of culture is a reaction to the perceived economic reductionism of the Marxian inspired world-system approach (Robertson and Lechner 1985: 107; Robertson 1990: 16). As Robertson puts it, 'I try to turn world-systems theory "on its head" by emphasizing *culture* and the *agency* aspect of the making of the global system' (1990: 28). Because of its origins in political economy, world-system theory does indeed tend to stress only the capitalistic, *Gesellschaft*-like dimension of the interrelations between nations across the globe. This approach is a variant of Marxist theories of imperialism of Lenin and Hilferding (Arrighi 1978) and later theories of dependency.[1] A polarized model of class struggle is mapped on to the world's nations. There are the upper class, rich, exploiting nations of the core and the lower class, poor exploited nations of the periphery, with a 'middle-class' stratum in between, the semi-peripheral nations (Chirot 1977: 8; Ragin and Chirot 1985: 298). Interstate rivalry and the global territorial conflict of the twentieth century are explained as expressions of the market-seeking logic of Western capitalism. This process is also held to explain the apparent obstacles to the imagined internationalization of revolutionary socialism via the world's underprivileged classes.

It is a commonplace that an important point of departure for the sociological pioneers of the last century and the early years of this century was to insist that economic regularities had to be understood sociologically. Economic patterns are only a species of social regularities in general. As Karl Mannheim later put it: 'when the Physiocrats and Adam Smith demonstrated the important role of competition in economic life, they were in fact only discovering a *general social relationship* in the particular context of the economic system' (Mannheim 1928: 195). For generations of sociologists it was necessary to fill in the cultural and social-psychological factors without which structured, repeated economic relations would not be possible – the so-called 'non-contractual' aspects of contract, in Parsons' words, paraphrasing Durkheim. So, the mainstream sociological tradition has always regarded Marx as in error when he tried to read off politics and culture as 'spheres' determined in some way by a separately conceived economic base and to reduce all forms of alienation to expressions of economic alienation.

The recent work of the cultural critics of Wallerstein emphasizes people's sense of solidarity, their reflexivity, the meaning they give to their lives as well as their identity formation, as also crucially implicated in the globalizing of social life. This accentuation forms a corrective to the analysis of globalization solely in terms of international trade and capital flows emanating to and from the core countries. These responses to Wallerstein thus reiterate an important formative dialogue in the development of sociology, but this time in relation to theorizing at the global level. Robertson has acknowledged this: 'I have set out to provide, as Weber did in his Protestant Ethic thesis, an "equally plausible" cultural account of globalization, in the face of the "materialism" of world-system theory' (1992: 320).

Much of the recent work of the cultural critics of Wallerstein draws on the once much maligned, but now to some extent rehabilitated, Parsonian paradigm, albeit construed in an adapted fashion so as to remove the naive functionalist connotations (Münch 1987; Holton and Turner 1986; Robertson 1990: 18). Following the general thrust of the sociological tradition, in which he was well versed, Parsons also distantiated himself from the economistic Marxist theory of society. He tried to accomplish this by analytically distinguishing separate, fictitious 'spheres' of society, including the economy, culture and communal life, then positing their different modes of 'interpenetration', as a device for explaining subsequent patterns (Münch 1987: 28, 67, 199). As Robertson also says, 'I am insisting that both the economics and the culture of the global scene should be analytically connected to the general structural and actional features of the global system' (1990: 18). This manoeuvre also provided Parsons and the later writers in this tradition with a way of bringing a pattern to a social reality implicitly assumed, very much in line with Simmel and Weber, to have no structure of its own. However, this ingenious artifice carried the danger of reproducing the dualism of culture/structure, which is a distant echo of the subject/object and thought/reality polarities of Western philosophy. Robertson is clearly aware of this problem, when he says that his (neo-Parsonian) strategy 'is only a prologue to a statement which transcends the cleavage between "material" and "idealistic" approaches' (1992: 320).[2]

Arguably, the processual approach of Elias can be seen as a synthesis which, amongst other things, tries to do just that, that is, to move away from action theory and its attendant dualisms such as culture/structure, as well as its voluntaristic overtones (Kilminster 1989). Like Parsons, Elias moved beyond political economy, but rather than positing analytically distinguished social 'spheres', he starts from the structured process of interwoven interdependent people in the plural, for which he coined the concept of figuration. For him people are simultaneously bonded to each other in various ways because of the multiple functions (affective as well as economic and political) which groups and individuals perform *for each other* (Elias 1978: 134ff).

The next two sections comprise two short excursions into some of the forerunners of global thinking from the eighteenth and nineteenth centuries, including Turgot, Condorcet, Herder, Hegel and Marx. Of necessity this coverage is somewhat schematic, but hopefully sufficient for present purposes. These are to illuminate the current sociological controversies about globalization by showing how the character of ideas on the subject of humankind as a whole as well as more systematic models of the functioning of social relations on a world level, are closely bound up with the nature of the phase of development of national differentiation and international integration at which they are articulated. This should help us to guard against uncritically employing today theories or concepts on this subject which were developed at earlier stages of development. Without these references to the balance of social forces in the societies in which these forerunners lived, and between nations at the time, I do not think it is possible fully to understand the character of their ideas on the subject of nations and their interrelations.

These excursions are thus an organic part of my argument about the concept of globalization being an emergent one developed to capture the contours of the recent integrative spurt in the level of social integration comprising the bonds between nation states. Even though I have used the works of historians of ideas in these sections, it would be a misunderstanding of my sociological approach to assume from that fact that what follows is simply an interesting exercise in the history of ideas tacked on to the analysis of contemporary theories of globalization so as to provide some historical 'background'. Nothing could be further from my intention.

I will return in the two sections after that to the basic sociological questions which have come to the surface again in the current debate about thinking and theorizing at the global level. I will conclude with some reflections on orientation and disorientation in the present period of extensive and bewildering change and the relevance of my preceding discussions as a contribution towards our better orientation.

FORERUNNERS

Even though they consist largely of adaptations to theories handed down to us as part of sociological traditions, the models of global social structure discussed in the Introduction to this chapter are still nevertheless a product of the current phase of the development of national and international dependencies. It is in the present period that the need to elaborate global sociological models has been perceived as an imperative. It is no accident that it is a period where accelerating global interdependence is more clearly visible around us and is shaping our fate in more compelling ways. However, as Johan Goudsblom has pointed out, 'global interdependence is far less recent than we may have been led to believe' (1989: 25). At no point in the past, he argues, has the history of any people been unaffected by that of their neighbours and theirs by their neighbours, and so on. These interconnections have been obscured in the earlier attempts by, say, Herodotus in the Ancient world or by St Augustine in the medieval period, to write histories of humanity as whole, which were in fact disguised histories of particular peoples or other selective trajectories.

I discovered by simply looking in the dictionary that the word humanity, derived from the Latin *humanitas* and corresponding to the French *humanité*, is first recorded as being in use meaning the human race in 1579 (OED). Today, the word humankind has come into currency as the non-sexist alternative to mankind, but in fact it is not a neologism but a revival. As a synonym for humanity, the word humankind dates from 1645.

Philosophers in the European Enlightenment such as Herder, Turgot and Condorcet, as well as later social scientists such as Marx and Comte, prefigured (which is not the same thing as anticipated) current debates about humankind as a whole and the relations between nations. The same is true of the writings of Hegel, particularly his *Philosophy of History* (1830). They addressed somewhat abstractly the fate of the human species and the linkages between nations, linguistic groups and civilizations, and the development of human knowledge as a whole.

Even if they were not always successful in their attempts, they all genuinely tried to transcend specific national allegiances and preferences. But they did so in different ways, according to different national traditions, such that it is misleading to specify one eighteenth-century view on the subject of nations and their linkages as being that of *The* Enlightenment. They also did not have the benefit of the enormous growth of knowledge about human societies that is so easily available to us. Hence, their attempted syntheses of the perceived trend towards human unification and the development of human knowledge, were rather premature (Elias 1991: 89, 120; Goudsblom 1989: 11–12).

Philosophies of history, such as those of Herder, Vico or Hegel, are as William H. Dray (1964: 59) pointed out, attempts to find meaning or significance in the historical events studied empirically by historians. They are often shot through with preconceived values or unconscious wishes and fears, stemming from the political hopes of their authors or from their national or class habitus. In the writings of Johann Gottfried Herder[3] in the 1770s and 1780s, particularly his *Also a Philosophy of History* of 1774, the nation is regarded as the only relatively stable entity in the flux of history. It is an organism, a non-rational, vital centre of human association and the source of all secular human truth. It was to be understood not through reason, but through empathy. For Herder, history is benevolent: all that has grown naturally, historically, including nations, is good. All nations are of equal worth and all contribute to the richness of humanity as a whole (Iggers 1968: 34ff).

This romantic-conservative view was relativistic and suffused with metaphysical and theological undertones (Baumer 1977: 295). However, what is interesting from the point of view of my argument is that Herder, like many of the other German 'historicists' of his time, had a conception of a common humanity which expressed itself in those national manifestations. His nationalism was not of the exclusive or chauvinistic kind that we find in the late nineteenth and twentieth centuries, but was, rather, a 'cosmopolitan culture-oriented nationalism' (Iggers 1968: 30) undergirded ultimately by a theological view of human unity.

The *Humanitätsideal* that Herder shared with Winckelmann, Humboldt and Goethe specified – contrary to the more rationalistic view of humankind found elsewhere in the Enlightenment, particularly in France – that humans are diverse, the rational and irrational aspects of the human personality being unified in a harmonious whole. Humboldt declared that 'Mankind as a whole exists only in the never attainable totality of all individualities that come into existence one after another' (quoted by Iggers 1968: 38).

These formulations, I would argue, represent a way of visualizing humankind as a whole when national self-images were strong in people's thinking, particularly in that of aristocratic elites, but not so strong as to block their prominent articulation of what they have in common with people of other nations (Elias 1968: 240ff). At this stage, such commonality was expressed rhetorically and at a high level of generality, largely by representatives of aristocratic strata whose confidence of their status and their *real international bonds* enabled them to visualize peoples of other nations with a cosmopolitan magnanimity. As Hans Kohn (1971: 120) has pointed out, the internationalist consciousness came from the European educated upper classes of the eighteenth century. Turgot's statement, quoted as the motto of this chapter, visualizes nations developing closer ties with each other in a similarly visionary and hence rather unspecific way.

During the French Revolution, Condorcet distinguished between intra- and international social relations, as well as raising the question of judging the improvement of humankind as a whole. In keeping with the more politicized nature of the French Enlightenment compared with that of Germany or England, Condorcet felt compelled to express the issue in the high moral tone of social criticism:

> Our hopes, as to the future condition of the human species, may be reduced to three points: the destruction of inequality between different nations; the progress of equality in one and the same nation; and lastly, the real improvement of man.
>
> (quoted by Baumer 1977: 232–3)

The kinds of nations all these writers have in mind are still dominated by dynastic and ecclesiastical elites – they are not yet nation states dominated by industrial classes and characterized by highly exclusionary and competing nationalistic ideologies. They talked about the unity of all nations in the most lofty and general terms, long before the territorial rivalries of this century and long before harbingers of its real possibility had begun to be observed, without anyone planning it, more tangibly around us, thereby generating the concept of globalization. It has been the nineteenth- and twentieth-century interstate conflict and rivalry that has produced the more exclusionary and chauvinistic forms of modern nationalism, blinding us to the developing international interdependencies which those ideological antagonisms belied. Herder's internationalist consciousness was, and still is, somewhat ahead of its time:

> The scholars who study [the] customs and languages [of the European nationalities] must hurry to do so while these peoples are still distinguishable: for everything in Europe tends toward the slow extinction of national character.
>
> (cited by Kohn 1971: 120).

At the later stage of the twentieth century, the interstate conflicts have, in a series of waves, raised the level of social tension within and between nation states, generating fear images in people's thinking. From the point of view of people in richer, more powerful, higher status nations, the peoples of other, poorer, less powerful, lower status nations are often regarded as subhuman, as ethnically inferior or in other ways as of low social worth. It is only in these circumstances that, at the level of interstate conflict, the conditions for the achievement of 'mutual identification' (Elias) between conflicting international antagonists become both a practical and a sociological problem. At the earlier stage, the lower level of international tension and the domination of loosely integrated European nations by pre-industrial elites, produced, depending on national context, conditions more conducive to cosmopolitan internationalism or to generalized theories of the moral or political progress of humankind, such as those of Condorcet, and Turgot (1750).

KARL MARX'S SYNTHESIS

Marx is an important actor in the drama because he was one of the first to try to develop social-scientific concepts systematically to deal with the social regularities and patterns set in train by the rapidly extending global trade networks of his time. It is worth dwelling on the global aspect of his theory of capitalism, since it has provided the framework upon which later exponents of the most influential contemporary model in the field – the theory of the world capitalist system – have in their own ways built. His work can be seen as a synthesis of Enlightenment ideas about humanity as a whole with a theory of the emerging global market which he found discussed in the works of political economists (Gay 1973: 344–68). He combined the two in the utopian projection of a world communist society, a vision he shared with many other socialist radicals of his time (Evans 1951).

The gist of the early sections of *The German Ideology* on this subject (Marx 1845: 39ff especially) is that communism is the empirical realization of the oneness of the human species, made possible by the development of social bonds of cooperation on a world scale. Communist society will put 'world historical . . . universal individuals in place of local ones' (ibid.: 47). Marx also suggests that social processes within nations will tend to become increasingly determined by the relationships *between* nations. He describes this process cryptically as the contradiction between 'national consciousness and the practice of other nations, i.e. between the national and the general consciousness of a nation' (ibid.: 43). Marx argues that this process could only be expressed metaphysically by Hegel because the productive forces and modes of human cooperation were insufficiently developed on a world scale to permit the realization of human unity in reality. In the *Paris Manuscripts*, written just a year before, he projects into the communist society 'the complete return of man himself as a *social* (i.e. human) being – a return become conscious, and accomplished within the entire wealth of previous development' (Marx 1844: 95).

Invoking Hegel and Adam Smith, Marx says that international trade and exchange and the whole world economic process, appear to operate independently of individual people, setting up empires, causing nations to rise and fall and to rule the earth with a 'hidden hand'. He concludes that Hegel and his followers had mistaken these alienating effects of the broadening of the division of labour and modes of human cooperation across the globe, as the existence of an external spirit-force driving the history of the world's peoples. Marx revels in making these basic sociological points over and over again against the Hegelians.

> In history up to the present it is certainly an empirical fact that separate individuals have, with the broadening of their activity into world-historical activity, become more and more enslaved under a power alien to them (a pressure which they have conceived of as a dirty trick

on the part of the so-called universal spirit, etc.), a power which has become more and more enormous and, in the last instance, turns out to be the *world market*.

(Marx 1845: 49)

Marx genuinely tried to render the issues of the structure of history and the possibility of human global unification amenable to empirical investigation. He looked for what he called the 'anatomy' of this process, which he variously terms – in his dualistic, philosophical way – the material 'substratum' or 'substructure', in political economy, the only developed social science at his disposal. At the stage of functional differentiation at which he stood, self-regulating, autonomous economic activities had outstripped the integrating social and political institutions, thus producing the illusion that the economic 'sphere' was a separate entity, independent of the state. Economic activity was so prominent and its representatives so powerful, that it probably seemed indubitable to Marx that the patterned human activities analysed by political economy – production and consumption – constituted the basic determining level of society and the driving force of all historical change. It was understandable that he should have seen society this way. He was not the only one in his time who did so – it was a model that he shared in essentials with the liberals.

However, the whole way in which Marx integrated scientific concepts from political economy into his theory was shaped by his confrontation with the philosophy of Hegel. And this, in turn, was overwhelmingly coloured by his socialist politics. He takes as his starting point Hegel's philosophy of history and claims, as we saw above, that it was a disguised representation of a real historical process of alienation. Marx's science of the development of historical modes of production purported to show empirically that international socialism and communism were the assured outcome of history: indeed they were written into it as its telos. What Hegel called the Absolute Ethical Life, that is, universal human freedom, Marx implicitly translates into real world communism, or democratic cooperation on a global scale, which progressively manifests itself in world history (Marx 1845: 49–50; Kilminster 1983).

Marx's synthesis gave him a 'scientific' version of socialism which politically subsumed all other versions. It was Marx's political commitments to socialism (and ultimately to communism) that fatefully drove him to translate one 'universalizing' philosophy of history into another, thus failing to make a clean break with the genre (Kilminster 1982 and 1983). Marx's social-scientific theory was thus burdened with the same teleology as that of the metaphysical theory he was claiming to supplant.[4]

Few who have followed Marx in developing theories of imperialism, dependency and world-system out of his observations on the global, market-seeking logic of capital accumulation, have used the dialectical-categorial method in which his work was couched. This is the method whereby (like Hegel) he moved in his inquiries from the abstract to the concrete, using concepts and empirical materials to construct the concrete totality of bourgeois civilization – including its worldwide manifestations – 'in thought', as he puts it.[5]

I cannot go into this obscure subject here, but suffice it to say that this method was integral to the way in which Marx investigated bourgeois civilization and its tendencies on a global scale. It was not a purely technical matter, nor an optional extra. The later Marxist writers have probably left it out because they wanted to jettison the metaphysical baggage in Marx, whilst retrieving the basic theory of economic power and exploitation for their own political purposes. However, by so doing, they by no means eliminated that baggage, but only obscured it. It remains true that Marx conspicuously failed completely to break with the philosophy of history. Hence, uncritically to appropriate his work without correction for this carries a number of risks, one being teleology.

It is worth bearing this in mind when considering Wallerstein's theory of the functioning of the world capitalist economy which comes packaged, not in the highly wrought categorial sequences of Hegel's *Logic* or Marx's *Capital*, but in the wrappings of contemporary empirical social science, including standard theories of economic cycles and a veneer of rigorous methodology. Wallerstein, like other contemporary Marxists, appears to have jettisoned the metaphysical hangovers which pervade Marx's work and salvaged the 'rational kernel' of his theories of economic power and of world capitalism. However, despite appearances and his disclaimers to the contrary (Wallerstein 1991: 225ff), at a deeper level of tacit assumptions, Wallerstein's theory still carries teleological overtones, which are the marks of its origins in Marx's partial overcoming of metaphysics. Wallerstein writes:

> It is precisely because [the world system] will continue to function as it has been functioning for 500 years, in search of the ceaseless accumulation of capital, that it will soon no longer be able to function in this manner. Historical capitalism, like all historical systems, will perish from its successes not from its failures.
>
> (Wallerstein 1991: 15)

Developing a sociological theory that can deal with the shape of the present stage of the global integration of nations, without falling into the economism and finalism of Wallerstein or the excessive abstraction of the cultural corrective of Robertson, is the sociological task in this field at the present time. The Marxian tradition and later elaborations broadly within this paradigm, have been looking decidedly unserviceable for some time. The reasons for this lie not just in recent events such as the collapse of communism in the European revolutions of 1989. They also lie a long way back in Marx himself who left us the legacy of a one-sidedly economistic theory about the developing global human circumstance which was skewed not only by metaphysical but also by mythological elements. The way in which his work is often portrayed today in summaries of his theory of class power in sociological textbooks and the ways in which it has been developed on the global level in world-system theory, have hidden from view just how arcane it actually was (see Kilminster 1983).

The one line from Hegel that every sociologist knows is that 'the Owl of Minerva spreads its wings only with the falling of the dusk' (Hegel 1820: 13). Never was this phrase more applicable than to the empirical research of Marx into the dynamics of bourgeois civilization on a world scale. In a profound discussion of Marx's method, Joseph J. O'Malley (1977: 26) pointed out that Marx's later writings and letters are studded with references to new crises and developments and to economic and political phenomena entering new phases, but which are not yet developed enough to a point where their significance could be grasped. As a good Hegelian, he knew that only when an institution or sphere had reached its nodal point of world-historical development and was in decline, could we fully understand it and its genesis. Changes in the national and world economies thus prevented, or delayed, Marx's work of scientific synthesis. It is possible that this is one reason why Marx's masterwork which he called *The Economics* was never finished. O'Malley asks if in the later letters of Marx we can detect 'a growing awareness that the world which he was seeking to grasp and to depict in its totality and in a scientific way had not yet grown old enough for him to do so?' (1977: 26).

THINKING GLOBALLY

The formation of sociologists' 'we' and 'I' identities within one or other of the mostly richer and more powerful nation states, unconsciously shapes the ways in which they fashion sociological concepts. During the period of intense European national territorial rivalry from the late nineteenth century onwards, to which the theorists of imperialism were responding, national self-images became entrenched in the consciousness of most people living in European countries. Hence, the macro-sociological concepts such as social system, social structure and total society which sociologists and other social scientists have subsequently developed, although of considerable explanatory usefulness, were none the less effectively synonyms for 'nation' (Elias 1968; Tiryakian 1990). This has made both the intellectual and emotional leaps into developing concepts adequate to the emerging level of integration above the national one formidably difficult. The integrity of the personalities of people living in nation states is to a very large extent still dependent upon the emotional security of a national 'we-identity', because 'nations were born in wars and for wars' (Elias 1991: 208). Nation state-based thinking seems therefore indubitable and provides for most social scientists the outer horizon of what is sociologically visualizable. Thinking about humankind as a whole or even new transnational regional identities, have little or no emotional significance.

It *may* be getting a little easier, during the current intensification of globalization, to begin to think about human association, bonding and patterning at the global level, as the process impinges on us in reality in a more pressing, rapid and unavoidable way. The conditions for greater 'mutual identification' between peoples may be becoming more favourable. But it nevertheless still represents a challenge to the sociological imagination. In this respect Wallerstein has to be given credit as a pioneer. He has contributed much to the collective leap of imagination and detachment that is needed to begin to think about (and thence to develop concepts adequate to) social reciprocities and interdependencies integrated at a level above that of the nation state.

Unfortunately, however, as in the case of his predecessor Marx, the cast of Wallerstein's thinking has been very considerably shaped by a strong sense of political mission. Following Ragin and Chirot's penetrating analysis (1985: 301ff), the first priority of Wallerstein's theory from the beginning was to inform a political and ideological programme, which they convincingly trace from his biography. Only secondarily is it intended to be a contribution to the comparative scientific understanding of historical origins of contemporary societies. From the model of the world capitalist system it can be predicted, to the satisfaction of its adherents anyway, that the system will be transformed into a socialist world system. The theory is not, they maintain, based on propositions that can be proved or falsified. It can only be illustrated. Furthermore, considered from a social-scientific point of view, it is this political impetus that is the source of many of the lacunae of the theory. These include not only its radical externalism and teleology, but also in particular its neglect of culture.

For the most part Wallerstein's model explains all important internal changes in countries, particularly economic changes, 'exogenetically' by their relative power position in the wider world system that produces such events. But this does not always explain why economic development affects extensive areas of the world with similar cultures in very similar ways, despite profound differences in their power position in the world system. To explain these cases, they argue, a concept of culture is necessary because clearly some countries are culturally more conducive to successful economic development than others. For Wallerstein, however, it is not a question of explaining the causes of change using a variety of concepts tentatively in close conjunction with evidence, but of finding more and more illustrations of the functioning of the world capitalist system. This is carried out solely in the service of demonstrating over and over again the exploitative nature of the capitalist world system in order to prepare the intellectual and political ground for the coming world socialist system. As Ragin and Chirot put it: 'those who make politics the first order of their intellectual agenda know what they are doing. It is unlikely that anyone could attempt as grand an enterprise as Wallerstein's without a powerful ideological vision of the world' (ibid.: 302). The parallel with Marx is striking.

The internationalist consciousness so typical of socialists such as Marx and taken for granted by Wallerstein later in the tradition, was not created by either of them. It arose from the cosmopolitanism of eighteenth-century thinkers such as Herder, that is from the confident magnanimity of the educated, privileged upper classes who had international links and experiences. It also depended heavily on new views of nature, society and man produced by the scientific outlook so prominent among the *philosophes* at the time (Wagar 1971: 114; Buchdahl 1961: 27; Gay 1973: 126–87). From the seventeenth century onwards, science was no longer subordinate to theology or metaphysics, reflecting in part a lessening of the relative power of the church *vis-à-vis* other groups. At the same time, the abstract ways in which these forerunners visualized international linkages and the lofty and rhetorical way in which they discoursed about humankind as a whole and its progress also corresponded to the properties of the stage of development of the integration of nations at which they, within their own nations, stood.

SOCIOLOGICAL ISSUES

The recent debate about the problem area of global interdependence has been dominated by a reprise of the traditional confrontation between political economy and sociology, but played out in relation to building models to understand global processes. Marxian political economy, as represented by Wallerstein's model of the world capitalist system, has become the leader in the field. Despite its flaws, even its sternest critics will concede its usefulness for explaining certain comparative patterns of historical change. However, it must be remembered that it has also become prominent partly through Wallerstein, driven by the monumental political mission that lies behind his theory, establishing a strong institutional base for its development and dissemination.

Quite understandably, as sociologists became aware of the materialistic cast of the theory, it has generated various cultural correctives. Most of these have been informed by the Parsonian social action approach, whereby culture is analytically distinguished from the economy as a structural feature of the global social system. Much of the current research and discussion revolves around positions taken within the framework of this time-honoured encounter and in terms of the antinomies thrown up by it.

Social relations at the level of integration above that of nations do not, however, represent in principle any particular technical difficulty of concept formation, provided a model of levels is employed to avoid reductionism (Elias 1987a). The main challenges to overcome in developing such models are (i) the achievement of relative distanciation from political convictions; (ii) going beyond political economy and the related materialism (structure)/ idealism (culture) confrontation; (iii) developing an interdisciplinary and cooperative approach towards the formidable task of data collection in this field; and (iv) rising above nation state-based thinking. The overcoming of these challenges is, however, not entirely in the hands of sociologists themselves, no matter how talented they may be. It is partly bound up with the precarious institutional autonomy of communities of sociologists as well as the professional closure of disciplinary boundaries, which militates against grasping the connectedness of social events and processes. At the same time, the raising of the level of tensions in the global interdependencies themselves and/or within nation states, can reinforce national self-images, hence the retrenchment of national and emotive thinking of all kinds, which spills over into sociological concept formation.

This chapter is partly an attempt to offer a programmatic 'third way' for sociological inquiry into globalization, moving between the economism of Wallerstein and the culturalism of Robertson. Or, to employ another metaphor, to proffer an alternative which comes up behind both of those approaches and goes round them. This is attempted by swinging the explanatory emphasis on to the conception of social relations as an emergent level of integration *sui generis* in the evolution of humankind out of physical, chemical and biological nature. The orderedness of the transnational level appears to be becoming increasingly autonomous, such that processes at the lower integrative levels (nation state, region, community, kinship) are in the present period becoming increasingly governed by the order of the higher level. This means that increasingly the range of decisions which can be taken at the nation-state level is decreasing as the continental and global levels increase in size and complexity (Elias 1987a and 1991).

Like the self-regulating, autonomous and impersonal nexus of events that came to be referred to at the national level as 'society', these higher, continental and global integrative processes are also operating as it were 'behind the backs' of the people whose intentional actions constitute them. But as such they by no means represent 'external' forces outside the effects of reciprocal human association and its unintended consequences. It would be a grave misunderstanding of my argument to read the terminology of levels of integration as indicative of metaphysical residues lingering in my own approach, even as I attempt to expose them in the work of others. The model is intended to be of use in empirical research and the concepts adequate to observable levels of the integration of human groups and the functions they perform for each other. The interdependencies between groups within nations and between nations across the globe, which has to be investigated much more on the empirical level, have properties which are the result of the unplanned consequences of those compelling relations, which exceed the scope of individual actions but are nevertheless only the result of those actions and the cumulative effect of the historical order of their development. My point is that their existence and concrete effects are empirically demonstrable.

The venerable sociological issue upon which this matter ultimately turns is that between sociological nominalism and sociological realism, played out this time in relation to higher integrative levels than that of the nation state. Over and over again in the history of sociology, writers who have tried to develop theories to explain the properties generated by one or other type or level of the widespread patterns of the interdependent relations of human groups have been accused of metaphysics. And so often the counterpoised alternative has been some form of individualism, carrying the danger of reduction to either psychology or biology.

The more sophisticated analytic approaches to sociology (e.g. Weberian, Simmelian, Parsonian) have wanted to preserve sovereign individuals at all costs, but at the same time to acknowledge the structured, patterned character of society. They have achieved this only by regarding society as in part the product of the cognitive organizing capacity of human beings (forms of sociation or culture) without which it would be structureless. The important work on globalization in the Parsonian tradition by Roland Robertson, however, shows equivocation on this issue, oscillating between nominalism and realism. Sometimes, consistently with the general cast of this approach, he feels compelled to put reality in inverted commas. For example, talking about transcending materialism and idealism he writes: 'In any case, "reality" has made it increasingly easy to do this, since economics and culture have become increasingly intertwined in the contemporary world' (Robertson 1992a: 320). Similarly, in other places he says that 'the concrete patterning of the world' is a 'heavily contested problem' and that 'the world' is merely 'the most salient plausibility structure of our time' (Robertson 1990: 20 and 21). Then, on the other hand, we find realist statements: 'there is a general autonomy and "logic" to the globalization process – which operates in relative independence of strictly societal . . . processes' (ibid.: 27–8).

Globalization is, then, viewed in this chapter as an emergent concept, which was created spontaneously to reflect people's experiences of the properties of an accelerating phase of the level of social integration comprising the bonds between nation states. The sociological concept of globalization is a more systematic version taken up from everyday usage and employed as a scientific concept. As I argued earlier, this emergent level of integration would appear in the present period to be beginning to canalize the levels below to a *greater* extent than before. The reasons for these unintended effects, brought about by the pressures being put on interdependent nations by each other, and by groups within them, is at present either reductively understood by Marxist political economy or attenuated by the abstract analytic sociology of the cultural corrective.

However, taken together, these two paradigms have located important problem areas and have begun to shift to an explanatory level above that of the nation state. But in so doing they have thrown up some characteristic antinomies, which need to be overcome. Once one enters the field attempting to correct, via 'culture', for the 'material' emphasis of world-system theory, then one has automatically reproduced the culture/structure dualism and its correlates. At the same time, Robertson has transferred the classical Parsonian 'problem of order' on to the global level, looking for cultural norms which would ensure the regulation of conflict at this level. He points to the importance of 'global norms' concerning national sovereignty, distinguishing the actual operation of state institutions from 'the development of regulative norms concerning the relationships between states', such as international law (1990: 23).

Following the figurational approach, on the other hand, there is no necessity to posit, on the lines of Parsons, a distinction between the factual order and the normative order for the purpose of explaining social cohesion, let alone to transfer this to higher levels. Rather, the focus is on the figurational compulsion of the web of social interrelations at the national, regional and global levels. It is the particular nature of the relatedness and interdependence of groups within nations and between them which exerts constraint over each one. Clearly, differing power ratios between the participants plays an important part in structuring the options and possible outcomes of struggles. For example, Elias (1987a: 74ff) traces the potentially dangerous consequences of the fact that at the interstate level there is no effective equivalent of the monopolization of the means of force by state institutions which exists within most internally pacified nation states. Each individually armed country feels much less inhibited in using violence internationally to settle disputes than do individuals or groups within nation states. Whether they do or not depends not so much on the existence of international 'regulative' norms as their place in the structured network of national and international power, which determines the 'price of violence' at any stage. As Elias (1978: 78ff) has pointed out, in trials of strength between groups of antagonists the outcome will depend on whose potential for withholding what the other requires is greater and who, accordingly, is more or less dependent on the other.

Applied to the level of transnational processes, the figurational approach anticipates the focus on economic power of the world-system analysis, as well as the accent on lived experience in the cultural corrective. It extends the former into other forms of the monopolization of means of social power and incorporates as a matter of course their embodiment in the structure of the interpersonal relations of everyday life. In this paradigm, the global structure of economic and political power is seen from the outset as intertwined with the monopolization of the means of force by nations as another source of power. Elias takes for granted the simultaneous embodiment of all three dimensions at the level of personality and interpersonal relations and in international communications, i.e. at the level of 'culture' (see discussions in Arnason 1987; Kilminster 1989; Wouters 1990).

The proponents of the world-system model have, however, made an important contribution in highlighting the global inequalities between nations, considered from the economic point of view. True to the history and tradition of this form of inquiry, however, its accent is on international inequality seen from the point of view of the weaker, exploited nations, with an eye always on developments which could be construed as leading towards greater equality between nations and a 'democratic world order' (Wallerstein 1991: 134–6).

However, it has been pointed out by a number of writers (e.g. Lenski and Lenski 1987: 313; 333; Wouters 1990: 69ff) that whilst the long-term trend this century within Western industrialized nation states has been towards a *decrease* in power, status and wealth differentials between social groups, the trend in the relations between nations across the globe has been towards an *increase* in the gap between powerful rich and less powerful poor countries. It is clear that it is a phase of this latter polarizing international trend that has attracted the attention of the world-system theorists. The problem of inequality and the hope of revolution had to be transferred to the international level. The underprivileged (often still referred to by the older mythical word proletariat) were now seen as a potentially united worldwide stratum.

The growing economic inequality gap between nations was of course real, but my point is that the Marxists were *politically* drawn to it, once the long-term, *intra*-national trend towards relative social equalization had given the lie to hopes of increased class polarization producing proletarian revolutions within Western nations (leaving aside short-lived polarizing phases). There is evidence that this impetus was certainly behind the genesis of Wallerstein's programme (Ragin and Chirot 1985: 278–84).

The explanatory fruitfulness of looking at the intertwining of economic and non-economic factors in globalizing developments, rather than analytically distinguishing them, is brought out in the work of Wouters (1990) in the figurational paradigm. He sees structural parallels between social developments which took place between groups within Western nation states in the last 300 years and processes occurring subsequently in the relations between nation states. If one looks beyond the criterion of income when assessing the gap between the rich and the poor nations, a more nuanced – and in view of current orthodoxies, controversial – picture emerges. Since the end of colonialism between the 1940s and the 1980s, so far as power and prestige are concerned, the gap between them has in fact *diminished*. The rich nations are now less likely to use violent means to settle disputes between themselves and the poor nations: they have been compelled to show them more respect than in the days of colonialism. Why is this, when they still have overwhelming power and military force on their side?[6]

The increasing restraints on military intervention worldwide brought about during the Cold War by the nuclear threat (Benthem van den Bergh 1992) created favourable conditions for remarkable commercial and financial growth in this period, hence raising standards of living in the richer countries. This helped to produce the well-known gap between rich and poor countries. This process parallels the cumulative effect of the internal pacification of European nation states from the sixteenth century onwards on the efficiency of organized work, which was considerably to increase it, thus contributing one of the conditions necessary for the origins of capitalism and the subsequent conflicts between social groups that flowed from it. Within Third World countries, the growth of institutions and organizations of administration has meant that more individuals have been compelled to regulate their conduct in a more even and stable manner, in ways comparable with the pattern of foresight and self-restraint which came to dominate personality formation of people in the industrial nations of the West.

The mechanism which led to the end of colonialism was therefore the beginning of a shift in the balance of power in favour of the colonized, paralleling the democratization between strata which – after an intense polarization shortly after the French Revolution – has accelerated *within* Western nations. Within these nations functional democratization[7] has closed social distance between people to a greater degree, producing greater mutual identification and a sensibility more conducive to taking the side of the international underprivileged. This, in turn, has fed into the economic and military dimensions of the relationship between the richer and the poorer nations. Put another way, the augmentation of the power potential of the poorer nations cannot be grasped without considering the relations between interdependent people in the round, not just economically.

Controlling the world market is beyond the power of any nation on its own, whatever its ideological hue or degree of wealth. In this context, the countries heavily in debt to the richer nations can still exercise constraint on them. The more serious the debt crisis, the more strenuous have become the loan conditions and the collective, cooperative policies for stimulating economic development. The poorer countries need the loans and the transnational companies operating within these countries are dependent upon the loan-demanding governments of those countries.

The process whereby in the West there was a reduction in the contrasts between groups, but an increase in their differences, via democratization and the informalization of behaviour codes, is likely to be repeated on the global level, producing, argues Wouters, a commingling of patterns of conduct. What seems to be a formalization of conduct and behaviour and manners in Third World countries, with the adoption of Western formal dress and orderly meetings, is in fact, in relation to the older traditional codes of these countries, an informalization, thus reproducing again one of the trends of Western nation-state formation.

The point is that the present informalized pattern of self-regulation of Western people *functions as a power resource*, an instrument of dominance, at the negotiating tables of the world and is a great advantage in a situation whereby the balance of power is shifting towards the outsider nations. It is not just an adjunct. It is *constitutive* of the balance of power. The older, formal codes of conduct of the colonial administrator now seem ridiculous because they reflected an earlier phase where the dividing lines between classes, generations and the sexes were much stronger within Western nations and were played out in the colonial context by upper-class representatives of those nations.

CONCLUSION: ORIENTATION AND DISORIENTATION

Speculating about future societal scenarios is not illegitimate, if it is done realistically. It forms a valuable part of the contribution that sociology can make. Following on from the previous argument, I would argue, along with Wouters, that the tendency in the relations between rich and poor nations has been for the poorer ones to be attracted to the products of the industrial economies, as well as to the models of behaviour and feeling characteristic of people living within them. The dominant direction of change at the international level, brought about by the structural compulsion of the power relations between nations themselves, is towards the more *modern* models of behaviour, conduct and organization. If the development of inter-group relations within European nations is anything to go by, the compulsion to adopt the aspirations, lifestyle and modes of conduct of the more powerful is very strong and probably will, in the long run, prove irresistible at the global level as well. Sociologically speaking, in contrast to what people might or might not wish to happen, this seems a very likely long-term scenario.

The counter-trend towards fundamentalism in beliefs and lifestyle has been highlighted by the culturalist theories of globalization and is undoubtedly important. This counter-current has arisen in opposition to the intermingling of Western and traditional attitudes and behaviour. It is likely to be prominent in nations which find themselves, through no fault of their own, structurally at the lower end of the international stratification ladder which is dominated by the Western and Western-orientated nations.

In the present period, national disintegration goes hand-in-hand with transnational reintegration at a higher level, particularly the continental, with an accompanying reinvigoration of ethnicity. In my view to concentrate on the fragmentary – or centrifugal – movement alone corresponds with a pluralistic conception of many different nations, which informs the so-called 'postmodern' worldview. This outlook is a symptom of disorientation brought about by people's experiences of the logic of the current phase of the continental and global levels of integration, which are more rapidly than hitherto disturbing national societies and individual identity formation, confusing people's orientation generally.

Since 1945, in the advanced countries, our orientation has been profoundly shaped by the relatively stable Cold War phase of international tension and the related economic prosperity thus made possible within the richer countries. As Hans Joas has aptly said, recently we have seen 'the return to a multipolar world after decades of bipolarity' (1991: 63). The postmodern outlook represents the sensibilities of younger generations of intellectuals and radicals in Western societies, which have undergone far-reaching democratization and informalization processes internally during this period. The conviction that the nations of the Third World have now increasingly to be taken into account, to be shown respect, suggests a shift in conscience formation has gradually occurred in the dominant countries. Hence, in the current phase people are searching for an alternative to the self-satisfied model of civilization associated with European colonialists and are experimenting with alternative ideals and moralities. The postmodern worldview is a product of this search for alternatives – an overreaction to European–American hegemony in the direction of cultural *pluralism*, elevated to an almost absolute status. From a purely sociological point of view, one is entitled to surmise that it is driven by the guilt of the younger generations in the dominant countries who have been historically speaking, fortuitously comparatively privileged and whose societies have undergone far-reaching, but unplanned, democratization and informalization processes.

In sociological and related debates in adjacent fields in the current period, this new sensibility plays itself out in the Lyotardian aversion to the 'grand narratives', such as Marxism or evolutionism. These are associated with the older civilizational ideal of the dominant European colonialists and the stage of the polarization of group conflicts and accompanying greater social distance that they represented. This aversion would rule out in advance the development of any general theory of globalization in the name of the highly 'informalized' concept of narrative, as opposed to theory. But this criticism simply overlooks that theories are not narratives. It is perfectly possible to have a general theory of global integration (without teleology) for the 'next step' in the process which, at the same time, acknowledges the extent of ethnic/national autonomy continuing at a given stage. The postmodern sensibility simply picks up the latter side of the current phase and infuses it with positive ethical-political evaluations. This reflects, as I argued above, the sensitivity of democratized younger intellectuals and others within Western nations whose structural position in the world network of interdependent nations is shifting.

My belief is that now the dust has settled from the explosion of interest in globalization, some clear theoretical and empirical stocktaking is needed, particularly on the issue of developing new sociological concepts and models to capture the emergent global level of integration. This does not mean, however, as Tiryakian (1990) seems to think, that the *whole* of sociology has to be 'internationalized', root and branch. This seems to me to be, at this stage, an overreaction.

Sociologically speaking, the apparently fragmented character of national societies and the world circumstance in general in the contemporary period could simply bespeak a phase and not an end-state of international pluralism. Many recent commentators have made this mistake. For example, in the influential writings of Zygmunt Bauman we find the following diagnosis of the contemporary situation: 'The main feature ascribed to "postmodernity" is . . . the permanent and irreducible *pluralism* of cultures . . . or the awareness and recognition of such pluralism' (1992: 102; emphasis in original. See also ibid.: 64). This statement confuses the moral and political ideal of cultural pluralism with its permanent empirical actuality. It rules out the possibility of longer-term continental, or regional alliances, or mergers of nations, which could considerably reduce cultural plurality or lead to further episodes of territorial expansion and conquest by the new hegemonic centres of power, during which cultures and even whole nations could be, in the longer run, assimilated or destroyed.

The doctrine of cultural pluralism presupposes a level of 'mutual identification' (Elias) between people, brought about by far-reaching democratization and informalization processes within the Euro-American nation states we call the West (as does the postmodern sensibility). In the longer term, however, the hegemonic struggles involved in the development of emergent, larger, regional centres of international social power could throw these democratization and informalization processes into reverse, steepening power gradients and social distance between groups within those new units. This would thus create social conditions conducive to new doctrines of civilizational superiority over lower-status groupings or nations. The current assertion that cultural pluralism is the final shape of the world reality and its enthusiastic advocacy as an absolute doctrine, or goal to work towards, is surely naive and unrealistic. At a future point it could seem as quaintly anachronistic as cosmopolitan internationalism seemed during the interstate rivalry of the period of European colonialism. These remarks are intended only to be a sober sociological judgement of real possibilities, nothing more.

Some, at least, of the apparent harbingers of 'social chaos' (Loye 1991: 12) discovered in the contemporary world are probably a matter of a faulty conceptualization, skewed by fear images.[8] But in so far as strife, conflicts and crises of various kinds are discernible on an increasing scale in the present period (more clarificatory work is needed in this field), my guess is that they are manifestations of complex realignments of social forces and behaviourial readjustments taking place as the pressures nations are increasingly putting on each other are unintendedly pushing the ordering principles of social development on to higher integrative levels.

It may be that on the global stage at the present time the centrifugal movement towards national and ethnic fragmentation just has the upper hand over the centripetal tendencies towards regional alliances of nations. The European Union suggests an incipient continental integration. Maybe others will emerge in the Far East. There is also the pact for a free trade zone consisting of Canada, the USA and Latin America recently entered into under US leadership. There are also international institutions such as the World Bank, United Nations, Red Cross, Amnesty International and the

World Health Organization. In the absence of a world polity these bodies are not yet strictly speaking 'world' organizations, but could be seen in that regard as nascent, although still skewed by US dominance, particularly in the case of the UN. But it is a question of keeping a longer-term view of these developments and not jumping to conclusions as to outcomes, which might be centuries in the future. The assumption of the opposite outcome to pluralism and endemic fragmentation – that of central political institutions and the pacification of the whole planet – is just as one-sided and utopian. As Elias writes of such institutions:

> But anyone who has studied the growth of central institutions knows that integration processes which are precipitated in the setting up of central institutions at a new level often need *a run-up period of several centuries* before they are somewhat effective. And no one can foresee whether central institutions formed in the course of a powerful integration may not be destroyed in an equally powerful disintegration process.
>
> (1991: 227; my emphasis)

New hegemonic regional alliances or even coalescences of nation states could emerge in the longer term, but the dominant shape of the next phase is just not clear enough at present to warrant a hasty judgement about cultural pluralism. The longer view suggests that any *relatively* stable and enduring new regional or global integrative pattern of nations (including possibly the long-term death of nations through absorption) could take a very long time to crystallize, well beyond the lifetimes of most of us living today.

The current situation is a disorientating one, which encourages speculation and rash social diagnosis. A further example is that some contemporary social scientists have uncritically applied to social development varieties of disequilibrium theory and 'chaos theory' taken from the biological and physical sciences. In doing so, they have assumed that what they take to be widespread 'crises and discontinuities affecting increasingly larger segments of the world population' (Loye 1991: 12) are indicative of a novel situation of *chronic* crisis. Others have talked of the current national and global situation as 'underpatterned' and have even gone so far as to say that it necessitates therefore wholly new sociological concepts, theories and assumptions (e.g. Bauman 1992: 65, 191ff). In my view these judgements are somewhat premature.

Speculating on the possibility of the globalization of manners, Stephen Mennell asks rhetorically:

> What are the implications now for a world-wide civilizing process, considered as changes in ways of demanding and showing respect, when Europe and Europe-over-the-ocean no longer occupy the hegemonic position? Or do they?
>
> (1990: 369)

The force of my previous discussion leads to the definite answer of 'yes' to the last question. In the present phase and for the foreseeable future, the relative power potential of the USA is and will probably remain decisive in social developments on a world scale. The rise of newly industrializing countries (the so-called NICs) in what we in Europe call the Far East and the breakup of the former Soviet Union are symptoms of a shift in the global balance of power between nations, which involves the relative decline (but by no means total fall) of American global hegemony. The former superpower confrontation of the Cold War has been transformed, but the Gulf War of 1990 was a telling reminder of the continuing power of the alliance of nations led by the USA. As Susan Strange has rightly said, 'The decline of U.S. hegemony is a myth – powerful, no doubt, but still a myth. In every important respect the United States still has the predominant power to shape frameworks and thus to influence outcomes' (1989: 169).

It is noticeable that whilst sociologists of the first rank have emerged in poorer, so-called 'peripheral' countries (Albrow and King 1990: 101ff) they are not yet institutionally strong. There still exists a powerful, US–European led, English-language, global hegemony in social science. This pre-eminent sociological archetype originates in the dominant world bloc of rich, powerful, high-status nations (Oommen 1991). This bloc also provides the standards of living, lifestyle and behaviour to which, as a matter of sociological fact, people of other nations (no matter what their ideological persuasion) seek to aspire. It is likely that the compelling force of this structure of power will, in the long run, prove irresistible. This sociological diagnosis is not synonymous with the prophetic 'triumph of capitalism' or 'end of history' scenarios that have become prominent in the present period. Nor does it carry an evaluative preference.

The global migration of people across borders has become an issue in many countries. The problem for many governments is how to open borders for global trade and at the same time keep them closed for those whom they perceive as unwanted immigrants. This illustrates very well the paradox of internationalization going hand-in-hand with the protection of nationhood. Globalization both fosters forms of cosmopolitan consciousness *and* stimulates feelings and expressions of ethnicity. It is not surprising, therefore, that the dominant contemporary sociological conception of globalization is of a Janus-faced process of global incorporation and local resistance. The younger generation of social scientists who emphasize the Janus-faced character of globalization themselves work within those dominant nations which are structurally affected by globalization in ways that are conducive to their psychological ambivalence. This may account for the strong evaluative weighting that has become attached to the latter component of the conception of the Janus-faced tension, i.e., 'resistance', as well as to the ideal of cultural pluralism.

Both tendencies correspond to a sensibility at least partly explicable by the changing conscience formation of these highly democratized social scientists and intellectuals based in the Euro-American hegemonic bloc of nations. These social scientists (including all involved in this book) are operating in a new situation where the nations in which they have grown up and in which they live and work are being increasingly put under pressure to show respect for and restraint in relation to the weaker, poorer, lower-status nations, with which they are interdependent. At the same time, these social scientists cannot escape the fact that although from the point of view of prestige (if not wealth) the gap between the richer established and the poorer outsider nations has narrowed, taken overall, the hegemonic group of nations of which their own nation is a part none the less still possesses the higher power ratio, whether they as a group approve of it or not.

NOTES

I am very grateful to Stephen Mennell, Conrad Russell and Cas Wouters for their comments on an earlier draft.

1 Within the Marxist tradition there are, of course, various theories of imperialism and dependency and many controversies between them. Not all Marxists, for example, would regard Wallerstein's work as faithful to the spirit and letter of Marx. But for the limited purposes of this chapter, I did not think it necessary to digress into the shades of difference between the Marxist variants nor the many positions taken in the debates between them, which often have political undertones. For a comprehensive review of the Marxist literature on imperialism, see Brewer 1980.

2 Interestingly, Wallerstein has expressed similar sentiments in responding to what he saw as the false and tendentious contrast by Roy Boyne of his economistic theory with one that emphasizes culture: 'Emphasizing "culture" in order to counterbalance the emphases others have put on the "economy" or the "polity" does not at all solve the problem; it in fact just makes it worse. We must surmount the terminology altogether' (Wallerstein 1990: 65).

3 My treatment of Herder's ideas on nations and internationalism is only the tip of the iceberg of insights to be found in his works (see Barnard 1965; Mueller-Vollmer 1990). He had much to say on art, philosophy, language and metaphysics and other commentators have also found in his works discussions of issues which have a contemporary resonance. For example, Richard S. Leventhal (1987: 187–9) has convincingly shown that Herder anticipated the current scepticism about 'foundationalism', as well as discoursed at length on what we would today call reflexivity and the institutional embeddedness of power/knowledge. And Michael Morton (1987: 171) has shown how Herder developed a theory of symbolism comparable with contemporary 'semiotics', a word that Herder also used.

4 The subject of Marx's critique of Hegel is much more complicated than I have been able to report in the text. As I have argued at length elsewhere (Kilminster 1979: Part one), Marx's inversion of Hegel's dialectic makes no sense because Hegel's dialectic was never on its head. Nor is there in Hegel an assumed spirit force driving history forward to self-knowledge. Nor does Hegel's philosophy of history necessarily imply an end-state of human perfection, but rather, as Gillespie has rightly said, 'a circular process that continually finds and continually loses

its perfection' (1984: 115). The explanation for why Marx insists on a crudely teleological, dualistic and spiritual reading of Hegel lies in Marx's prior moral–political commitment to the communist movement. His critique of Hegel was one that produced a theoretical result which enabled him to maximize his chances of success in the competition between groups of socialists for the prize of the most complete 'scientific' theory of socialism.

5 The place in his writings where Marx grapples with the conceptual expression of these heady matters is in his unpublished drafts on the dialectical method, a neglected and often misunderstood aspect of Marx's work (Marx 1857). Here Marx takes seriously Hegel's depiction of history as the filling out of many 'determinations' of concrete universals, even agreeing with Hegel that the historical movement of categories from abstraction to concrete fullness is a real sequence. But he disagrees with the conclusion that Hegel apparently drew from those sequences, i.e. that their driving force is pure absolute thinking communing with itself via the categories (Marx 1873: 19–20). See note 4.

6 There is a common explanation of the declining likelihood that the powerful, richer Western states in particular will resort to military violence against weaker states: it is held to have less to do with growing 'respect' for poorer nations and more to do with the fact that it is becoming increasingly difficult to mobilize popular support for war in post-industrial countries. This political explanation has been argued, for example, by Martin Shaw (1991). But we need to look more closely into the sociological preconditions that lie behind this trend. Why have people's attitudes changed in such a way that it has become more and more difficult, politically, to convince public opinion towards accepting the need to go to war? The far-reaching democratization and informalization processes that have taken place in the advanced societies, mentioned in the text, have, amongst other things, brought about greater mutual identification and mutually expected self-restraint between people. This has arguably created greater respect for others in general, including peoples of other nations, one manifestation of which is a widespread anti-war sensibility.

7 The concept of functional democratization is being used here in the specific sociological sense developed by Norbert Elias. It refers to the long-term, unplanned process of the lessening of the power gradients and social distance between interdependent groups in differentiated societies. This has gradually come about because groups have become more interdependent by virtue of the specialized functions that they perform for each other (see Mennell 1992: 124ff). The concept should not be confused with the term democratization used by political scientists to describe the extension of political representation and the development of democratic political institutions on Western lines through which conflict can be peacefully managed. The general diminution of permanent hierarchies of rank over a long period in the history of Western societies has, of course, long been recognized from Alexis de Tocqueville onwards, and others have written about this general trend of the lessening of power differentials between groups, employing more general concepts such as 'equalization' (Scheler) or 'fundamental democratization' (Mannheim).

8 For example, David Loye (1991: 12–13) lists as symptoms of the breakdown of systems which can lead to social chaos a wide range of trends, events and processes which are of different kinds, working at different levels, which he, along with others who invoke systems theory, calls 'crises and discontinuities'. These are described as being of a financial, food, political and military nature and all said to be 'driven' by changes in technology, ecological problems, the gap between rich and poor countries, the degradation of fertile land and population pressures.

It is unclear how these items are related to changes in the relations between groups within nations, or in the relations between them. The analysis is further vitiated by the alarmist language which makes it less than successful as a contribution to our orientation in the present period: food crises are said to be 'ravaging' Africa; there is ecological 'devastation'; there is the 'desertification' of productive land; all brought about by what is obscurely described as 'the churning of history' (ibid.).

13

WIDER HORIZONS WITH LARGER DETAILS

Subjectivity, ethnicity and globalization

Cesare Poppi

The more reification there is, all the more subjectivism will there be.
T.W. Adorno, *In Search of Wagner*

THE TERMS OF THE PROBLEM

Globalization theory – like 'postmodernism theory' of which it represents one of the correlates – is as much the premise for the phenomenon that it describes as it is the result of extra-theoretical historical developments. Its advocated self-reflexive nature constitutes perhaps the most ambitious attempt to date to theorize *ex prae-facto*. In this sense, in the age when intellectual apparatuses appear less to denote a reality 'external' to them than to carve out for themselves intellectual capitals of discursive legitimacy, in many ways the discourse of globalization creates what is coterminous with it.[1] As such, it cannot be accepted or rejected: it is a historical development, which is also the precondition for it becoming the subject of sociological investigation. The problem therefore is to what extent the *concept* (as distinct from the *phenomenon*) of 'globalization' is or is not a useful tool to understand and explain certain central developments of late capitalist society.[2]

In the context of the present collection, my aim will be to explore the articulations between globalization and ethnicity. Ethnicity, one of the fastest-growing contemporary social phenomena (Cohen 1986), appears to give the lie to modernist assumptions about the obsolescence of localized, bounded institutional and cultural apparatuses.[3] The thrust of the argument presented here, however, will be that the contemporary growth of ethnicity is *at the same time* the demonstration that the 'imagined communities' upon which the modern nation states are established (in Anderson's well-known argument) have indeed met their historical *nemesis*, but *also* that the very same terms of their constitution are reproduced, *mutatis mutandis*, in the constitution

284

of the new 'ethnic' – as distinct from 'national' – subjectivities. The claim for the recognition of 'imagined communities' which are less imaginary – as it were – than the former nation states, nevertheless follows by and large the same logic. Most crucially, like nationalism, ethnicity cannot 'work' except within the frame of shared assumptions concerning the universality of subjectivity and its legitimacy. In turn, the legitimacy claim of subjectivity is the legacy of modernity, only taken a step further by the process of globalization. In this sense, the thesis of the crisis of the nation state is not only compatible with but also necessary for the understanding of ethnicity as yet another movement in the unfinished project of modernity with its globalizing implications.

More generally, as I try to analyse the key aspects of the connection between ethnicity and globalization, it will emerge that globalization must be understood as the condition whereby localizing strategies become systematically connected to global concerns. This happens *both* at the level of the *Lebenswelt* (or what others might call social practice) and at the level of the *theories* – or of what might be better called the 'representational elaborations' – which attempt to account for it. Thus, globalization appears as a dialectical (and therefore contradictory) process: what is being globalized is the tendency to stress 'locality' and 'difference', yet 'locality' and 'difference' presuppose the very development of worldwide dynamics of institutional communication and legitimation.

This thesis is, of course, not new, and it has been variously predicated by social theorists.[4] Therefore, if there is any originality in the thesis proposed below, it rests in the attempt to treat the contemporary redefinition of subjectivity *inside* metropolitan social formations on the one hand, and the attempts to break *away* from them on the other, as processes both underpinned by the ongoing expansion of globalization. In much contemporary social theory the 'fragmentation' of the subject is celebrated to the point of becoming the new, theoretical foundation of the concept. Simultaneously, though, an imagery of unity and integration is reconstructed *outside and away* from the metropolitan condition in the growth and theorization of ethnicity. The two processes complement each other: wider horizons have come to contain larger, and more crowded, details.

This confers on globalization a character both in line with and contradicting the universalizing tendencies of capitalist expansion in the modernizing stages of its developmental cycle. The fact that '*autonomie et différance*' are coming to replace '*liberté et égalité*' is to be seen as the coming of age of the dialectics implicit in the movement of modernity (one feels tempted to muse here that the crisis of the family and kinship is taking care of '*fraternité*'). Globalization does have limits: they are at once implicit in the aporias of the cultural logic of late capitalism, but they are also exploding the never delivered promises of modernization.

GLOBAL SUBJECTIVIES:
THE THEORETICAL TURN

The end of the millennium is witnessing a reassessment of the parameters within which subjectivities were constituted in the modern age. This process of revision provides the quasi-transcendental conditions for ethnicity to become a *plausible discourse* – and one for which a legitimate case can be made as the foundation of emerging subjectivities. Far from being the resurgence of obsolete, 'archaic' or 'primordial' feelings, as some liberal thinkers in despair still appear to think in the face of the onslaught in Bosnia and Rwanda, ethnicity is but one specification of the contemporary renegotiation of the terms of engagement between the local and the global, the specific and what used to be called 'the universal'. It is therefore important to understand its specificities in the context of dynamics that are of crucial import even in the domains where ethnicity, as such, matters not.

Central to the postmodernist developments of cultural theory is the notion that the 'master narratives' of modernism encoded a project of global domination which overlooked those crucial and 'radical' power relations, such as race and gender, now at the forefront of critical cultural discourse.[5] Key analytical and operational concepts such as 'class', under which the leading theories of the modernist Left intended to subsume (and often subordinate) the emancipatory processes of race and gender, have been exposed as compromised along with the project of the Hegelo-Marxist teleological view of history and its inherent authoritarianism.[6] Here the clash appears to be between an alleged notion of immanent subjectivity (the 'actualization' of Hegel's Transcendental Subject in the *Phenomenology*), waiting to be delivered from and through the unfolding of the contradictions of the capitalist system, to be summoned to action by transcendental 'laws of history' teleologically orientated, as against a celebration of subjectivity which stresses fluidity, contingency, non-identity, creativity, 'fractal' individuality (Wagner 1991) and the like (Chambers 1994 amongst a variety of other authors).[7] The observation that in the contemporary situation 'the alienation of the subject is displaced by the latter's fragmentation' (Jameson 1991: 14) applies not only to the phenomenology of the subject, but also to the paradigmatic shift in the social sciences. This favours agency over sociological determination, the subjective over the structural and, as a further determination of subjectivity, the individual versus the collective implicit in the Durkheimian/Parsonian (but also, to an extent, in some radical formulations, Weberian) paradigms.[8]

Thus, as against the objectivizing tendencies of both structuralist and functionalist approaches, a great deal of literature in the social sciences is currently devoted to the reintroduction of 'the subjective' in the theory of social action. In the field of anthropology monographs are devoted to the exploration of identity, personhood and therefore choice and identity negotiation (Battaglia 1990; Jackson and Karp 1990; Hardin 1993 among others).

Leading theorists propose to eschew the notion of society altogether from the conceptual apparatus of the discipline. The alternative concept of 'sociality', stressing the subject-centred character of social interaction, and therefore the fluid, negotiated nature of societal norms, carries the day in anthropological debates (Ingold 1990).[9] Along the same lines, earlier proponents of a theory of social action that attempted to animate the connection between the structural and the subjective – namely Giddens and his concept of 'structuration' – appear to favour, in their latest writings, a more subjectivizing approach (Giddens 1992). Often the two notions of 'identity and personhood' are unified in the analytical/operational concepts of 'agency' and 'empowerment'. The last are understood as the active input of individuals against the background of socially structuring rules and expectations, and are seen as the independent variables to be reinstated against the – implicit or explicit – positivistic trends of the classical tradition in the social sciences (Rapport 1995).[10]

Such new trends tend to play the social dimension of subjectivity increasingly on the stage of culture. Described in the literature on globalization as 'the ideological battleground of the modern world-system' (Wallerstein 1990) the debate on culture has come to substitute for the debate on 'structure' (namely *economic* structure) of the modernist Left in the social sciences.[11] This happens both at the level of the phenomenology of social relations (in this it is fully an 'objective' phenomenon, or – perhaps – *a fact*) and at the level of epistemological theorization. A stress on cultures as the incommensurable, bounded wholes of post-structuralist cultural theory and anthropology implies a view of the social sciences as subjective readings, translations at best, more revelatory of the enquiring subject's own culture than they are of the object of theorization.[12]

It appears as if the structural rearrangements in the process of production and reproduction of capital have finally been granted leave to obtain the dream of the classical economists: a market that follows its own internal logic of production and reproduction free of constraints and impingements from the 'superstructural'.[13] This also implies that the latter is enabled to pursue its own freedom of expression relatively unfettered by economic *determinations*.[14] In this sense, the old critique of ideology which consisted essentially in exposing the *necessary nexus* between certain cultural expressions and the process of capitalist production and reproduction appears obsolete. What survives of the old critical intention turns into a 'theory of culture' in Gramscian terms. Here, the connection sought and theorized is no longer that between the political economy and its expressions in the cultural domain, but that between diverse (or occasionally alternative) cultural expressions independent of their 'real determinations'.[15] The logic of capitalist reproduction works out its own devices, while above and away from it the conflictual aspects of the global social formation are played out in the realm of representations. In this domain, 'the cultural' accrues by its own dynamics. These dynamics do not presuppose and do not include (as it was by definition in the classical anthropological concepts) the economic instance. In short: you do not need to produce and consume within a specific economic system to have a different culture – at most you need to have different economic *attitudes vis-à-vis* consumer's choice.

In this respect, it is significant that the most recent trend in the analysis of the economic instance in social relations stresses the subjective, culturally determined and therefore specific/exclusive behaviour of 'the subject' *qua* exchanger and consumer. The latest determination of subjectivity is seen as making cultural choices in the process of self-creation – its status of producer dealing with still rather objective conditions of capitalist *production* having been written off the scholarly agenda (Miller 1987; Dilley 1992; Evers and Schrader 1993; Friedman 1994b; along this line see also the culturalist/neo-substantivist positions in economic anthropology contained in Hugh-Jones and Humphreys 1992).[16] To this state of things still applies, *mutatis mutandis*, the age-old critique produced by Marxist economists against the idealism governing non-Marxist theories, where the stress is put upon the offer/demand dynamics – and therefore consumer's choice in the new, subjectivist analyses – rather than on production, its objective constraints and inbuilt contradictions.

What Jameson has called the contemporary 'effacement of the traces of production' (1991: 314) has transmigrated from the domain of social phenomena into the domain of theory. The phenomenological invisibility of the moment of production in an economy dominated by the tertiary sector on the one hand, and by anonymous financial capital on the other, has been imported into sociological thinking as both a theoretical premise and a methodological consequence: that which is a fact has been transformed into a truth. Theory, here, is not asking *at which structural conditions* the subjectification of social life appears to be *the* condition of postmodernity. The 'fragmentation' induced by 'movements of cultural autonomy, nationalist movements, ethnic movements . . . local autonomy and community self-control' (Friedman 1994a: 86) has not only been taken on board as an object of sociological enquiry. It is also being theorized as a legitimate new way of thinking of the social as such.

Confronted by this resurgence of subjectivism on the one hand, and by the way the phenomenon is being incorporated into the conceptual apparatus of the new social sciences on the other, the question must be asked of how much the tensions underpinning 'the subjective' in the life-world are not themselves the result of objective trends taking new forms, in the first instance, within the realm of the structural, the (would-be) normative – and more specifically in what the historical-materialistic strand in the social sciences used to conceptualize as their enduring tensions. The assumption is, therefore, that the lines along which subjectivity is strategically played and personhood subjectively constructed are themselves the product of structural lines of attrition arising within late capitalism. The new historical subjectivites may be indeed the product of their own choices, so to speak, but the question must at least be posited of how much the notion of 'choice' itself is a specific emergence developing out of the universalizing drive of modernity. How much is the 'will to subjectivity' – together with its conceptual subsumption within the new social sciences – itself the product of historically objective processes – and, for the purposes of the present chapter, the product of globalization?

Ethnicity is one facet of the 'new subjectivity' which has taken unprece dented form both in the life-world and in the conceptual apparatuses of contemporary theorizing in the social sciences.[17] Its entanglements with the unfinished process of modernity, and namely with the tantalizing project of a coherent cultural and social identity pursued in the formation of the nation states (Gellner 1983; Smith 1981 and 1991), show that the claim to subjectivity it carries can only be understood as part of a global process of identification which ethnicity – also and nevertheless – contradicts. Ethnicity is *both* 'local' in its claim and 'universal' in its implications: if X and Y can constitute themselves as legitimate, recognized subjects, why then not W and Z? Its fast growth on the contemporary world scene articulates the process whereby 'subjectivity' can be demonstrated to be an instance of the objective consequences of globalization.

ETHNICITY: FROM DIVERSITY TO DIFFERENCE

One of the main areas of agreement to emerge in the debate over identity, ethnicity and culture is that ethnicity is a subjectively constructed phenomenon. In this sense, the definition of the parameters of an ethnic claim to difference are left to the actor's own perspective. A constructivist understanding of ethnicity thus seems to constitute a point of wide agreement in one of the fastest growing bodies of literature in the social sciences (Tonkin, McDonald and Chapman 1989; Jackson and Penrose 1993; Eriksen 1993 among others). A corollary to this position is that ethnicity is a relational concept: it takes at least two to be ethnic (Barth 1969; Cohen 1986). Cultural traditions as boundary markers are 'invented' and put into place according to selective agendas whose rationale is entirely determined by contingent circumstances (Hobsbawm and Ranger 1983).[18] Although the literature stresses the 'processual' character of such invention – and therefore puts a strong emphasis on its historical nature – the conceptualization of historicity that seems to prevail here is of a functionalist/instrumentalist kind. Timewise, the rationale for 'constructing ethnicity' is placed synchronically: it is the agenda of the present that shapes up an image of the past (the 'myths' of ethnicity) for its own unmediated consumption. Here history is fully 'contemporaneized' and made dependent upon subjective choices and agendas which are specific to a given *point* in time, the 'here and now'. It is as if the set of circumstances which come together to build up a given ethnic project appear simultaneously, 'lined up' – so to speak – on a front which is both homogeneous in its time dimension and systematically and coherently organized as to its purposes. In this sense, ethnic subjectivity becomes a function in the old Parsonian sense: a set of quasi-natural 'pre-requisites' which need to be met and enforced, in the same way that 'individuality' constituted the functional requisite for the working of former Liberal ideological regimes of subjectivity. Against this reduction of the circumstances for historical actions to what their protagonists – quite literally – make of and with them, the objective moment of the constitution of subjec-tivities needs to be salvaged:

> The 'reasons' of history are 'invented' by historical subjects, but they appoint their own cast of characters. Each generation finds the condi-tions upon which to operate as a conscious subject already set by its predecessor, in a form which appears to the actors as objectively given: each generation's agenda is written on the former.
>
> (Poppi 1992: 133)

If these are the conditions under which ethnicity emerges, how can a notion of ethnicity which stresses the 'simultaneity' of both contemporary projectuality and the conditions of its coming into being, account for what of a given social formation's distinctive characteristics remains 'outside' the ethnic project? A theory of ethnicity which reduces historical dynamics to their subjective perception (and strategic implementation) and to an aligned front marching on simultaneously, cannot account for what historical devel-opments expurgate from the focus of self-awareness and subjectification. Self-consciousness and choice can only cover the entire spectrum of what is historically relevant by an idealistic *fiat* – implicit in the New Subjectivism – whereby little matters besides (and behind) what the acting subject 'decides' to implement. If this perspective were to be right, Minerva's owl ought not to take off at dusk, but should be there ever since dawn, to subsume under the wing of consciousness even that which will have become opaque and ultimately invisible at dusk, when self-consciousness begins its nocturnal march.

A theory that aims at accounting for both successes and failures in history, for what alternatively emerges as relevant in the constitution of subjectivity or else sinks into oblivion, has to work with a more sophisticated theory. Namely, we must account the differential rates at which some aspects of 'identity' and 'culture' appear on the scene of the negotiation of ethnicity, while others remain in the dark background. We have already seen how the instance of production has been eschewed from the theories of the New Subjectivism. This alone testifies, on the one hand, that the instance of pro-duction belongs to the 'non-negotiable' features of subjectivity, while, on the other hand, 'culture' is programmatically emptied of the productive instance as one of its determining features. The result is that both the productive and the cultural aspects of subjectivity become reified: the former as a non-negotiable, objective constraint, the latter as a container to be filled after a pick-and-choose fashion. But a theory of ethnicity that aims at going beyond the positivistic acceptance of what *de facto* appear to be the visible, self-conscious cultural traits selected in the process of the construction of ethnicity, must account for that selection against the background of wider, unreflected processes of cultural homologation.

In this respect, theorists of ethnicity have stressed the importance of language difference recognition as one of the cornerstones of the ethnic struggle. Why is it that the process of ethnogenesis, especially in the parliamentary democracies of Europe and North America, has become focused on the issue of linguistical difference as the core issue of ethnicity (Bourdieu 1982)? Language is the most 'abstract' expression of cultural identity. It is a form that can express many contents, and one that can retain its exchange value as a marker of cultural distinctiveness even when its import in terms of use-value is the same as that expressed by the majority language. In late capitalist social formations, the 'meanings' expressed have become largely homologous, and therefore the formal difference in the media through which these are conveyed is set at the forefront of the cultural struggle. In other words (and with the awareness that I am pushing my thesis here): it is because all other cultural traits have become widely homologated to the wider context that the language issue is stressed as the defining marker of difference. A theory of ethnicity must account for this beyond the simple recognition of a subjective 'choice': it has, in other words, to trace the emergence of 'difference' (and difference as the 'becoming focused' of certain 'markers') as part of the historical obliteration of 'diversity'.

The process of globalization can be characterized as one of articulation of hitherto unrelated life-worlds. The emergence of 'difference' – drummed to the point of conceptual noiselessness by the theorists of 'Otherness' – is the form taken by such articulation at the moment it presents itself to reflection. Yet, as Fredric Jameson has pointed out in his conceptualization of the postmodern condition 'difference *relates*' (1991: 31; emphasis mine). This is a notion that has been long present in anthropological thinking, and namely in what remains to date one of the most intriguing and thoughtful reflections on the nature of difference in the social domain. In Bateson's *Naven* (1958, but also see Bateson 1973), the concept of schismogenesis accounts for the emergence of sets of differential cultural traits within one single system. For a set of differential, individuating characteristics to become schismatic, they need to be organically articulated with one another as parts of a system (in a power system 'aggression' cannot exist without 'submissivity', 'dominance' without 'subordination', etc.). In this sense and in the age of multiculturalism, it is no longer the case that 'alterity is a negative category of the Same' (Mudimbe 1988: 12 and *passim*) as it used to be in the imperialist stage of world history. At the time when cultural relativism has rounded

291

up the diversities of the life-world and assigned to each a measure of difference, the Other has become altogether an instance of the Same in the global system of culture.

An inter-cultural (as opposed to an intra-cultural) schismogenic process needs not to be articulated in complementary, alternative traits of the kind mentioned above, nor, eventually, in the readjustment of their relative standing *vis-à-vis* an intervening 'third factor'. Several (although increasingly less so) are the situations within which schismogenesis does not lead to confrontation, and these are most often those in which a schismogenic process of the 'complementary' kind can be found. When two groups – say one of pastoralists and one of agriculturalists – occupy and exploit different niches in the same ecological environment, their schismogenetic articulation can be altogether peaceful. When, however, the two begin to compete for the same resources – namely the control of the State and related 'modern' agencies – then the fight begins.[19]

In this respect, what is crucial for the present argument is that the legitimacy of the schismogenic process advocated (i.e. the claim to autonomy or 'minority rights') is predicated upon a type of moral economy whose *form*, at least, is shared by all contestants. Thus, for instance, the schismogenically antagonistic aspects of the process of constitution of Basque nationalism are grounded in the *fueros* of the sixteenth and seventeenth centuries, which granted *hidalguía* ('nobility') to the entire Basque population. Since then, the notion of 'collective nobility' has been 'a key notion in Basque nationalist doctrine in which it is regarded as a primordial attribute of all Basques' (Heiberg 1989: 26). On the basis of their *equality* with the Spanish nobility, the Basques began to claim special rights *vis-à-vis* the Spanish State, and this in due course became systematically articulated with the whole gamut of traits and provisions for national independence.

Be it the First Amendment of the US Constitution or the UN Charter for Human Rights, ethnicity appeals to the international *shared and acknowledged* set of principles of the moral economy to vindicate its legitimacy. In this sense '[E]thnicity describes both a set of relations and *a mode of consciousness*' (Comaroff and Comaroff 1992: 54; emphasis mine). If it is also true, as is stated in a recent assessment of the literature on ethnicity for a wide audience, that 'every distinction – no matter how "objective" or "natural" it may seem to us – needs to be codified culturally in order to be recognised' (Eriksen 1993: 156), what needs to be stressed here is that such cultural codification needs to become shared *across the board* for ethnicity to take the crucial step that turns it into 'a mode of consciousness' at the global level. As has been pointed out, the feelings of communality engendered by the singing of the national anthem may indeed owe their appeal to the perception of a 'simultaneity' of attitudes which they foster in their singers (Anderson 1991: 145). But the results of that 'simultaneity' feed back not only *within* a given national or ethnic formation: they also, and most importantly, apply *across* different subjectivities. Each national anthem sounds exclusive and specific – 'ours' – because it sounds like all others – 'theirs'.

In this light, difference can be defined as the process by which structural features of the system of cultural and sociological diversities (selected *elements* of which come to constitute 'ethnicity'), emerging under specific historical circumstances, are historically negotiated to become the common ground for negotiating further trans-specific differences in the contemporary life-world. This negotiation implies in turn a dialogical process, by which common relevant grounds are firstly individuated, then selectively decided as relevant (or not) to the dialogical situation and then, eventually (but not necessarily), transformed into grounds of more or less extreme contention. Following this line of analysis, what is needed to explain ethnicity is a *theory of articulation* between hitherto *diverse* sociocultural systems turned into *differing* systems. Globalization, in turn, is the process which facilitates such articulation. It is the process by which the choice of 'selected traits' in the dialogical situation comes to cover an ever broader spectrum, so that the original, 'sectorial' diversities between contenders in the ethnic arena become organically connected to all the other features of the system: from a 'diversity' in religious ideology to a 'difference' in overall political outlook; from a diversity in 'language' to 'political autonomy' and so on (Poppi 1991).

The educated, literate classes, the agents which are most of all articulated *externally*, are the main sociological operators of the *internal*, organic connection (Gellner 1983). The differences that matter in terms of locality and specificity are therefore defined within a wider, global connection. The differential intervals implemented in the construction of identity respond to a global interpolation, a kind of 'alignment' whereby diversities become commensurable and therefore appear as differences. The expansion of globalization – the media, close interaction/confrontation in urban/migrant settings, etc. – speeds up the process and provides the minimal common denominators upon which differential intervals between ethnic, cultural and other 'minority' groups can be organized as plausible *representations* of identity to global audiences. What have been termed 'rituals of traditionalization' follow the same revivalist pattern of staged performances throughout the globe, from National Days to the opening of international sports events and a variety of outsiders-orientated affirmations of identity (Bendix 1985; Boissevain 1992; Herle and Phillipson 1994; Manning 1983; Sharp and Boonzaier 1994; van Binsbergen 1993 in a growing body of literature). It is at this juncture of specific identities and global *desiderata* that the changing attitude to 'the Past' can be gauged. From formerly having a sense only in relationship to its background context *within* the unreflected, since undetected and unmonitored, borders of the ethnic group, the common denominator of 'tradition' now finds its sense in the difference it marks at the boundary with other similar, because different, events throughout the globe.

Ethnic and national festivals – from Notting Hill to the Trinidad and Rio Carnivals – become a performative genre, 'ones of a kind', summoned and lined up by the globalization of particularism. Ethnicity in the postmodern age is therefore expressed not so much in the *internally* context-specific *diversities between* cultural formations, but between the *externally* context-specific *differences across* cultures. If in pre-colonial days I would have had to be acquainted with the internal organization and symbolism of the Barotse royal court in order to understand the 'meaning' of the *Kazanga* royal festival (van Binsbergen 1993), today I have first of all to look outside the Barotse social formation – or, rather, at the boundary which constitutes the individuation of Barotse ethnicity – to understand it as an 'ethnic festival' meant to 'beat the boundary' of difference. Barotse kingship, that was in pre-colonial time a context-specific functional institution, is now functional to a process which begins *outside* the former context.

The issue of 'authenticity' (however 'invented' or 'constructed') is one of the hotbeds of postmodernist theoretical elaboration and itself a by-product of globalization. It emerges in the context of the shifting grounds of significance induced by cultural homologation. 'Tradition' is constituted in the selection of cultural traits that the process of modernization has expounded from the life-world as redundant and irrelevant to its own process. Yet, tradition becomes an object of representation of locality and specificity. In the age of globalization, subjectivity cannot express itself but in this mediated, objectified form: the self is its own spectacle that only others can see.

INSCRIBING THE SUBJECTIVE: WHAT IS GLOBALIZED?

What is globalized as a specific yet commensurable difference, acquires its meaning within the widening canvas of world culture. As Frederic Jameson glosses in his reassessment of Adorno's critique of modern subjectivity: '[E]xchange value, then, the emergence of some third, abstract term between two incomparable objects ... constitutes the primordial form by which identity emerges in human history' (1990: 23). As long as specificity and subjectivity cannot liberate themselves of 'identity' as a historical necessity, they will fatefully have to come back to the ideological stock exchange to have their claims assessed and rated against all other similar currencies. In this sense, 'cultural values' represents the ongoing fixing of exchange rates on the global market.[20] The cry-foul that punctuates each of Benetton's (the cynical Venetian merchant!) advertising campaigns certifies the pain and confusion that each trespass of the use-value/exchange-value boundary still carries within itself. But it provides, by the same token, also a measure of the *necessity* of the reification of subjectivity, this time in the form of global morality, under the existing conditions.

Yet, not all use-values of cultural products are suitable to be turned into exchange-values. The global division of ethnic cultural labour allocates skills, production quotas as well as ideological markets to each identity-carrier. The terms are negotiated internationally, cast as they are in the vocabulary of a – by now – global ideology. The text accompanying a collection of ethnic pictures published on occasion of the World Conference of Indigenous People (Rio de Janeiro 1992), and signed by the General Co-ordinator of the Intertribal Committee, Marcos Terena, is worth quoting in full and *verbatim* (emphasis mine):

> Manipulation [*sic*, but a literal translation of the Spanish original would have read 'Management'] of the Earth and Environment has always been an act of wisdom of our people. There was a time, therefore, when we were rich. We dominated completely nature itself, healing herbs, its feeding potential and, even, an architecture of the jungle. Afterwards, the colonizer arrived, a 'civilization' was imposed upon us, our land invaded, our homes destroyed, our voices silenced. Nevertheless, the teachings of our fathers are still alive in our minds, five hundred years later. Love [the] earth that feeds you. Live the dreams of our wise men: let us be human beings, forgetting a time when, *just for the fact of being different, we were taken as useless.* The Indigenous People Earth Chart is so simple and understandable as the song of birds and the sight of children.

What are then the circumstances under which 'different' people stop being perceived as 'useless' and become, instead, *useful?* What are the conditions by which a use-value that was (once) specific to 'them' can turn into an exchange-value with global (never mind how contested) rating for 'all'? The boundaries of difference, their very significance and meaning, are re-built upon inter-cultural/global concerns which involve both contexts of the 'cultural' divide. Some are allocated the 'ecological niche' because their difference is now built upon the inter-culturally shared environmental issue and its predicaments. Inuit people, while struggling to keep their land from the encroachment of oil companies, are granted (partial) exemption from the ban on whaling on condition that they keep it as a feature of their 'cultural identity': small scale and, in the wider market, competitively irrelevant.

However, those less suitable cultural traits which would probably score little global agreement as 'useful differences' are – to paraphrase Wittgenstein – passed over in silence. And those who – nevertheless – made it to the world stage are taken care of by the growing cultural relativism of the post-modernist kind. Reduced to 'constructions of the Other', uncomfortable ethnographies are agreed to be subjective, 'authorized' points of view. As such they are negotiated into irrelevance: *de facto* by the ever-expanding, if never ending, homologation to UN-sanctioned decency, and *de jure intellectus* by their epistemological incorrectness.

Things become more complicated when the construction of the boundary of difference is set *within* a wider social formation and comes to overlap with already set cultural isobars. Here the aporias of multiculturalism have to be considered: why is it that same cultural traits come to be accepted and enforced as legitimately 'somebody's culture', and others cannot? The Catch 22 'Rushdie Paradox' on freedom of expression, the First Amendment Debate – and a number of other less newsworthy instances – are cases in question ('are guns part of American culture' – and therefore in – or are they part of its criminal tendencies – and therefore out? [And – in the context of the present argument – why is it that 'culture' does not seem to be allowed any longer to include criminal tendencies?]). Why is it that the attitude towards 'human rights' in China, Somalia and other parts of the world comes under the inventory of 'human rights politics' and not that of ('their') 'culture' – and can therefore be safely contested? Things become even more complicated when the construction of the boundary of identity intersects cultural issues *within* metropolitan social formations confronted with 'minority cultures': how 'cultural' are *purdah* and *chador*? And, on a wider scale, how much legitimacy as a boundary marker in the division of the ethnic labour can female circumcision claim and attain? Here, liberal-minded critics find themselves caught between the rock of exhausted symmetries predicated upon a universalism no longer suitable as a 'grand narrative' ('your freedom ends where mine begins') that the process of glob-alization has finally made both hopelessly porous and ferociously transitive, and the hard place of the new 'cultural racism' (Balibar and Wallerstein 1991), whereby 'different' peoples should indeed be allowed 'to pursue their own cultural values' and – for that very reason – are to be thrown out of the country.

The problem here is that the obsolescence of the grand, universalist narra-tives of modernism, that is claimed to constitute one of the reasons for the legitimation of multiculturalism, runs up against the difficulty of specifying (and legislating about) which traits of a given culture can become accept-able blocks for the construction of difference.[21] There is therefore a problem of selectivity and articulation – the very same processes that the present analysis set earlier at the core of the globalization of difference. If the *fatwah* and the *jihad* cannot be treated as legitimate markers of difference in the international division of the cultural labour, then this means that a powerful – albeit contradictory – process of selection is at work. The criteria for this selection are dictated by a global culture which still owes some allegiance to the 'modernist' criteria of bourgeois Enlightenment – as well as suffering from the same schizophrenia that the double bind of the ideology of freedom inescapably carries within itself. Particularism implies universalism: each preys on the other as both its begetter and foe.

Failure to acknowledge the relational, *social* nature of ethnic schismogenesis – its character as a negotiated process which begins from a globalized, shared and undersigned discourse of difference – exposes the liberal-minded notion of multiculturalism to what has been termed 'differentialist racism' (Taguieff 1984, quoted in Balibar and Wallerstein 1991: 21). As was remarked earlier in this chapter, the notion by which cultures are self-contained, incommensurable wholes has gained a certain currency in anthropological literature of the postmodernist persuasion. Here, the notion of difference has been applied to cultures as their inherent *nature*. As Etienne Balibar has pointed out, this 'naturalization of culture' is at the ideological roots of the new racism, whereby the justification of racist policies is no longer predicated upon a genetic theory of race (by now fundamentally bankrupted), but upon a culturalist theory of the ontology of cultures and their irreducible differences. Hence an 'attack from the rear' which exploits what appeared to be, at its beginnings (and still undoubtedly is for its promoters), the soft underbelly of a radically liberal outlook (Balibar and Wallerstein 1991: 21–4).

Thus, globalization is responsible for selectively sieving which markers of difference can be deployed in the process of constructing the international division of ethnic and cultural labour. Not all cultural traits can sing in the multicultural chorus, only some. Which of them will be auditioned and finally make it to the actual performance remains to be seen. However, it is possible – and evidence for this is already at hand – that in the process parts will be distributed that will become the specific 'song line' of cultural formations identified more and more by a few dominant, subject-specific traits. The rest – the unredeemable traits from the point of view of globalization – will be quietly swept under the carpet. They will either be forgotten or grouped under an inventory ('politics/power') within which some hierarchy of discourse will be still legitimately practicable: here an attempt will be made finally to repress them.

WIDER HORIZONS WITH LARGER DETAILS – AND ALL THAT THEY CONTAIN

This chapter has attempted to understand the phenomenon of ethnicity as a specific instance of what I have called the New Subjectivity. This emerges from the ashes of de-subjectivized, post-structuralist social theorizing. Of its probably recalcitrant father, it retains a *penchant* for contingency and fragmentation as the 'true' condition of the postmodern subject. The New Subjectivity emerges in conditions whereby 'the structural' has sunk to the bottom, has become invisible, and subjectivity can float free of objective determinations. In this sense, a notion of 'culture', expurgated of its structural/functional economic instance, has become the ideological battlefield of the postmodern era.

It has been argued that this is true both as a social fact and as a trend in contemporary social theory. This is underpinned by the specific form taken by the process of global production and reproduction of capital in its late stage of development: the predominance of the tertiary sector and of financial capital over materially productive capital has made the instance of production fade out of focus. 'Ethnicity' emerges in the social sciences along-side a theory of subjectivity as a bundle of more or less unsystematically related, situation-dependent, social networks.

Following this general lead, constructivist theories of ethnicity show a tendency to reduce 'the reasons of history' to the subjective 'choices' made by the actors of the ethnic process within contexts whose time dimension is synchronically given. They assume that the historically given background to contemporaneity has no bearings upon the process of selection of what has to be 'ethnicized'. What is at work in history are the agendas of the synchronic subject producing itself, and not (*also*) the objective legacy of the diachronic process that brings about contemporaneity.

To counter such subjectivist trends in the theory of ethnicity, a theory of selection and articulation has been advocated. The process of ethnogenesis can be understood as an instance of the process of schismogenesis. In Bateson's formulation, this is the systematic articulation of a differential set of characteristics between sectors of a social formation. The 'making' of ethnicity's differential articulations is an instance of this process, as it widens under the impulse of globalization. Globalization provides the context for the systematic articulation of differences. As it moves on, the differential traits of a given cultural formation are made commensurable, and their difference can be made to appear as a determination of the ethnic subject. This has been expounded as the process by which 'diversities' turn into 'differences'. Finally, it has been argued, the process of the constitution of differences brings about the notion of identity as exchange-value between cultural traits hitherto confined to their local, specific – and 'useless' – use-values. However, not 'everything which is cultural' makes it to globalization.

To invert Marx's famous saying, not all fluids that enter the mainstream of historical developments coagulate into anything solid. Globalization selects and negotiates which hitherto diverse and unrelated cultural traits will 'make it' as the building blocks of ethnic difference. A new form of cultural hege-mony is thus being created, whereby schismogenesis implies systematic articulation and commensurability. Meaningful differences exist – like the Saussurian signifier – only as part of a differential structure. Globalization is the process that takes care of the syntagmatic aspects of the process, while 'culture' provides the paradigmatic materials to be organized. That which is left out will constitute the inarticulable and, eventually, the repressed debris of history.

Cast in this light, the paradox of ethnicity consists of the fact that for two (or more) cultural formations to become schismogenic they have to become first of all commensurable with one another. In the terms of the present study, it is not when they correspond simply to diverse use-values in relatively confined life-worlds that they become 'ethnic', but when they are attributed

298

different exchange-values. In order for their difference 'to make sense' they have to differ from something they have in common: 'identity' is the form both of their identification as well as their subsumption *qua* instances of the global. Thus, social formations become ethnic not when they are too dissimilar, but when they have become too similar to one another.

Does this mean, as it has been proposed, that 'the dehegemonization of the Western-dominated world is simultaneously its dehomogenization' (Friedman 1994: 117)? In line with the analysis conducted in this chapter, the answer to that question has to be negative: there is probably no more and no less 'homogeneity' today in the world than there has always been. Only, the homogeneity which is produced on a larger scale, does in fact disturb the narrow-range view in the process of incorporating local details. Each regional conflict is – potentially – the beginning of a global conflagration.

If these are the terms of the question, Hegel is still right: globalization is the (latest? final?) ruse of reason. It is the movement whereby the *Zeitgeist* rounds up diversity, selects the traits which are compatible with its own realization, and encircles what is historically left of the Other in history to recognize it as yet another determination of the Identical. All human beings are equal because they are all different. By the same token, Hegel is still wrong: the limits of globalization are the limits to which the operation of encirclement and subsumption can be carried out in full. With globalization the differential details of each emergent cultural/ethnic formation do not disappear. They are, instead, magnified as the process moves on and the picture of the world system also expands. The limits to which this process can be carried out *ad infinitum*, so that the boundary defining each detail in the widening picture will not come to interfere and finally clash with its neighbours' – with potentially devastating effects for the wider context – are also the limits to which the enlarged reproduction of capital can be carried out at the present rate.

The transferral of the battle onto the cultural grounds defined (and fostered!) by what has been called 'the absence of the structural' in the New Subjectivism, would make it appear as if 'the structural' can quietly run its course at the bottom undisturbed by what is going on at the surface. But the process of the reification of culture takes care that what was previously simply diverse in its small-scale capacity as cultural use-value acquires, in the process of ethnic differentiation, also a powerful (possibly ultimately unadministrable) exchange-value. Global *hybris* may still turn into global *hubris*.

This progressive transformation, whose consequences are already visible in the growth of the 'ethnic lawsuit' and the capitalization of copyrighted 'cultural property', develops its own costs and comes to impinge upon the submerged structure. Whether the structural submarine will be able to withstand the pressure which is building up by enforcing a further distinction between 'civil' and 'cultural' society (as it once succeeded in drawing a line between the 'civil' and the 'political', to secure the corner-stones of the ideology of the free market), and therefore dodge having to emerge and confront the battle at the surface – it is too early to tell. But that is the as yet unwritten story of a new subjectivity which will, perhaps, build the difference that will finally count.

NOTES

1 The literature stemming from the debate on globalization has grown in the last decade beyond any individual's capability of extracting a workable definition of the concept. In a sense the meaning of the concept is self-evident, in another, it is as vague and obscure as its reaches are wide and constantly shifting. Perhaps, more than any other concept, globalization *is* the debate about it. In the present chapter, therefore, I will not give 'a definition' as is customary in Anglo-American sociology. I will rather let the concept 'do its work' by focusing on its conditions of existence on the one hand, and on its implications on the other.

2 Authors such as A. G. Frank and B. K. Gills have argued that the implications of the concept of globalism must be extended to cover a process of *longue durée* stretching back to antiquity and beyond (see Frank and Gills 1993). Jonathan Friedman has propounded an altogether sociological theory of globalism, whereby the global dimensions of the process of reproduction represent a *constitutive* feature of the very concept of social formation. This, in Friedman's view, ought to counter the tendency of both functionalist and Marxist approaches to treat social formations *qua* closed, self-contained systems as is the case with the concept of mode of production (Friedman 1994a, esp. ch. 2). Friedman's sociologism, however, overlooks the issue of the *relative* import of global relations *vis-à-vis* the internal arrangements and specific dynamics of a given mode of production considered, in the first (and only in the first) instance, as a 'closed' system. If it cannot indeed be denied that 'globalism' is an aspect of modes of production present at any point in time (Marx's critique of Crusoe's economicism applies as much to social formations as it does to individuals), the issue of the *articulation* between modes of production is one that must be treated as an analytically distinct problem from that of the internal articulation of a mode of production. In fact, the impact of global relations upon the process of reproduction of a given social formation (which becomes in Friedman's perspective crucial in order to understand historical change) is surely different when it leads to a rearrangement of the internal relations of production (as it is the case with the Central African material he brings to bear upon his argument) than when it affects simply the appropriation and distribution of goods obtained on the 'global exchange' circuit. The two processes are of course often historically linked, and the latter may indeed lead to the former, but this question is of an empirical and not of a theoretical nature, as Friedman instead seems to claim. In this sense 'globalism' in Friedman's sense and 'globalization' in Wallerstein's terms are two separate – if related – issues. In particular, the globalization induced by capitalism is historically specific in that it prompts the collapse of local modes of production by reaching at the very heart of the relations of production and by *subsuming* them within an increasingly integrated world system. This becomes dominated by *one* mode of production and is no longer characterized by an articulation between different modes as was formerly the case. Once again, in line with the general argument of this study, in spite of Friedman's neo-classical

insistence upon reproduction/circulation, the crucial and overlooked issue still remains the issue of production.

3 The reference is, of course, to Hobsbawm's pedigreed (Hegel, Marx and – partly – Weber) thesis of the demise of the nation state in the waning of the modern age and to Anderson's early attempt to re-think nationalism away from mere ideology and superstructural romantic deception (Hobsbawm 1996; Anderson 1991). A clear assessment of the issue is contained in Balakrishnan 1995.

4 Thus, for instance, in an early debate about the concept, J.-M. Benoist said that the study of identity must 'oscillate between the poles of disconnected singularity and globalizing unity' (in Lévi-Strauss *et al.* 1977: 15). A more recent formulation of the problem of identity states, along the same line, that 'groups may actually become culturally more similar at the same time that boundaries are strengthened' (Eriksen 1993: 38). For a development of this general line of analysis closer to the concerns of the present essay see Friedman 1990.

5 Beyond the political implications of the concept, I am using 'radical' here in its etymological sense. The issue of how notions of gender and race are 'prior' or to be prioritized *vis-à-vis* historically rooted and historically specific phenomena of social grouping such as 'class' is, of course, a thorny one. The terms of the ongoing debate appear to contrast the Hegel–Marx (and *partly* Weber) line which argues for the historical rootedness – and therefore immanent contingency – of power arrangements, with a Nietzsche–Foucault–Derrida (and postmodernist epigones) line which instead stresses the *quasi*-anthropological, transcendental (in a Kantian sense) embeddedness of overlapping notions of 'power and knowledge' as the very precondition of historical discourses. The terms of the debate have been laid out in Habermas 1987b (esp. Lectures IX and X) and Callinicos 1989 (esp. ch. 3). A clear rendition of the ambiguities inherent in the power/ knowledge conflation of postmodernist cultural theorists from a feminist perspective is contained in Mascia-Lees *et al.* 1989.

6 The obvious reference here is to Lyotard's *The Postmodern Condition*. A number of similarly orientated works, detailing the general positions contained in Lyotard's *Urtext* have since followed. It is worth pointing out, in the general economy of the present chapter, how in Lyotard's early work it was nowhere made clear whether he was simply recording a matter-of-fact development in contemporary culture at large (which would have made the thesis work *sociologically* plausible), whether he was subscribing to the demise of the secular deities, as it were (which would have been less agreeable), or both. I would think that the latter is rather the case, or so it has been assumed by a range of both pro- and anti-postmodernist theorists. However, the observation is worth making in that to record this ambiguity in Lyotard's work (and all the more so in that of his epigones) uncovers the underlying, ultimately *positivist* stance of postmodern theorizing. Having subscribed to the philosophical premise of an identity between power and knowledge, and the reduction of the latter to the former, no room is left for a *relative* autonomy of thought from the reasons of its constitution: with Heidegger, gnoseology is reduced to an instance of ontology. Having thus renounced the very possibility of thought as a function of an emancipatory process which might at least *posit* its own normative project over and above the existing situation, critique is reduced to an exercise in the deconstruction of what already positively exists: critical thought stalks what is already in place, only in reverse gear. Deconstruction, because of its self-proclaimed *reflexive* nature, thus functions wholly within the limitations of contemporary agendas – *including its own*. As is for instance the case of 'radical' theorists *à la* Richard Rorty, the figure of engagement of critical elaboration with 'reality' is then sceptical, armchair

'liberal irony' (Callinicos 1995: 204–11). Things get edgy, though, when enthusiastic theoreticians *à la* Fukuyama spill the beans and bring the normative aspirations of postmodernist theorizing out of the woodwork, and triumphantly (and embarrassingly) announce that the 'spirit of the contingent time' is altogether *the Zeitgeist* (Fukuyama 1992). Here the Hegelian positive identity of subject and object dovetails with the implicit positivism of postmodernist theorizing.

7 The notion that the Marxian notion of subjectivity is inherently teleological, scientistic and quasi-religious in its 'transcendental historical necessity' – not much better than Hegel's philosophy of history – appears to be *quaestio soluta* both among the old Marxist theoreticians of Althusserian persuasion as well as among both their liberal and conservative opponents. For the former, history is essentially the history of *structures* and not (also) of *praxis* – the problem of subjectivity having been reduced altogether to the question of the so-called 'superstructure', whereas for the latter the issue of subjectivity is reduced to a question of individuality-cum-human-nature – anything else smacking of idealistic metaphysics (e.g. Gellner 1992). Yet, the allegation of teleological idealism raised against Marx's view of historical subjectivity is hardly defensible in a philologically accurate reading of Marx's philosophy of the subject (Schmidt 1971, ch. 3). This runs against a theory of history *qua* history of structures expounded of subjectivity pursued by Althusser and much 1970s French (and Anglo-American) Marxist thinkers (Schmidt 1972 and 1981). The current misrepresentation came out of a widely accepted Althusserian reading of Marx, which the critics of historical materialism still take to be the 'correct' (and therefore philosophically, politically and morally bankrupt) interpretation. Sadly and paradoxically, both Bucharin and Zinov'ev's Leninist attacks and Kautsky's 'right-wing' criticism of Lukács' ontologizing views of the proletariat's role in world history in *History and Class Consciousness*, demonstrate that a Hegelian view of 'the Subject' was extraneous to the Marxist tradition even at the lowest ebb of its development (Lukács 1973; also see the Introduction by A. Spinella in the same volume). A vigorous and balanced reassessment of the general issue is contained in Callinicos 1995. An assessment of the Left's uneasy relationship with emerging 'identity politics', pushed to the point of making the two incompatible, is contained in Hobsbawm 1996.

8 For a recent reiteration of such trends in radical cultural theory see Mestrovi'c 1993.

9 It is important here to stress that the views expressed by M. Strathern and C. Thoren against the concept of 'society' in the work cited are directed as much against the notion of 'society' as they are directed against the notion of the 'individual' – which both authors see as the conceptual correlate of an untenable dichotomy they wish to overcome. Yet, their views remain 'subjectivist' in that by eliminating the tension implicit in the classical dichotomy between a normative, intersubjective and 'reified' social domain and individual (or – for that matter – collective) attempts to renegotiate and redefine them, they reduce sociality to the sum total of the relationships between 'persons'. These, in M. Strathern's view, contain the potential for relationships with others as much as they are embedded in them (Strathern 1988: 10, but a theoretically complete formulation was already present in the concept of the person as 'dividual' elaborated in Strathern 1988). In this sense, 'structure' is reduced to a network of person-generated relations, a line of reflection which theorists of cultural complexity expand to cover transcultural relations (Hannerz 1992a). In all such theoretical developments, the moment of the objectivity of societal structures is lost to theorization. It becomes extremely difficult to understand for which reason

302

people should share the same 'meanings' – or, for that matter, even quarrel over them. Before being in the concept 'society', reification is in *the thing* the concept attempts to grasp in thoughts. The fact that 'it looks ugly' is no reason to dispatch it. Finally, the argument here is not about the validity of concepts such as the 'dividual' as appropriate tools of analysis for the specific social realities which they set off to explain. It is, rather, about their validity as general theoretical apparatuses. When such claim is put forth, the thought cannot be escaped that if the modernist concept of the individual shaped the entire world after the self-image of the bourgeoisie, the new concept universalizes, instead, the 'networked', multiple individualities of late capitalism. Postmodernist revisions remain as ideological as Durkheimian reifications.

10 The re-elaborations of Mauss's notion of 'the person' (Mauss 1979), together with the reappraisal of Maurice Leenhardt's ethnography of 'the person' in Melanesia by one of the inaugurators of the postmodernist critique of Durkheimian anthropology (Clifford 1982), have paved the way to a body of literature stressing the mental and psychological aspects of individuality over its social, objective determinations (Carrithers *et al.* 1985). However, an emphasis on the dialectics between individuality and social normativity was already found in the work of the most lucid of functionalist anthropologists. In M. Fortes' essay on the concept of the person among the Tallensi, a tension is maintained to exist at all times between individual projects and the normative aspects of the context in which they operate. Fortes' notion of 'the moral domain' – which is as much external to as it is internalized by individuals – works as the *trait-d'union* between subjective pulsions and social norms. These remain, however, irreducible to one another. It is on this irreducibility that the very necessity of a moral domain is predicated: unlike postmodernist conceptions, 'morality' is as much subjectively interpreted as it is objectively grounded (Fortes 1987: 247–86).

11 The body of literature concerned with the mutual implications of culture and globalization grows almost by the day. The collections edited by M. Featherstone 1990, A. D. King 1991, and S. Lash and J. Friedman 1992 – as well as the works by U. Hannerz 1992b and J. Friedman 1994a, provide a wide and complex view of the *problematiques* and positions connected to the issue.

12 For a summary of the state of the debate and a cogent critique of such tendencies see Kuper 1994 and the earlier essay by P. Steven Sangren 1988. The exchange between J.-P. Olivier de Sardan 1988 and 1989 and P. Stoller 1989, and the debate between C. Geertz 1992 and J. Goody 1992, provide a clear-cut view of the positions in question.

13 In this sense, E. Mandel (1975) has described 'late capitalism' as the stage in which the logic of capitalist accumulation appears in its 'purest' form. Mandel's analysis is grounded in the tradition of the 'theory of disembeddedment' in historical-materialistic studies, from Marx to Polanyi. For an application of the theory to the analysis of globalization, see Altvater and Mahnkopf (chapter 14) in the present collection.

14 This does not mean, however, that the superstructural is freed of economic constraints – i.e. cultural expression still 'needs money' to realize itself, but this time as a means to an end, and not as a determinant of its very form of expression.

15 The presupposition of a separation between the spheres of 'culture' and 'production' in the contemporary life-world appears to grant leave to write off altogether the *vexata quaestio* of the relationship between structure and superstructure. Authors of a former Marxist persuasion are perhaps the most eager to dump the problem as one overcome by the *de facto* developments of contemporaneity. Thus, Jonathan Friedman writes of ethnic nationalism in Europe as characteristic

of a situation in which 'the cultural sphere is separated from the process of reproduction' (Friedman 1994a: 87). Instead of asking the materialistic and dialectical
question of which are the *structural* conditions for 'the cultural' *to appear and constitute itself* as a 'separate domain', Friedman and a number of like-minded radical
thinkers assume such separation as a *fait accompli*, and they take it as a starting
point of their analysis. This trend is perhaps best illustrated by Gorz's controversial theory of the necessary separation between the 'heteronomous' domain
of production, where objective constraints operate, and the 'autonomous' domain
of the *lebenswelt* as the area of subjective fulfilment (Gorz 1982).

16 To assume *the phenomenon* of the appearance of 'the cultural' as disengaged from
'the economic' as both an analytic and theoretical *premise* of current cultural
theory (rather than to investigate the conditions for that appearance of autonomy
as themselves determined by the specific conditions of late capitalist production)
is yet another instance of the paradoxical positivist tendencies in contemporary
cultural theory (see note 5 above). Even F. Jameson, an otherwise strong critic
of postmodernist cultural theory, although keen on stressing the 'globally material' nature of the media, still analyses them not in their structural/economic
determinations, but in terms of aesthetic and social phenomena providing the
key paradigm of 'the cultural' in postmodernism (Jameson 1991).

17 The entry 'Ethnicity' in the Subject Directory of the 1994 Register of the
European Association of Social Anthropologists lists 93 professionals dealing with
the subject, while the entry 'Politics' lists only eight (Hubinger 1994).

18 The reference here is, obviously, to Hobsbawm and Ranger's *The Invention of
Tradition* and to the staggering amount of literature the central concept of the
work has inspired since its publication. The general thrust of this intellectual
production is that the 'reasons of history' are to be reduced to the agendas of
those who interpret them according to the needs of synchronicity (to their 'invention'). This approach reduces history to a subjective construction as much with
respect to its *making* as with respect (and all the more so!) to its *interpretations*. As
was the case with the new social sciences discussed above, in postmodernist histo-
riographies the determinations of the object of enquiry are conflated with the
requirements of theory and methodology. Even if it might be *plausible* that the
reasons of history are actually 'invented', this ought not to be imported uncritically within the reflection on the process of knowledge. The old dialectical tenet
that 'people make history as much as history makes people' is here reduced only
to the first part of the equation. This radical departure was perhaps not the
intention of the authors of the original text, as – perhaps – a recent revisitation
of the concept demonstrates (Ranger 1993).

19 This is the case of so-called 'tribalism' in Africa. The indigenously acknowledged
diversity of ethnic groups in the pre-colonial situation turned into administra-
tively bound differences in the colonial period. Each group was subsumed within
the wider context by having its specificities measured up against the requirements
of the administration. Once reduced to commensurable 'units', each with the
same attributes of the other (a language, a culture, a history, etc.), ethnic groups
began to fight over the control of the very same frame which generated them
as different units in the first place. African 'tribalism' can be understood, in this
sense, as an attempt to articulate a set of hitherto heterogeneous diversities into
a coherent, bound set of organized differences. Once the asymmetries of the
schismogenic process outlined above turn into the symmetries shared by historical
subjects competing over *the same* terms of existence, then the process of articulation turns into a process of contested hegemonization.

20 The recent attempt to break away from the vicious encirclement of Otherness
by Sameness carried out in Vincent Mudimbe's celebrated work *The Invention of*

304

Africa, ends up by postulating either rather vague and unsubstantiated notions of incommensurability between an ever-elusive African *gnosis* which would have (supposedly? hopefully?) escaped the siege of 'Western' construction, or else by advocating a (future?) self-definition of 'identity' whose fundamental difference from any ideological elaboration of a nationalist – or, specifically, Panafrican – ideology remains hard to see. In the light of the present argument, this is the necessary outcome of an attempt to reconstruct a notion of cultural specificity within the conceptual constraints of 'identity'. Identity is bound to remain nailed within the circle of Otherness and Sameness because it is constituted from within that circle, and namely – as it has been argued – by the process which sets exchange-values as the rate against which use-values are rendered commensurable. The emergency exit would be to think subjectivly both within and without the circle constitutive of identity. But this would mean – once again – to be able to abolish the process of formation of exchange-values. It would entail, in other words, the critique of the political economy.

21 For a forceful and concise critique of multiculturalism, which dialectically sees 'multiculturalism' *itself* as a specification of a wider 'American culture', see Jacoby 1994.

14

THE WORLD MARKET UNBOUND

Elmar Altvater and Birgit Mahnkopf

In *The Great Transformation* the eminent economic historian Karl Polanyi proposed the following thesis:

> the idea of a self-adjusting market implied a stark utopia. Such an institution could not exist for any length of time without annihilating the human and natural substance of society; it would have physically destroyed man and transformed his surroundings into a wilderness. Inevitably, society took measures to protect itself, but whatever measures it took impaired the self-regulation of the market, disorganized industrial life, and thus endangered society in yet another way. It was this dilemma which forced the development of the market system into a definite groove and finally disrupted the social organization based upon it.
>
> (Polanyi 1957: 3–4)

Only towards the end of the eighteenth century and then with a vengeance in the nineteenth century did the labour market, gold standard and free trade convert the 'previously harmless market pattern into a societal monstrosity' (Polanyi 1979: 138). The economic system took on a life of its own to such an extent that in the end social relations 'became embedded in the economic system' (Polanyi 1979: 114) instead of the economy remaining a social product. The 'mechanisms of systemic and social integration' 'get separated from each other' as Habermas puts it (1987a: 164) in order to show that the segmentary differentiation of the life-world is more complex than is suggested by Polanyi' s 'disembedding' thesis.

After the industrial revolution it is not the market itself which is historically new, but rather the all-encompassing reach and enormous tempo of market transactions, that is, the exchange of goods and services in the form of commodities. By 'reach' is meant not only the physical and spatial extension to the whole planet, but also the functional-spatial process of the integration of everything into a system of cool calculating market-like exchange. No longer was it only what Marx called the 'vulgar commodity rabble' [*ordinärer Warenpöbel*] which was exchanged for money on the commodity market, but in addition labour power was transformed into a commodity to be bought and sold on the labour market. Human life became dependent upon the market. Even money, which is as a rule (mis)understood by economists as a pure medium of exchange (medium of circulation) and therefore as a 'money veil', becomes a commodity and therefore completely integrated in the market processes. A money market emerges which today is expanded on to a global scale in which different moneys (national currencies) are traded like sides of pork, iron ore or soya beans with, as we shall see, fatal consequences for national economies. Finally, bits of nature are marketed and thus subordinated to a logic of valorization which has little or nothing to do with their natural conditions. There also emerges a property market in which not the thing itself – e.g. real estate – but certainly the deed of title to a particular property becomes an object of transaction.

In this totality of exchange relations in which only owners of commodities or monetary wealth can participate there is little room for inter-subjective bonds via gifts or offerings, for reciprocity and solidarity (Latouche 1994; Mauss 1990), for reciprocal 'generosity' (cf. Aristotle' s *Nicomachean Ethics*) or for human 'community'. Thus the historical process of 'disembedding' is indeed a 'great transformation' from traditional to modern relations. In place of the exchange of products, which has a very long history, all areas of human communication are taken over by forms of commodity exchange. 'Market economization' [*Vermarktwirtschaftung*] means the domination of commodity production and circulation ('commodification') and the subordination of all relationships to its logic.

The tendency of the market to separate from its social bonds and to neglect the nature of planet earth in the course of fierce economic globalization is nothing new. It was already a subject of the analytical part of the Marx and Engels *Communist Manifesto*. Marx occupied himself with this reality in his analysis of the commodity form and criticized it as reification; as the 'fetish character' of commodities, money and capital. These disembedded relations are human creations which, however, exercise an 'objective compulsion' [*Sachzwang*] over their creators.[1] They become external constraints because their social origins are no longer traceable and their mechanisms of domination no longer intelligible without critical efforts aimed at their transformation.

GLOBAL DISEMBEDDING

Economic forms take on a fetishized life of their own and the unfolding of their logic now dominates society. This is reflected in economic theory; in the wide-reaching abstraction of social relations with the intention of constructing a 'pure' economic theory whose rationality then in turn 'imperialistically' (Kenneth Boulding) percolates throughout society. Just as the economy divides itself off from society, so in the economic sciences the economy is no longer conceived as a socially or naturally bound phenomenon. Von Hayek was therefore quite consistent in avoiding the word 'economy' [*Wirtschaft*] because of its institutional connotations and falling back instead on the concept 'catalactic' (study of exchange) which had already been used by John Stuart Mill. This separating out of economic theory from the social-scientific conceptual store and then the converse attempt – because model building is just so much easier – to project the no longer socially mediated, 'disembedded' and therefore 'pure' rational principle on to society seems to determine the trajectory of economic science.

As one can see from reading any economic history, markets have a long history reaching back several thousand years to post-neolithic times (Cameron 1993; Ponting 1991; Frank and Gills 1993). However, the 'market economization-tionization' of land, natural resources, labour power and money is of a later date. Only since the industrial revolution can we speak of the 'market economy' as a totality. Before this we are dealing at most with a 'patchwork of market economy'. 'Free wage labour' has existed only quite recently as the generalized and globalized social form. As the early history of the capitalist means of production shows, wage labourers had to be forced to be 'free'. Fernand Braudel dates this 'great transformation' to before the time of the industrial revolution (Braudel 1986: 44), Polanyi to the late eighteenth and early nineteenth centuries – in any case as far as England is concerned (Polanyi 1957). We can offer good grounds for either view, the plausibility of which, however, depends on what is understood by 'market economy'. As Braudel convincingly argued against Polanyi, markets and complex trans-regional pricing processes are very old.[2] The total market economy, which transforms money, nature and labour power into commodities and places them under a regime of capital accumulation, has existed only since the epoch of the industrial revolution, as Polanyi correctly demonstrated.

Clearly, the 'great transformation' of 'disembedding' did not reach its conclusion in the nineteenth century. It is one of the capitalist system's tendencies which was later and is still at work. What Polanyi identified in the transition to a market economy in England continues elsewhere and 'commodification' envelops the global system. Market economization drives not only towards as yet unaffected geographical areas, but also inwardly, into the refuges of social life. We are dealing here with that process characterized by Habermas (and before him Rosa Luxemburg) as the 'colonialization of the lifeworld' (Habermas 1987a, esp. 332ff); a process which has triggered the 'communitarian' critique not only because of the loss of meaning which unavoidably accompanies the rationalizing economization of social relations, but also because of the considerable loss of efficiency which societies experience when they give up their communal resources in the process of disembedding.

We can thus justifiably assume that, first, there are steps in the disembedding process which were not surveyed by Polanyi, and that second, it certainly did not run its course without contradictions or contrary movements. The intensity of the process of disembedding is also increased due to, third, money form taking on a life of its own *vis-à-vis* the 'disembedded market' and, fourth, the economy becoming globalized. In this way the economy can to a large degree escape from policies of economic regulation by nation states and the international system of nation states or international institutions. Not without significance for the dynamic of disembedding is, fifth, that a global spatio-temporal regime has emerged. The capitalist imperative of the new age is 'time is money'. Life time, free time, work time, time for oneself and time for others have to obey this motto unconditionally. There emerges a world time in which the history of humanity for the first time runs its course ruled by a unified time regime. With this, concrete spaces also disappear; the borders between them become meaningless. Different spatial experiences get lost because they have become irrelevant. The new time regime has little to do with the spatio-temporal representation of peoples in historical societies. It is for this reason that it has taken so long to break the resistance against the time regimes of the factory (in nineteenth-century Europe) and the global financial market (at the end of the twentieth century in all places). The perpetuation of the disembedding mechanism (Giddens) was possible only because, sixth, it has been supplied with a powerful fuel in which biotic, spatially and temporally limited energy sources are replaced by fossil and nuclear energy.

'Disembedding' is not a completed process, but one which – still today – continues and whose consequences feed back onto society as *Sachzwänge* to which the society must accommodate itself. How this accommodation occurs becomes a question of *zweckrational*, decision-making which is prepared and scientifically accompanied by 'expert systems' (Giddens 1990). Are there good arguments against the necessity of subordination to conditions of competitiveness? Can a country effectively defend itself from currency crises? Can the welfare state be defended against cost reductions? Can employment policy be pushed through when control over interest rates has been lost? Can borrowers avoid interest deadlines and repayment schedules? The possibility of offering alternative answers to these questions in the face of the compulsion of integration into the global system is extremely limited. In the course of 'disembedding' the still harmless appearance of the 'fetish character' of commodities and money which Marx analysed has transformed itself into an *ubiquitous fetish* which exercises a global power over its creators within the contemporary world market. Some of these dimensions of 'disembedding' are illustrated in Figure 14.1.

Mechanisms of political and economic disembedding

The 'first stage of disembedding' is characterized in Polanyi's description of the separation of the economy from the society. This is clearly only a

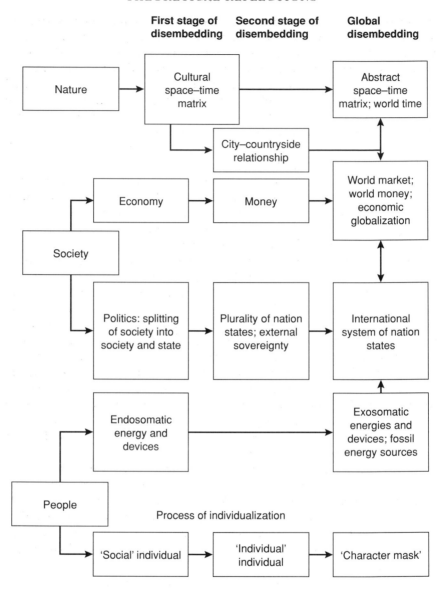

Figure 14.1 Mechanisms of disembedding

part of a much more extensive process of disembedding ('disembedding mechanisms' are at work here according to Giddens 1990: 21–9) whose different dimensions are represented in Figure 14.1. The separation of economy from society is firstly only an aspect of a process of 'splitting of the society into society and state' (Marx after Hegel), i.e. an element of

310

the rationalization of bourgeois modernity through the differentiation of specialized functional spheres or subsystems in society. At that moment in which the economic bourgeois step onto the stage of world history, the citizen is born as citizen of a nation state which, at least within European modernity, becomes a *Rechtsstaat* and later develops into a democratic and social *Rechtsstaat* (see Habermas 1987a: 356ff). With the disembedding of the economy, society will clearly be held together only through the cool market process, 'naked interest' and the 'cash nexus' (Marx), i.e. through communication with the binary code of 'payment/non payment' (Luhmann 1987) and no longer through gifts and generosity.

In pointing towards the installation of 'expert systems' which are clearly not exclusively confined to the state, Anthony Giddens also emphasizes these aspects of disembedding: 'by expert systems I mean systems of technical accomplishment or professional expertise that organize large areas of the material and social environment in which we live today' (1990: 27). The example of groups of experts (lawyers, architects, doctors, etc.) offered by Giddens suggests that functionaries bear a particular responsibility in the 'risk society's' 'division of labour which is indispensable for normalizing social action: expert systems are disembedding mechanisms because, in common with symbolic tokens, they remove social relations from the immediacies of context' (1990: 28). This disembedding mechanism clearly lacks the drama which is characteristic of spatio-temporal abstraction and money. We are dealing here with the necessary specialization of the division of labour which, even in traditional societies, always represents the division of domination and therewith the alienation of social relations from the people who have entered into them. However, it can be pointed out with some justification that with the increase of risk in the 'risk society' the alienation/disembedding of expert systems assumes proportions unknown in pre-capitalist/pre-industrial societies. This requires a degree of trust in a frictionless functioning system based on the division of labour – which in turn assists the establishment of expert systems: the education system for doctors, lawyers, architects; the bodies which guard over qualification and expertise; customer protection organizations and courts who determine responsibility for mistakes, etc. – all these functionaries and institutions act as regulators within a widely deregulated market society.

Because we live in a culture dominated by a specific world system of rationality, the 'disembedding tendency' is itself 'embedded' in rationalization. This is one reason why it is so potent and bare of historically effective resistance. This is often most apparent in those contexts in which a specifically 'Fordist' culture has emerged; where the commodity form of relations between people and likewise between humans and nature is accepted as an unquestionable self-evident truth. The universalization of wage labour attains a particular end point in all regions of the world only in the age of Fordism. Household production is pushed out by mass production whose products are present in almost all corners of the world where modern distribution centres – supermarkets and shopping malls – are to be found and purchasing power to be counted upon. Mass production and mass consumption, which entail rendering cultural patterns of social communication uniform, have in time created a rich cultural soil for disembedding yielding a paradox: disembedding results in a renewed embedding; the 'disenchanted world' (Max Weber) acquires a new enchantment.[3] All this clearly does not mean a reversal of disembedding and disenchantment. On the contrary, it creates a cultural buffer which enables the effects of the 'mechanisms of disembedding' and the processes which they bring about to have a 'soft landing'.

The political implications of the disembedding process are also considerable, particularly for the chances of political participation. The market not only frees itself from society, but also imposes its logic upon politics. Theoretically these conditions were considered by Max Weber, by Schumpeter, Downs, Samuelson, Eucken and others, but clearly without taking the critical turn towards a theory of disembedding. Disembedding of the economy from society can express itself as the destruction of political democracy to the advantage of the 'economic democracy of the dollar or the deutschmark ballot paper'. Social participation is then possible through commodity ownership or better still through monetary wealth. The contours of classical democracy with their institutions of the separation of powers, legitimation, representation and selection are swept in the direction of Plutocracy. In other words, economic disembedding can undermine political democracy.

Space and time: expansion and acceleration

This also becomes clear when we observe the effects of disembedding on time and space regimes. The coordinates of the 'spatially and temporally compressed' globe (Fraser 1993) are almost identical in all areas of the world. Today it is credit schedules which determine the rhythm of global time regimes. The maturing of debts and no longer – as in Agrarian societies – the harvest cycle or the rate of circulation of fixed capital – as in 'large-scale industry' – define the horizon of action and the periodization of the cycles within globalized finance capitalism. In this way money's logic dominates the global society. Here lies also the gateway for every globalization of culture which lies like a mildew over national and local cultures and whose integrative effect is significant due to the simultaneity of local presence and global scope. In the course of globalization the cultures of the world are melting into a worldwide hybrid culture.

Milton Santos (1994) observed that people organize their everyday life into 'banal space' and 'banal time'. Space and time are banal because humans, like all life-forms, are natural creatures and nature is unimaginable outside space and time. All creatures are naturally 'grounded' [verortet] in rhythms of day and night; alertness and tiredness; hunger and thirst; sometimes good, sometimes bad moods, etc. However, such forms and radii of thought are enveloped by abstract reason, that is by a transcultural, global spatio-temporal matrix. Global relations run in networks which conform to an abstract logic just as the Spanish town planners in Latin American set cities into the landscape abstractly with scant regard to the natural condition and attending only to the cities' function within the system of domination. Buarque de Holanda (1995) uses the metaphor of 'tiling' the landscape just as one would tile any old room to capture this.

The 'debanalization' of space and time has always been grounded in economic mechanisms. As the 'disembedding thesis' suggested, in the market which has rid itself of its social conditions the present is 'omnipresent' (Lechner 1994) because the historical time span is reduced to a single point in time whose coordinates are to be found in the economic rather than the natural domain of reason. Even within non-economic social subsystems, the market economization of transactions has meant forgetting the past just as it has meant losing the future as a project. The present dominates both past and future. The future appears in the present merely as a non-discounted value or as a simple extrapolation, and in this way becomes at a later time a present abstracted from history. The primacy of the present means the dissolution of concepts of 'diachronic solidarity' (Ignacy Sachs 1993) between generations and thus also of 'synchronic solidarity' within a generation because the proximity to others within an abstract space is transformed into an equidistant indifference towards all. All-encompassing contemporaneity is responsible for the conservatism within otherwise highly dynamic 'quick living' market economies. Because future interest on loans depends upon innovation, bankers should be open minded about innovation, but this is only possible within the framework of highly conservative guidelines because, first, they are used to discounting the future against the present, and, second, because the realization of credit from future projects requires securities which have been accumulated in the past.

The best future is therefore the one which is the same as the present but enlarged to that degree which will sustain interest rates. That the Left, too, in the abstraction of its political models from real time is not immune to this kind of Newtonian trajectory between past and future has been powerfully expressed by Jorge Castaneda: 'The only thing left to fight for is a future that is simply the present, plus more of the same' (Castaneda, quoted in Dunkerley 1994: 28). The market economy thereby dissolves historical time into a physical-logical time as Nicholas Georgescu-Roegen (1971) in his critique of neo-classicism has so convincingly shown. The future in this representation is quantitatively bigger – expressed prognostically, 'present plus' – and the past is its mirror image: 'present minus'. The axis of time is not a historically irreversible time arrow, rather it is like a spoke revolving around a centre which is the present. Hence the frustration that social-scientific predictions about the historical future always turn out wrong. There is nothing other than systematically false prediction (they can only be accidentally 'right') because events in real time run a different course from prognostications constructed in terms of abstract time. The only exception would be if the prognosticating sciences were like Maxwell's or Laplace's 'demons' and thus not exposed to historical contingency and armed with perfect knowledge about initial and final states (see Prigogine 1992).

Similarly, political life is gripped by this present-orientated thought. The past is just as important for the social memory and consciousness relevant to action, for the identity of the individual and the history of societies as is the 'future-orientated project': the assumption that you can shape the future according to wishes, needs and utopias of citizens which are the object of permanent conflict-laden discourses. Without this time and space boundedness, a democratic society is in principle impossible. But the rhythms of the political process create a systematic over-emphasis on the present *vis-à-vis* the future; on the interests of the present generation over those of future generations. Prognoses rather than utopias are required. We must prolong the present rather than think out and project something quite different, that is, as against the tendencies and counterfactual programmes and subjects brought together within the sphere of political negotiation. Market rationality forces its way into the political processes. Decisions and the consequences of decisions are considered and implemented from the short-term perspectives of a systematically short-sighted (myopic) actor.

Disembedded and empowered energy

In terms of material and energy, the widening of horizons hinted at is only possible because in the course of capitalist rationalization available energies have been rationally used and the energy base has shifted from a biotic to a fossil energy source (it is this which characterized the industrial revolution). Rationalization begins with endosomatic energy and the use of wind and water power (Debeir *et al.* 1989). These are, however, essentially fixed and localized energy sources, and thus hardly support the suggested expansion of horizons and the process of abstraction and disembedding. The boundaries are in fact very tightly drawn. This is demonstrated with great clarity in Leonardo da Vinci's technically brilliantly thought-out and highly modern apparatuses where the narrow bounds of the energy and energy transformation systems stood in the way of realizing or appropriately translating them into practical operation and utilitization. Only since the transition to the wide use of exosomatic energy (above all fossil fuel) from the eighteenth century have we had the expansion of human capacities and at the same time freedom from spatial and temporal limitations. Only now is the acceleration of time possible which creates the modern time regime. Now space can also be explored with new means of transportation and communication in such a way that the narrowness of the parish (of those 'four English miles' which according to Lawrence Sterne formed the world of Tristram Shandy's nurse) is overcome and the spatial coordinates of individual and collective rootedness can be globalized. 'Global thinking' can only then become a political formula. Now the market can grow out of the social 'bed'; something it had been unable to do in the long course of human history.

We should not forget that markets as an economic place of exchange and as a social institution are ancient. They came into being after the neolithic revolution when it became possible to produce a tradable surplus. Market money has also had a longer history than that of market-economy modernity. Only since the 'disembedding mechanisms' have been driven by fossil energy sources have they been able to develop that power which put historians' and sociologists' tools for analysing instrumentally rational patterns of behaviour on the agenda. Now that there are fossil energy sources and appropriate technical energy transmission systems (unlike for Leonardo who had to put up with bio-endosomatic energy sources) the madness of abstract reason can easily be followed through, so as to translate its blueprints into reality. With these experiences, which at the same time open up possibilities unknown before the beginning of the age of fossil energy, the limits of 'embeddedness' are experienced as a Procrustean bed. The process of disembedding is experienced as a widening of horizons. Only now is slavery – the use of 'human coal' – a backward form of economic exploitation, now 'the idiocy of rural life' really is passé and the adventure of the 'big wide world' can begin.

Disembedded money

The 'second stage' of disembedding, as shown in Figure 14.1 above, characterizes a development of the process described by Polanyi to which he was able to pay only rudimentary attention. The characterization as 'second stage' should not necessarily be taken to mean a sequentially later event, but rather as a step which follows logically from the 'first' and which may well occur along side it. This is particularly so for money and market. Here we reach the fourth dimension of the 'disembedding process'. The separation of economy and society is only possible where a money economy develops; when money is also unbound from society and can become a money fetish in the Marxist sense. A market without commodities is unthinkable nonsense, but money without commodities all the more so. But money is not only a medium of communication or circulation that as such obeys fully the laws of commodity exchange. Rather it develops 'as money' a life of its own such that it is justified to speak of a 'second stage' of disembedding. We are dealing here with that abstraction of which Aristotle was already suspicious: 'the striving for the accumulation of wealth' which disregards the criterion of the 'good life' in society. As soon as there is money there are further grounds for the development of the process of disembedding.

First, money in combination with the fossil energy sources lifts the 'great transformation' onto a global level. Now for the first time 'globalization' is possible as more than merely an individual journey of discovery or as a historically specific campaign of conquest. There emerges a global financial system as a monetary sphere decoupled from the real economy. The sphere of economic functioning is globalized in this fashion. In contrast, the sphere of politics is much more territory-bound than the economy; it remains national or at most extends to international politics.[4] The thesis of the separation of the economy and society is above all relevant to market-economic regulation within nations. Thus, due to the nature of political processes within institutions and among actors at the level of the nation state, disembedding on the national scale is never as complete as it is on the global scale which knows only partially political regulation.

Second, Keynes had already disposed of the classical and neo-classical assumption that markets through the price mechanism in principle, equally, and in all cases lead to a market balance of full employment. Were this really so, then the separation of markets from society would do no harm. Things are, however, not as simple as in the 'ideal world of the economists' (Ward 1979). It is much more the case that a capitalist economy creates a specific hierarchical order of markets: the money market directs the goods market whose development directs the labour market, i.e. the system (and the level) of employment. Marx was quite right when he showed in his form-analysis of value how work as the final creator of all value becomes socialized through the circulation of money. Market economies are, as the 'monetary Keynesians' emphasize, money economies, and money decodes their laws of movement. Thus distantiation between persons through money becomes possible, thus the economy disembeds itself from society, and thus money becomes decoupled from the real economy in order to impose its logic on the economy which in turn forces society to obey it as 'Sachzwang'. Thus money becomes 'an inherent part of modern social life' (Giddens 1990: 26). It is defined 'in terms of credit and debt' (Giddens 1990: 24), i.e. as money that no longer functions only as a medium of circulation within the commodity cycle. It is 'money as money'. This fact is regularly ignored in the doleful attempts to interpret money sociologically. Luhmann's interpretation of money unambiguously rests upon its function as a means of communication for the circulation of commodities, which leaves the dimensions of the global money society unexplained. Deutschmann (1995) too sees money as a medium of exchange and not as credit, as means of payment or as treasure, although in reality on the global currency markets more than US$1000 billion circulate daily, while for world export (yearly US$3600 billion) daily only US$10 billion are needed. Viewed quantitatively, the sociological theory of money can claim explanatory power for 1 per cent of the money turnover, but not for the remaining 99 per cent.

Marx showed, in contrast to Simmel or Keynes, how, first, the money form is already contained in the commodity form, and, second, how it can be

316

determined more exactly in terms of its functions: the function of the measurement of value is still bound in its entirety to the individual commodity; the function of the medium of circulation still to the exchange of commodities among and against each other. Here the room for the autonomizing tendencies [*Verselbständigungstendenzen*] is restricted; here the commodity owner appears in markets in social contact – even where Marx grounds these simple determinations of form in the possibility of crises – in the end buying and selling can take place far apart in spatio-temporal terms. However, the spatio-temporal distances responsible for the crisis have something to do with the available energy which can be used to overcome space and destroy time. The economic and social crisis is in its turn an expression of disembedding (if you wish, an accident of the disembedding process) because the socially uncontrollable economic tendencies feed back in ways which certainly do not accord with the plans of market actors.

The self-propulsion of money as money comes to fruition only when the material and energy become available to detach time and space from the immediacy of a banality limited by the everyday world. Only then does money appear as the superbly suitable instrument – as genius (not loci, but globi)[5] – not only to connect distant times and spaces and to mediate the respective interests based there through arbitrage, but above all to re-organize temporal and spatial coordinates. While commodity owners must still be spatially and temporally present in order to exchange their wares, this is no longer necessary for the owners of money. What matters is that obligations stemming from money relations are fulfilled within the agreed time scale. These time scales and the agreed places in which obligations are to be met determine the space–time matrix of world society.

REPERCUSSIONS: THE DISEMBEDDED WORLD MARKET BECOMES A 'SACHZWANG'

In the chapter on money in Volume One of *Capital* there is a short section on 'world money' following the discussion of money as money which frequently goes unnoticed. Here we find the suggestion, not fully worked out, that world money – at that time gold which gets its nationality stamped upon it by the currency – is something more than mere gold bars. Problems of exchange rates play a role here which can only be treated appropriately if the balance of trade, of visibles and invisibles, and of capital are drawn into the analysis. Now we see what 'disembedding' is: the emergence of 'synthetic indicators' (as furnished by the sub-balances of the balance of payment) with which societies are comparatively evaluated in the abstract functional space of the global market. Such evaluations would be harmless if they were only about the judgements on the national economy by interested politicians or scientists. But they define the comparative position of a currency area within the global economy and thus the context of a nation's currency area within global currency competition. Just

317

as sovereignty in nineteenth- and early twentieth-century thought remained bound to the territoriality of states, so now it defines itself in a world of world money through a currency area whose borders are defended at the counters of the foreign exchanges or within the global 'swift-network' of internationally operating banks.

The mechanisms of disembedding have the fatal consequences that through them a reality is produced according to standards which are binding even when their effects should irk society. Once delivered into the hands of market mechanism and subordinated to global time and space regimes and dependent upon the price of money (interest and exchange rate), societies must accommodate themselves to the disembedded economic mechanisms. That is to say, they must implement in perpetuity 'structural adjustment programmes' in order to maintain their competitiveness, or alternatively tolerate subordination to such a programme through the intervention of international organizations such as the World Bank or the IMF. Thus we have not only the 'disembedding mechanisms' represented by Figure 14.1 but also the 'mechanisms of objective compulsion' [*Sachzwangmechanismen*] stylized in Figure 14.2.

The world market with its time and space regimes, with the global monetary and credit system that is maintained through the fossil fuel sources and their associated material and energy conversion systems is the frame of reference for sociation. Accommodation to quickly changing standards is a decisive element in the process of modernization whose social (and ecological) costs can clearly be very high. The diagram represents the 'first stage of disembedding' as the much sociologically discussed separation of the market and its logic from the society and its patterns of symbol-mediated interaction. A 'second stage of disembedding' is now money's acquisition of a life of its own in relation to the 'real economy'; the 'decoupling of monetary from real accumulation'; and the crystallization of a globally operating financial system which is subordinated to neither social norms nor political direction. Money is no longer a reified medium of communication with socially destructive autonomizing tendencies *vis-à-vis* those actors who use it to enter into communication – as those who rely on Simmel claim (Deutschmann 1995: 387) – but rather a societal relationship between creditors and debtors. This 'autonomization' [*Verselbständigung*] as money transforms the global society into a *society of monetary wealth owners*. But with monetary wealth comes obligations (debts) which have created a global *debt-society*. One social relationship therefore means two societies, which already indicates how much money works as a bacterium, now, however, on a global scale. A society of monetary wealth and debt as an expression of global disembedding lacks all those social bonds which are still found in regional or national-state bounded societies, whether traditional or modern. The 'realm of necessity' spreads and tightens its grip against expectation that it would emerge into the 'realm of freedom'.

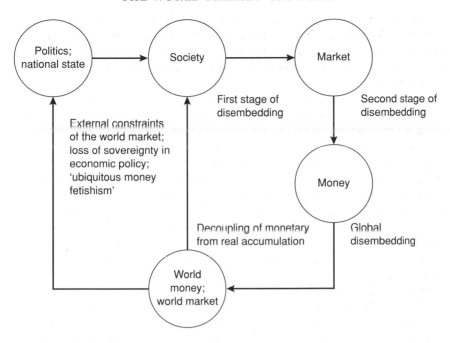

Figure 14.2 From disembedding to the external constraints of the world market and the loss of sovereignty in economic policy

As schematically suggested in Figure 14.2, disembedded powers therefore feed back on to social relationships and systems of political institutions as *Sachzwänge*. This finds expression in the 'hierarchy of markets' already described by Keynes when he counted neo-classicism: the money market steers with prices the market in commodities, and this is in turn relevant for demand on the labour market. In terms of the life practices of dependent employees, disembedding means therefore that their chances on the labour market are directed by processes on the global market which they cannot influence at all. For the political system this same process is responsible for the loss of sovereignty in economic policy. When interest and currency rates are no longer determined politically by legitimate institutions of the nation state but rather are formed by global markets, the market dynamic can no longer be politically regulated according to directives which are *incompatible* with it. Then in reality as well as theoretically, ideologically and finally politically the ratification of these conditions of global disembeddness appears as a politics of 'deregulation'. Politics does not disappear, but its rationality is synchronized with the economy.

Here we see again that mechanisms of disembedding represent not only the negative side of the separation of economic processes from social and political regulation, but can actually become a historically powerful project which as a 'neo-liberal counter revolution' (Friedman 1976) has dominated for decades the politics of entire continents.[6] Social relations come to be thought of and treated as a mere market medium. In light of disembedding of money from the market and then the globalization of the 'mechanisms of disembedding', this project comes to demand subordination into the world market and world money; the 'opening' to the outside of society bounded culturally, regionally and by nation states. Consequently, 'open up the world market' becomes the motto of the deregulating project. This principle goes unquestioned even in those newer conceptions in which disembedding is reined back in for the sake of civil society. Therefore we should ask what is meant when we speak of the self-evidence of markets and their external constraints (*Sachzwänge*).

THE MARKET: THAT UNKNOWN THING . . .

Niklas Luhmann casually remarks that 'we [lack] an adequate theory of the market even or precisely in the economic sciences' (Luhmann 1990: 107). He is not so far out. One could, however, extend the dictum to money and work by adding that this theoretical gap becomes wider the more one enters into the world market for commodities, labour, money and capital. Here most social and economic theoreticians come to a breathless halt. The market, due to the disembedding tendencies presented here, is a simple opportunity free of all social and political residues. One could conceive of it as a functional place of exchange processes thus avoiding any representation of the economy as a phenomenon bound in space and time and, with F. A. von Hayek (and J. S. Mill), conceptualize the economic process as a pure catalactic; as an unending series of price-regulated exchanges which in the end produce an equilibrium in which no agent of the market has reason to revise his/her plans. Already for Cournot this was a horrible image because at the point at which change in action becomes irrational, history comes to an end (cf. Anderson 1983). Even von Hayek was against it because it is imbalances which stimulate innovations. The market is not a balanced phenomenon but rather a 'voyage of discovery' (von Hayek 1968). Here too, he, like Luhmann, was not so far off the mark. The market is in practice an extraordinarily complex and thus theoretically complicated phenomenon which is not simple to decode.[7] To show this a whole range of arguments can come into play.

First, the process of disembedding does not go so far as to leave the society and its institutions with no role in the regulation of the market. Globalization, as already indicated, meets its limits; globalism is never attainable. Rather it is the case that disembedded markets which follow an 'asocial' and 'non-natural' logic and can conform to economic rationality require social regulation. Money relations are in principle contractual relations which require legal regulation via an independent body which is itself no party to the contract. In contrast to neo-liberal assumptions that more market means less state, market economizations produce an enormous demand for legal regulation of money relations which increases state intervention at least with respect to regulations.[8] The Freiburg School around Eucken knew this, and in Great Britain, too, deregulation has only been possible because new regulations have been developed. If only between the lines, the IMF too is concerned in its analysis of 'emerging equity markets' (*World Economic Outlook*, May 1994: 26) about the stability of global financial markets and pleads for some regulation by nation states whose capacity to intervene has been reduced precisely by market economization introduced under the direction of the IMF's 'structural adjustment programmes'. Similarly, in the transitional countries of Eastern and Central Europe we hear the call for order, for contractual and legal security so that the private 'investors' can make their decisions under conditions of calculable 'risk'. Even the tendency for further privatization of money through the introduction of the 'electronic purse' requires public regulation.

In this way the state with its 'regulatory policy', which neo-liberals developed against 'process politics', comes into play. For Walter Eucken, private property rights (and this means in each case clearly established property rights guaranteed by the public authorities), clear rules of liability, a policy of ensuring currency stability and the restriction of money supply by public institutions such as the Central Bank together form the 'core' of regulation policy. The securing of the 'functioning price system' is the 'economic-constitutional basic principle' (Eucken 1959: 160f). So it is that economic deregulation is followed by regulatory law and political re-regulation. The pure disembedded market economy is thus a mirage. Economically, social disembedded market economies and political authoritarianism share a family resemblance.

Second, as Emile Durkheim (1933) has shown, contractual and thus also money relations always contain extra-contractual (and by implication, extra-market) preconditions which are unavoidable for the functioning and efficiency of the market and money economy. The sociological critics of the neo-classical rational model of money and market-mediated sociations (Etzioni 1988; Granovetter 1985) start for this 'moral dimension' in order to show, rightly, that empirical societies have always produced non-economic networks (beyond market and hierarchy) in order to cope with the economic *Sachzwänge* which they have themselves created. This suggests that a complete separation of the economy from society – a total disembedding – is in fact damaging not merely for the social substance but also for economic efficiency.

Extra-market networks of social relations however depend on the competence of *civil society* and on its power to socialize individuals as market participants; on access to information; on trust and reciprocal relations; and on consensus and mutual recognition. All these connections of the economy as a social-communicative system are inadequately explained within the economic theory of the market: the 'invisible hand' is so invisible that no one asks about the anatomy of the body whose instrument it is. Moreover, market theoreticians are usually satisfied with the 'invisible' hand without asking about the second, the 'visible' hand (Chandler 1977), or even the 'third hand' (Elson 1990). Here we find ourselves in the midst of the debate about 'governance', i.e. the institutional binding of market processes into networks (see Messner and Nuscheler 1996). Civil-societal 'networks' have a material dimension to which Polanyi refers when he quotes R. G. Hawtrey:

> In contrast to the nomadic peoples, the cultivator commits himself to improvements *fixed in a particular place*. Without such improvements human life must remain elementary, and little removed from that of animals. And how large a role have these fixtures played in human history! It is they, the cleared and cultivated lands, the houses, and other buildings, the means of communication, the multifarious plant necessary for production, including industry and mining, all the perma- nent and immovable improvements that tie a human community to the locality where it is. They cannot be improvised, but must be built up gradually by generations of patient effort, and the community cannot afford to sacrifice them and start afresh elsewhere.
>
> (Hawtrey, quoted in Polanyi 1957: 184)

Third, anyone who speaks today of the 'market' must speak of the world market. In doing so we must analyse not only world trade, but also the world money market. Here restrictions on money are created which are imposed upon market actors in order to stimulate them to high levels of performance in global competition. Curiously and fatally the sociological debate about 'money as a social construct' does not ascribe significance to this fact (e.g. Deutschmann 1995). The science of society has no clue that society at the end of the twentieth century is a money-mediated world society.[9] So the cynical and fatalistic assessment gains plausibility that the world market provides a constant context for dealing with the welfare state [*Sozialstaat*] and that the only option is to adopt internal adjustments to it. In this way the welfare state becomes a mere cost factor. These costs are intervention variables and are at the same time nationally accessible. Money's constraints are written into 'social nature' in the *form* of the global processes of reproduction, but paradoxically within the world economy they find their expression in political *institutions* such as the International Monetary Fund, the World Bank, GATT or the WTO, namely, in the 'conditionality' of 'structural adjustment programmes'.

The following schema (Figure 14.3), which builds on and extends that of Michel de Vroey (1991), indicates the complexity of the market. Every field in the schema demands theoretical clarification. We are dealing here with a well-known social scientific problem; that of structure and action, and thus 'structuration' (Giddens). How is it that prices are formed when all the market agents act as price takers in the model of complete competition (see Box 2.1)?

How is the structuration of a market price system to be conceptualized *ex ante* through individual non-selected actions? The relevance of the questions is disguised by the fact that the outcomes are always ratified by the market *post festum*. How can independent 'individual' decisions be justified when all market participants simultaneously use a common social ambiance (through common language, habitus and norms, cultural practices) and natural environment and then transform it by creating externalities (positive or, as in most cases, negative) (Box 5.1), that is, when they thrive on the same social yeast? Is the assumption of 'methodological individualism' still justified although it represents the basis of 'rational choice' (Box 1.1)? Where there are no independent decisions, the basic assumption of autonomous individuals who enter into free contracts is questionable (Box 1.1; 1.2). They find themselves already in relations which strengthen them and sometimes also bind and restrain them ('lock-in effect'), and which require a mediation through cultural – public political – regulation and not private law. This is particularly spectacular in the case of so-called 'positional goods' which may no longer be exchanged as commodities. For them the market is not a suitable mechanism of coordination. How does an equilibrium – the reference point of market theory – come about in practice if market participants strive not for an equilibrium of market processes but for maximum profitability of single capitals and for the highest satisfaction of needs of individual consumers (Box 1.3; 2.3)? Is 'perfect competition' – like 'perfect computation' – only imaginable as a game external observers play with market agents as though they were their marionettes, not as a game among market participants themselves (Box 4.2; 4.3)? By the way, how do markets come into being where there is no participant actively 'making' it happen? This question about 'market makers' is significant for the transitional economies of Eastern Europe. All honour goes to Say's Theorem according to which every supply already creates its own adequate demand. But demands for services (e.g. investment goods) must appear in order for commodity markets to come into being and production to get fully underway. As Keynes (and naturally Marx) has shown, a minimal level of 'marginal efficiency of capital' – a minimum profit rate – is required.

And the world market? What Marx characterized as the 'propagandistic tendency' to bring the world market into being is no longer an abstraction which can only be understood by an analytical mind. It is rather a reality of capitalist modernity. It is more than exotic produce, long-distant travel, casino capitalism and multinational enterprise. The world market is an ensemble of economic and social forms and political institutions of money, commodities and labour markets. In the process of disembedding, the market goes beyond the trade in goods to other aggregate forms of capital: a world market for money and capital come into being, for labour and even for nature's bounty. What Polanyi had already shown for the national labour and money markets can now be seen on a global level, namely the development of institutions

	Actor	Process	Coordination
Actor	**1.1** Decentred individual; 'methodological individualism'; interdependency and interference	**1.2** No knowledge of the market system's consequences for action	**1.3** Spontaneous non-anticipated consequences for action 'behind the back of the actor'
Process	**2.1** Actors as reactors ('price takers'). If all are price takers, who determines the price?	**2.2** Market interferences, market hiearchies: labour market dependent upon goods and finance market	**2.3** Result: balance and optimization. How are they to be defined? How do they come together in the conditions of the market process?
Coordination	**3.1** Rules of the game; external restrictions; property rights; 'Sachzwang'	**3.2** Alternative types of market processes: from full competition to monopoly	**3.3** Total balance in the system is impossible
Observer; economist	**4.1** Actors are like marionettes in a game directed by the observer; model building	**4.2** The observer knows the logic of the market. To realize this logic, he/she acts like an auctioneer	**4.3** Result of the process under conditions of competition comparable to those of planned economies: 'perfect competition = prefect computation'
The market's environment	**5.1** Actors use and influence the social and natural environment. Thereby emerges non-market-like interference; externalities; extra-contractual elements on contractual relations	**5.2** Incomplete information and erroneously introduced processes; short-sightedness; market failure	**5.3** The materialism of coordination; the energy side of the information flow

Figure 14.3 The complexity of the market

and organizations, i.e. a formation of a regime, if only as a partial and under-developed regulation of elements of the world market. All over the world market nation states are also present. In no way do these disappear in the course of globalization even if the political sovereignty necessary for economic regulation is limited in the process. However, what is forgotten by global bodies of regulation and nation states in their function as global players in world market competition is that we are dealing here with market institutions not political ones. The difference is important because only political institutions of democratic legitimation require consensus and react to the logic of hegemonic stability and the participatory demands of civil society. Political market institutions, e.g. the IMF, the World Bank, the WTO, do not find this consideration necessary except in so far as civil society forces them. Herein lies the meaning – or from the perspective of these institutions, the scandal – of the newer actors on the international stage (non-governmental organizations, e.g. Greenpeace)

NOTES

This chapter is an abbreviated translation of Chapter 4 of Elmar Altvater and Birgit Mahnkopf, *Die Grenzen der Globalisierung. Politik, Ökonomie und Ökologie in der Weltgesellschaft* (Verlag Westfälisches Dampfboot, Münster, 1996). A version also appeared in *The Review of Political Economy* 4/3, 1997.

1 This is a Faustian dilemma: 'Beim ersten sind wir frei, beim zweiten sind wir Knechte' [By the first we are free, by the second serfs]. With these deeds the conditions of action are set which as restrictions and as *Sachzwänge* impose 'dependency upon a path' on all later actions and actors. Only with bifurcation is free choice returned to the path; only then can the serf successfully become master of his own fate.
2 Frank and Gills (1993) date the emergence of markets and capitalist relations far back into antiquity. But they only succeed at the cost of abstraction from each and every historical process, which Marx characterized in his analysis of the conditions of production of 'relative surplus value' as the 'real subsumption of work under capital'.
3 Habermas also seems to have this process in mind when he criticizes – not, however, on the whole very convincingly – the Marxist theory of value: 'Marx has no criteria by which to distinguish the destruction of traditional forms of life from the reification of post-traditional lifeworlds' (Habermas 1987a: 340).
4 As a consequence of this there is no 'earth policy' (Weizsäcker 1989). This label is only a metaphor for the many-sided, usually helpless attempt to regulate processes through trans- and international policies which have been largely removed from the reach of nation state and international regulation within the global disembedded functional space. The territory of the earth knows not that single sovereignty which the nation state claims in order to be.
5 The genius of money is not the 'genius loci', but from the beginning a 'genius globi'.
6 The dominance and fetish character of the mechanisms of disembedding also finds expression in the fact that the style of thought associated with it has been uncritically absorbed by the once critical social sciences.
7 Sombart' s definition is therefore too simple to do justice to the complexity of the market. He writes: 'With the word market we understand in general and abstract sense the epitome of possibilities of selling and opportunities to sell' (Sombart 1987 [1916], Vol. 2: 185). This follows only the view of the producer ('Seen from the vantage point of the producers/traders' (ibid.: 188)) and therefore Sombart is interested above all in the 'enlargement of the market' on the basis of 'demographic', 'administrative', 'political', 'commercial' and 'technical' factors (ibid.: 187). 'When we speak of a local or national markets or of a world market: we assume the vantage point of one interested in the business of commodities' (ibid.: 188).
8 Ironically, in the original country of deregulation – Great Britain – the number of regulatory measures in the 1980s grew more than in, say, France or Finland;

namely by about 600 per cent (from 1980 to 1991). In France the rate of growth between 1976 and 1990 was 100 per cent, in Finland from 1980 to 1993, 200 per cent. The data is presented in a 'Regulatory Report' of UNICE (1995: 6) in the course of a plea for further deregulation. But even here the agreement of its members about some measure of intervention and regulation by states is demonstrated.

9 Luhmann says explicitly that society today is a world society, but does not draw any consequences from this assessment for the media and codes of social system regulation. Nor has Habermas any conception of a global society.

BIBLIOGRAPHY

Ackerman, R. J. (1988) *Wittgenstein's City*, Massachusetts: University of Massachusetts Press.

Ackroyd, S., Burrel, G., Hughes, H. and Whitaker, A. (1988) 'The Japanization of British Industry?', *Journal of Industrial Relations*, 19, 1: 11–23.

Adorno, T. W. (1987) 'Fetish character in music and regression of listening' in A. Arato and E. Gebhardt (eds) *The Essential Frankfurt School Reader*, New York: Urizen Books.

Aglietta, M. (1979) *A Theory of Capitalist Regulation*, London: New Left Books.

Albrow, M. (1992a) 'Interpreting the emergence of the concept of globalization', Unpublished paper presented to the Research Committee for the History of Sociology, ISA, Budapest, 9 April.

Albrow, M. (1992b) 'Globalization' in T. B. Bottomore and W. Outhwaite (eds) *The Blackwell Dictionary of Twentieth Century Social Thought*, Oxford: Basil Blackwell.

Albrow, M. and King, E. (eds) (1990) *Globalization*, London: Sage.

Amin, A. (ed.) (1994) *Post-Fordism: A Reader*, Oxford: Blackwell.

Amin, A. and Goddard, J. (1986) *Technological Change, Industrial Restructuring and Regional Development*, London: Allen and Unwin.

Amin, A. and Robins, K. (1990) 'The re-emergence of regional economies? The mythical geography of flexible accumulation', *Environment and Planning D: Society and Space*, 8: 7–34.

Amin, A., Robins, K. and Schoenberger, W. (1992) 'Lean production (an update)'. Paper presented to the 'Lean Production and European Trade Union Co-operation Conference' TGWU Centre, 6–11 December 1992, Eastbornc, England.

Amin, A. and Smith, I. (1990) 'The British car components industry: leaner and fitter?' in P. Stewart (eds) *Restructuring for Economic Flexibility*, Aldershot: Avebury.

Amin, A. and Thrift, N. (1993) 'Globalization, institutional thickness and local prospects', *Revue d'Economie Régional et Urbaine*, 3: 406–27.

Anderson, B. (1983) *Imagined Communities: Reflections on the Origin and Spread of Nationalism*, London: Verso.

Anderson, B. (1991) *Imagined Communities: Reflections on the Origin and Spread of Nationalism*, Revised and Extended Edition, London: Verso.

Ang, I. (1985) *Watching Dallas*, London: Matthews.

Appadurai, A. (ed.) (1986) *The Social Life of Things*, Cambridge: Cambridge University Press.

Appadurai, A. (1990) 'Disjunction and difference in the global cultural economy' in M. Featherstone (ed.) *Global Culture: Nationalism, Globalization and Modernity*, London: Sage.

Archer, M. (1990) 'Theory, culture and the post-industrial society' in M. Featherstone (ed.) *Global Culture: Nationalism, Globalization and Modernity*, London: Sage.

327

Arnason, J. (1987) 'Figurational sociology as a counter-paradigm', *Theory, Culture and Society*, 4, 2/3: 429–56.
Arrighi, G. (1978) *The Geometry of Imperialism*, London: New Left Books.
Attali, B. (1994) *Les guerres du ciel: cinq ans aux commandes d'Air France*, Paris: Fayard.
Aydalot, P. and Keeble, D. (eds) (1988) *High Technology Industry and Innovative Environments*, London: Routledge.
Badcock, C. R. (1975) *Lévi-Strauss: Structuralism and Sociological Theory*, London: Hutchinson.
Bagnasco, A. (1977) *Tre Italia: La problematica territoriale dello sviluppo economico Italiano*, Bologna: Il Mulino.
Bagnasco, A. and Trigilia, C. (1993) *La Construction Sociale du Marche*, Paris: Presses ENS Cachan.
Balakrishnan, G. (1995) 'The national imagination', *New Left Review*, 211: 56–69.
Balfour, A. (1990) *Berlin: The Politics of Order*, New York: Rizzoli International.
Balfour, J. (1993) 'The control of state aids in the air transport sector', *Air and Space Law*, 18, 4/5: 199–204.
Balfour, J. (1994) 'Air transport – a community success story?', *Common Market Law Review*, 31: 1025–53.
Balibar, E. and Wallerstein, I. (1991) *Race, Nation, Class: Ambiguous Identities*, London: Verso.
Balme, R. (1994) 'Le territore en Europe au prisme de ses paradigmes' in R. Balme and Alii (eds) *Le territore pour politiques: variations européennes*, Paris: L'Harmattan.
Balme, R. and Le Galès, P. (1997) 'Stars and black holes, French regions and cities in the European galaxy' in M. Goldsmith and K. Klausen (eds), *Local Authorities and the European Integration*, London: Edward Arnold.
Banister, D. and Button, K. (eds) (1991) *Transport in a Free Market Economy*, Basingstoke: Macmillan.
Barnard, F. M. (1965) *Herder's Social and Political Thought: From Enlightenment to Nationalism*, Oxford: Clarendon Press.
Barth, F. (ed.) (1969) *Ethnic Groups and Boundaries: The Social Organization of Cultural Difference*, Bergen and London: Allen and Unwin.
Barthes, R. (1978) *A Lover's Discourse*, Harmondsworth: Penguin Books.
Barthes, R. (1985a) *The Fashion System*, London: Jonathan Cape.
Barthes, R. (1985b) *The Grain of the Voice*, New York: Hill and Wang.
Barthes, R. (1990) *The Pleasure of the Text*, Oxford: Basil Blackwell.
Bateson, G. (1958) *Naven: A Survey of the Problems Suggested by a Composite Picture of a Culture of a New Guinea Tribe Drawn from Three Points of View*, Stanford: Stanford University Press.
Bateson, G. (1973) 'Culture contact and schismogenesis' in G. Bateson (ed.) *Steps to an Ecology of Mind*, London: Granada Publishing.
Battaglia, D. (1990) *On the Bones of the Serpent: Person, Memory and Mortality in Sabarl Island Society*, Chicago: University of Chicago Press.
Bauman, Z. (1973) *Culture as Praxis*, London: Routledge.
Bauman, Z. (1978) *Hermeneutics and Social Science*, London: Hutchinson.
Bauman, Z. (1992) *Intimations of Postmodernity*, London: Routledge.
Baumer, F. L. (1977) *Modern European Thought: Continuity and Change in Ideas, 1600–1950*, Basingstoke: Macmillan.
Baumol, W. J. (1982) 'Contestable markets: an uprising in the theory of industry structure', *American Economic Review*, 72, 1, March: 1–15.
Beccatini, G. and Sengenberger, W. (1990) *Industrial Districts*, Geneva: ILO.
Beck, A. (1993) 'The arts policy of British Government in the Thatcher years', Paper to PSA Conference, University of Leicester.

Beck, U. (1992) *Risk Society: Towards a New Modernity*, London: Sage.

Beck, U. (1994) 'The reinvention of politics' in U. Beck, A. Giddens and S. Lash (eds) *Reflexive Modernization*, Cambridge: Polity.

Bendix, R. (1985) *Progress and Nostalgia: Silvesterklausen in Urnasch, Switzerland*, Berkeley: University of California Press.

Benington, J., Geddes, M. and Mair, A. (1992) 'Europe: the new arena for local economic policy', in M. Geddes and J. Benington (eds) *Restructuring the Local Economy*, London: Longman.

Benko, G. and Lipietz, A. (eds) (1992) *Les régions qui gagnent*, Paris: PUF.

Bennett, R. J. (ed.) (1990) *Decentralisation, Local Government and Markets: Towards a Post-Welfare Agenda?*, Oxford: Oxford University Press.

Benthem van den Bergh, G. (1992) *The Nuclear Revolution and the End of the Cold War: Forced Restraint*, London: Macmillan.

Berbaux, F. and Muller, P. (1992) 'Les interventions économiques locales', *Pouvirs*, 60: 99–114.

Berger, P. L. (1986) *The Capitalist Revolution: Fifty Propositions about Prosperity, Equality, and Liberty*, New York: Basic Books.

Berger, P. L. (1988) 'An East Asian development Model?' in P. L. Berger and M. Hsin-Huang Hsiao (eds) *In Search of an East Asian Development Model*, New Brunswick: Transaction.

Bergesen, A. (1990) 'Turning world-system theory on its head', in M. Featherstone (ed.) *Global Culture: Nationalism, Globalization and Modernity*, London: Sage.

Berggren, C (1988) '"New production concepts" in final assembly – the Swedish Experience' in B. Dankbaar, U. Jurgens and T. Malsch (eds) *Die Zukunft der Arbeit in der Automobilindustrie*, Berlin: WZB.

Berggren, C. (1993) 'The end of history?', *Work Employment and Society*, 7, 2: 163–88.

Berlin Museum Catalogue (1994) *Friedrich Gilly 1772–1800 und die Privatgesellschaft junger Architekten*, Berlin: Verlag Willmuth Arenhövel.

Bernal, M. (1987) *Black Athena: The Afroasiatic Roots of Classical Civilization*, Volume 1, London: Free Press Association.

Betthausen, P. (1983) *Karl Friedrich Schinkel*, Berlin: Henschelverlag.

Bhaba, H. (1993) 'Remembering Fanon: self, psyche and the colonial condition' in P. Williams and L. Chrisman (eds) *Colonial Discourse and Post-colonial Theory*, Hemel Hempstead: Harvester Wheatsheaf.

Bianchini, F. and Parkinson, M. (eds) (1993) *Cultural Policy and Urban Regeneration: The West European Experience*, Manchester: Manchester University Press.

Boissevain, J. (ed.) (1992) *Revitalizing European Rituals*, London: Routledge.

Borenstein (1992) 'The evolution of US airline competition', *Journal of Economic Perspectives*, 6, 2: 45–73.

Borraz, O. (1994) 'Le gouvernement des villes, une comparison de deux villes française et deux villes suisses', unpublished Doctoral thesis, IEP, Paris.

Bottomore, T. B. (1996) 'Problems and prospects of a socialist economy in Europe' in R. Kilminister and I. Varcoe (eds) *Culture, Modernity and Revolution: Essays in Honour of Zygmunt Bauman*, London: Routledge.

Bourdieu, P. (1982) *Ce que parler veut dire: l'economie des echanges linguistiques*, Paris: Fayard.

Boyer, R. (1986) *La theorie de la regulation: une analyse critique*, Paris: La Decouverte.

Boyne, R. (1990) 'Culture and the world-system' in M. Featherstone (ed.) *Global Culture: Nationalism, Globalization and Modernity*, London: Sage.

BPI (1993) *BPI Statistical Handbook 1993*, London: BPI.

Braudel, F. (1986a) *Sozialgeschichte des 15.–18. Jahrunderts*, 2 volumes, Munich: Kindler.

Braudel, F. (1986b) *L'Identité de la France*, Paris: Arthaud/Flammarion.

329

Bremmer, I. and Taras, R., (eds) (1993) *Nations and Politics in the Soviet Successor States*, Cambridge: Cambridge University Press.

Brewer, A. (1980) *Marxist Theories of Imperialism: A Critical Survey*, London: Routledge and Kegan Paul.

Brindley, T., Rydin, Y. and Stoker, G. (1989) *Remaking Planning: The Politics of Urban Change in the Thatcher Years*, London: Unwin Hyman.

Brinkerhoff, D. B. and White, L. K. (1991) *Sociology*, third edition, St. Paul: West Publishing Company.

Brotchie, J., Hall, P. and Newton, P. (eds) (1987) *The Spatial Impact of Technological Change*, London: Croom Helm.

Brusco, S. (1994) 'La leçon des districts et les nouvelles politiques industrielles' in A. Bagnasco and C. Sabel (eds) *PME et développement économique en Europe*, Paris: La Découverte.

Bruun, O. (1995) 'Political hierarchy and private entrepreneurship in a Chinese neighbourhood' in A. Walder (ed.) *The Waning of The Communist State*, Berkeley: University of California Press.

Buarque de Holanda, S. (1995) *Die Wurzeln Brasiliens*, Frankfurt am Main: Suhrkamp Verlag.

Buchdahl, G. (1961) *The Image of Newton and Locke in the Age of Reason*, London: Sheed and Ward.

Bulpitt, J. (1983) *Territory and Power in the United Kingdom*, Manchester: Manchester University Press.

Bunch, C. (1987) *Passionate Politics*, New York: St. Martin's Press.

Butler, J. (1990) *Gender Trouble: Feminism and the Subversion of Identity*, London: Routledge.

Button, K. (ed.) (1991) *Airline Deregulation: International Experiences*, London: David Fulton Publishers.

Button, K. and Swann, D. (1989) 'European Community airlines – deregulation and its problems', *Journal of Common Market Studies*, 27, 4: 259–82.

Button, K. and Swann, D. (1991) 'Aviation in Europe' in K. J. Button (ed.) *Airline Deregulation: International Experiences*, London: David Fulton Publishers.

Byrd, P. (1985) 'The development of the peace movement in Britain' in W. Kaltefleiter and R. L. Pfaltzgraff (eds) *The Peace Movements in Europe and the United States*, London: Croom Helm.

Cabral, A. (1993) 'National liberation and culture' in P. Williams and L. Chrisman (eds) *Colonial Discourse and Post-colonial Theory*, Hemel Hempstead: Harvester Wheatsheaf.

Callinicos, A. (1989) *Against Postmodernism: A Marxist Critique*, Cambridge: Polity Press.

Callinicos, A. (1995) *Theories and Narratives: Reflections on the Philosophy of History*, Cambridge: Polity Press.

Cameron, R. (1993) *A Concise Economic History of the World: From Palaeolithic Times to the Present*, Oxford: Oxford University Press.

Campbell, M. (ed.) (1990) *Local Economic Policy*, London: Cassell.

Canadian Auto Workers (1990) *CAW Statement on the Reorganisation of Work*, CAW.

Carrere d'Encausse, H. (1979) *The Decline of Empire: The Soviet Socialist Republics in Revolt*, New York: Newsweek Books.

Carrere d'Encausse, H. (1991) *The End of Empire*, New York: Basic Books.

Carrithers, M., Collins, S. and Lukes, S. (eds) (1985) *The Category of the Person: Anthropology, Philosophy, History*, Cambridge: Cambridge University Press.

Carter, A. (1992) *Peace Movements: International Protest and World Politics since 1945*, Harlow: Longman.

Cassirer, E, (1944) *An Essay on Man*, New Haven: Yale University Press.

Cassirer, E. (1953/55/57) *The Philosophy of Symbolic Forms*, 3 volumes, translated by R. Manheim, New Haven: Yale University Press.

Castells, M. (ed.) (1985) *High Technology, Space and Society*, Beverly Hills, Calif.: Sage.

Castells, M. (1989) *The Informational City*, London: Edward Arnold.

Caygill, H. (1990) 'Architectural postmodernism: the retreat of an avant-garde?' in R. Boyne and A. Rattansi (eds) *Postmodernity and Society*, Basingstoke: Macmillan.

Caygill, H. (1993) 'The place of graffiti', *Journal of Philosophy and Technology*, 1, Fall: 22–9.

Chambers, I. (1994) *Migrancy, Culture, Identity*, London: Routledge.

Chandler, A. D. (1977) *The Visible Hand: The Managerial Revolution in American Business*, Cambridge, Mass.: Harvard University Press.

Cheng, B. (1962) *The Law of International Air Transport*, London: Steven and Sons.

Chenus, A. and Tabard, N. (1994) 'Les transformations socio-professionnelles du territoire français', *Population*, 6: 122–58.

Chevigny, P. (1991) *Gigs: Jazz and the Cabaret Laws in New York City*, New York: Routledge.

China Statistical Publishing House (CSPH) (1995) *China Statistical Yearbook 1995*, Beijing: China Statistical Publishing House.

Chirot, D. (1977) *Social Change in the Twentieth Century*, New York: Harcourt Brace Jovanovich Inc.

Chu, Godwin and Ju, Y. (1993) *The Great Wall in Virus*, Albany: State University of New York Press.

Civil Aviation Authority (1993) *Airline Competition in the Single European Market*, CAP 623, Cheltenham: CAA.

Cixous, H., (1986) 'Sorties: out and out: attacks/ways out/forays', in H. Cixous and C. Clements *The Newly-Born Woman*, translated by B. Wing, Manchester: Manchester University Press.

Clarke, S. (1991) (ed.) *The State Debate*, Macmillan: London.

Clifford, J. (1982) *Person and Myth: Maurice Leenhardt in the Melanesian World*, Durham, NC: Duke University Press.

Clinton Commission (1993) *Change, Challenge and Competition: A Report to the President and Congress*, The National Commission to Ensure a Strong Competitive Airline Industry, Washington DC: Government Printing Office.

Cohen, A. P. (ed.) (1986) *Symbolising Boundaries: Identity and Diversity in British Cultures*, Manchester: Manchester University Press.

Comaroff, J. and Comaroff, J. (1992) *Ethnography and the Historical Imagination*, Boulder: Westview Press.

Comité des Sages (1994) *Expanding Horizons: A Report by the Comité des Sages for Air Transport to the European Commission*, Brussels: European Commission.

Commission of European Community (1987) *Public Administration and the Funding of Culture in the European Community*, Brussels: Commission of European Community.

Confederation of Japan Automobile Workers' Unions (1992) 'Towards coexistence with the world, consumers and employees', February.

Continho, J. V. (1974) Preface to P. Freire's *Cultural Action for Freedom*, Hamondsworth: Penguin Books.

Daly, M. (1979) *Gyn/Ecology: The Metaethics of Radical Feminism*, London, Women's Press.

Dankbaar, B., Jurgens, U. and Malsch, T., (eds) (1988) *Die Zukunft der Arbeit in der Automobilindustrie*, Berlin: WZB.

Dawisha, K. and Parrott, B. (1994) *Russia and the New States of Eurasia*, Cambridge: Cambridge University Press.

Deakin, N. and Edwards, J. (1993) *The Enterprise Culture and the Inner City*, London: Routledge.

Debeir, J.-C., Deléage, J.-P. and Hémery, D. (1989): *In the Servitude of Power: Energy and Civilization Throughout the Ages*, London: Zed Books.

De Coninck, F. (1992) *European Air Law: New Skies for Europe*, Paris: ITA Press.

de Kadt, E. and Williams. G. (1974) *Sociology of Underdevelopment*, London: Tavistock Publications.

Demesteere, S. and Padioleau, J. G. (1992) 'La planification stratégique', *Annales de la Recherche Urbaine*, 51: 28–39.

Department of Research on Party Literature, Central Committee of the Communist Party of China (1987), from a talk between Deng Xiaoping and Vice-President Ali Hassan Mwinyi, United Republic of Tanzania, 1985 in a collection of Deng's speeches, *Fundamental Issues in Present-day China*, Beijing: Foreign Languages Press.

Derrida, J. (1981) *Dissemination*, Chicago: University of Chicago Press.

Derrida, J. (1987) *The Truth in Painting*, Chicago: University of Chicago Press.

Descartes, R. (1968) *Discourse on Method and the Meditations*, Harmondsworth: Penguin Books.

de Sola Pool, I. (1990) *Technologies Without Boundaries*, Cambridge, Mass.: Harvard University Press.

de Swaan, A. (1988) *In Care of the State*, Cambridge: Polity Press.

Deutschmann, C. (1995) 'Geld als soziales Konstrukt. Zur Akutalität von Marx und Simmel', *Leviathan*, 23, 3: 376–93.

de Vroey, M. (1991) 'Der Markt – von wegen einfach', *PROKLA*, 82: 7–22.

Dicken, P. (1992) *Global Shift: Industrial Change in a Turbulent World*, London: Harper and Row.

Dilley, R. (ed.) (1992) *Contesting Markets: Analyses of Ideology, Discourse and Practice*, Edinburgh: Edinburgh University Press.

Diuk, N. and Karatnycky, A. (1993) *New Nations Rising: The Fall of the Soviets and the Challenge of Independence*, New York and Chichester: John Wiley.

Doganis, R. (1991) *Flying Off Course: The Economics of International Airlines*, London: HarperCollins.

Doganis, R. (1993) 'The bilateral regime for air transport: current position and future prospects' in OECD, *International Air Transport: The Challenges Ahead*, Paris: OECD.

Douglas, M. (1992) *Risk and Blame: Essays in Cultural Theory*, London: Routledge.

Dray, W. H. (1964) *Philosophy of History*, Englewood Cliffs, NJ: Prentice-Hall.

Duncan, S., Goodwin, M. and Halford, S. (1993) 'Regulation theory, the local state and the transition of urban politics', *Environment and Planning D: Society and Space* 11, 1: 67–89.

Dunkerley, J. (1994) 'Beyond Utopia: the state of the Left in Latin America', *New Left Review*, 206: 27–43.

Durkheim, E. (1933) [1893] *Division of Labour in Society*, translated by G. Simpson, New York: Free Press.

Durkheim, E. (1969) [1898] 'Individualism and the intellectuals', translated by S. Lukes and J. Lukes, *Political Studies*, 17: 16–30.

Durkheim, E. (1995) [1912] *The Elementary Forms of Religious Life*, translated by K. E. Fields, New York: The Free Press.

Dyson, K. and P. Humphreys (eds) (1986) *The Politics of the Communications Revolution in Western Europe*, Special Issue of *West European Politics*, 9, 4.

Einem, E. von (1987) *Die Rettung der kaputten Stadt*, Berlin: Transit.

Einem, E. von (1991) 'Warten auf Schinkel: Der Genus loci und das Mühen um die Berliner Stadtplanung' in *Aesthetik und Kommunikation: Hauptstadt Berlin*, 76: 56–63.

Eisenschitz, A. and Gough, J. (1994) *The Politics of Local Economic Policy: The Problems and Possibilities of Local Initiative*, Basingstoke: Macmillan.

Elger, T. and Smith, C. (1994) *Global Japanisation? The Transnational Transformation of the Labour Process*, London: Routledge.

Elias, N. (1968) 'Introduction' to the 1969 [German] edition, translated and reprinted in N. Elias (1978) *The Civilizing Process, Volume 1: The History of Manners*, Oxford: Blackwell and as Appendix I in N. Elias (1994) *The Civilizing Process*, Oxford: Blackwell.

Elias, N. (1978) *What Is Sociology?*, London: Hutchinson.

Elias, N. (1987a) *Involvement and Detachment*, Oxford: Blackwell.

Elias, N. (1987b) 'The retreat of the sociologists into the present', *Theory, Culture and Society*, 4, 2–3, June: 223–47.

Elias, N. (1991) *The Society of Individuals*, Oxford: Basil Blackwell.

Elias, N. (1994) *The Civilizing Process: The History of Manners and State Formation and Civilization*, translated by Edmund Jephcott, Oxford: Blackwell.

Eliot, T. S. (1972) *Notes Towards the Definition of Culture*, London: Faber.

Elkins, T. H. (1988) *Berlin: The Spatial Structure of a Divided City*, London: Methuen.

Ellingham, M., McVeigh, S. and Grisbrook, D. (1994) *Morocco: The Rough Guide*, London: Rough Guides Ltd.

Elson, D. (1990) 'Markt-Sozialismus oder Sozialisierung des Marktes?, *PROKLA*, 78: 60–107.

Elworthy, S. (1989) 'Nuclear weapons decision-making and accountability' in C. Marsh and C. Fraser (eds) *Public Opinion and Nuclear Weapons*, Basingstoke: Macmillan.

Eriksen, T. L. (1993) *Ethnicity and Nationalism: Anthropological Perspectives*, London: Pluto Press.

Erlich, C. (n.d.) 'Socialism, anarchism and feminism' in *Quiet Rumours: An Anarcha-Feminist Anthology*, London: Dark Star.

Espérou, R. (1990) 'L'échange bilatéral des droits de trafic aérien est-il condamné?', *Revue française du droit aérien*, 193–211.

Esping-Andersen, G. (1990) *Three Worlds of Welfare Capitalism*, Cambridge: Polity Press.

Etzioni, A. (1988) *The Moral Dimension. Towards a New Economics*, New York: The Free Press.

Eucken, W. (1959) *Grundsätze der Wirtschaftspolitik*, Reinbek: J. C. B. Mohr.

Evans, D. (1951) *Social Romanticism in France 1830–1848*, Oxford: Oxford University Press.

Evers, H.-D. and Schrader, H. (eds) (1993) *The Moral Economy of Trade: Ethnicity and Developing Markets*, London: Routledge.

Fainstein, S., Gordon, I. and Harloe, M. (1992) *Divided Cities: New York and London in the Contemporary World*, Oxford: Blackwell.

Featherstone, M. (ed.) (1990) *Global Culture: Nationalism, Globalization and Modernity*, London: Sage.

Featherstone, M. (1993) 'Global and local cultures', in J. Bird, B. Curtis, C. Putnam, G. Robertson and L. Tickner (eds) *Mapping the Futures: Local Cultures, Global Change*, London: Routledge.

Ferguson, M. (1992) 'The mythology about globalization', *European Journal of Communications*, 7, 1, March: 69–94.

Ferrante, J. (1992) *Sociology: A Global Perspective*, Belmont: Wadsworth.

Fiske, J. (1989) *Understanding Popular Culture*, London: Routledge.

Fortes, M. (1987) *Religion, Morality and the Person: Essays on Tallensi Religion*, edited and with an Introduction by Jack Goody, Cambridge: Cambridge University Press.

Foucault, M. (1970) *The Order of Things*, London: Tavistock Publications.

Foucault, M. (1972) *The Archaeology of Knowledge*, London: Tavistock Publications.

Foucault, M. (1977a) *Discipline and Punish*, Harmondsworth: Penguin Books.

Foucault, M. (1977b) *Language, Counter-Memory, Practice*, New York: Cornell University Press.

Foucault, M. (1983) *This is Not a Pipe*, Berkeley: University of California Press.
Frank, A. Gunder (1969) *Latin America: Underdevelopment or Revolution?*, New York: Monthly Review.
Frank, A. Gunder and Gills, B. K. (1993) *The World System: Five Hundred Years or Five Thousand?*, London: Routledge.
Fraser, J. T. (1993) *Die Zeit. Auf den Spuren eines vertrauten und doch fremden Phänomens*, Munich: dtv Sachbuch.
Frazer, G. and Lancelle, G. (1994) *Zhirinovsky: The Little Black Book*, Harmondsworth: Penguin Books.
Freche, G. (1990) *La France Ligoté*, Paris: Albin Michel.
Freire, P. (1972) *Pedagogy of the Oppressed*, Harmondsworth: Penguin Books.
Friedman, J. (1990) 'Being in the world: globalization and localization' in M. Featherstone (ed.) *Global Culture: Nationalism, Globalization and Modernity*, London: Sage.
Friedman, J. (1994a) *Cultural Identity and Global Process*, London: Sage.
Friedman, J. (ed.) (1994b) *Consumption and Identity*, Chur, Switzerland: Harwood Publishers.
Friedman, M. (1976) *Kapitalismus und Freiheit*, Munich: dtv.
Frith, S. (1988) *Music For Pleasure*, Cambridge: Polity Press.
Frith, S. (ed.) (1989) *World Music, Politics and Social Change*, Manchester, Manchester University Press.
Frith, S. (1991) 'Critical response' in D. Robinson (ed.) *Music at the Margins*, London: Sage.
Frith, S. (ed.) (1994) *Music and Copyright*, Edinburgh: Edinburgh University Press.
Fucini, J. F. S. (1990) *Working for the Japanese*, New Jersey: The Free Press .
Fukuyama, F. (1992) *The End of History and the Last Man*, London: Hamish Hamilton.
Gallacher, J. and Odell, C. (1994) 'Airline alliances: tagging along', *Airline Business*, July, 25–42.
Garnham, N. (1990) *Capitalism and Communications*, London: Sage.
Garrahan, P. and Stewart P. (1992) *The Nissan Enigma: Flexibility at Work in a Local Economy*, London: Mansell.
Garrett, W. R. (1992) 'Thinking religion in the global circumstance: a critique of Roland Robertson's globalization theory', *Journal for the Scientific Study of Religion*, 31, 3: 296–332.
Gay, P. (1973) *The Enlightenment: An Interpretation, Volume Two: The Science of Freedom*, London: Wildwood House.
Geertz, C. (1973) *Interpretation of Cultures*, New York: Basic Books.
Geertz, C. (1992) '"Local knowledge" and its limits: some *Obiter Dicta*', *The Yale Journal of Criticism*, 5, 2: 129–35.
Gellner, E. (1964) *Thought and Change*, London: Weidenfeld and Nicolson.
Gellner, E. (1983) *Nations and Nationalism*, Oxford, Blackwell.
Gellner, E. (1992) *Reason and Culture: New Prespectives on the Past*, Oxford: Blackwell.
Georgescu-Roegen, N. (1971) *The Enthropic Law and the Economic Process*, Cambridge, Mass.: Harvard University Press.
Gerbaux, F. and Muller, P. (1992) 'L'intervention économique des collectivés locales', *Pouvois*, 60: 99–114.
Geron, L. (1990) *Soviet Foreign Policy Under Perestroika*, London: RIIA/Pinter.
Giddens, A. (1990) *The Consequences of Modernity*, Cambridge: Polity Press.
Giddens, A. (1991) *Modernity and Self-Identity: Self and Society in the Late Modern Age*, Cambridge: Polity.
Giddens, A. (1992) *The Transformation of Intimacy: Sexuality, Love and Eroticism in Modern Societies*, Cambridge: Polity Press.

Giddens, A. (1993) *Sociology*, second edition, Cambridge: Polity Press.

Gillespie, M. A. (1984) *Hegel, Heidegger and the Ground of History*, Chicago: University of Chicago Press.

Giroux, Henry A. and McLauren, P. (eds) (1994) *Between Borders: Pedogogy and the Politics of Cultural Studies*, London: Routledge.

Gleditsch, N. P. (1990) 'The rise and decline of the new peace movement' in K. Kodama and U. Vesa (eds) *Towards a Comparative Analysis of Peace Movements*, Aldershot: Dartmouth.

Goldman, M. I. (1991), *What Went Wrong With Perestroika?*, New York and London: W. W. Norton.

Goldsmith, M. (1993) 'The Europeanisation of local government', *Urban Studies*, 30, 4/5: 683–99.

Goldstein, M. and Ku, Y. C. (1993) 'Income and family support among rural elderly in Zhejiang Province, China', *Journal of Cross Cultural Gerontology*, 8, 3: 197–233.

Goldthorpe, J. H. (1971) 'Theories of industrial society: reflections on the recrudescence of historicism and the future of futurology', *Archives européennes de sociologie*, 12: 263–88.

Goody, J. (1992) 'Local knowledge and knowledge of locality: the desirability of frames', *The Yale Journal of Criticism*, 5, 2: 137–47.

Gorbachev, M. (1987) *Perestroika: New Thinking For Our Country and the World*, London: Collins.

Gorz, A. (1982) *Farewell to the Working Class: An Essay on Post-industrial Socialism*, London: Pluto.

Goudsblom, J. (1989) 'Human history and long-term social processes', in J. Goudsblom, E. Jones and S. Mennell (eds) *Human History and Social Process*, Exeter: University of Exeter Press.

Granovetter, M. (1985) 'Economic action and social structure: a theory of embeddedness, *Americal Journal of Sociology*, 91, 3: 481–510.

Gray, C. (1993) 'The network for cultural policy in Britain', Paper to PSA Conference, University of Leicester.

Gray, J. (1989) 'The end of history – or of liberalism?', *National Review*, 27 October: 33–5.

Gray, J. (1993) *Beyond the New Right: Markets, Government and the Common Environment*, London: Routledge.

Gray, J. (1994) 'Against the world', *Guardian*, Tuesday 4 January: 18.

Green, A. E. (1994) *The Geography of Poverty and Wealth*, Warwick: Institute for Employment Research.

Greenham Common Women Against Cruise Missiles (1984) New York: Center for Constitutional Rights, Legal Education Pamphlet.

Grey, C. and Mitev, N. (1995) 'Re-engineering organisations: a critical appraisal', *Personnel Review*, 24, 1: 6–18.

Griffin, S. (1978) *Women and Nature*, New York: Harper and Row.

Gurnah, A. (ed.) (forthcoming) *Culture for Social Renewal*, London: NIACE.

Gurnah, A. and Scott, A. (1992) *The Uncertain Science*, London: Routledge.

Habermas, J. (1984a) *Communication and the Evolution of Society*, Oxford: Polity Press.

Habermas, J. (1984b) *Theory of Communicative Action, Volume One: Reason and the Rationalization of Society*, translated by T. McCarthy, Cambridge: Polity Press.

Habermas, J. (1987a) *Theory of Communicative Action, Volume Two: The Critique of Functionalist Reason*, translated by T. McCarthy, Cambridge: Polity Press.

Habermas, J. (1987b) *The Philosophical Discourse of Modernity*, Oxford: Polity Press.

Habermas, J. (1990) 'What does socialism mean today? The rectifying revision and the need of new thinking on the left', *New Left Review*, 138: 3–21.

Hall, P., Breheny, M., McQuaid, R. and Hart, D. (1987) *Western Sunrise: The Genesis and Growth of Britain's Major High Tech Corridor*, London: Allen and Unwin.

Hall, P. and Markusen, A. R. (eds) (1985) *Silicon Landscapes*, Boston, Mass.: Allen and Unwin.

Hall, S. (1993) 'Cultural identity and diasporas' in P. Williams and L. Chrisman (eds) *Colonial Discourse and Post-colonial Theory*, Hemel Hempstead: Harvester Wheatsheaf.

Hanlon, P. (1996) *Global Airlines: Competition in a Transnational Industry*, Oxford: Butterworth, Heinemann.

Hannerz, U. (1990) 'Cosmopolitans and locals in world culture' in M. Featherstone (ed.) *Global Culture: Nationalism, Globalization and Modernity*, London: Sage.

Hannerz, U. (1992a) 'The global ecumene as a network of networks' in A. Kuper (ed.) *Conceptualizing Society*, London: Routledge.

Hannerz, U. (1992b) *Cultural Complexity: Studies in the Social Organization of Meaning*, New York: Columbia University Press.

Hardin, K. (1993) *The Aesthetics of Action: Continuity and Change in a West African Town*, Washington: Smithsonian Institution Press.

Harding, A.(1991) 'The rise of urban growth coalitions, UK-style?', *Government and Policy* , 9, 3: 295–319.

Harding, A. (1994) 'Conclusion: towards the entrepreneurial European city?' in A. Harding, J. Dawson, R. Evans and M. Parkinson (eds), *European Cities in the 1990s: Profiles, Policies and Prospects*, Manchester: Manchester University Press.

Harding, A., Dawson, J., Evans, R. and Parkinson, M. (eds) (1994) *European Cities in the 1990s: Profiles, Policies and Prospects*, Manchester: Manchester University Press.

Harding, A. and Garside, P. (1994) 'Urban and economic development' in P. Stewart and G. Stoker (eds) *Local Government in the 1990s*, Basingstoke: Macmillan.

Harvey, D. (1989) *The Condition of Post-Modernity*, Oxford: Blackwell.

Hastings, E. H. and Hastings, P. K. (eds) (1982) *Index to International Public Opinion 1978–1980*, Westport, CT: Greenwood Press.

Hastings, E. H. and Hastings, P. K. (eds) (1984) *Index to International Public Opinion 1982–1983*, Westport, CT: Greenwood Press.

Hausner, V. (ed.) (1986) *Critical Issues in Urban Economic Development, Vol. 1*, Oxford: Clarendon.

Hausner, V. (1987) *Economic Change in British Cities: Five Case Studies*, Oxford: Clarendon.

Hausner, V. (1988) *Critical Issues in Urban Economic Development, Volume 2*, Oxford: Clarendon.

Hay, C. (1993) 'Crisis, what crisis? Global economic dynamics, state crisis and the emergence of new forms of local governance', Paper to the Ninth Urban Change and Conflict Conference, University of Sheffield, 14–16 September.

Hayek, F. von (1968) 'Der Wettbewerb als Entdeckungsverfahren', Lecture at the Institut für Weltwirtschaft, Universität Kiel, *Kieler Vorträge* 56.

Hayward, S. (1993) *French National Cinema*, London: Routledge.

He, Zhao Fa, S., Chen, C. Yan and Y. Li (eds) (1991) *Zhujiang Sanjiaozhou Zizhen yu Jumin – Shehuixue di Shequ Yinjiu* [Town Groupings and the Residents in the Pearl River Delta – A Sociological Study on the Community], Guangzhou: Huanan Ligong Daxue Chubanshe.

Hegel, G. W. F. (1820) 'Preface' to *The Philosophy of Right*, translated with notes by T. M. Knox, Oxford: Oxford University Press, 1971.

Hegel, G. W. F. (1956) [1830] *The Philosophy of History*, translated by J. Sibree, New York: Dover Publications, 1956.

Heiberg, M. (1989) *The Making of the Basque Nation*, Cambridge: Cambridge University Press.

336

Heinrich, G. (1993) *Rot-Grün in Berlin. Die alternative Liste in der Regierungsverantwortung 1989–1990*, Marburg: Schüren Pressverlag.

Held, D. and McGrew, A. (1993) 'Globalization and the liberal democratic state', *Government and Opposition* 28, 2: 261–89.

Helmer, S.D. (1985) *Hitler's Berlin: The Speer Plans for Reshaping the Central City*, Ann Arbor, Mich.: UMI Press.

Henderson, J. and Castells, M. (eds) (1987) *Global Restructuring and Territorial Development*, London: Sage.

Henry, I. (1993) *The Politics of Leisure Policy*, Basingstoke: Macmillan.

Herle, A. and Phillipson, D. (eds) (1994) 'Living traditions: continuity and change, past and present', Special Issue of *Cambridge Anthropology*, 17, 2.

Hickman, J. (1986) 'Greenham Women Against Cruise Missiles and others versus Ronald Reagan and others' in J. Dewar *et al.* (eds) *Nuclear Weapons, the Peace Movement and the Law*, Basingstoke: Macmillan.

Hill, J. (1993) 'Government policy and the British film industry, 1979–90', *European Journal of Communications*, 8, 2: 203–24.

Hines, C. and Lang, T. (1995) 'Globalization of the market', letter to *Guardian*, 29 March.

Hirst, P. Q. and Thompson, G. (1992) 'The problem of "globalization": international economic relations, national economic management and the formation of trading blocs', *Economy and Society*, 21, 4: 357–96.

Hirst, P. Q. and Thompson, G. (1994) 'Globalization, foreign direct investment and international economic governance', *Organization*, 1, 2: 277–303.

Hirst, P. Q. and Thompson, G. (1996) *Globalization in Question: The International Economy and the Possibilities of Governance*, Cambridge: Polity Press.

Hirst, P. Q. and Zeitlin, J. (eds) (1988) *Reversing Industrial Decline?*, Oxford: Berg.

Hirst, P. Q. and Zeitlin, J. (1991) 'Flexible specialization versus post-Fordism', *Economy and Society*, 20, 1: 1–56.

Hobbes, T. (1972) *Léviathan*, London: Fontana.

Hobsbawm, E. (1996) 'Identity politics and the left', *New Left Review*, 217: 38–47.

Hobsbawm, E. and Ranger, T. (eds) (1983) *The Invention of Tradition*, Cambridge, Cambridge University Press.

Hoffman, J. (1995) *Beyond the State*, Cambridge: Polity Press.

Hoffmann-Axthelm, D. (1990) 'Ausfahrt Potsdamer Platz,' *Bauwelt*, 4 May: 864–7.

Hohenberg, P. M. and Lees, L. H. (1985) *The Making of Urban Europe 1000–1950*, Boston, Mass.: Harvard University Press.

Holloway, J. (1994) 'Global capital and the nation state', *Capital and Class*, 52: 23–49.

Holton, R. J. and Turner, B. (1986) *Talcott Parsons on Economy and Society*, London: Routledge.

hooks, b. (1993) 'Postmodern blackness' in P. Williams and L. Chrisman (eds) *Colonial Discourse and Post-colonial Theory*, Hemel Hempstead: Harvester Wheatsheaf.

Hosking, G. (1990), *The Awakening of the Soviet Union*, London: Heinemann.

Hubinger, V. (ed.) (1994) *EASA Register 1994*, Praha: EASA.

Hugh-Jones, S. and Humphreys, C. (eds) (1992) *Barter, Exchange and Value: An Anthropological Approach*, Cambridge: Cambridge University Press.

Hutchinson, J. (1994) *Modern Nationalism*, Glasgow: Fontana.

Hutton, W. (1994) 'Markets threaten life and soul of the party', *Guardian*, Tuesday 4 January: 13.

Hutton. W. (1995) *The State We're In*, London: Jonathan Cape.

IFPI (1990) *World Record Sales 1969–1990*, London: IFPI.

Iggers, G. (1968) *The German Conception of History: The National Tradition of Historical Thought from Herder to the Present*, Middletown, Conn.: Wesleyan University Press.

Ingold, T. (ed.) (1990) *The Concept of Society is Theoretically Obsolete*, Manchester: GDAT.

Internationale Bauausstellung Berlin 1987 (1987a) *Projektübersicht*, Berlin: IBA.

Internationale Bauausstellung Berlin 1987 (1987b) *Idee, Prozeß, Ergebnis: Die Reparatur und Rekonstruktion der Stadt*, Berlin: IBA.

Ionescu, G. (1993) 'The Impact of the information revolution on parliamentary sovereignties', *Government and Opposition*, 28, 2: 221–41.

Irigaray, L. (1985) 'Any theory of the "subject" has always been appropriated by the masculine', in *Speculum of the Other Woman*, New York: Cornell University Press .

Jackson, M. and Karp, I. (1990) 'Introduction', in M. Jackson and I. Karp (eds) *The Experience of Self and Other in African Cultures*, Washington: Smithsonian Institution Press.

Jackson, P. and Penrose, J. (1993) *Constructions of Race, Place and Nation*, London: UCL Press.

Jacoby, R. (1994) 'The myth of multiculturalism', *New Left Review*, 208: 121–6.

Jahn, E. (1989) 'The role of governments, social organizations and peace movements in the new German and European peace process', in M. Kaldor, G. Holden and R. Falk (eds) *The New Detente*, London: Verso.

Jameson, F. (1990) *Late Marxism: Adorno, or, the Persistence of the Dialectic*, London: Verso.

Jameson, F. (1991) *Postmodernism, or, the Cultural Logic of Late Capitalism*, London: Verso.

Jayaweera, N. (1987) 'Communication satellites: a Third World perspective', in R. Finnegan, G. Salaman and K. Thompson (eds) *Information Technology: Social Issues*, London: Hodder and Stoughton.

Jessop, B. (1988) 'Regulation theory, post-Fordism and the state: more than a reply to Werner Bonefeld', *Capital and Class*, 34: 147–68.

Jessop, B. (1990) 'Regulation theories in retrospect and prospect', *Economy and Society*, 19, 2: 153–216.

Jessop, B. (1992) 'The Schumpeterian workfare state: or "On Japanism and post-Fordism"', Paper to the Conference of Europeanists, Chicago, 27–29 March.

Jessop, B. (1994) 'Post-Fordism and the state' in A. Amin (ed.) *Post-Fordism: A Reader*, Oxford: Blackwell.

Joas, H. (1991) 'Between power politics and pacifist utopia: Peace and war in sociological theory', *Current Sociology*, 9, 1: 47–66.

John, P. (1994) *The Europeanisation of British Local Government: New Management Strategies*, Luton: Local Government Management Board.

Johnson, G. (1993) 'Family strategies and economic transformation in rural China: some evidence from the Pearl River Delta' in D. Davis and S. Harrell (eds) *Chinese Families in The Post-Mao Era*, Berkeley: University of Californian Press.

Jones, D. (1992) 'Lean production (an update)', paper presented to the 'Lean Production and European Trade Union Cooperation Conference', 6–11 December, TGWU Centre, Eastborne, England.

Joseph Rowntree Foundation Inquiry Group (1995) *Inquiry into Income and Wealth*, volumes 1 and 2, York: Joseph Rowntree Foundation.

Julius, D. (1990) *Global Companies and Public Policy*, London RIIA, Pinter.

Juppke, C. (1994) 'Revisionism, dissidence, nationalism: opposition in Leninist regimes', *British Journal of Sociology*, 45, 4: 543–61.

Kaldor, M. (1982) *The Baroque Arsenal*, London: Deutsch.

Kamen, E. (1994) 'Erst kamen die Ideen – jetzt kommt die Architektur', *Foyer*, 11, June.

Kaplan, F. (1984) *Wizards of Armageddon*, New York: Simon and Schuster.

Kasper, D. M. (1988) *Deregulation and Globalization: Liberalizing International Trade in Air Services*, Massachusetts: The American Enterprise Institute/Ballinger Publishing Company.

338

Kassim, H. (1996b) 'Theories of integration and their limits: European Community policy developments in the air transport sector, 1957–1992', D.Phil. thesis, University of Oxford.

Kassim, H. (1996a) 'Air transport' in H. Kassim and A. Menon (eds) *The European Union and National Industrial Policy*, London: Routledge.

Katz, E. and Tamar, L. (1985) 'Mutual aid in decoding *Dallas*: preliminary notes from a cross-cultural study' in P. Drummond and R. Patterson (eds) *Television in Transition*, London: BFI.

Kedourie, E. (1966), *Nationalism*, London: Hutchinson.

Keeble, D. and Wever, E. (eds) (1986) *New Firms and Regional Development in Europe*, London: Croom Helm.

Kenny, A. (1973) *Wittgenstein*, Harmondsworth: Penguin Books.

Kerbo, H. R. (1989) *Sociology: Social Structure and Social Conflict*, New York: Macmillan.

Kerr, C., Dunlop J., Harbison T. and Myers, C. A. (1960) *Industrialism and Industrial Man*, Harmondsworth: Pelican Books.

Khasbulatov, R. (1993) *The Struggle for Russia: Power and Change in the Democratic Revolution*, London: Routledge.

Kilminster, R. (1979) *Praxis and Method*, London, Routledge.

Kilminster, R. (1982) 'Theory and practice in Marx and Marxism' in G. H. R. Parkinson (ed.) *Marx and Marxisms*, Cambridge: Cambridge University Press.

Kilminster, R. (1983) 'From the standpoint of eternity', *Theory, Culture and Society*, 2, 1: 118–33.

Kilminster, R. (1989) 'The limits of transcendental sociology', *Theory, Culture and Society*, 6, 4, November: 655–63.

Kilminster, R. (1992) 'Alienation' in T. B. Bottomore and W. Outhwaite (eds) *The Blackwell Dictionary of Twentieth Century Social Thought*, Oxford: Basil Blackwell.

Kilminster, R. (1994) 'The Symbol Theory as a Research Programme', Paper presented to the Ad hoc Sessions on Figurational Sociology, XIII ISA World Congress of Sociology, Bielefeld, 18–23 July.

Kim, Kyong-Dong (1994) 'Confucianism and capitalist development in East Asia' in L. A. Sklair (ed.) *Capitalism and Development*, London: Routledge.

King, A. D. (ed.) (1991) *Culture, Globalization and the World-System*, London: Macmillan.

King, Amborse Yeo-chi (1991) 'Kuan-si and network building: a sociological interpretation', *Daedabus*, 120, 2: 79.

King, Y. (1983) 'All is connectedness: scenes from the Women's Pentagon Action USA' in L. Jones (ed.) *Keeping the Peace*, London: Virago.

Kleihues, J. P. (ed.) (1987) *750 Jahre Architektur und Städtebau in Berlin*, Berlin.

Knieper, H., Machleidt, M., Schäche, W. and Engel, H. (eds) (1991) *Potsdamer und Leipziger Platz: Dokumentation*, Berlin.

Kohn, H. (1971) 'Nationalism and internationalism' in W. Wagar (ed.) *History and the Idea of Mankind*, Albuquerque: University of New Mexico Press.

Korpi, W. (1983) *The Democratic Class Struggle*, London: Routledge and Kegan Paul.

Kuper, A. (1994) 'Culture, identity and the project of a cosmopolitan anthropology', *Man*, 29, 3: 537–54.

Labour Party (1993) *Music: Our Cultural Future*, London: Labour Party.

Laclau, E. (ed.) (1992) *The Making of Political Identity*, London: Verso.

Laclau, E. and Mouff, C. (1985) *Hegemony and Socialist Strategy*, London: Verso.

Lapeyronnie, D. (1993) *L'individu et les minorités, la France et la Grande-Bretagne face à leurs immigrés*, Paris: PUF.

Lash, S. and Friedman, J. (eds) (1992) *Modernity and Identity*, Oxford: Blackwell.

Lash, S. and Urry, J. (1987) *The End of Organised Capitalism*, Cambridge: Polity Press.

Lash, S. and Urry, J. (1994) *Economies of Signs and Space*, London: Sage.

Latouche, S. (1994) *Die Verwestlichung der Welt*, Frankfurt am Main: dipa.

Law, C. (ed.) (1991) *Restructuring the Global Automobile Industry: National and Regional Impacts*, London: Routledge.

Le Galès, P. (1993) *Politique Urbaine et Développement Locale*, Paris: L'Harmattan .

Le Galès, P. (1994) 'Questions sur les villes entrepreneurs', in S. Biarez (ed.) *Les Nouvelles Politiques Urbaines*, Grenoble: Cahiers du Cerat.

Le Galès, P. (1995) 'Du gouverenment des villes à la gouvernance urbaine', *Review Française de Science Politique*, 45, 1: 57–95.

Le Galès, P. and Mawson, J. (1994) *Management Innovations in Urban Policy: Lessons from France*, Luton: Local Government Management Board.

Lechner, N. (1994) 'Marktgesellschaft und die Veränderung von Politikmustern', *PROKLA*, 97: 549–62.

Lefebvre, C. (1994) 'Les politiques institutionnelles visant à constituer des autorités d'agglomération dans les pays industrialisés' in S. Biarez and J. Y. Nevers (eds) *Gouvernement des villes et politiques urbaines*, Grenoble: CERAT.

Lefort, C. (1988) *Democracy and Political Theory*, translated by D. Macey, Cambridge: Polity Press.

Lenski, G. and Lenski, J. (1987) *Human Societies: An Introduction to Macro-sociology*, New York: McGraw Hill.

Leventhal, R. S. (1990) 'Critique of subjectivity: Herder's foundation of the human sciences' in K. Mueller-Vollmer (ed.) *Herder Today*, Berlin and New York: Walter de Gruyter.

Lévi-Strauss, C (1967) *The Scope of Anthropology*, London: Jonathan Cape.

Lévi-Strauss, C (1968) *Structural Anthropology*, Hamondsworth: Penguin Books.

Lévi-Strauss, C. (1966) *The Savage Mind*, London: Weidenfield and Nicolson.

Lévi-Strauss, C. et al. (1977) *L'Identité. Seminaire Interdisciplinaire Dirigé par Claude Lévi-Strauss, 1974–75*, Paris: Presses Universitaires de France.

Levinas, E. (1987) 'Humanism and Anarchy', *Collected Philosophical Papers*, translated by A. Lingis, The Hague: Martinus Nijhoff.

Levy, M. J. Jr. (1949) *The Family Revolution in Modern China*, Cambridge, Mass.: Harvard University Press. .

Levy, M. J. Jr. (1955) 'Contrasting Factors in the Modernization of China and Japan' in S. Kuznets, W. E. Moore, and J. J. Spengler (eds) *Economic Growth: Brazil, India, Japan*, Durham, NC: Duke University Press.

Libas International, (1993) Volume 6, Issue 3, London: Libas International Ltd.

Liddington, J. (1989) *The Long Road to Greenham: Feminism and Anti-Militarism in Britain Since 1820*, London: Virago.

Ligachev, Y. (1991) *Tbilisskoe delo*, Moscow: Kodeks.

Ligachev, Y. (1993) *Inside Gorbachev's Kremlin*, New York: Pantheon.

Linton, R. (1989) 'Seneca Women's Peace Camp: shapes of things to come' in A. Harris and Y. King (eds) *Rocking the Ship of State: Towards a Feminist Peace Politics*, Boulder, Col.: Westview Press.

Linton, R. and Whitham, M. (1982) 'With mourning, rage, empowerment and defiance', *Socialist Review*, 12, 3/4: 11–36.

Little, R. (1995) 'International relations and the triumph of capitalism', in K. Booth and S. Smith (eds) *International Relations Today*, Cambridge: Polity Press.

Loder, J. (1986) 'The economics of scheduled and non-scheduled aircraft operation: the impact of regulation' in National Consumer Council (1986) *Air Transport and the Consumer: A Need for Change?* London: HMSO: 135–67.

Logan, J. and Molotch, H. (1987) *Urban Fortunes: The Political Economy of Place*, London: University of California Press.

Lorrain, D. (1991) 'De l'administration reépublicaine au gouvernement flexible', *Sociologie du Travail*, 4: 461–84.

Lorrain, D. (1995) 'France, le changement alleneieux' in D. Lorrain and G. Stoker (eds) *Les provitisations des services urbains en Europe*, Paris: La découvert.

Lovering, J. (1988) 'The local economy and local economic strategies', *Policy and Politics*, 16, 2: 145–57.

Loye, D. (1991) 'Chaos and transformation: implications of nonequilibrium theory for social science and society' in E. Laszlo (ed.) *The New Evolutionary Paradigm*, New York: Gordon and Breach Science Publishers.

Luard, E. (1990) *The Globalization of Politics*, Basingstoke: Macmillan.

Luhmann, N. (1987) *Soziale Systeme. Grundriß einer allgemeinen Theorie*, Frankfurt am Main: Suhrkamp Verlag.

Luhmann, N. (1990) *Ökologische Kommunikation*, Opladen: Westdeutscher Verlag.

Lui, Tai Lok (1994) *Chinese Entrepreneurs in Context*, Hong Kong Institute of Asia Pacific Studies Centre, Hong Kong: Chinese University of Hong Kong.

Lukács, G. (1973) *Storia e Coscienza di Classe*, Milano: Mondadori.

Lukes, S. (1973) *Individualism*, Oxford: Blackwell.

Luo, Cheng-fei (1993) *Zhongguo Dangdai Zhengzhi Zidu* [Political Systems in Contemporary China], Guangzhou: Zhongshan Daxue Chubanshe.

Lyotard, J.-F. (1984) *The Postmodern Condition: A Report on Knowledge*, Manchester: Manchester University Press.

McAuley, M. (1984), 'Nationalism and the multi-ethnic state' in N. Harding (ed.) *The State and Socialist Society*, Basingstoke: Macmillan.

McCannel, D. (1973) 'Staged authenticity: arrangements of social space in tourist settings', *American Journal of Sociology*, 79, 3: 589–603.

MacDonald, S. (ed.) (1993) *Inside European Identities – Ethnography in Western Europe*, Providence: Berg Publishers.

McGowan, F, and Seabright, P. (1989) 'Deregulating European airlines', *Economic Policy*, 9, 283–344.

McGrew, A. (1992) 'Conceptualizing global politics' in A. McGrew and P. Lewis (eds) *Global Politics: Globalization and the Nation-State*, Cambridge: Polity.

McGrew, A. and Lewis, P. (eds) (1992) *Global Politics: Globalization and the Nation-State*, Cambridge: Polity.

Macintosh, M. and Wainwright, H. (eds) (1989) *A Taste of Power: The Politics of Local Economics*, London: Verso.

McQuail, D. and Siune, K. (eds) (1986) *New Media Politics*, London: Sage.

Malm, K. and Wallis, R. (1993) *Media Policy and Music Activity*, Manchester: Manchester University Press.

Mandel, E. (1975) *Late Capitalism*, London: New Left Books.

Mann, M. (1987) 'War and social theory: into battle with classes, nations and states' in C. Creighton and M. Shaw (eds) *The Sociology of War and Peace*, Basingstoke: Macmillan.

Mannheim, K. (1928) 'Competition as a cultural phenomenon' in *Essays on the Sociology of Knowledge*, London: Routledge and Kegan Paul, 1952.

Manning, F. E. (1983) *The Celebration of Society: Perspectives on Contemporary Cultural Performance*, Bowling Green: Bowling Green University Popular Press. .

Marcuse, P. (1995) 'Not chaos, but walls: postmodernity and the partitioned city' in S. Watson and K. Gibson (eds) *Postmodern Cities and Spaces*, Oxford: Blackwell.

Marshall, A. (1919) *Industry and Trade*, Basingstoke: Macmillan.

Martin, P., McLean, D., Martin, E. and Margo, R. (1984) *Shawcross and Beaumont Air Law*, fourth edition, London: Butterworths.

Martin, S. and Pearce, G. (1992) 'The internationalization of local authority economic development strategies: Birmingham in the 1990s', *Regional Studies*, 26, 5: 499–503.

Marx, K. (1844) *Economic and Philosophic Manuscripts of 1844*, translated by Martin

341

Milligan, Moscow: Progress Publishers, 1956.

Marx, K. (1845) (with Friedrich Engels) *The German Ideology*, London: Lawrence and Wishart, 1965.

Marx, K. (1857) 'Introduction' to *A Contribution to the Critique of Political Economy* (ed.) Maurice Dobb, London: Lawrence and Wishart, 1971.

Marx, K. (1873) 'Afterword' to second German edition of *Capital*, London: Lawrence and Wishart, 1970.

Marx, K., (1973) *Grundrisse*, translated by M. Nicolas, London: Penguin Books.

Marx, K. and Engels, F. (1975) *Selected Correspondence*, Moscow: Progress Publishers.

Mascia-Lees, F., Sharpe, P. and Ballerino-Cohen, C. (1989) 'The postmodernist turn in anthropology: cautions from a feminist perspective', *Signs*, 1: 7–33.

Mauss, M. (1979) *Sociology and Psychology – Essays by Marcel Mauss*, London: Routledge and Kegan Paul.

Mauss, M. (1990) [1950] *The Gift: the Form and Reason for Exchange in Archaic Societies*, translated by W. D. Halls, London: Routledge and Kegan Paul.

Mauter, H., Földenyi, L., Pfeiffer, U., Kernd'l, A. and Schröder, T. (1993) *Der Potsdamer Platz: eine Geschichte in Wort und Bild*, Berlin: Nishen.

Mayer, M. (1994) 'Post-Fordism in city politics' in A. Amin (ed.) *Post-Fordism: A Reader*, Oxford: Blackwell.

Melucci, A. (1989) *Nomads of the Present: Social Movements and Individual Needs in Contemporary Society*, London: Hutchinson Radius.

Mennell, S. (1990) 'The globalization of human society as a very long-term social process: Elias' theory', in M. Featherstone (ed.) *Global Culture: Nationalism, Globalization and Modernity*, London: Sage.

Mennell, S. (1992) *Norbert Elias: An Introduction*, Oxford: Basil Blackwell.

Messner, D. and Nuscheler, F. (1996) *Global Governance. Herausforderungen an die deutsche Politik an der Schwelle zum 21. Jahrhundert*, Bonn: Stiftung Entwicklung und Frieden, Policy Paper 2.

Mestrovi'c, S. G. (1993) *The Barbaric Temperament: Toward a Postmodern Critical Theory*, London: Routledge.

Meyer, M. M. (1991) 'Welche Hauptstadt braucht Berlin?,' *Asthetik und Kommunikation: Hauptstadt Berlin*, 76: 10–25.

Mill, J. S. (1977) *Essays on Politics and Society*, Volume 20, London: Routledge and Kegan Paul.

Miller, D. (1987) *Material Culture and Mass Consumption*, Oxford: Basil Blackwell.

Mises, L. von (1977) [1929] *A Critique of Interventionism*, New Rochelle: Arlington House.

Mishra, V. and Hodge, B. (1993) 'What is Post(-)colonialism?', in P. Williams and L. Chrisman (eds) *Colonial Discourse and Post-colonial Theory*, London: Harvester Wheatsheaf.

Moharty, C. T. (1993) 'Under Western eyes: feminist scholarship and colonial discourse' in P. Williams and L. Chrisman (eds) *Colonial Discourse and Post-Colonial Theory*, Hemel Hempstead: Harvester Wheatsheaf.

Moharty, C. T. (1994) 'On race and voice: challenge for liberal education in the 1990s' in Giroux and McLauren (eds) *Between Borders: Pedagogy and the Politics of Cultural Studies*, London: Routledge.

Mönninger, M. (1991) *Das Neue Berlin*, Frankfurt am Main: Insel Verlag.

Moore, W. E. (1966) 'Global sociology: the world as a singular system', *American Journal of Sociology*, 71: 475–82.

Morrison, S. A. and Winston, C. (1986) *The Economics Effects of Airline Deregulation*, Washington DC: Brookings Institute.

Morrison, S. A. and Winston, C. (1995) *The Evolution of the Airline Industry*, Washington DC: Brookings Institute.

Morton, M., (1990) 'Changing the subject: Herder and the reorientation of philosophy' in Kurt Mueller-Vollmer (ed.) *Herder Today*, Berlin and New York: Walter de Gruyter.

Mudimbe, V. (1988) *The Invention of Africa: Gnosis, Philosophy and the Order of Knowledge*, Bloomington Ind.: Indiana University Press.

Muegge, H. and Stohr, W. B. (eds) (1987) *International Economic Restructuring and the Regional Economy*, Aldershot: Avebury.

Mueller-Vollmer, K. (ed.) (1990) *Herder Today*, Berlin and New York: Walter de Gruyter.

Müller, J. (1990) 'Der Potsdamer Platz in Berlin: Zur Geschichte eines zentralen Platzes', *Arbeitsheft des Instituts für Stadt- und Regionalplanung*, Berlin: Technische Universität.

Münch, R. (1987) *Theory of Action: Towards a New Synthesis Going Beyond Parsons*, London and New York: Routledge.

Murphy, B. (1983) *The World Wired Up*, London: Comedia.

Murray, R. (1991) *Local Space: Europe and the New Regionalism*, Manchester: CLES/SEEDS.

National Consumer Council (1986) *Air Transport and the Consumer: A Need for Change?* London: HMSO.

Naveau, J. (1989) *International Air Transport in a Changing World*, Brussels: Bruylant, Martinus Nijhoff Publishers.

Negus, K. (1992) *Producing Pop*, London: Edward Arnold.

Nelson, C. and Grossberg, L. (eds) (1988) *Marxism and the Interpretation of Culture*, Basingstoke: Macmillan.

Nietzsche, F. (1979) 'On truth and lies in a nonmoral science' in D. Breazeale (ed.) *Philosophy and Truth*, Atlantic Highlands: Humanities Press Inc.

Nisbet, R. (1976) Introduction to Emile Durkheim's *The Elementary Forms of Religious Life*, London: Allen and Unwin.

Novarina, G. (1993) *De l'urbain à la ville, Les transformations des politiques d'urbanisme dans les grandes agglomérations. L'example de Grenoble 1960–1990*, Paris: Commissariat Général du Plan.

Offe, C. (1995) 'Schock, Fehlkonstrukt oder Droge? Über drei Lesarten der Sozialstaatskrise', *Jahrbuch Arbeit und Technik 1995: Zukunft des Sozialstaats*, edited by W. Fricke, Bonn: Dietz Nachfolger GmbH: 31–41.

Ohmae, K (1991) *The Borderless World: Power and Strategy in the Interlinked Economy*, London: Fontana.

Ohmae, K (1993) 'The rise of the region state', *Foreign Affairs*, Spring: 78–87.

Ohmae, K. (1995) 'Putting global logic first', *Harvard Business Review*, January–February: 119–25.

Oliver, N. and Wilkinson, B. (1992) *Japanization of British Industry: New Developments in the 1990s*, Oxford: Blackwell.

Olivier de Sardan, J.-P. (1988) 'Jeu de la Croyance et "je" ethnologique: exotisme religieux at ethno-égo-centrisme', *Cahiers d'Études Africaines*, 28, 3/4: 527–40.

Olivier de Sardan, J.-P. (1989) 'Le réél des autres', *Cahiers d'Études Africaines*, 29, 1: 127–35.

O'Malley, J. J. (1977) 'Marx, Marxism and method', in A. Shlomo (ed.) *Varieties of Marxism*, The Hague: Martinus Nijhoff.

Oommen, T. K. (1991) 'Internationalization of sociology: a view from developing countries', *Current Sociology*, 39, 1: 67–84.

Panitch, L. (1994) 'Globalization and the state' in R. Miliband and L. Panitch (eds) *Between Globalism and Nationalism: Socialist Register*, London: Merlin Press.

Parkinson, M., Bianchini, F., Dawson, J., Evans, R. and Harding, A. (1993) *Urbanisation and the Functions of Cities in the European Community*, Luxembourg: Commission of the European Community.

Parsons, T. and Smelser, N. J. (1956) *Economy and Society: A Study in the Integration of Economic and Social Theory*, London: Routledge and Kegan Paul.

Peck, J. and Tickell, A. (1992) 'Local modes of social regulation? Regulation theory, Thatcherism and uneven development', *Geoforum*, 23, 3: 347–65.

Peck, J. and Tickell, A. (1994) 'Searching for a new institutional fix: The after-Fordist crisis and global-local disorder', in A. Amin (ed.) *Post-Fordism: A Reader*, Oxford: Blackwell.

Perulli, P. (1994) 'La Stato delle citta', *Il Mulino*, 353: 479–90.

Peters, G. (ed.) (1987) *Zur Baugeschichte Berlins, East Berlin*, Berlin, East: Berlin Verlag.

Picciotto, S. (1991) 'The internationalization of the state', *Capital and Class*, 43: 43–63.

Pickvance, C. and Preteceille, E. (eds) (1991) *State Restructuring and Local Power*, London: Pinter.

Piore, M and Sabel, C. (1984) *The Second Industrial Divide: Possibilities for Prosperity*, New York: Basic Books.

Planque, B. (1982) *Le Développement Décentralisé, Dynamique Spatiale et Planification Regionale*, Paris: LITEC/GRAL.

Plant, S. (1992) *The Most Radical Gesture: The Situationist International in a Postmodern Age*, London: Routledge.

Polanyi, K. (1957) [1944] *The Great Transformation*, Boston: Beacon Press.

Polanyi, K. (1979) *Ökonomie und Gesellschaft*, Frankfurt am Main: Suhrkamp Verlag.

Policy Studies Institute (1992) *Cultural Trends 1992*, London: PSI.

Ponting, C. (1991) *A Green History of the World*, Hamondsworth: Penguin Books.

Poppi, C. (1991) 'The contention of tradition: legitimacy, culture and ethnicity in Southern Tyrol' in Biblioteca Comunale di Trento (a cura di) *Per Padre Frumenzio Ghetta, O.f.M. etc . . . In Onore del Settantesimo Compleanno*, Trento: Comune di Trento-Istitut Cultural Ladin.

Poppi, C. (1992) 'Building difference: the political economy of tradition in the Ladin Carnival of the Val di Fassa' in J. Boissevain (ed.) *Revitalizing European Rituals*, London: Routledge.

Porter, M. (1990) *The Competitive Advantage of Nations*, New York: Free Press.

Presse und Informationsamt des Landes Berlin (1990) *Berlin im Aufbruch: Bilanz eines Jahres rot-grüner Politik*, Berlin.

Preteceille, E. (1988) *Mutations Urbaines et Politiques Locales*, Volume 1, Paris: CUS.

Prigogine, I. (1992) *Vers un humanisme scientifique*, Naples: Instituto Italiano per gli studi filosofici.

Pryke, R. (1991) 'American deregulation and European liberalization' in D. Banister and K. Button (eds) *Transport in a Free Market Economy*, Basingstoke: Macmillan.

Ragin, C. and Chirot, D. (1985) 'The world system of Immanuel Wallerstein: sociology and politics as history' in Theda Skocpol (ed.) *Vision and Method in Historical Sociology*, Cambridge: Cambridge University Press.

Randle, M. (1987) 'Non-violent direct action in the 1950s and 1960s' in R. Taylor and N. Young, *Campaigns for Peace: British Peace Movements in the Twentieth Century*, Manchester: Manchester University Press.

Ranger, T. (1993) 'The invention of tradition revisited: the Case of Colonial Africa' in T. Ranger and O. Vaughan (eds) *Legitimacy and the State in XX Century Africa*, Oxford and London: St. Anthony's College/Macmillan.

Rapp, L. and Vellas, F. (1992) *Airline Privatization in Europe*, second edition, Paris: ITA.

Rapport, N. (1995) 'Postmodern and realist versions of culture', *Anthropology Today*, 11, 3: 22.

Redhead, S. and Street, J. (1989) 'Have I the right? Legitimacy, authenticity and community in folk's politics', *Popular Music*, 8, 2: 177–84.

Reich, R. (1991) *The Work of Nations*, New York: Knopf.

Reporters Sans Frontiers (1993) *1993 Report: Freedom of the Press Throughout the World*, London: John Libbey.

Rhodes, R. (1988) *Beyond Westminster and Whitehall*, London: Unwin Hyman.

Rigby, B. (1991) *Popular Culture in Modern France*, London: Routledge.

Robertson, R. (1990) 'Mapping the global condition: globalization as the central concept', *Theory, Culture and Society*, 7, 2/3: 15–30.

Robertson, R. (1992a) '"Civilization" and the civilizing process: Elias, globalization and analytic synthesis', *Theory, Culture and Society*, 9, 1: 211–27.

Robertson, R. (1992b) *Globalization: Social Theory and Global Culture*, London: Sage.

Robertson, R. and Chirico, J. (1985) 'Humanity, globalization and world-wide religious resurgence: a theoretical exploration', *Sociological Analysis*, 46: 219–42.

Robertson, R. and Lechner, F. (1985) 'Modernization, globalization and the problem of culture in world-systems theory', *Theory, Culture and Society* 2, 3: 103–17.

Robinson, D., Buck, E. B. and Cuthbert, M. (1991) *Music at the Margins*, London: Sage.

Rocca, J.-L. (1994) 'The new elites' in Maurice Brosseau and C. K. Lo (eds) *China Review 1994*, Hong Kong: Chinese University of Hong Kong.

Roseneil, S. (1993) 'Greenham revisited: researching myself and my sisters' in D. Hobbs and T. May (eds) *Interpreting the Field*, Oxford: Oxford University Press.

Roseneil, S. (1994) 'Feminist political action: the case of the Greenham Common Women's Peace Camp, unpublished PhD thesis, London School of Economics and Political Science.

Roseneil, S. (1995) *Disarming Patriarchy: Feminism and Political Action at Greenham*, Buckingham: Open University Press.

Rossi, A. (1981) *A Scientific Autobiography*, Cambridge, Mass.: MIT Press.

Rossi, A. (1982) *The Architecture of the City*, Cambridge, Mass.: MIT Press.

Rouanet, S. P. (1995) 'Die brisilianische Kultur im Zeitlulter der Internationalisierung' in R. Sevilla and D. Ribeiro (eds) *Brisilen – Land der Zukunft*, Unkel and Bad Honnef: Horlemann.

Sabel, C. F. (1988) 'Flexible specialisation and the re-emergence of regional economies', in P. Hirst and J. Zeitlin (eds) *Reversing Industrial Decline?*, Oxford: Berg.

Sachs, I. (1993) *Estratégias de transicao para o século XXI. Desenvolvimento e meio ambiente*, Sao Paulo: Studio Nobel, Fundap.

Said, E. (1983) *The World, the Text, and the Critic*, Cambridge, Mass.: Harvard University Press.

Said, E. (1991) *Orientalism*, Harmondsworth: Penguin Books.

Sakwa, R. (1989) *Soviet Politics: An Introduction*, London: Routledge.

Sakwa, R. (1993) *Russian Politics and Society*, London: Routledge.

Sampson, A. (1984) *Empires of the Sky: The Politics, Contests and Cartels of World Airlines*, London: Hodder and Stoughton.

Santos, M. (1994) 'O retorno do território' in M. Santos, M. A. de Souza and M. L. Silveira (eds) *Território – Globalizacao e Fragmentacao*, Sao Paulo: Editora Hucitec.

Sassen, S. (1991) *The Global City: New York, London, Tokyo*, Princeton, NJ: Princeton University Press.

Schmidt, A. (1971) *The Concept of Nature in Marx*, London: New Left Books.

Schmidt, A. (1972) *Storia e Struttura: Problemi di una Teoria Marxista della Storia*, Bari: De Donato.

Schmidt, A. (1981) *Oltre il Materialismo Storico: la Scuola di Francoforte e la Storia*, Roma-Bari: Laterza.

Scott, A. (1996) 'Bureaucratic revolutions and free market utopias', *Economy and Society*, 25, 1: 89–110.

Scott, A. (1997) 'Modernity's machine metaphor', *British Journal of Sociology*, 48, 4.

Scott, A. J. (1988) 'Flexible production systems and regional development: the rise of new industrial spaces in North America and Western Europe', *International Journal of Urban and Regional Research*, 12, 2: 171–86.

Senatsverwaltung fur Stadtentwicklung und Umweltschutz (1990) *Der Zentrale Bereich*, Berlin.

Sengenberger, W. (1993) 'Local development and international economic competition', *International Labour Review*, 132, 3: 313–29.

Sharp, J. and Boonzaier, E. (1994) 'Ethnic identity as performance: lessons from Namaqualand', *Journal of Southern African Studies*, 20: 3: 405–15.

Shaw, M. (1991) *Post-Military Society: Militarism, Demilitarism, Demilitarization and War at the End of the Twentieth Century*, Cambridge: Polity Press.

Shenton, H. (1994) 'US international aviation policy: the last of yankee imperialism?', *Avmark Aviation Economist*, November: 2–5.

Siu, H. F. (1992) 'Cultural Identity and the Politics of Difference in Southern China', Mimeo, Paper Presented at the Centre For International and Areas Studies, Yale University.

Sklair, L. (1991) *Sociology of the Global System*, London: Harvester Wheatsheaf.

Smith, A. D. (1981) *The Ethnic Revival in the Modern World*, Cambridge: Cambridge University Press.

Smith, A. D. (1986) *The Ethnic Origins of Nations*, Oxford: Blackwell.

Smith, A. D. (1990) 'Towards a global culture?' in M. Featherstone (ed.) *Global Culture: Nationalism, Globalization and Modernity*, London: Sage.

Smith, A. D. (1991) *National Identity*, Harmondsworth: Penguin Books.

Smith, A. D. (1993) 'The ethnic sources of nationalism', *Survival*, 35, 1: 48–62.

Smith, G. B. (1988) *Soviet Politics: Continuity and Change*, Basingstoke: Macmillan.

Snodin, M. (ed.) (1991) *Karl Friedrich Schinkel: A Universal Man* (catalogue), New Haven, Conn.: Yale University Press.

Snyder, J. (1993) 'Nationalism and the crisis of the post-Soviet state', *Survival*, 35, 1: 5–26.

Sochor, E. (1991) *The Politics of International Aviation*, Basingstoke: Macmillan.

Solzhenitsyn, A. (1991) *Rebuilding Russia*, London: Harvill.

Sombart, W. (1987) [1916] *Der moderne Kapitalismus*, 3 volumes, Munich: dtv Reprint.

Sreberny-Mohammadi, A. (1991) 'The global and local in international communications' in J. Curran and M. Gurevitch (eds) *Mass Media and Society*, London: Edward Arnold.

Städtebaulicher Wettbewerb Potsdamer/Leipziger Platz (1990) *Ergebnisprotokoll*, Berlin.

Starr, F. (1983) *Red and Hot: The Fate of Jazz in the Soviet Union*, Oxford: Oxford University Press.

State Statistical Bureau (SSB) (1990) *China: The Forty Years of Urban Development*, Hong Kong: China Statistical Information and Constancy Service Centre and International Centre for the Advancement of Science and Technology Ltd.

Steele, J. (1994) *Eternal Russia: Yeltsin, Gorbachev and the Mirage of Democracy*, London: Faber.

Steven Sangren, P. (1988) 'Rhetoric and the authority of ethnography – 'postmodernism' and the social reproduction of texts', *Current Anthropology*, 29, 3: 405–35.

Stewart, P. (1996) 'Beyond Japan, beyond consensus? From Japanese management to lean production', in P. Stewart (ed.) *Beyond Japanese Management: The End of Modern Times*, London: Frank Cass.

Stewart, J. and Stoker, G. (eds) (1989) *The Future of Local Government*, Basingstoke: Macmillan.

Stewart, J. and Stoker, G. (eds) (1994) *Local Government in the 1990s*, Basingstoke: Macmillan.

Stewart, P. and Garrahan, P. (1995) Employee responses to new management techniques in the auto industry', *Work Employment and Society*, 9, 3: 517–36.

Stewart, P., Garrahan, P. and Crowther, S. (eds) (1990) *Restructuring For Economic Flexibility*, Aldershot: Avebury.

Stoller, P. (1989) 'Speaking in the name of the real', *Cahiers d'Études Africaines*, 29, 1: 113–25.

Storper, M. (1993) 'Regional "worlds" of production: learning from innovation in the technology districts of France, Italy and the USA', *Regional Studies*, 27, 5: 423–55.

Storper, M. and Walker, R. (1989) *The Capitalist Imperative: Territory, Technology and Industrial Growth*, Oxford: Blackwell.

Strange, S. (1989) 'Toward a theory of transnational Empire' in Ernst-Otto Czempiel and James N. Rosenau (eds) *Global Changes and Theoretical Challenges*, Lexington: Lexington Books.

Strathern, M. (1988) *The Gender of the Gift: Problems with Women and Problems with Men in Melanesia*, Berkeley, Calif.: University of California Press.

Street, J. (1993) 'Global culture, local politics', *Leisure Studies*, 12: 191–201.

Strinati, D. (1992) 'The taste of America' in D. Strinati and S. Wagg (eds), *Come on Down? Popular Media Culture in Post-war Britain*, London: Routledge.

Suny, R. (1992) 'Roots of the national question' in G. W. Lapidus and V. Zaslavsky with P. Gordon (eds), *From Union to Commonwealth: Nationalism and Separatism in the Soviet Republics*, Cambridge: Cambridge University Press.

Swyngedouw, E. A. (1992) 'The Mammon quest. "Glocalisation", interspatial competition and the monetary order: the construction of new scales' in M. Dunford and G. Kaftalas (eds) *Cities and Regions in the New Europe: The Global–Local Interplay and Spatial Development Strategies*, London: Belhaven.

Taylor, Mark C. and Saarinen, E. (1994) *Imagologies: Media Philosophy*, London: Routledge.

Teissenc, P. (1994) *Les politiques de développement économique local*, Paris: Economica.

Tilly, C. (1978) *From Mobilization to Revolution*, Reading, Mass.: Addison-Wesley.

Tilly, C. (1992) *Coercion, Capital, and the European States, AD 990–1992*, revised paperback edition, Oxford: Blackwell.

Tiryakian, E. A. (1990) 'Sociology's great leap forward: the challenge of internationalization', *International Sociology*, 1, 2: 155–71 (also in M. Albrow and E. King (eds) (1990) *Globalization*, London: Sage).

Tomlinson, J. (1991) *Cultural Imperialism*, Leicester: Pinter Publishers.

Tonkin, E., McDonald, M. and Chapman, M. (eds) (1989) *History and Ethnicity*, London: Routledge.

Tu, Wei Ming (1989a) 'The Confucian Dimension in the East Asian Development Model', Mimeo, paper presented at the Chinese Institute For Academic Research, Taipei, Taiwan.

Tu, Wei Ming (1989b) 'The Rise of Industrial East Asia: The Role of the Confucian Values', Mimeo, paper presented at The Centre for East Asia Studies, University of Copenhagen.

Tunstall, J. and Palmer, M. (1991) *Media Moguls*, London: Routledge.

Turgot, A. R. J. (1750) 'A philosophical review of the successive advances of the human mind', in Ronald Meek (ed.) (1973) *Turgot on Progress, Sociology and Economics*, Cambridge: Cambridge University Press.

Tyrni, I. (1987) 'Teamwork and promotion: interdependence in the Japanese management system' in T. Blumenthal (ed.) *Japanese Management At Home And Abroad*, Bersheva: Ben-Gurion University Press.

van Binsbergen, W. (1993) 'The Kazanga Festival: ethnicity as cultural mediation and transformation in Central Western Zambia', paper presented at the 1993 Grahamstown Conference on Ethnicity (in press).

Veillard-Baron, H. (1994) *Les banlieues française ou le ghetto impossible*, La Tour d'Aigus: Editions de l'Aube.

Vellacott, J. (1993) 'A place for pacifism and transnationalism in feminist theory: the early work of the Women's International League for Peace and Freedom', *Women's History Review*, 2, 1: 23–56.

Veltz, P. (1993) 'Logiques d'entreprise et territoires, les nouvelles regles du jeu', in M. Savy and P. Veltz (eds) *Les nouveaux espaces de l'entreprise*, La Tour d'Aigus: Editions de l'Aube/Datar.

Vinçon, S. (1991) *Rapport de la commission de contrôle chargée d'examiner la gestion administrative, financière et technique de l'entreprise nationale Air France*, Sénat Second Ordinary Session 1990–1, Document No. 330, Paris: Journaux Officiels.

Wachtel, D. (1987) *Cultural Policy and Socialist France*, New York: Greenwood Press.

Wagar, W. (1971) 'The Western tradition' in W. Wagar (ed.) *History and the Idea of Mankind*, Albuquerque: University of New Mexico Press.

Wagner, R. (1991) 'The fractal person' in M. Godelier and M. Strathern (eds) *Big Men and Great Men*, Cambridge: Cambridge University Press.

Wallerstein, I. (1979) *The Capitalist World Economy*, Cambridge: Cambridge University Press.

Wallerstein, I. (1990) 'Culture as the ideological battlefield of the modern world-system', in M. Featherstone (ed.) *Global Culture: Nationalism, Globalization and Modernity*, London: Sage.

Wallerstein, I. (1991) *Geopolitics and Geoculture: Essays on the Changing World-system*, Cambridge: Cambridge University Press.

Wallis, R. and Malm, K. (1983) *Big Sounds from Small Peoples*, London: Constable.

Wang, Gangwu (1988) *Trade and Cultural Values: Australia and the Four Dragons*, Current Issues in Asian Studies Series No. 1, Victoria, Australia: The Asian Studies Association of Australia.

Wank, D. C. (1995) 'Bureaucratic patronage and private business: changing networks of power in urban China' in A. Walder (ed.) *The Waning of The Communist State*, Berkeley, Calif.: University of California Press.

Ward, B. (1979) *The Ideal World of Economics*, New York: Basic Books.

Ware, R. X. (1992) 'What good is democracy? The alternatives in China and the West' in A. J. Parel and R. C. Keith (eds) *Comparative Political Philosophy: Studies Under the Upas Tree*, New Delhi: Sage: 115–40.

Waters, C. (1990) *British Socialists and the Politics of Popular Culture*, Manchester: Manchester University Press.

Watkin, D. and Mellinghof T. (1987) *German Architecture and the Classical Ideal 1740–1840*, London: Thames and Hudson.

Weber, M. (1951) *The Religion of China: Confucianism and Taoism*, New York: The Free Press.

Weber, M. (1958) *The City*, edited by D. Martindale and G. Neuwirth, London: Collier-Macmillan.

Weber, M. (1994) [1918] 'Parliament and government in Germany under a new political order' in P. Lassman and R. Speirs (eds) *Weber: Political Writings*, Cambridge: Cambridge University Press.

Webster, D. (1988) *Looka Yonder! The Imaginary America of Populist Culture*, London: Routledge.

Weizsäcker, E.U. von (1989) *Erdpolitik, Ökologische Realpolitik an der Schwelle zum Jahrhundert der Umwelt*, Darmstadt: Wissenschaftliche Buchgesellschaft.

Wenders, W. and Handke, P. (1989) *Der Himmel über Berlin*, Frankfurt am Main: Suhrkamp Verlag.

Wheatcroft, S. and Lipman, G. (1986) *Air Transport in a Competitive European Market*, London: Economist Intelligence Unit.

Wheatcroft, S. and Lipman, G. (1990) *European Liberalization and World Air Transport*, London: Economist Intelligence Unit.

White, S. (1994) *After Gorbachev*, Cambridge: Cambridge University Press.

White, S., Pravda, A. and Gitelman, Z. (eds) (1992) *Developments in Soviet and Post-Soviet Politics*, Basingstoke: Macmillan.

Williams, K., Haslam, C., Adcroft, A. and Johal, S. (1993) 'The myth of the line: Ford's production of the Model T at Highland Park, 1909–16', *Business History*, 35, 3: 66–87.

Williams, K., Cutler, T., Williams, J. and Haslam, C. (1987) 'The end of mass production', *Economy and Society*, 16, 3: 404–38.

Williams, K., Haslam, C., Williams, J., Cutler, C., Adcroft, A. and Johal, S. (1992) 'Against lean production', *Economy and Society*, 21, 3: 321–54.

Williams, K., Haslam, C. and Williams, J. (1992) 'Ford – v – "Fordism": the beginning of mass production?', *Work Employment and Society*, 6, 4: 517–55.

Williams, K., Haslam, C., Johal, S. and Williams, J. (1994) *Cars: Analysis, History, Cases*, Providence and Oxford: Berghahn Books.

Williams, P. and Chrisman, L. (eds) (1993) *Colonial Discourse and Post-colonial Theory*, London: Harvester Wheatsheaf.

Williams, R. (1981) *Culture*, London: Fontana.

Williams, R. (1983) *Keywords*, London: Fontana.

Willis, P. (1990) *Common Culture*, Milton Keynes: Open University Press.

Wilson, B. (ed.) (1970) *Rationality*, Oxford: Blackwell.

Winch, P. (1958) *The Idea of a Social Science*, London: Routledge and Kegan Paul.

Wittgenstein, L., (1953) *Philosophical Investigations*, Oxford: Basil Blackwell.

Wittgenstein, L. (1975) *The Blue and Brown Books*, Oxford: Basil Blackwell.

Wittner, L. (1988) 'The transnational movement against nuclear weapons 1945–1986: a preliminary summary' in C. Chatfield and P. van den Dungen (eds) *Peace Movements and Political Cultures*, Knoxville, Tenn.: University of Tennessee Press.

Womack, J. P., Roos, D. and Jones, D. T. (1990) *The Machine That Changed The World*, New York: Rawson.

Wong, Siu-Lun (1994) 'Chinese entrepreneurs and economic development' in J. Unger and B. McCormick (eds) *China's Prospects: Lessons From Eastern Europe and East Asia*, New York: M. E. Sharpe.

Wood, S. (ed.) (1989) *The Transformation of Work*, Basingstoke: Macmillan.

Woolf, V. (1938) *Three Guineas*, London: Hogarth Press; reprinted 1977, Harmondsworth: Penguin Books.

Wouters, C. (1990) 'Social stratification and informalization in global perspective', *Theory, Culture and Society*, 7, 4: 69–90.

Wright, V. (1995) 'The state and major enterprises in Western Europe: the enduring complexities' in J. Hayward (ed.) *National Enterprise and European Integration: From National to International Champions*, Oxford: Oxford University Press.

Yanarella, E. and Green, W. (1990) *The Politics of Industrial Recruitment: Japanese Automobile Investment and Economic Development in the American States*, New York: Greenwood Press.

Young, A. (1990) *Femininity in Dissent*, London: Routledge.

Young, K. and Mason, C. (eds) (1983) *Urban Economic Development: New Roles and Relationships*, Basingstoke: Macmillan.

Zhang, Zhizheng and Zupei Shi (1992) *Gaige Kaifeng Zhong de Guangdong Jingji* [Guangdong economy in reforming and opening], GuangzHou: Zhongshan Daxue Chubanshe.

Zohler, G. (1994) 'Erblast des Mythos: das Verfahren Potsdamer/Leipziger Platz: Ruckblick nach vier Jahren' in M. Vittorio Mangnano and R. Schneider (eds) *Ein Stück Großstadt als Experiment: Planung am Potzdamer Platz in Berlin*, Stuttgart: Verlag Gerd Hatje.

INDEX

NOTES

NOTES

NOTES

NOTES